Spy Stories

Spy Stories

Inside the Secret World of
the R.A.W. and the I.S.I.

Adrian Levy and Cathy Scott-Clark

juggernaut

JUGGERNAUT BOOKS
C-I-128, First Floor, Sangam Vihar, Near Holi Chowk,
New Delhi 110080, India

First published by Juggernaut Books 2021

10 9 8 7 6 5 4 3 2 1

P-ISBN: 9789391165147
E-ISBN: 9789391165154

For sale in the Indian Subcontinent only

Typeset in Adobe Caslon Pro by R. Ajith Kumar, Noida

Printed at Thomson Press India Ltd

For Z&A

"It is always better to admire the best among our foes rather than the worst among our friends"

Viet Thanh Nguyen, *The Sympathizer*

Contents

Acknowledgements and a
Note on Sources and Methods

What follows are personal accounts – and, occasionally, the regretful recollections – of rival officers and analysts working to outwit and trap one another in the ground zero of the spy wars. The principals in this book are from India's Research and Analysis Wing (R.A.W.), which is rarely talked about at all, and has been denigrated as a bureaucratic viper's nest, while its enemies, in Pakistan's Inter-Services Intelligence (I.S.I.), are spoken about all the time, but mostly portrayed as mysterious, self-serving, and deadly.

These are politically tinged tropes, and in the pages that follow spies from both secret services appear altogether different, as they describe how they became (and some still are) invisible protagonists, knee-deep in chaos, a few of them becoming militant, some losing traction, others having religious and political epiphanies, some going rogue, a few becoming crazy. Many of the events they participated in are well-known outrages, but they have redrawn them in the book in intimate, and revelatory ways, shedding new light, providing finger-tip context, and drawing, sometimes, contrary, and shocking, conclusions.

Their stories are deeply subjective, sometimes confessional, and nearly always partial thanks to operational security that throttled their vision so that often they only saw their own inputs and outputs. On other occasions, their vehemence reflects the hold their outfits still have over them, framing everything they see and do. Some who began as hawks and arch pragmatists have become pacifists, now believing in dialogue over warfare, advocating for negotiation as the path to resolution. A small number who have never stepped into the sunlight remain committed to hot-metal solutions, impatient with the tangles in democracy.

The (religious and secular) insurgents in India and Pakistan that these spies tracked, recruited, ran as assets, or tried to kill, over two decades, emerge anew in the following pages too, as a small band of capable, relentless, and ruthless antagonists, with names that are familiar but whose goals and antecedents are surprising. And, like a crimewave family, a small band of men (and the thousands they recruited and sent to their deaths) triggered a cascade of incidents, small and large, that almost engulfed the entire region in war, and raised nuclear hackles. Also here are extracts from their liturgy, the powerful creation stories, and religious justifications, drawn all the way back from the conspiracy in 1981 to kill President Anwar Sadat of Egypt, and re-purposed for the 9/11 levies.

This is not a book about the Central Intelligence Agency (C.I.A.) but it is everywhere, framed by two secret missions. One was the Gary Powers spy-plane calamity in 1960, which glued together an early version of the I.S.I.–C.I.A. pact, after an American long-range U2 surveillance plane was permitted to take off from a base near to Peshawar (to carry out a deep, unparalleled reconnaissance mission over the Soviet Union). The second was in 2017, as Donald Trump became the surprise pick for president and actioned a covert plan to spring from a Pakistan jail a local doctor accused of conspiring with the C.I.A. to track and kill Osama bin Laden. These waystations in history saw the Agency balancing its *need* for the I.S.I. (it now mistrusts) against a *desire* for India (and the R.A.W., which the C.I.A. now prefers) to grow as a strategic buffer to China, while opening-up its markets to American industry.

Wooed by those it shunned, pandered to by its current protégés and partners, the C.I.A., as the stories that emerge here suggest, was a catalyst for change and security in Pakistan and India, when it did well. But when C.I.A. officers went off the rails, their brutal excesses were aped too by the I.S.I. and the R.A.W., dragging on the democracies of India and Pakistan, to devastating effect.

Stories from this precinct have been told brilliantly from Langley's perspective. We all have our favourite books, documentaries, and movies. The C.I.A.'s management of its myth is perhaps its greatest work. And even though India–Pakistan remains a global flashpoint, an understanding of which is key to knowing where we have come from and where we might end up, there are very few accounts that emanate from the blind tower off Lodhi Road (where the R.A.W. resides) or the cool, grey, granite-and-marble precinct of Aabpara (where the I.S.I. rules). Some of this is down to secrecy laws, and a concept of operational security borrowed from the British and Israelis. Also at play are thin-skinned governments and administrations of all colours in both countries that have cracked down on spies talking and journalists asking.

However, despite the risks, a huge number of officials from the security services in India and Pakistan, well over a hundred, taped over the decades, helped to make this book happen, after years of asking by our long-term friend, editor, and publisher Chiki Sarkar, whom we first met when she was at Penguin India.

Many of these interviewees, whom we saw multiple times, cannot be name checked and would be grateful if we never mentioned their role. So, here's to you, respecting your need for anonymity.

The Pakistan High Commission in London was in for the marathon and often open to us, even when Islamabad, sometimes, was not, as in the years we were blacklisted by one section of the military, while being engaged by another. Diplomats and military officers stationed in London talked candidly, and we surprised each other, agreeing and disagreeing. The High Commission magnified our requests, fielded our disappointment, and cheered with us when things worked out. Irritated by a hostile reading of Pakistan in the West that was often Islamophobic, it was keen to explore how to set that right.

Many officers at every level in the Pakistan military–intelligence services combine heard us out, and relived encounters, successes, and failures with candour, and in the kind of detail we have never heard before. We talked to almost all XI Corps commanders, and among the clearest thinkers were Lt. Gen. Masood Aslam and Lt. Gen. Khalid Rabbani, who between them endured much of what the "war on terror" years could chuck at the Pakistan military.

We engaged with Joint Intelligence chiefs, and with seven former I.S.I. chiefs, including General Ehsan ul-Haq, who has a profound regional view and who remains close to European and U.S. thinking, as well as that in the Gulf states, Singapore, and Turkey. We interviewed many of the I.S.I.'s Deputy Director Generals and their support staff for the "war on terror" years, to finesse an overlapping picture. Inside intelligence, but more overwhelmingly inside the military, Lt. Gen. Javed Alam Khan is a capable raconteur with a passion for history like no other. Within counter-insurgency, Major General Ghulam Qamar remains a sharp tool, engaging with a wide international audience, and a deep constituency in Pakistan. We spent time with I.S.I. regional desk officers in Khyber Pakhtunkhwa, and veterans like Asad Munir and many others whose names have never made it into the public domain, and instead are known by their service legends: Chacha, Tariq, Qasim, Abdallah, and Ibrahim. Their counterparts in Sindh and Punjab opened doors for us, including among political factions, like the Jamaat e-Islami Pakistan and the Muttahida Quami Movement.

Equally forthright was the police, and the judiciary, who spent days and months with us, pushing back. Included are those who ran the Federal Investigation Agency, when it was winning more than it was losing. Its counter-terror specialists inside the Special Investigations Group, and their first scenes of crime lab and bomb squad officers, showed us the ways of the new terror, its chemistry and physiognomy, describing the insider threat, drawing for us in-depth profiles of the enemies they sought. And we continued to nag these officers when they moved back to the parent outfits in Punjab and Sindh, hoping they would write books too. Tariq

Khosa never stops working and writing, even in hostile times, and is always demanding and counterintuitive in his thinking. Tariq Parvez has seen civilian intelligence and counter-terrorism work from the ground up and is an eloquent guide as has been Syed Asif Akhtar, from his days in the F.I.A. and Interpol. Likewise, Khalid Qureshi, former S.I.G. chief at the F.I.A., navigated political and sectarian waters. Mohammed Shoaib Suddle, who took us from Baluchistan to Karachi via Islamabad, is a reformer, innovator, and, mostly, a stubborn pragmatist, who refuses to let go of the idea of change.

Dr Sohail Tajik has tracked, from the ground up, terror, extortion, and organized crime, and was, when we last spoke, heading into a role in the Punjab government. Along the way he has had his life's work hacked and stolen on a laptop, and met protagonists who have eluded most Western intelligence officers. His own book, when it comes, will be compulsory reading as will those in the pipeline by Rahimullah Yusufzai, who as a journalist and interlocutor, based in Peshawar, has sat down to eat with most people commonly regarded as insurgents, terrorists, or outlaws, strung out along the Durand Line in Khyber Pakhtunkhwa. Rabia Akhtar and Adil Sultan, both deep divers, provided challenging narratives.

Thanks too to the conservative religious parties and fighting groups, including office holders and clerics in Lashkar-e-Toiba, the Hizbul Mujahideen, Jamaat-e-Islami Pakistan, and Hizb ut-Tahrir, as well as sectarian veterans of Lashakar-e-Janghvi, who, after some cajoling, talked frequently, sometimes cryptically, occasionally hectoring and threatening, but also welcoming.

In London, the Indian High Commission has often helped us in every way imaginable, and thanks to all there who facilitate, critique, listen, and counter. In India, several senior diplomats who served in Pakistan and Europe guided and inspired us, as they have done for many years, especially T.C.A. Raghavan, whose own writing on the neighbour next door is compelling. We spoke at length to six former heads of R.A.W. (including the late Girish Saxena), who, over the years, we met many

xvi   Acknowledgements and a Note on Sources and Methods

times, along with a clutch of Joint, Special and Additional Secretaries, as
well as some of the founding figures in India's strategic thought world,
who served in the Prime Minister's Office, in the Intelligence Bureau
(I.B.), the Defence Intelligence Agency, Military Intelligence, Rashtriya
Rifles, and the Border Security Force.

It is easy to forget that the strategic domain – as a discipline and tool –
is relatively new in India and those who came first or became prominent
(like the late K. Subramanyam, who we spoke to often, and the team
he led on the Kargil post-mortem) had to jostle to be heard, working
against the left-leaning mainstream, and surviving regular demotions
and politically contrived career setbacks. The R.A.W. and the military,
now feted on Netflix and in Bollywood, have also been despised and
ghosted by past governments.

A key vector in India for this book was Nitin A. Gokhale and his
Bharat Shakti, one of the several security-facing think tanks he runs.
Nitin is an industry, jostling with the liberal media, to produce an
enormous output of books, podcasts, videocasts, and commentaries
that record the country's nationalist tendency, tracing its evolution, the
campaigns, and strategies. He is now working like an unofficial Indian
external affairs agency, hoping to transform foreign opinions on India
but also countering Western (and Chinese) narratives, supplanting
them with a subcontinental, nationalist take on events, and one that is
unashamedly assertive. To be a self-reliant conservative or a religious
nationalist in an industry of secular liberals, and in a country of
peaceniks, can be the hardest place to be, but Nitin is resilient, and
has access to the post-2014 circle of national security chiefs in every
wing and sector. We agreed to disagree in some areas – especially
Kashmir – while finding consensus in others, including on jihad and
the mujahid epochs.

Syed Asif Ibrahim is a stone-cold thinker, for the I.B. and,
afterwards, the broader security and intelligence community, with a
tool chest of practical experience in the subcontinent but also within
the wider region. His practitioner's knowledge was honed on multiple

vicious operations spanning three decades that somehow he survived. Many of them ran parallel to those orchestrated by I.B. officer (and then service chief) Ajit Doval, a deadly, pragmatic hand who was integral to fighting the putsches and insurgencies accelerated by Pakistan, as well as authoring strategic relations with countries that were historically opposed to India. Doval, a pessimist, became an officer who made his own luck, shaping narratives across the subcontinent. We met with him in and out of service, during his years at a conservative think tank in Delhi, and since 2015 in his new incarnation as the National Security Adviser, and head of the National Security Advisory Board, where he supported the idea of this book, fishing for details on security dynamics in Pakistan.

Rajinder Khanna, a work-horse detective, served in many difficult, complex field stations in Europe and Southeast Asia before becoming service chief, and is a deep decoder of Pakistan and the wider region. Khanna suspects the worst, hoping for the best, and has a deep memory as well as a nose for conspiracies and their proliferation. We satellited around him when he was undercover, and in recent years, more openly, to debate the past and the future, sharing a passion, especially, for Southeast Asia and beyond.

R.A.W. officers like Rana Banerji and Tilak Devasher, two quite different temperaments, have never stopped developing their theses on India's neighbours and borderlands, on insurgencies and Islamism. The latter is by character a political economist, and the former a data collector.

Dozens of journalists in India and Pakistan – who are among the best on their beats in the world – have helped us along the way, and some cannot be thanked. Saleem Shahzad, a long-time confederate, was murdered and many others who survived him cannot operate freely, with Pakistan 145th on the World Press Freedom Index, falling three places, but India has slipped too, two places, to 142. One journalist we can acknowledge is Josy Joseph, an inveterate optimist, who shares a love for primary sources. We have shared data, ideas, and connections over the recent years, and there are few who are as driven.

The high khaki class in Pakistan and India are cousins, which makes the spy war in some ways a family dispute. Everyone, on both sides, wondered about our repetitive technique. Over how many breakfasts and lunches would we rake the past? Generosity was stretched to breaking point. For the record, tessellating spy stories takes time and however far we have travelled, the officials who talked – and fed us – have gone that much further than anyone else. And who does not want to spend time with men and women who for three decades have listened into the maelstrom, humming its tunes.

Finally, thanks to David and Heather Godwin and Philippa Sitters (at the D.G.A.). Thanks to Kirsty McLachlan, who now has her own agency in London. At Juggernaut, thanks to everyone who helped us through the marathon process, and especially to our editor, Jaishree Ram Mohan.

Prologue

In the 1990s, the Central Intelligence Agency (C.I.A.) decided on a facelift and appointed a Tinseltown liaison, Chase Brandon, a cousin of the star Tommy Lee Jones but also from the old order.[1] Brandon had spent four decades in espionage, almost twenty-five years of it undercover for the Agency in regions including Latin America.

He got to work in 1996 engaging studio heads, directors, stars, and writers, encouraging them to project a different kind of spy in their scripts. In the two decades before, the C.I.A. had been accused of acting illegally, immorally, and without constraint, experimenting with group conditioning and hallucinogens, doping volunteers, and spiking the unsuspecting. Abroad it was seen to have commissioned assassinations and coups, with officers involved in torture and death squads.[2] Democracy appeared to be the flats of a stage, behind which the Agency toiled.[3]

But now, Brandon maintained, the Agency had changed. "We've been portrayed erroneously as evil and Machiavellian. It took us a long time to support projects that portray us in the light we want to be seen in," he said.[4] What came were shows including *The Agency*, which aired in 2001 on CBS, depicting diligent, workaday spooks who solved ferocious problems through fortitude and hard work.

More followed. There was Jennifer Garner in the TV show *Alias*, where she played a C.I.A. undercover officer, regularly saving the world, and *The Bourne Identity*. Stars were now given privileged tours of Langley in Virginia, which featured in movies for the first time.

However, the most sensational intervention came post-9/11 when the Agency faced its nadir. Accused of sitting on intelligence that might have helped other agencies in cinching the conspiracy, it faced rising condemnation for abducting suspects, concealing them off the grid in black sites, and creating an interrogation programme that was ruled to be torture. To shift the narrative, the Agency got involved in *Zero Dark Thirty*, sharing intelligence with the writer and the director.[5] It was a film that presented a case that the brutal programme was not only necessary but effective, generating vital intelligence that saved countless lives. For a service of secrets, the C.I.A. was filled with knowing leakers, who constantly briefed American authors, journalists, documentarians, and film makers in a way most other Western clandestine services rarely, if ever, do.

Apart from repointing history, much of what emerged created tropes out of parts of the world that were actually bearing the brunt of insurgencies and Islamism's death cults. Cities from Karachi to Peshawar that resounded with suicide bomb strikes seldom featured at all, replaced with locations in Jordan and India. Moreover, the spies and police from Rawalpindi and Mumbai became clumsy bit-part players portrayed as venal, servile, and ill-educated. The C.I.A.'s – and much of Hollywood's – versions of its operations ignored their impact on these countries, their leaders, and their security services.[6]

Six years ago, we began trying to reveal more of the covert scaffolding in South Asia and the impact on it of the C.I.A.'s "war on terror" years. Criss-crossing between New Delhi and Islamabad, travelling in the Gulf, Europe, and the United States, we found soldiers and spies from the subcontinental perma-military, whom we encouraged to come out, like C.I.A. officers and contractors were doing, to reveal some of the hidden world.

Some of those we talked to were from the Research and Analysis Wing (R.A.W.). This is not an agency, or a service, like the C.I.A. or MI6, the Secret Intelligence Service in Britain, but an adjunct of the Prime

Minister's Office (P.M.O.), without a charter or legislative oversight, contrary to most other services in Europe and the U.S.

It is based in a tower off Lodhi Road that was as corporate as utilitarian Delhi allowed in the 1980s, the era when it was constructed for Rs 98 crore – tall and blind, eleven storeys high and with little natural light. The budget generated for the R.A.W. headquarters strained relations with civil servants and other arms of government, as did the very idea of a secret foreign intelligence service.[7] Inside Lodhi Road, R.A.W. officers from that time complained, it was like working in a government school where the students had gone feral. But the R.A.W. hardly ever wrote about itself and came down hard on those who did, like Major General V.K. Singh (not to be confused with the cabinet minister), who, having served for four years, rising to the rank of Joint Secretary, composed a mild memoir, and in 2007 had his home raided and his passport, computer, and papers seized.[8]

Others we interviewed worked for the Inter-Services Intelligence (I.S.I.) directorate in Pakistan, established in 1948, just months after the country was founded following Partition. Widely caricatured as thugs, they are often at the centre of bloody pandemonium in Pakistan and regarded by Western and Indian voices as the evil protagonists in a region in which R.A.W. is often portrayed as white knights.

Shadowy and misunderstood, and also resisting active oversight from civilian governments, the I.S.I. is regularly referred to as Aabpara, the name of the comfy Islamabad district where it is headquartered.[9] After 9/11, the military erected a new polished campus there, financed by millions of U.S. dollars, derived from bounties paid for capturing high-value al Qaeda suspects. The monolithic, gleaming-grey edifice looms like Pakistan's very own Tyrell Corporation.

Much has been written about the R.A.W. and the I.S.I. by foreign observers, correspondents, and analysts, but most of it is voiced by competing Western operators, officers, and government officials from outside the region who sparred with these outfits. One of the few substantial books that came from within was co-authored in 2018 by retired I.S.I. chief Lt. Gen. Asad Durrani and retired R.A.W. boss Amarjit Singh Dulat, with the former blackballed by the Pakistan military that went apoplectic and prevented him from leaving the country for a time, while the latter, modest and combative, rode out the brickbats, also brushing off the praise.[10]

Two tight-lipped services drawn from the same DNA, these days they intermittently talked to one another, via backchannels managed, secretly, by Saudi Arabia and also a Gulf monarchy. But on the ground they remained locked in a death spiral, sometimes winning, occasionally losing, and hardly ever finding common ground or understanding.

Advice on how to approach R.A.W. came from a veteran Indian diplomat whom we met over masala cheese toast at a South Delhi club. Only institutional support would work – otherwise "no one will talk openly at all." This set the bar high.

A senior officer in the Intelligence Bureau (I.B.) warned: "R.A.W.'s great achievement is to endure brickbats for its presumed pacifism and inactivity when it is frantically sculpting India's image as a benign state. Its second achievement is spilling blood *invisibly*. To explain the second would be to undermine the first. So good luck!"

We crossed over at the Wagah border, and drove to Islamabad, where I.S.I. secrecy was fiercely maintained to protect the state (and its military businesses). We asked for endorsements and connections, calming nerves, trying to reason our way around deep-seated suspicions, discussing books and movies as reference points.

In Rawalpindi, officers derided the TV series *Homeland*, which cast the I.S.I. as duplicitous and savage, showed Indian cars driving down presumed Pakistan streets, and tribal cities where boys conversed in Urdu instead of Pashto. But still they watched it. Although it was officially banned, *Zero Dark Thirty*, which showed the I.S.I. as Osama bin Laden's protector, had also become compulsive viewing.

We suggested watching *Argo*, which polished the C.I.A. role in an international plan to free U.S. citizens who were hostages in Iran after the revolution of 1979. Look at *Black Hawk Down*. Screen *Gatekeepers*. The last of these was the least well known and did not polish the U.S. national interest. Its focus was another formidable outfit, Shin Beth, Israel's domestic intelligence service, motto: "The Defender that Shall Not be Seen". But the film makers drew out silent men and crafted a compelling covert history of Israel–Palestine.

No means maybe. The I.S.I. see-sawed. The Analysis Wing worried that Pakistan would not benefit from the I.S.I. talking. "The C.I.A. can say whatever it likes. But we are not a superpower and we are vying for small advantages in a kinetic backyard – why would we want to expose ourselves?" argued a deputy director general (D.D.G.) in C-Wing, which is responsible for counter-intelligence, counterterrorism, counter-espionage, and domestic intelligence. Another pointed to every occasion we had criticized Pakistan over two decades, telling the then I.S.I. chief, Lt. Gen. Naveed Mukhtar: "We can never trust them." Mukhtar's circle pushed back, suggesting that writers who had been both "for" and "against" Pakistan were *credible*, which made this an *opportunity*.

It was *Black Hawk Down* that triggered a rethink. In the 1993 battle for Mogadishu U.S. Special Forces tried to capture allies of the warlord Mohamed Aidid. However, two Black Hawk helicopters were downed, and a convoy of soldiers deployed to rescue the crew. They came under heavy fire, with hundreds of Somalis killed, as well as eighteen U.S. operators, with seventy-three more injured. Footage of U.S. corpses being dragged through the streets scarred the American military.

Senior I.S.I. officers who watched Ridley Scott's movie saw how it turned U.S. war fighters into heroes even in the face of disaster, and they were irritated by it. Pakistani troops had been there too, playing a significant but unsung role. A contingent working as U.N. peacekeepers had given up their lives; yet no one had told their story. A D.D.G. in B-Wing, or external intelligence, told Mukhtar: "Highlighting success and memorializing failure is something that Pakistan dismally fails at – and so no one ever knows what we did and what it cost."[11]

A chink of light. A lunch was arranged at the Rawalpindi Polo Club and an officer asked many questions as his daughter cantered over the scrub, and havildars in maroon brought snacks, napkins, and ketchup. Who exactly did we want to talk to? What would we ask? Where would the material go, if they gave it? Could they maintain editorial control?

The officer, who had once been a fighter pilot, believed in the project but did not want to *own* it, because he liked his life. We described a method – survey the top level of chiefs and their deputies who served in the "war on terror" years, and then interviews with a second tier of operators who saw things from the street corner. He referred it up the chain of command, with our caveat that only a book without any constraints would be credible.

Spies of all countries sign iron-cast secrecy agreements not to welch on other spies. But we compiled wish lists for both sides of the Line of Control (LoC) and began to feel our way through the murky world of clandestine operators, case officers, subject matter experts, targeters, and analysts. Some names in Pakistan and India drew grimaces. The I.S.I. crossed out a third immediately. One man was "under a cloud." Another had "political issues." A senior officer in the R.A.W. who once ran interference operations against Pakistan, and who we thought was out, could not talk now, as he was on his way back in.

On both sides, some officers suggested correctives, putting forward stalwarts who they said did not toe the line or advocate for any government, but who "did their job." In Pakistan, a full colonel talked about "malcontents and patriots." He said: "Your list is filled with flag-wavers but not everyone was for the U.S. war on terror, although they were Pakistan patriots."[12] A similar conversation in Delhi pointed to analysts who had served during the most tumultuous episodes, but who complained of the increasing politicization of intelligence, which they feared was stoked by Hindu chauvinists. We listened to them all.

Maybe means yes. We drove to Lahore for discussions, crossing over at Wagah, and heading for Delhi. The Indian intelligence community had begun to share thoughts with us shortly after we wrote *Deception*, a book about the A.Q. Khan nuclear proliferation network, and invited us to the third floor of Sardar Patel Bhavan, to talk to the National Security Adviser (N.S.A.), Ajit Doval.

We were ushered into a darkened "situation room" from where, off to the side, he conducted marathon eighteen-hour days. He was a youthful, conspiratorial workaholic, who, restless and slight, concealed his seventy-four years. Doval was intrigued by our I.S.I. vs R.A.W. idea. It was an opportunity to cherry-pick key kinetic episodes over the last eighteen years, rather than retelling all of it, and so gaining some input in helping us select which battles to focus on that would benefit India too. Hearing we had been with I.S.I. officers in Rawalpindi the day before, Doval asked: "How was it over there?" His smile flickered like a room in the Overlook Hotel. He would not be visiting Pakistan any time soon. R.A.W.–I.S.I. relations were mostly sub-zero, barring the on–off backchannel meets, like the sessions that took place between Doval and his counterpart from Pakistan, Lt. Gen. Nasir Khan Janjua, in Bangkok, Thailand, from 2015 to 2018. And the more recent second-tier discussions that sought to end the LoC shelling.[13]

Doval stepped out to greet a Saudi delegation, a project that typified his ambition for India to make its way in new territories that had previously shunned Delhi, he said. But it was a doubly interesting fixture for what went unsaid, as the Saudis continued their role as intermediary, bringing news from Rawalpindi.[14]

Later a colleague of Doval told us a story that had electrified officers in the I.B. and the R.A.W. At the end of the Cold War, as Germany readied for unification, the C.I.A. met the K.G.B. in a house in Karlshorst, in Berlin's eastern sector. Milton Bearden, chief of the C.I.A.'s Soviet division, and Hugh Price, its chief of counter-intelligence, were summoned by their Soviet counterparts, Rem Krassilnikov and Leonid Nikitenko, the heads of K.G.B. counter-intelligence. They wanted to understand the high level of defections from the East to the West.

What fascinated this officer was not the chit-chat. It was the mechanism that had got bitter adversaries into a room in East Berlin shortly before the wall was dismantled.[15] It was known as the Gavrilov channel, named after an eighteenth-century Russian poet, a top-secret telephone hotline linking Langley to the Lubyanka that could call meetings on short notice, and had commenced in 1983. Without Gavrilov there was nothing, and this hotline reduced tensions, leading to a post-Soviet relationship between the C.I.A. and the K.G.B. successor outfits, finding common ground on narcotics trafficking and terrorism.

Publicly, politicians in India claimed they had nothing to talk about to Pakistan, but privately even hard-line spies worried, continually, about hearing a rival agency (mostly) via eavesdropping, as everything became misdirected, muffled, and potentially misconstrued. "We have zero deep, trusting connections to the I.S.I.," Doval's colleague complained. The pitter-patter of messages carried by others. A few foreign jaunts. "And – by and large – what we know about them is what we overhear, and they tap us too, both sides whispering lies, which can't be good."

Later Doval called us back. "These are critical times." Was he talking about the Saudi water carrying? "There is no detail that is too small when it comes to the I.S.I. I need to study every scintilla. They are our forever enemy and we can never, ever know enough," he said, agreeing to the project.

We were also Gavrilov.

Part 1

The Back Story
1968–2000

Iftikhar

Major Iftikhar was the nom de guerre for an operations officer, which meant he had worked undercover for the I.S.I. (in rotations that saw him deployed at home, abroad, and with his regiment). From 1995, he had taken part in some of the agency's most controversial operations. After leaving in 2011, apparently under a cloud, he had gone dark.[1]

Tech-savvy and trained in security and counter-surveillance, Iftikhar had done everything he could to throw people off his scent. As he always did, the major charged his phones so they had enough battery to remain live for a day and placed one into a padded envelope that he had couriered to Quetta. He had another sent to Karachi. A third went to Lahore. He used a V.P.N. to shield his I.P., making it seem as if he was in Nepal, where spies often ran for cover, and from this virtual bolthole he cancelled all his old email accounts. He also burned his laptop because he knew how much data was recoverable from a hard drive, even when it had been formatted.

To avoid being compromised by Indian–Israeli tech tie-ins that went after WhatsApp, Facebook and even iPhones (that Apple maintained were fortresses but that some private spyware firms had repeatedly breached), he used a Nokia "brick" for personal calls and internet cafes for data.[2] Iftikhar registered for an email account with Proton – feeling reassured that it was created by coders and scientists who formerly worked for CERN, the Euro-nuclear research centre. He used that address to open an account with Wire, a Swiss messaging package, so he could ping people around the world.

He created go-bags, with currencies, fake passports, bogus ID cards, and clothes, and bought cryptocurrencies, using an offline wallet to store them. Cramming his belongings into a small holdall without even saying goodbye to his family, he took a flight out of Pakistan, possibly to the Gulf. Iftikhar had disappeared. No one was going to catch him unless he wanted to be caught.

We messaged a Wire account and waited. After several weeks, a floral emoji and blessings came back. That was better than we had expected, but if he agreed to meet, should we go? We did not know what he had done, and we did not want to get tangled up with dangerous people who did. Pakistani journalists with more street smarts than us had been abducted and killed for rubbing up against I.S.I. business. After Saleem Shahzad had described al Qaeda penetration of the armed forces post the U.S. raid on Abbottabad in 2011, the journalist vanished, only to turn up dead in a storm drain, his body showing signs of torture.[3]

Then a second message from Major Iftikhar came through, suggesting a time and place in the United Arab Emirates. Almost immediately, his handle was deleted, but we decided to take a chance.

At al-Satwa, a busy neighbourhood of Dubai, packed with market stalls, shops, and apartment blocks, we had been told to look out for a "Balochi" who sold generic medicines to worshippers at the Obai bin Kaab masjid. With its crisp, cream minarets, the mosque was easy to locate, but we saw no one matching the description. A day later, we returned after the noon prayer, salat al-zur, and noticed a crowd standing around an upright, pale-skinned man handing out strips of pills. When they dispersed, we approached, and beside him was a wiry man, more legs than torso, and the cuffs of his oatmeal kameez rode up revealing muscly forearms. His wore his cola-black hair a little above shoulder length, with a well-tended parting, which was more marketing man than military.

"You're late," he said irritably. Leading us to a nearby cafe, looking to the left and the right, he ordered khuzi, the U.A.E.'s national dish, baked lamb falling off the bone served on a bed of rice. He had chosen a busy venue and seated us near the very noisy exit, next to a TV screen blaring Arabic hip-hop. He produced two notepads one on top of the other to leave no indentations. There was no sign of a mobile phone and we had been told to leave ours behind. This was his tradecraft.

He ate, ravenous, or perhaps he had a big appetite. We sat, too tense to pick at our food. Finally, breaking the ice, we asked what he got up to these days. His mood darkened. "Exporting to Syria and Iraq, Aleppo and Diwaniyah. Just splints and bandages. Trauma dressings. That's *all* . . ." he said, exposing a badly fitting dental prosthetic that covered a hole in the roof of his mouth. He caught us staring. "This?" he asked. He spun it around with his tongue making it click and clack. "It's a surgical plate and it covers a deep wound in the roof of my mouth. I was blown up in the field. Attacked by a man I spent years trying to kill."

The recent past was painful. The present was uncomfortable. So we changed tack and asked him to go further back in time and tell us how the I.S.I. had recruited him.

~

Islamabad, F6, 1995. After the evening prayer, salat al-'ishr, Iftikhar headed out of the Jamia Masjid Farooqia in a comfortable neighbourhood of Islamabad. But in the car park, a hand grabbed his elbow.

"Like to have a glass of something, Major?"

Iftikhar said the man looked like a recognizable type. A compact sort, well into his retirement, not much over 173 centimetres, but lithe with helicopter arms. He was dressed in a pressed khaki shalwar kameez, wore black Peshawari chappals, his hair cropped like a winter cane field.

"The stranger was well informed, as my promotion had only just been listed," Iftikhar told us. "So, I said, 'Why not...'"

Iftikhar allowed himself to be steered towards an idling car, and was driven to Iqbal Markaz, a semicircular market that hummed with picture framers, grocers and snack stalls, where they perched on stools and chatted over spicy mix-tea and greasy aloo naans, delivered on old pages of the *Nawa-i-Waqt* daily.

"His generosity stopped me from leaving," Iftikhar recalled.

Lesson one: *a free meal is disabling*.

"Finally, the stranger asked me a question: '*What do you think of the I.S.I.?*' That was a showstopper!"

Monisha

She called herself Monisha. At first all we had was a low-res JPEG of a woman, raven-black hair cut into a shoulder-length bob, an oblong face tapering into a cleft chin, her skin pale, her eyes hazel. Mid-height, perhaps 157 centimetres, she was middle-aged but with a runner's body, and a love for argyle sweaters.

A former veteran R.A.W. analyst, she, like Iftikhar, had quit her outfit after several decades of service. Monisha had initially gone back to working as a bureaucrat, then resigned or retired, changed her name, and left the subcontinent, for reasons that were, a friend told us, "personal but political."

We eventually located her near Seattle, at a start-up (begun by Silicon Valley all-stars). On our first call we went slowly and asked if she had graduated from the prestigious Lal Bahadur Shastri National Academy of Administration in Mussoorie, the institution where India's civil service – administrative, police, foreign, etc. – trained. After a long pause, she asked us to switch to Wire, the same discreet Swiss app that Iftikhar relied upon.

Monisha told us how her team was working on real-time analytics in a company that was trying to reduce latency – the length of time it took for a message to move from a server to a device, controlling a smart home with a mobile phone for example. She was not coding but fishing for angel investors and her path from security to tech was a well-beaten one, pursued by many in the intelligence community who jumped into the well-funded private sector to make up for years of Spartan government life. "After so long inside the bureaucracy, I've become a speed freak," she riffed. Monisha was clearly a polymath, but why was she in the U.S.?

She blamed her mother.

~

Hazrat Road area, Ballygunge, Kolkata, 1970s. She grew up with money but no father, dead to a heart attack when she was still in her teens. Her mother, who ran the family's upmarket culinary club, was distracted for as long as she could remember.

Bookish Monisha was obsessed by world history. She recalled her mother taste-testing strudel at the kitchen table, as she studied the history of World War II. With the smells of the buttery pastry filling the house, Monisha wondered how Austrian Christians could plot the annihilation of their fellow Jews when they shared such a deep love for the country's rich *konditorei*.

"I told everyone that I was going to study political science, but no one was listening," she said. The domestic "climate of indifference" made her independent and ultimately successful. When she won a university place, her mother was away working in the Gulf, and when, miraculously, she got into the I.A.S., a stranger picked up the phone at the family home. He said he was a house guest and was giving classes on making Morroccan *mechoui*. He would pass on her news, but no one rang back.

Monisha graduated and entered the civil service, before being led into the foothills of the R.A.W. by one of her lecturers. When, in the early 1980s, she finally embarked on a career that she was unable to talk about, there was no one left to tell. "At thirty years old I experienced my first dead drop," she said, recalling how her mother had relocated to Dubai and could only be communicated with via a P.O. Box.

Her first impression of the R.A.W. was that background checks were poor and that they never got to the root of her. Psych tests were ad hoc. Later, there were polygraphs but if the machine and the candidate were not properly prepped the results were ambiguous. When her turn came, she was strapped to a cold machine with no baseline established. Security was manual – ledgers, sign-in registers, analogue identity cards.

By contrast, on a training visit to Israel she learned that the Mossad scoped potential recruits for months in stress tests that plumbed their physical and mental depths and then continued throughout a service career, the attrition rates severe.

"Welcome to the wing," an instructor at an R.A.W. training camp told her. They were stationed in a hostel on the outskirts of Delhi. "Remember you work for the Cabinet Secretariat," he said, referring to the body that administers the Indian government. "And it answers to the prime minister." He paused. "So, enjoy this privilege today. You are among the very few. But from now on never mention the R.A.W. again, not even to each other. You will only refer to I.A.S. Or the Secretariat. Call it the company. The workshop. The office. The department. But the R.A.W. – or the Wing – does *not* exist."

Unsurprisingly there was no signboard at headquarters off Lodhi Road, leading her to make several false turns before she got to the new tower that had only recently opened. Excited, she entered. "What a surprise. The plumbing clanked. The offices were sweltering, the air coolers were deafening. The air was stagnant." Someone told her that if a pot-plant was put outside a meeting room that meant it was occupied. "It was like being inside a hatchery."

The early years

During her induction, Monisha soaked up India's history of espionage, learning how for the four decades after Independence there was no dedicated external intelligence at all, but only the I.B., which operated like a police special branch and was staffed by Raj-trained Indian Police Service (I.P.S.) officers.

The I.B. existed in a "tragic-comic state of helplessness."[4] The British had left the service with a legacy of colonialism and a "lot of broken furniture." But Partition was also a forge, as one of the largest and most violent mass migrations in human history got under way with millions of Muslims heading out of India and into Pakistan, while Hindus and Sikhs travelled in the opposite direction. The security services were a microcosm of the tectonic shift, with the majority of capable Muslim officers choosing new Pakistan, leaving the I.B. depleted. The Hindus and Sikhs left behind in the Indian service, and their new Muslim rivals over the border, were transformed by the harrowing vista of torture, rape, mass murder, and arson which tempered everyone's perceptions.

War in 1965 intensified these divisions. In August of that year, Pakistan infiltrated Indian Kashmir, sending thousands of soldiers over the contested border dressed as local fighters in an operation code-named Gibraltar. India was blind-sided and both sides suffered thousands of casualties in the battles that followed. It would end inconclusively, as had an earlier combat between India and China in 1962, when despite the United States warning India of an imminent invasion, Delhi had not acted. Both conflicts, according to veteran I.B. officers, demonstrated a lack of analysis and foresight, with few fixes.[5]

Incoming prime minister Indira Gandhi could see India required an external intelligence agency to combat Pakistan and China. Cabinet Secretary D.S. Joshi chose its name – Research and Analysis Wing – and it came into being on September 21, 1968. Its motto, "Justice protected, protects," was as intangible as its remit. Staffed by 250 I.P.S. officers from the I.B.'s China and Pakistan desks and backed by a shoestring budget of less than half a million U.S. dollars, the R.A.W. was ordered to build a competent and aggressive foreign intelligence agency, like the C.I.A. – although not exactly the same, as one of Langley's first revealed budgets from this period was estimated to be $750 million.[6]

~

Pakistan was decades ahead. Born out of the first India–Pakistan war of 1947, the Inter-Services Intelligence directorate was the brainchild

of Major General Sir Robert Cawthome, an Australian by birth who
served in the British Indian Army but who had become Deputy Chief
of Staff in the newly formed Pakistan Army in 1947, where he first set
up a Signals Corps.

The I.S.I. was his response to the Pakistan military's dismal showing
in its first war with India just two months after Independence, deploying
a proxy force of irregulars, made up of Pathans from Waziristan, to
the princely state of Kashmir where the maharaja had been debating
independence. However, four days after the invasion, pressurized by
India, the maharaja acceded to Delhi.[7] Outnumbered and overpowered
by the better armed and equipped Indian Army, Pakistan lost six men for
every Indian soldier and retreated. Cawthome concluded that Pakistan
would have to resort to the force multipliers of fear and manipulation
in the future.

Originally located in the first Pakistani capital of Karachi and
housed in a building opposite Zainab Market on Old Victoria Street,
the newly formed I.S.I. was tasked with collating and analysing insights
and intercepted communications gathered by all three fighting forces.
Its officers were warned not to get bogged down in domestic politics.
Weakening a mighty neighbour was their primary goal. But Cawthome
could see that India's sheer size and ambition made it vulnerable:
hundreds of millions of people of different castes and creeds all locked
together in a single country.

After seizing the Pakistani presidency by military coup in 1958,
General Ayub Khan ordered the I.S.I. to create a Covert Action Division
(C.A.D.) to act upon Cawthome's insights. It began by boosting
an insurgency in India's North-East, where battles for autonomy,
compounded by rival ethnicities, were raging. To beef up his military,
Khan had already reached out to the U.S., realizing that Pakistan sat on
a Cold War fault line. Rawalpindi was funded and equipped in exchange
for leasing covert bases for American intelligence collection on Chinese
and Soviet nuclear testing. In May 1960 an American U2 spy plane,
piloted by Gary Powers, was shot down by the Soviets over the Ural

Mountains, causing an international furore. Little known was the fact that it had taken off from Peshawar. According to a classified letter from the Pentagon, the Peshawar base was "one of a very limited number of important overseas intelligence gathering stations."[8] The I.B. in Delhi noted that Pakistan mattered to the C.I.A.; soon Indian intelligence's yearning to catch Langley's attention would come to define it too.

~

Delhi recruited for the new R.A.W. One of them was Bahukutumbi Raman, known by foreigners with poor language skills as "B," or just Raman. He had entered the I.P.S. in 1961, seven years before the R.A.W. existed, working in the Madhya Pradesh police cadre. Inducted into the I.B., he was moved into the new external intelligence service the year it was set up. With a prodigious memory, and rigorous work ethic, Raman quickly became one of R.A.W.'s most valuable officers, eventually leading the counterterror section in the 1980s. But he never realized his true place in the outfit, stymied by the bureaucratic and rigid promotional structure, inherited from the police service, which favoured the trigonometry of seniority over talent.

Frugal with everything but his intellectual capital, Raman – Delhi's George Smiley – sauntered into work every day at dawn clutching a battered leather briefcase. He only left when his brain could not ingest any more data. He famously called into Lodhi Road several hours after his mother's funeral. And whenever he got home, he allowed himself a glass or two of whisky.

In the early 1980s, Raman was among the first to develop relationships with foreign intelligence officers, in the days when the R.A.W. was suspicious of liaisons and doubted the benefits of reaching out to rival outfits. He went undercover in Paris, posing as a journalist with *The Hindu*. There, he quietly excavated a channel to the new clerical regime in Iran that had been proscribed by the U.S., after the fall of the Shah. Still ignored by Washington, India opted for a high-risk strategy of courting its enemies. "The U.S. was Delhi's forever obstacle," Raman told us at a dinner after his retirement when he remained an influential voice. "Unless India becomes so powerful, economically, intellectually, or militarily, that Washington can ill afford to overlook us. Or alternatively, if Pakistan becomes a failed state and China's economy mushrooms, only then will India be needed by the U.S. as their buffer. And China will not like that one little bit." Given the China–India showdowns of 2020, Raman, who died in 2013, was prescient.

One of R.A.W.'s greatest victories came early on. A source inside the office of military dictator General Yahya Khan, the third Pakistani president, and intelligence from eavesdropped and decrypted messages from East Pakistan gave warning of air strikes against India on December 3, 1971 and, days later, pinpointed intelligence about the whereabouts of the East Pakistan cabinet that narrowly survived an air strike.[9]

This marked the beginning of Pakistan's greatest ever military defeat, which saw the loss of half its country, and the creation of Bangladesh, a crisis enabled with Indian backing of proxies and insurgents, a favourite ploy of the C.I.A., mimicked in Pakistan by the I.S.I. However, there was also good technical intelligence wielded by the R.A.W. and poor fieldcraft observed by Pakistan, where senior officers talked freely on open lines.

A few years on, in 1975, R.A.W.'s deep human intelligence (or HUMINT) uncovered a coup plot against Sheikh Mujibur Rahman, Bangladesh's first president. R.N. Kao, the R.A.W. chief, flew undercover to Dhaka to warn Mujib. Here a valuable lesson was learned. Truth was sometimes not enough. Mujib ignored the advice and was killed alongside most of his family that year.

When Indira Gandhi fell in 1977, after twenty-one months of Emergency during which all democratic norms were stifled in favour of rule by decree, the country's deep state was loathed. The Janata government of Morarji Desai reversed directions and culled the R.A.W., slashing the agency's budget and operations, and knocked back I.B. too. According to a commentator writing at the time, the R.A.W. was "reduced to a pathetic parody of a government department, with bureaucratic backstabbing, favouritism and jockeying for plum assignments or extensions of service, which has become almost routine."[10]

The 1980s: I.S.I. soars

With the start of the Soviet–Afghan war in the 1980s, the Cold War manifested itself in Pakistan. The country became awash with cash from the C.I.A. (and Saudi Arabia) while mujahids from all over the Middle East, North Africa, and the Caucuses converged on Peshawar. The R.A.W.'s demoralization, on the other hand, deepened. It had moved into its new tower on Lodhi Road, only to become beset by internal tensions.

Overworked, under pressure, miserably paid, and ruled by decree, officers followed the lead of I.B. officers and tried to set up a staff association. In both services, staff bridled at being given extra duties, for no more money, having their working lives forcibly altered with little consultation. By the summer of 1980 the association had taken up complaints against a new security regime that was said to be heavy-handed and imperious. It was epitomized by the moving of the loathed Counter-intelligence Service, known to everyone by its initials, C.I.S., from South Block to Lodhi Road.

Insular and paranoid, C.I.S. thrived on being outsiders. It hunted for spies and saboteurs inside its own ranks, while looking for covert plays by foreign services. The C.I.S. demanded a higher standard of operational security and brought higher standards for personnel checks and registration, demands that riled long-standing officers outside that section who were not consulted on the arrangements. There were also allegations of high-handedness and bullying. One assistant director, Colonel Bagchi, was accused of slapping a junior for damaging the leg of a sofa, as he helped to move his furniture into the new building.

A boisterous crowd of R.A.W. agents sang and shouted inside and outside a secret building whose occupants demanded absolute discretion. The R.A.W. demonstrators charged into the office of C.I.S. Deputy Director M.D. Dittia and would not leave or allow him, and two colleagues, to go, making it clear they were hostages. "There were speeches in the corridors of the office also. Insubordination, indisciplined activities, abstention from work, moving around in and outside the building, threatening the willing workers and making speeches inciting the staff to abstain from work and defy orders were resorted to," according to an affidavit made by one R.A.W. executive officer. "The slogans were obscene, abusive, threatening, and personal in nature. Slogans were also shouted regularly in favour of the employees' association."[11]

A negotiator tried to end the deadlock, but the only demand made by the men barricaded inside the C.I.S. office was one that R.A.W. would not agree to: the easing of the new security protocols.

The C.I.S. called for backup and at 8.30 p.m. coaches of police and paramilitaries streamed in, beating 31 R.A.W. officers badly and arresting them, the group jailed until bailed 12 hours later. The police action forced the immediate suspension of the protesters as they could no longer serve having been charged. The move triggered a "pen down" strike in Lodhi Road, with officers reaching out to other R.A.W. offices, including the Special Bureau in Lucknow, where officers did the same. Eight officers from Delhi and two from Lucknow were fired. But that move triggered a legal action, the courts asked to overturn the sackings, leading to more unrest, during which the outfit was crippled by dissent and loathing. India's inability to deal with internal R.A.W. grievances – or govern fairly – meant Pakistan was hardly being watched at all.[12]

The staff association formed on February 14, 1980 was finally quashed, and the petition for the reinstatement of the eight, backed by a young field assistant and fifty-one others, reached the Delhi High Court. There it failed, with the ousted officers complaining that the judiciary had been leant on.

Afterwards, the R.A.W. continued to shrink, its internal structures slimmed down and shaken up. In the same way that the U.S. "peace dividend" – the process of streamlining and cutting back defence spending at the end of the Cold War – denuded the C.I.A. of experience and officers (which come 9/11 would have devastating consequences for the Agency and the U.S.), the R.A.W. failed to retain the best or diversify its staff.

Meanwhile, the I.S.I., which had begun receiving U.S. training for its Covert Action Division (CAD), readied an assault on another Indian fault line, identified by Cawthome. Men with guns slipped into the Indian Punjab, reaching out to leaders of the Sikh independence movement fighting for a homeland called Khalistan, the Land of the Pure. The I.S.I. contacted diaspora Sikhs too, who sent money from the U.K. and Canada to stoke an uprising.

"R.A.W. was getting seriously left behind," Raman grumbled.[13] Realizing that India was stuck between warring superpowers, he began encouraging Chinese language tuition for R.A.W. specialists. He also created a Chinese-centric study group, watching the giant to the north, when almost the only thing Chinese in India was plates of Gobi Manchurian.

"We also studied how the U.S. deepened its friendship with the I.S.I. during the 1980s, especially with the advent of America's war against the Soviets in Afghanistan," said Raman. Fighting America's wars remotely was a tactic the C.I.A. had nurtured during the Vietnam conflict, when it recruited Hmong tribes in Laos to wage a secret war against the neighbouring North Vietnamese, whose resupply lines, known as the Ho Chi Minh Trail, ran through the jungles bordering both countries.

The Agency honed the idea of using proxy armies in Latin America during the 1970s and 1980s when the Nicaraguan Contras learned how to torture in secret C.I.A. training camps located in the Honduran jungle. Some of these operations were covertly funded by the sale of weapons to Iran, via Israel, its supposed nemesis. In the covert world, insurgencies and putsches, trafficking of arms, people, and drugs, were strategies to keep an enemy off balance. As the dictator General Zia ul-Haq famously told his spymaster General Akhtar Malik, looking towards Afghanistan, the water had to "boil at the right temperature."

Raman studied joint U.S.–Pakistan intelligence operations that R.A.W. believed had sought to undermine Indira Gandhi. He learned that the C.I.A. had encouraged the I.S.I. to publicize in foreign newspapers in Europe how forty of Gandhi's Congress parliamentarians received cash from a Moscow slush fund, allegations that were likely a mirage.[14] Acting on behalf of the C.I.A., the I.S.I. flagged up the (phantom) existence of a "Soviet presence" at Indian naval bases in Visakhapatnam, a port city in Andhra Pradesh, and the Andaman Islands, in the Bay of Bengal.

After Indira Gandhi green-lit Operation Blue Star and sent the military into the Golden Temple complex in Amritsar in June 1984, a calamitous raid that killed many worshippers and damaged part of the holy site, thousands more Sikhs flocked to join an independence movement, as that year the I.S.I. floated the rumour, again in the European media, that "a K.G.B. detachment" had advised Gandhi on the tactic. In October 1984, the prime minister was killed in her own garden by two Sikh guards, in what was seen as a catastrophic intelligence failure by the I.B. and the R.A.W.

One positive development at Lodhi Road was the creation in 1983 of a dedicated R.A.W. spy school, the Research and Analysis Service (R.A.S.). Previously, R.A.W. recruits had been selected from within the I.P.S. and retrained in espionage at an ad-hoc facility on the outskirts of Delhi. Even those taken straight into the service, like Monisha, had only received basic induction. From now on some spies would be plucked from college, like they were in the U.S. and U.K., fresh minds that could be shown the basics of espionage. One of those to benefit from direct entry was Rajinder Khanna, who would become a formidable officer with a stellar career with foreign postings to France and Myanmar, and who in 2014 would become the first R.A.W. chief drawn from its own cadre.

Apart from transforming its training regime, the R.A.W. also had to revolutionize how it ran operations and the regions it would operate in.

Having studied how the I.S.I. and the C.I.A. worked, the R.A.W. began experimenting with proxies steered through two counter-intelligence units, CIT-X and CIT-J. "X" worked on Pakistan while "J" targeted Pakistan-backed groups operating inside India.

After Indira Gandhi's killing, these two units converged to mount a string of revenge bombing and public disobedience campaigns that lit up Punjab and Sindh in Pakistan. "Equivalence became, secretly, the *theme*," Raman once told us. "When the I.S.I. sends men to strike in Manipur, Karachi finds itself fighting fires. When Amritsar was ungovernable, Lahore succumbed to blasts and riots." He aped the I.S.I., whose relationship with the C.I.A. was deepening and aggravating the R.A.W. that reached out to the Mossad in the late 1980s, a tricky manoeuvre given that India's first prime minister, Jawaharlal Nehru, had recognized the state of Israel in 1950, but as a nod to Palestinians declined to establish full diplomatic relations. Nehru worried that permitting Israel to open an embassy in New Delhi would damage wider relations with the Arab world, and this position was maintained, officially, until 1992.

The covert Israel manoeuvre was blessed by the new R.A.W. chief, the outfit's sixth, Anand Kumar Verma, a blunt I.P.S. officer from an intake for Madhya Pradesh and who took charge in 1987, becoming a close counsellor to prime ministers before an official post was created, one that would culminate in the creation of Ajit Doval's position today, as consiglieri and unofficial director of national intelligence.[15] Verma, who had spent many years in the I.B., had got noticed by being both operationally bold and analytically incisive, when officers were more usually one or the other. "It was Verma who made the R.A.W. more muscular," recalled Raman, "and made us bite again." In 1988 Raman and another were directed to set up several companies – including Piyush Investments and Hector Leasing and Finance – and use them to buy two interconnected apartments in the Gauri Sadan residential building on Hailey Road, New Delhi. Mossad's station chief travelled to India undercover on an Argentinian passport and used it as his safehouse.

The R.A.W. also edged into the sensitive South Africa conflict, where a young Mahatma Gandhi had raised a family and advocated non-violent resistance to campaign for civil rights. India still had a sizeable diaspora there and Indian trainers and spies aided the African National Congress, fighters schooled in situ and outside the continent too, in an expensive exercise whose counterbalance was an exploratory (and controversial) relationship with the apartheid regime. Playing off one's enemies against one's friends was a useful Machiavellian trait learned from the I.S.I. and Israel too.

A similar two-sided push–pull took place in Sri Lanka, where covertly R.A.W. trained the Liberation Tigers of Tamil Eelam (L.T.T.E.) and other Tamil armed groups, while flick-flacking to give secret support to the Sinhalese government in Colombo, as Israel did, selling attack boats to the government and anti-attack-boat marine engineering to the Tigers.[16]

Verma initiated some dangerous experimentation with low-key anti-Chinese measures, sending weapons to rebels on the Burmese border, including the Kachin Independence Army and Wa insurgents, who were fighting a pro-Chinese government, run by the ethnic Burmese in Rangoon and Chinese security forces to the north. Two veterans involved in these operations claimed that the Wa and Kachin funded their re-arming through trafficking heroin and the sale of jadeite hacked from slave-run pits. Simultaneously, Verma worked to establish a backchannel with Beijing via its Ministry for State Security.

But the R.A.W. continued to remain a poor cousin to the I.S.I.

Monisha

At a secret R.A.W. training hostel on the outskirts of Delhi, Monisha studied signals traffic from I.S.I. field detachments. It was a good way of understanding a complex outfit that cloaked its units and detachments with frequently changing numerical codes. At night, and taking the taskmaster Verma as her guide, Monisha worked on critical thinking, exploring theoretical pathways to knowledge, using books provided by instructors.

All birds have feathers, and all robins are birds. Therefore, robins have feathers. Deduction was supposedly the easiest process, in that a conclusion was drawn from facts that were gathered to build a case. But when an officer was undercover, evidence was often the hardest thing to come by, instructors warned her.

All brown dogs in the park today are small dogs. Therefore, all small dogs must be brown. Induction relied on probability, as it sought to draw a general conclusion from specific, incomplete instances. The R.A.W. thrived here and could identify significant beats and was able to produce conclusions from these that in all probability were true, which did not make them factual. The R.A.W. utilized these skills in perception operations, one of the outfit's strengths, where they wielded a selection of events to colour a person or country in ways that were persuasive, but not necessarily true.

When it rains, the grass gets wet. The grass is wet, it must have rained. The R.A.W., Monisha felt, was least capable when it came to abductive reasoning. It required analysts to stretch to a conclusion from whatever information was available, or at least arrive at *the best explanation possible*, the quality of the answer depending on the elasticity of the mind set the task. It required something that went far beyond a good education, or even brilliance, and, as Verma endlessly told officers in Lodhi Road, to think differently was not enough – what was required was an intellectual all-wheel drive.

In the early hours, as Verma suggested, Monisha polished her languages, hoping, at some point, to make the transition from analysis to clandestine service, which for a woman in the R.A.W. felt like a reach.

In the same way that post-9/11 the C.I.A. realized it had few Arabic speakers with clearances, languages were a blind spot at Lodhi Road. Only a small number of officers spoke key regional tongues like Pashtun and its variants, or the other languages of the North-West Frontier Province, Baluchistan, and Sindh. The outfit was filled with Hindus,

Sikhs, Christians, and atheists, but almost no Muslim senior officers were inducted at all. Monisha said her instructors did not hide their hostility to Islam. This made missions inside Islamic nations doubly dangerous as non-Muslims acting the part tended to overlook a detail.

Money, money, money

Nothing R.A.W. did matched the plushness of Pakistan's partnership with the C.I.A. in Afghanistan, which became a template for the I.S.I. and made Pakistan's spy agency rich. Raman, who was disgusted with the U.S. State Department and the C.I.A., wrote a series of alarm-ringing, bad-tempered reports suggesting that opium processing and heroin refining over the border had generated billions of untraceable dollars. He warned that "the reins of this business have been taken over by I.S.I. officers who used the cash for operations in Indian-administered Kashmir, the Punjab and North-East."[17] Pakistan's covert nuclear programme, the R.A.W. believed, was also underpinned by drug cash. Classified and largely gung-ho estimates suggested that the heroin business was 20 per cent larger than the Islamic republic's legitimate economy.[18] R.A.W. reports highlighted the inexplicable wealth of individual I.S.I. officers, one of them said to have $400,000 in foreign exchange bearer certificates, eight Pakistani Union Bank accounts containing $42 million, a dollar account at Deutsche Bank containing a further $19.1 million, three houses and three industrial units.[19]

General Zia too became concerned by the deep wealth of many spies and soldiers in Pakistan, belatedly concluding the security state had become rapacious.[20] A wealthy man himself, he expressed concern that the Pakistan military was officially spending almost 7 per cent of the country's G.D.P., but the actual figure, taking into account military purchases, salaries, and military-owned businesses, as well as interest on debt repayment, was likely over 40 per cent of the country's annual budget.[21] Dismayed, only an officer as unpredictable as Zia could have decided to do the unthinkable, and explore a tryst between Pakistan's and India's spy chiefs to discuss ways to de-escalate so that some of that cash could be repurposed into development. The order to talk fell to Lt. Gen. Hamid Gul, the intelligence chief.

On the face of it, this was an extraordinary gesture with an unlikely interlocutor. Gul did not conceal the fact that he despised India with a passion. Described in Indian newspapers as a "monster," he rubbed shoulders with senior C.I.A. officers but also Afghanistan's mujahideen leaders like Gulbuddin Hekmatyar and Jalaluddin Haqqani, whom he referred to as his "true friends." However, while Gul's public persona was of an unbending, chauvinist fairground barker, these words were often intended to hurt more than actually meant, and privately he described himself as pragmatic and anti-colonial.

In Lodhi Road, R.A.W. chief Verma, who hated Pakistan almost as much as Raman despised the Reagan Administration, was sufficiently concerned about black cash and off-the-books operations that he recommended the talks to Prime Minister Rajiv Gandhi. Verma sat down with Gul, a Pashtun from the Yusufzai tribe, in Amman. The secret meeting, in 1988, was hosted by Crown Prince Hassan of Jordan, who had opened-up his palace after a personal request from Rajiv Gandhi, endorsed by the C.I.A., which remained exceedingly close to the monarch.

"It was like a mongoose meeting a cobra," Raman told us. Verma warned Pakistan its cities would burn (again) if the Indian Punjab continued to simmer. "And if U.S. Stinger missiles intended for Afghanistan ever appeared in Kashmir, it would be war," Raman said. "And low and behold, Gul and Verma secretly got on exceedingly well." Gul confirmed this, bashfully, telling us he admired Verma's forthrightness. "Privately, we continued to exchange messages with one another," Hamid Gul claimed. "Our own backchannel." He contrived two more secret meetings, and even pondered peace. Negotiations, which were mostly conducted overseas, came close to settling disputes in the high Himalaya as well as de-escalating Kashmir. However, not everyone on the Pakistan side wanted rapprochement. In Delhi too there were hawks born for war.

Zia, aged sixty-four, died later that year, inexplicably, when his air force transporter exploded mid-air. The crash also claimed ten senior army officers, the U.S. military attaché, and the U.S. ambassador, Arnold Raphel.[22] Eight hours after the disaster, Gulam Ishaq Khan, the leader of the Senate, who assumed power, warned that "sabotage cannot be ruled out"; the crash would never be convincingly explained, giving way to decades of conspiracy theories that variously blamed the C.I.A, the Mossad, MI6, and the R.A.W., the Saudis, Jordanians, and even the Turkish. A version conjured a supernatural rapture that enveloped the crew. Gul survived by not getting on that transporter, but his career imploded, and he was removed from office the following year. "The talks, lacking deep-state backing, broke down," he told us. "Even I began to believe that the permanent war between nations was far too profitable to be quashed."

Verma clung on. He also hoped that detente could be kick-started but switched directions anyhow. If Pakistan had gone cold, he pondered a grand strategy of reaching out to another of Rawalpindi's sponsors, strengthening a backchannel to Beijing. But despite this and many other successes, the brilliant Verma, a lateral thinker and non-conformist, remained unloved at Lodhi Road, where the R.A.W. was once again impoverished, its numbers dwindling, with a 25 per cent shortfall in recruitment and a budget so fragile reform remained too expensive.

A domineering workaholic, Verma expected everything from his officers. But what they faced was an I.S.I. that continued to widen the base of its operations. By the 1990s, in Chennai, where Monisha was sent to work, analysts would spot I.S.I. fingerprints on Tamil regional politics, where black cash was funnelled to antagonize Delhi. And over the Palk Strait, Raman saw the I.S.I.'s footprints in Colombo and the Sinhala hinterland, where Islamist groups that were clients of Pakistan began seeding, as they did in the Mauritius.

In Kolkata, in the new millennium, R.A.W. analysts, like the resourceful Rana Banerji, studied every kidnapping and bank robbery for signs of I.S.I. input, as common crimes were often used to raise black cash.[23] A coiled ball of energy, Banerji, would become one of R.A.W.'s premier Pakistan watchers and eventually rise to Special Secretary in the Cabinet Secretariat.

Future R.A.W. chief Rajinder Khanna would do the same in Myanmar and Thailand where he came to identify I.S.I. glove puppets and false fronts, as well as their side businesses – flogging porn, trafficking in fake drugs, pressing counterfeit dollars and Indian rupees, acts that were profitable but that also sought to destabilize or demoralize India.

Iftikhar

In 1995, the I.S.I. talent scout dropped Iftikhar off at Omar Khayam Restaurant in the Blue Zone of Islamabad. Inside, his mother and father sat ready to celebrate his promotion to major, brimming with pride. "As the hot bread arrived, I did not tell my folks that I had just been tapped up," he recalled.

Lesson two: *secrecy severs a person from their moral anchors.*

Privately, Iftikhar was having second thoughts. In Pakistan, the I.S.I. was regarded anywhere between bacteria and an antibiotic. Most people tried not to talk about it at all. "The I.S.I. seldom referred to itself and often we used phrases like angels or ghosts," he said. "My friends called it the 'Other Place.' And spooks were *the Boys*."

He began to soul search: "Why had the I.S.I. zeroed in on me? I was not a bare-knuckle fighter or a blue blood. We were working people from Jhang."

His hands were smooth and his complexion fair – none of which tallied with lives spent in the wheat fields. We wondered about his antecedence. He stared at us, immediately reading our scepticism. "I take after my mother's side," he butted in. "They were traders from Kotli in Azad Kashmir." Pale-skinned workhorses, they came from the Pakistan-administered sector of the divided Kashmiri state.

And at that moment we glimpsed something that I.S.I. recruiters had likely seen too. This man who sensed our doubts was hyper-intuitive.

"Are *we* OK?" Iftikhar asked us.

"Sure. We're OK," we said.

"So . . . Walking into the I.S.I. . . ."

He recalled the entrance to the old building being inconspicuous. Bougainvillea tumbled over the barbed wire. An automated gate grumbled open and men with long guns wavered in the shadows. "Inside, there was no smell and doors were unnamed and unnumbered." Men and women milled around, like at any foreign corporation. Everything was compartmentalized. No part of the building encouraged co-mingling, even the mess hall. "There's chole and there's rice," Iftikhar said. Everyone used first names. Workers put thumbprints on oaths vowing not to talk.

Trainers came mainly from the Pakistan Army's School of Military Intelligence at Cliffden Camp, hidden away in the Murree hills, 55 kilometres outside Islamabad. The I.S.I. had almost no full-time instructors of its own but its goals and the military's intermingled: to promote Pakistan and destroy India. Iftikhar settled in and became steeped in the language and history of spying from Checkpoint Charlie to the Wakkhan Corridor.

Lessons began in everything from spotting and recruiting an asset, to breaking and entering, arranging a collect from an asset to leaving orders: the brush past and secure drops. He studied hard: collection and analysis, surveillance and counter-surveillance – working in teams and on his own. He learned to read a room or the street with the devotion his father had for an edition of the *Dosheeza* magazine when it arrived in the 1980s. Students worked on creating and maintaining a cover with all of its back stories and credentials. Some were tropes – known as Abdullahs. Others were as form-fitting as a diver's suit. We knew this man as Major Iftikhar, but that was just one of many identities he had assumed over the years. And to reach this point, there had been long periods of evaluation.

Pakistan was becoming far more conservative and religious because of the influx of mujahids and the opening of seminaries to train them, funded by Saudi Arabia. This fervour was felt in the armed forces too.

Espionage and the covert disciplines became taboos for religious troops who protested, claiming that spying was forbidden by the Quran, resulting in changes being made to Iftikhar's training.

He and his batch were introduced to a bearded tutor who smelled of curd and rice and who built a case for why prying *was* forbidden but spying – in defence of the faith and an Islamic republic – was permissible, even if it was on fellow Muslims.

Curd-&-Rice directed them to read a story about how the Prophet sent an emissary, Husayn, to roam the Arabian Desert sipping hibiscus cordial and gathering information from his sources among tribes who opposed Mohammed. He described the prophet as a master of misdirection, learning what his enemies were thinking by penetrating their cabals.

"War is information, but it is also deception," the tutor said, summarizing writings of, among others, Ibn Hajar al-Asqalani, a medieval Islamic scholar, who described how when Mohammed came to know what was expected of him he did the opposite. Al-Asqalani wrote that the Prophet believed tricks and deception prevented fighting.

The Prophet's life was steeped in covert practice. The first three years of his mission became known as the "Stage of the Secret Call," as his movements, the passing on of his message and practices, were concealed. "'He who keeps his secret keeps his choices,' Curd-&-Rice told us." He was echoing an Egyptian scholar, Al-Haythami. Writing in eighth- and ninth-century Cairo, the scholar concluded: "All war is cunning."[24]

Every morning, Curd-&-Rice would begin by reciting an extract from Verse 80 of his favourite Surah, known as *The Ornaments*: "Do they think that we do not hear their secrets and conspiracies? Yes indeed, our messengers are beside them, recording all."

He had one more piece of advice. "The use of arms should be the last resort," Curd-&-Rice told Iftikhar. "When the I.S.I. fails, Pakistan goes to war."

On a weekend's leave to Jhang, Iftikhar was taken to Yousaf Shah Road by his father and brothers for some warm carrot halwa. "It was then I spied a man who locked eyes and then turned away to pick at a mound of dahi bhalla."

Was Iftikhar being monitored or had the I.S.I. activated his peripheral vision, he wondered?

Lesson three: *the service is as unverifiable as it is deniable.*

The dangerous 1990s

Not only was the I.S.I. reaching out across the region, but it was also playing a more dangerous role inside Pakistan. "In August 1990 when a civilian prime minster, Benazir Bhutto, tried to ring-fence it, appointing her own nominee as chief, she was ousted," Raman observed. As prime minister, Nawaz Sharif did the same, appointing Lt. Gen. Javed Nasir as his D.G.-I.S.I. – only for Nasir to be barred from attending Corps Commanders conferences.

During Bhutto's second term – by which time the Soviet war was over and the C.I.A. had finally turned off its money tap – R.A.W. analysts concluded, in an internal report, that sections of the I.S.I. were "implicated in the murder of Bhutto's brother Murtaza, killed in September 1996."[25] The I.S.I. blamed the death on Benazir Bhutto's husband, Asif Ali Zardari, and eventually Bhutto herself, paving the way for her dismissal in 1996.[26]

The following year, on June 16, 1997, a slush fund of Rs 140 million (approximately $6.5 million) that was said to have been used by the I.S.I. to blacken Bhutto's Pakistan People's Party (P.P.P.) was exposed.[27] When Nawaz Sharif in his second term (which started in 1997) tried again to side-line the I.S.I., appointing the mild-mannered army engineer Lt. Gen. Ziauddin Butt as director general, the entire Joint Intelligence North (J.I.N.) was transferred to the Directorate-General of Military Intelligence (D.G.M.I.) by Pervez Musharraf, then the army chief, leaving the prime minister with an intelligence service that was a paper bag.

Outside the subcontinent, the R.A.W. was largely unknown and underrated, which are desirable adjectives for a secret organization but also demoralizing. In contrast, the I.S.I. triggered feelings of fear, wonder, hatred, and dismay. It was not down to its infallibility or its physical size. Employing about 10,000, the I.S.I. was twenty times smaller than the notorious F.S.B. in Russia (and about the same size as the R.A.W., if Lodhi Road was ever fully staffed). But the I.S.I. was battle-hardened, accomplished in unconventional warfare, tuned in to insurgencies all over the subcontinent, and flush with U.S. dollars and Saudi riyals. A powerful mythology was also spawned by the I.S.I.'s air of entitlement that acted like gun grease for some of its darker, pathological tendencies.

R.A.W., however, outstripped the I.S.I. in a few key areas. While it struggled with recruitment, funding, and its esprit de corps, grubbing around for political backing, it was, thanks to a burgeoning relationship with the Mossad, and tactical shopping expeditions in Africa, Europe, and the Middle East, becoming tech-savvy. As Langley refused to supply Aabpara with eavesdropping and surveillance equipment, arguing that these would be used against India, the I.S.I. fell behind.

It relied instead on the brute force of cold cash. In Pakistan, the ports and borders were seeded with paid informers. The Saudis were masters at this. Its General Intelligence Department, or Istakhbarat, recruited from among the thousands of impoverished Pashtun labourers (and those from India too) who came to the kingdom for work, only to return to their homes in Karachi and Kerala as informers for court in Riyadh.

Betrayals

Money (or income inequality) made both the R.A.W. and the I.S.I. uneasy. New officers, like Iftikhar and Monisha, were monitored by their respective counter-intelligence services. Foreign agencies, especially Russia's F.S.B. and the C.I.A., used hard cash to flip soldiers and spies, making deposits in foreign bank accounts. School or college-age children of C.I.A. assets were gifted free places at costly foreign institutions. Those who risked being exposed were offered new lives abroad. No one was immune to the lure of a better life, money, and power, as MI6, the C.I.A., and the F.B.I. – that were all deeply penetrated – knew well.[28]

The R.A.W. was betrayed profoundly at least nine times at the most senior levels. Sex was often the facilitator. Monisha recalled watching the fallout from a case that detonated in 1987 involving K. V. Unnikrishnan, a Kerala-born I.P.S. officer with a swagger and a family that he doted on.[29] "He had served for years in Sri Lanka, where he had done well," said Monisha, who worked with him. As a result, Unnikrishnan was transferred to Chennai and promoted, becoming one of R.A.W.'s most senior officers in the city, a deputy inspector general running a highly sensitive portfolio to covertly assist Tamils in Sri Lanka, including the deadly L.T.T.E.

But there was a shadow over his career. "We all suspected he had got himself into trouble in Colombo," said Monisha. He was alleged to have had an affair with a female U.S. consular official, according to a C.I.S. report that she saw, suggesting that they suspected this woman was working for the C.I.A. The relationship, Monisha said, demonstrated Unnikrishnan's lack of self-control. "That was downplayed, and we found ourselves working on the L.T.T.E. ticket."

A woman who said she was a friend of Unnikrishnan's old lover contacted him and he agreed to meet. A more straightforward officer who had already been imperilled would not have gone, Monisha said. "He should have reported the contact. These are the rules."

But Unnikrishnan made excuses to his colleagues and met with the caller, who claimed she was an American air hostess working for Pan Am out of Singapore. They saw each other a few times and she then sent the forty-seven-year-old an air ticket to join her in the island city state, where they had sex for the first time. "His absences were becoming more frequent, but no one seemed too worried," Monisha said. "There was a culture of male privilege," she claimed, "and hanging him out to dry would have harmed my career." Cash was also a consideration, she believed, with Unnikrishnan unable to provide for his children, one of whom was becoming an outstanding sportswoman.

Then the R.A.W. Sri Lanka desk began to flail. "Colombo seemed to know highly sensitive details about Indian operations," Monisha recalled. Secret arms shipments bound for the L.T.T.E. were seized. Finally, the R.A.W. launched a counter-intelligence inquiry in 1987, which would become one of the largest of its kind. At one point, most of the Madras Police Force was under investigation, until the inquisition settled on Unnikrishnan, who, cornered, was said to have admitted his guilt.[30]

His long-distance love affair had blown hot and cold, Monisha learned. And finally, after a few months, a C.I.A. case officer was waiting for him in Singapore in place of the Pan Am hostess. Confronting him with photos, the Agency had suggested a trade. Unnikrishnan had, Monisha recalled, taken the deal and over the next two years handed over to the C.I.A. some of India's most secret and sensitive intelligence, for which he was tried in camera, jailed and dismissed. "However, after one year in Tihar the spy was quietly released, and for reasons no one could fathom," Monisha said.

~

The R.A.W. and the I.S.I. both understood the power of sex. The I.S.I. went after lonely Indian army officers at staff college, who after an exchange of photos were blackmailed and recalled. The honeytrap evolved, operating in cyberspace often, spawning provocative and enthralling female and male avatars, who fished for gay and straight, male and female, Indian engineers, defence contractors, scientists, and diplomats, enticing them into private, intimate chats, which became eroticized and escalated.

Employees of BrahMos Aerospace, a joint venture between India's Defence Research and Development Organisation (D.R.D.O.) and the Military Industrial Consortium of Russia, was one outfit the I.S.I. targeted, ensnaring an engineer and a development scientist.[31]

The R.A.W. struck back in the new millennium. Major Iftikhar's boss, a blue-blooded I.S.I. executive officer sheltering beneath a diplomatic posting, was ambushed by a photographer (during the peak of the U.S. "war on terror") as he canoodled in the back of a car in Italy with a young South Asian woman.[32] Becoming aware of the cameraman, the I.S.I. officer fled so fast that he only realized when he made it back home that his wallet and phone were still in the footwell. The next day, as he sweated it out, wondering what to do, a visitor called at Pakistan's embassy. It was a courier hand-delivering the missing items, a signal that everyone understood. The officer's spying career was over.

These ploys were invariably greasy. An academic we met in Pakistan in 2017 described how, aged twenty-five, she was shopping around for work to help raise funds for a foreign grad school when she was approached by a government official. "A local woman came to see me in 2015 and said: 'We heard you are on the market right now. You're potentially a good fit for a job in government, if you have the strength of character: *a sense of yourself.*'"

Sharmeen straightened her turquoise dupatta and told us her story carefully. She was still processing what had happened. "I had been brought up by close, loving parents, who always wanted the best for me. So, I told the woman: 'I trust myself. My *parents* trust me.'"

The recruiter butted in and corrected her: "*They* can never hear about *this*."

Sharmeen had been startled and wished she had listened to her inner voice. "This was starting to feel like grooming. Who separates a kid from their parents? But I said to myself, *you need the cash.*"

She was instructed to browse online for profiles of visiting academics and businesspeople. She was told to create a LinkedIn profile (with photo) and contact executives and officials, asking for employment. Well educated, with languages, and immaculately presented, she got several responses almost immediately. Following instructions, she migrated the leads to WhatsApp. Then a trainer stepped in saying he would take over, while she dug for more leads.

Several days later, in an empty office, curiosity got the better of her and she attempted to log in to her WhatsApp account once more. Its username and password had not been changed and she scrolled through the messages. The online version of her was chilling. Her avatar had sent provocative messages which became flirtatious, the posts including attachments of movie clips and images – shots of a shoulder, a breast and then a thigh, purportedly filmed by her. These elicited a flurry of provocative and then explicit videos from her correspondent. She deleted the account and a day later was asked to leave.

Sharmeen swept some dust from her desk. She put her pens in a line. The electricity fizzed, the lights going dark, the desktop computer babbling as it powered down. "They paid me off," she said. Green tea arrived and a plate of almond crackers.

She sipped and nibbled, her face a map of self-doubt.

The late 1990s: New flare-ups

India's tech investment paid off by the late 1990s. Indian intelligence got inside the computer of Gen. Jehangir Karamat. The Chairman Joint Chiefs of Staff, a four-star general, Karamat had authorized Pakistan's testing of its nuclear bomb that year and remained adjacent to the security services after he retired.[33]

In May 1999, when a band of infiltrators occupied isolated peaks in the Himalaya on the Indian side of the LoC, they were lauded by Pakistan army chief Pervez Musharraf as "freedom fighters" from Kashmir. However, when Musharraf went on an official visit to Beijing, he used a hotel landline to consult with his Chief of the General Staff. The long-distance call was intercepted by Indian intelligence, and Musharraf was recorded referring to the intruders as Pakistan regulars, leading to a cringing withdrawal.

Following his own goal, on Christmas Eve that year, an Indian Airlines jet leaving Nepal was taken over by armed men from Pakistan and forced down in Amritsar. There, no Indian Special Forces raid materialized. Instead, the jet left India's airspace, circling the Gulf, where Delhi failed to persuade the authorities to let it land to enable a Special Forces raid. The pilot eventually put down in hostile Kandahar, in Afghanistan. There, the Taliban laid down a perimeter; however, I.S.I. officers were eavesdropped guiding negotiations from the control tower, according to Ajit Doval, one of the negotiators brought in by the I.B. to handle the crisis.

Doval had cut his teeth working the clandestine sector of the I.B., wading into brutal Pakistan-funded insurgencies in the North-East and the Punjab during the 1980s. These were pitiless campaigns where many thousands died on all sides, and that continue to traumatize the states. Apart from his drive and focus, Doval's superpower was to project certainty, evoke necessity, and escape public or political censure.

But during the Kandahar hijack, the I.B. officer felt frustrated and helpless. He described the IC 814 saga as a "diplomatic failure" for India.[34] Finally, after much agonizing, no raid was ordered, and the passengers were exchanged for prisoners in Indian jails. They included the British insurgent Omar Sheikh and the Pakistan cleric Masood Azhar. Osama bin Laden threw a celebratory dinner at his Kandahar airport compound, hailing the men as heroes. Their release would have an extraordinary impact on the future of the subcontinent. For Doval too this was a turning point. On the tarmac for the duration, he would never forget being outplayed and losing traction with a government in Delhi that chose flight rather than fight.

However, Doval was bitterly aware that the crisis was also a colossal intelligence failure. R.A.W. officer U.V. Singh, serving as second secretary in the Indian embassy in Kathmandu, had reported to his counsellor and fellow R.A.W. officer Shashi Bhushan Singh Tomar that an asset at the airport believed a hijacking was in the offing with the plotters coming from Pakistan. A car was said to have been driven to Tribhuvan Airport, registered to the first secretary of the Pakistan embassy, Arshad Cheema. He had claimed diplomatic immunity to prevent it being searched, the vehicle, R.A.W. believed, ferrying weapons airside. Cheema later denied this version.

But U.V. Singh's lead had not been developed. Instead, Tomar took flight IC 814 to Delhi and sat in 16C.[35] His presence then became a hindrance. He was travelling to see his wife, Sonia, whose sister was married to N.K. Singh, the powerful principal secretary to the Vajpayee government. Sonia's eldest sister, Shyama, was a Congress party candidate, who that year had successfully won the Lok Sabha seat for Aurangabad, in Bihar. She was married to Nikhil Kumar, the director general of the National Security Guards, whose outfit would have stormed the plane. These connections might have prevented another outcome. But there would be retribution, of a kind favoured by Doval.

In a third act, in April 2001, Nepali internal security received a tip-off about a bomb threat and launched a raid, arresting a couple, and finding 16 kilos of RDX, a military grade explosive. The detained man was Arshad Cheema, and he noisily protested that he had been set up. Cheema claimed diplomatic immunity *again*. But twice was too much for Nepal, and the diplomat, doxed by the R.A.W., was deported.[36]

After the IC 814 affair, a moratorium on R.A.W. hot actions in Pakistan, instigated in 1997, was lifted. Indian intelligence hit back repeatedly and secretly at the I.S.I. and its proxies. It commenced dizzying information wars that billowed like stage fog over the region, building a narrative about Rawalpindi being the prime manipulator of regional terror. In this version, India was a perennial victim and, as a result, many Western nations would also start to perceive Pakistan as toxic. If Doval learned anything from IC 814, it was that peace was not preferable to winning and that talking was overrated.[37]

Part 2

9/11 and Its Long Shadow

2001

In the fallout from the Kargil War, in October 1999, Army Chief General Pervez Musharraf seized power from Prime Minister Nawaz Sharif, whom he accused of running to the U.S. to seek sanctuary for his entire family, instead of remaining resolute over the incursions. Musharraf would elevate himself to chief executive and later president, moving General Mahmud Ahmed, a trusted confidant, into the I.S.I. as its chief. Musharraf wanted a battle-hardened war veteran – "a trustee" – to watch his back.[1]

General Ahmed, like Musharraf, had been a child at Partition and witnessed the killings and violence close-up. Born in Ludhiana, in the Punjab, he was religious and conservative and having fought in the wars of 1965 and 1971 became deeply anti-Indian. When he joined the I.S.I., Lt. Gen. Hamid Gul, a former I.S.I. chief, was a mentor. But in this new posting at the spy agency, Ahmed was unlucky. He was in Washington, D.C. on 9/11, meeting future C.I.A. director Porter Goss for breakfast, when the first plane crashed into the World Trade Center. "I knew he liked military history and I'd brought him a book," Goss told us.[2] "I was going to give it to him when we got to my office. But it never happened. He had to rush off. The book is still on my shelf, all wrapped up."

As Ahmed struggled to find a way out of the U.S., he experienced the full force of America's wrath. On September 12, Deputy Secretary of State Richard Armitage told him that Pakistan had to make a choice:

45

"You are either one hundred per cent with us or one hundred per cent against us – there is no grey area." That afternoon, he also met George Tenet, the C.I.A. director, who later told us he was "lobbying hard" to drop a C.I.A. hit squad into Afghanistan to take out Osama bin Laden and the Taliban leadership.[3]

Ahmed recalled that he advised Tenet that Mullah Omar, the Taliban chief, was a religious man, and not a violent one. It was a vital distinction. The cleric did not support what bin Laden had done and had not assisted the "planes operation," which he despised.[4] The best way to get to al Qaeda was to befriend the Taliban and use Mullah Omar as the intermediary, Ahmed believed.[5]

As a blood lust and real fear gripped America and George Tenet struggled for political survival at the C.I.A., this was not what he or the Bush administration wanted to hear or were ready to accept. It looked like appeasement, Tenet told us, while for Ahmed it was pragmatism.

Musharraf, back in Rawalpindi, had been galvanized by the crisis and had had a vision of a new Pakistan. The country needed a "drastic course-correction" and there could be no more back-room manoeuvring, he told us. Instead, a "controlled democracy" had to flourish. He called for a fresh strategic outlook, including, unusually, peace with India. The president's ideas were put down in a classified briefing note: "Can we survive a US-led Backlash against al Qaeda and Taliban?"[6]

Stamped "Secret," the briefing expressed itself with the kind of frankness that deep classification is intended to elicit. "Pakistan cannot win a military conflict with the US and yet we are heading for one," it concluded.

We must change, while 1. guarding our sovereignty and 2. protecting strategic interests.

The US will go to war over al Qaeda at some point, and the Taliban will become casualties for shielding them, unless we can persuade them otherwise – which is *doubtful*. Then, Pakistan will have to choose. And if Pakistan chooses Taliban, while this decision will be popular, it will also be disastrous.

Let us consider: 1. Taliban are mostly beyond ISI influence. 2. If we cannot get their attention, how do we protect our interests in Afghanistan? The task is capturing their attention and maintaining influence over the US. But also reaching out to India. War on every border is not desirable and, critically, unsustainable.[7]

The briefing tells a radically different version of events to that voiced in Washington, where the I.S.I. was projected as practically running the Taliban and colluding with al Qaeda.

Walking Musharraf's tightrope, spy chief Ahmed worried about Pakistan's failure to voice its national interest, and to develop a robust public voice. The military way was to work quietly and in secret without ever creating a public consensus.[8] He was sent on a mission to see the Taliban, hoping to re-engage the movement and safeguard it from a U.S. air war, while Rawalpindi tried to win them a deal.

The overworked Ahmed was then dispatched back to Washington, D.C., carrying a message of change (in Pakistan) and continuity (in Afghanistan). Ahmed was "stoic, honest and loyal," Musharraf said. He could be "relied on for straight talk."[9]

With the intel chief gone, more reports that Musharraf commissioned landed on his desk. One, entitled "The Role of the Gun," stated that after so many years of being a front-line state and a launch pad for jihad, Pakistan was bent out of shape. "Weapons are everywhere. They are currency," the brief concluded. Development would not happen without firearm amnesties. "This should be a priority."[10]

Musharraf also tasked the I.S.I. with ending communalism – the wars between Islamic sects – and asked his staff to think about what kind of democracy Pakistan might become. In the frankest terms, the briefs explored whether the nation could become more like Thailand, or Singapore, where the military dropped their uniforms to sit in parliaments rather than invisibly puppeteering democracy. Musharraf mused and decided that a clear-out was needed to enable him to move quicker. He wanted a new team of deeper thinkers.

Almost one month after 9/11, on the night of October 7, Musharraf called General Ehsan ul-Haq at home. A specialist in anti-aircraft warfare, the quietly spoken Pakistan Air Force officer had been commissioned from the Army Air Defence Command. He was a clinical and forward-thinking family man, with a son in an American college, which made him, Musharraf believed, a pragmatist. "Mahmud's gone," Musharraf told ul-Haq, who recalled it took him a minute to understand where this was leading.[11]

Pakistan needed a suave, plain dealer to tackle Washington. Ul-Haq was a former director general of Military Intelligence, and the outgoing XI Corps Commander based in Peshawar. He had graduated on a diet of noodles, engineering, and physics at the People's Liberation Army Air Force Aviation University in Zhengzhou, China. Musharraf knew that he would understand the geometry of the new Pakistan–U.S. pact, with its multiple narratives.

Ul-Haq would be ruthless in dead-heading the I.S.I., pruning the time-servers, and weeding out the worst of Hamid Gul's old protégés, those who would impede Musharraf or conspire against him as he manoeuvred closer to the U.S. to ensure his own political survival. Musharraf recalled that ul-Haq "was a crocodile," a lethal submarine capable of terminal aggression – which to his way of thinking was a compliment.[12] But the army, the largest and most powerful defence wing, traditionally ran the I.S.I. and ul-Haq's elevation as an air man to D.G.-I.S.I. would also see him leapfrog army men of seniority, creating deep bitterness. Musharraf did not care. And ul-Haq gave the impression that neither did he.

Musharraf doubled down on General Ahmed, using his departure to play to a U.S. audience that was still uncertain about Pakistan. Mahmud had been "the wrong man," Musharraf confided in U.S. officials, representing "old Islamist tendencies."[13] Ul-Haq told us this was not true. The Director General, Analysis (D.G.A.), General Javed Alam Khan, a secular officer who counted Ahmed as a friend, described it as "poppycock."[14] But it was useful for the U.S. to report Ahmed's ousting this way, ul-Haq recalled. "Back with your old enemy, Pakistan, you need a clean sheet, I guess," he said. "As for the U.S. and Indian headlines: I.S.I. is deradicalized. What rot! Rubbish. We never deradicalized, de-Islamized, downsized. But if Washington wanted to project that Pakistan – now a major ally – had reformed, with Ahmed purged, let them! We did not lose a man and the I.S.I. was about to grow."

As Pakistan struggled to realign itself with America, the permanent war with India got in the way. R.A.W., still livid over Kargil, and dismayed by the U.S. decision to back Pakistan, hoped to use the fallout from 9/11 to flag India as a preferential client.

~

Monisha had reached a personal realization. Once you learned to step around the politics and the chauvinism inside R.A.W., the uncles and the lotharios, the mansplainers and the Brahminical zealots, the spying life was invigorating. She loved it more than a marriage, she told herself. More than having a mother. More than a fat salary, fancy apartment, a car. More than regular hours, vacations, and a family lunch at Kolkata's Allen Kitchen, which had been a ritual. More even than public praise and recognition. She was starting to understand the seduction of the clandestine world, the pleasure of doing something that made history which would only ever be known by a handful of people. Right now, one of these R.A.W. deep plays unfolded, and she was on its coattails.

It began with the Press Trust of India scoop on October 7, 2001, at 23:08 I.S.T.:

While the Pakistani Inter Services Public Relations (ISPR) claimed that former ISI Director-General Lt-Gen Mahmud Ahmed sought retirement after being superseded on Monday, the truth is more shocking. Top sources confirmed here on Tuesday, that the general lost his job because of the evidence India produced to show his links to one of the suicide bombers that wrecked the World Trade Center (WTC).

The US authorities sought his removal after confirming the fact that $100,000 was wired to WTC hijacker Mohammed Atta from Pakistan by Ahmad Umar Sheikh at the instance of Gen Mahmud. Senior government sources have confirmed that India contributed significantly to establishing the link between the money transfer and the role played by the dismissed ISI chief. While they did not provide details, they said that Indian inputs, including Sheikh's mobile phone number, helped the FBI in tracing and establishing the link.[15]

The conclusion was stunning:

A direct link between the ISI and the WTC attack could have enormous repercussions. The US cannot but suspect whether or not there were other senior Pakistani army commanders who were in the know of things. Evidence of a larger conspiracy could shake US confidence in Pakistan's ability to participate in the anti-terrorism coalition.

The report raised the bogie of IC 814 and Omar Sheikh, the British prisoner released after the hijacking, all of which projected the U.S. as suffering from Stockholm Syndrome by partnering with Pakistan (where Washington was the victim who empathized with its abductor, Islamabad):

Indian officials say they are vitally interested in the unravelling of the case since it could link the ISI directly to the hijacking of the Indian airlines Kathmandu–Delhi flight to Kandahar last December. Ahmad Umar Sayeed Sheikh is a British national and a London School of Economics graduate who was arrested by the police in Delhi following a bungled 1994 kidnapping of four westerners, including an American citizen.

Within hours, the story was in the *Wall Street Journal*.

"Our Friends the Pakistanis ..."

Yesterday we noted a report from a Pakistani newspaper that Lt. Gen. Mahmud Ahmed had been fired as head of Islamabad's Inter-Services Security agency after U.S. linked him to a militant allied with terrorists who hijacked an Indian Airlines plane in 1999. Now the *Times of India* says Ahmed is connected to the Sept. 11 attacks:

Top sources confirmed here on Tuesday that the general lost his job because of the "evidence" India produced to show his links to one of the suicide bombers that wrecked the World Trade Center. The U.S. authorities sought his removal after confirming the fact that $100,000 were wired to W.T.C. hijacker Mohammed Atta from Pakistan by Ahmad Umar Sheikh at the instance of Gen Mahmud.

Senior government sources have confirmed that India contributed significantly to establishing the link between the money transfer and the role played by the dismissed I.S.I. chief. While they did not provide details, they said that Indian inputs, including Sheikh's mobile phone number, helped the F.B.I. in tracing and establishing the link.[16]

Back at Aabpara, senior I.S.I. officials were thrown into a panic by what they concluded was an I.B.–R.A.W. play. They knew that India had recently pounced on a real Islamist cell in West Bengal that had been remotely coached by the I.S.I. It was led by an Indian national, Asif Raza Khan (A.R.K.), jailed for the possession of explosives in 1994, the investigation revealing that he had flirted with insurgent groups in Pakistan that were heading for Kashmir.

In Delhi's Tihar Jail, A.R.K. had mixed with others housed in the terrorist wing – including Briton Omar Sheikh and preacher Masood Azhar – who persuaded him that he should launch a war on his release in 1999. A.R.K. did just that, and R.A.W.'s Rana Banerji had dived into A.R.K.'s operations – which included a series of kidnappings the following year – deducing that these were carried out to finance attacks on India.[17]

To stick the knife into General Ahmed, the I.S.I., and Pakistan in general, Indian intelligence bound truth and fiction, that A.R.K. was committed to terrorize India, and that the proceeds of his actions were wired via the I.S.I. to al Qaeda hijackers. "This was inductive thinking at its best," Monisha said, praising the way the intelligence community crafted a compelling false argument.

The suggestion that the 9/11 plotters had used a public figure like Ahmed to wire money to hijackers in Florida was patently unbelievable. In the month leading to the operation, Osama bin Laden had not even told his own shura about the brewing operation.[18] The eleven hijackers were briefed a few hours before boarding the planes. Only those trained to fly knew some but not all of what was coming. It had been a highly compartmentalized plan, which was one of the main reasons for it succeeding. Another was the advice al Qaeda gave to all fighters and fieldworkers – "Never trust the I.S.I."[19]

According to subsequent inquiries, the C.I.A. did not call for Ahmed's sacking or find him culpable.[20] German intelligence did not find any links between the I.S.I., Ahmed, and the hijackers.[21] And the only man who did know – and could reveal – where the money from the Kolkata crime wave went was A.R.K. He was shot dead by Indian cops in a contrived cold kill in Rajkot, Gujarat, in December 2001, which meant he could never take the stand.[22]

General ul-Haq said ruefully: "Our enemy is smart. I would have done the same if I was them." The story dragged on for years, even after the U.S. 9/11 Commission Report did not name General Ahmed or accuse the I.S.I. of culpability.[23] But the I.S.I. would struggle to shake off the building suspicion in the West, one that was shot through with Islamophobia: that a nation of Muslims was in league with al Qaeda.

So powerful was the idea that it would resurface in testimony by John Pistole, Deputy Assistant Director of the F.B.I.'s counterterrorism division, in 2003, only for his evidence to be corrected later by the Bureau. "The F.B.I. has clarified that Pistole meant the funds were traced back to [Khalid Sheikh Mohammad, the architect of 9/11] in Pakistan.

No actual bank accounts there have been identified."[24] But the R.A.W. version and Pistole's uncorrected earlier statement continued to gather momentum, contributing to comments made in a 2015 memoir by deep thinker Neeraj Kumar, a former Delhi police commissioner.[25]

It was a slugging match, with each side painting the other as zealots and sectarians. But India's beguiling narrative was winning in the West.

~

The U.S. invasion of Afghanistan began on the same day – October 7, 2001 – as the new intelligence chief was driven to the I.S.I. HQ. Inside, there were so many moving parts that needed rethinking and recalibrating, General Ehsan ul-Haq figured that he would be well into his retirement before the reforms were completed. It would take at least as long for Pakistan to become another kind of country.

Ul-Haq – who classed himself as an authoritarian democrat – chalked out a blueprint for I.S.I. Analysis, expanding it to consider new theatres of conflict – creating more desks and inducting language and area specialists. Internal, the I.S.I. C-Wing, was honed to better run political management in critical areas, especially the Punjab and Sindh, eventually making headway in the Federally Administered Tribal Areas (FATA) where the I.S.I. had fallen behind. C-Wing would also prop up Musharraf and his political party, the Pakistan Muslim League-Q, by bribing or threatening powerful factions as well as taking on news control.

Next, he focussed on I.S.I. counterterrorism. He shortlisted as chief an outsider, Brigadier Azmat Hyat. An armoured infantry officer, Hyat was an unusual but canny choice. "The army had been very kind to me," Hyat reflected.[26] He was a big man whose size was cloaked by his manners. Today he lives in a respectable, fading sector of Islamabad in a detached, practical villa. Gracious but cautious, ever worried by the watchers who could make trouble for him and his family, he chose a time that was far too late to be a formal supper and could be interpreted as an unannounced visit.

A marble-floored hall gave way to a secluded, sparse living room, and elderly staff who had served with him all over the country, rushed around bringing plates of hot snacks and sweet tea. He spoke unfalteringly, recalling everything he had done, while two phones constantly trilled, a TV blaring with headlines from an Urdu news channel. This was also his tradecraft.

The R.A.W. was watching the counterterror revamp too, but analysts were conflicted about Pakistan's goals and angered by the attention the U.S. was paying to Aabpara rather than Lodhi Road. Officers were also finding it hard to get over the fact that a nation that had used terror covertly ever since 1947 was now making a concerted push to counter it.

Hyat was a mystery for officers like Monisha. His rise in the military appeared to have been stymied by question marks over his temperament. Hyat would never roll over. That was one of his peccadillos, two of his colleagues claimed, and this might have capped his career at brigadier. He would never move if he believed an order was palpably wrong. He was righteous, a tad moralistic even, which was never a good thing as general officers were required to be pragmatic and loyal. Monisha said: "There was a touch of finger-wagging about Hyat, almost puritanism. Perhaps he had too much self-regard."

However, she saw something else too. I.S.I. instructors and senior executives repeatedly complained that most officers could never be posted outside Pakistan as they had seldom left the country unless making umrah and lacked international finesse. They rarely, if ever, had to dress in the modes of the Far East or the West and were unlikely to survive an Italian restaurant menu.

The doe-eyed son of a pious lieutenant general in Rawalpindi recently told us how his only contact with Americans had been in a battle-royale campaign on the game "Call of Duty: Modern Warfare," and then when he had asked the kids from Bedford Heights, Ohio, if they prayed, they asked him if he knew anyone in al Qaeda.

Brigadier Hyat, however, had fought, shat, and bled beside C.I.A. paramilitaries in foxholes in the Afghan war. He had crammed alongside them at the U.S. Army Infantry School at Fort Benning, Georgia, graduating in 1987. From then until 1996, he frequently visited the U.S., training and studying conflict in West Asia, Northern Africa, and Afghanistan. He was comfortable in the lecture hall and the taproom. He could boardslide around the rim of American culture. And then there was the question of Hyat's antecedence. Afghanistan was pivotal in the post-9/11 wars and he had his roots there. His mother came from a Pashtun family on the Durand Line.

There was another reason for ul-Haq's choice that R.A.W. could not see: Hyat's failure. His inability to break through into the upper echelons had left him dejected, and ul-Haq sensed that the herculean task as counterterror chief – even though it was a poisoned chalice – would be impossible for the man to refuse.

~

Key to shaping New Delhi's understanding of the I.S.I. manoeuvres was Syed Asif Ibrahim – who in 2012 would become the first and only Muslim officer to head I.B. He was a graduate of Jawaharlal Nehru University, in Delhi, and selected for the I.P.S. in 1977 as part of the Madhya Pradesh batch. His career began in the state's bandit-belt of Bhind–Morena, where *baaghis* hunted, like Malkhan "Dada" Singh, whose tilak looked like a broadsword and whose moustache grew like knotweed. Dada Singh's band hid away in the ochre ravines called *beehad*, from where Ibrahim oversaw their surrender.[27] Elsewhere, in Rajasthan, he ordered a phone tap on a gang thought responsible for the abduction of a wealthy jeweller, and the cops tasked with bringing him the data turned up with the phone booth on the back of a truck.

Ibrahim, wily and resilient, caught the attention of the I.B. He was part of the team that captured Omar Sheikh in 1994, after the Briton had abducted three Britons and an American, in Delhi, hoping to free the Punjabi cleric Masood Azhar.[28] He had been caught earlier in the year in Kashmir, travelling on a fake Portuguese passport and riding in an autorickshaw that stalled.[29] While India projected the I.S.I.-sponsored insurgency in Kashmir as terrifying and all-consuming, it was often penny-pinching and amateur as Azhar's case revealed. Omar Sheikh was put behind bars, where he was reunited with the plump preacher, and where Ibrahim continued to visit both with ever more questions that got him deeper into their heads. He also began to pay closer attention to the increasing zealotry in Pakistan that had leached into the armed forces, not to mention the rise of the Taliban and al Qaeda in Afghanistan, worrying about the backwash.

On one trip, we sat with Ibrahim in a well-guarded bungalow ringed by marigolds, in the heart of Lutyens Delhi. He ordered Chinese food, and over a plate of sweet and sour chicken, interspersed with cigarettes, he summarized a study he had done for the P.M.O. on India's vulnerability to Islamism.[30] "Would India experience an al-Qaeda-backed Islamist uprising and insurgency?" he asked himself. "Was there anything about India, in terms of the interpretation or worship of Islam, that might thwart al Qaeda?"

He read, canvassed opinions, and came up with a theory. Several hundred years ago, Muslim travellers and preachers came to India from Constantinople, via overland routes. These Ottomans mostly subscribed to the Hanafi school, one of the four principal thought silos in Sunni Islam, and whose laws were broadly based on consensus. The Hanafi school became the most popular stream of Islam in India.

Within the Hanafi college was a revivalist movement. It began in 1867 in Deoband, Uttar Pradesh, in the wake of the 1857 war of independence, where the British Empire became a common enemy for Muslims and Hindus. After Partition, the Darul Uloom, the house of knowledge, in Deoband, passed a fatwa against making jihad in the newly independent republic.[31] It ruled that India was not *dar al-harb* – in a state of war – and not *dar al-Islam* – an Islamic state. India was *dar al-aman* – a place of peace – because its new constitution provided for freedom of religion. This had bought India time. In Pakistan, on the other hand, Deobandis fuelled armed sectarians like the psychopathic Lashkar-e-Jhangvi (LeJ), which murdered and hounded Shia business leaders and clerics, as well as the Pakistan talibans known as the T.T.P., and the Afghan Taliban.[32]

Other sects would come to India via sea routes, like those that belonged to the Shafi'i school, but they only anchored in pockets along the western Konkan coast, including Kerala. In these enclaves, sporadic support for al Qaeda, and later the Islamic State, was incubated.

However, the majority of Indian Muslims were not turning to Islamism of any kind, Ibrahim reported back. He fired up another cigarette. "We concluded that Pakistan was far more of a threat to India than al Qaeda would ever be."

~

In June 2001, Major Iftikhar flew from Karachi to Bangladesh. At Mazhar Mistanna Bhandar, a well-loved sweet shop in old Dhaka, crowds queued for their *kalojam*, sponge fingers soaked in sugar, and Iftikhar picked up tickets there and a new identity. The documents said he was heading for Delhi, and he wondered if there was always so little time to learn a legend. One thing was for sure, he thought, studying his boarding card. Next time the I.S.I. deployed him to India he would insist on an aisle seat.

Officially, Iftikhar was here to enforce a Kashmir ceasefire, demanded by the U.S. and signed off by Musharraf, who had pledged to stop all Pakistan-backed insurgents fighting anywhere in India and concentrate on supporting President Bush's "war on terror". But it had to be the right kind of peace and secretly Iftikhar was also in Kashmir to disrupt R.A.W.–I.B. operations designed to encourage an Indian peace deal in the Valley that was favourable to Delhi and that would cast it in a better light in Washington.

Entering the humid terminal in Delhi, crumpled and sweating, he rushed to the toilet, locking himself into a cubicle. He needed a moment to compose himself. Crouching on the seat, he scanned his passport. Where was his boarding pass? He had left it in the seat pocket. Without it, customs officers could pull him aside as they would not be able to match it to his baggage tag. Too late.

At immigration he had role-played his part: a jovial greeting; his counterfeit passport open, the two-sentence idle chatter about the weather. The tired Indian officer did not even raise his eyes from his screen. Beyond the baggage carousel, a long line backed up into the hall as a pair of overworked customs inspectors in their white uniforms moved glacially. When it was his turn, they grabbed the tag from his case but did not ask for his pass. Pakistan and India were alike, Iftikhar thought. There were so many systems and such shoddy implementation.

Staring out of the open window of his non-A.C. taxi, absorbing the view, he realized he was in the capital of his imagination, the city from where the R.A.W. had filtered so many of its operations. *Secrete yourself somewhere busy.* As arranged, he instructed the driver to head for the middle-class grid of Jangpura, in the south of the city.

He checked into a small guest house and found himself staring at the Arabic prayer, behind the cashier. This was a Muslim establishment – and poor tradecraft. He was supposed to be among secular Western tourists. Next time, he would double-check every detail and not leave it to others. He dumped his bag, and ventured into the city, collecting drops close to the Chaat Wala. Among the things that had been left for him by unseen hands was a train ticket for Jammu, the winter capital of Jammu and Kashmir.

There was something appalling and thrilling about entering the Indian sector of the divided state, one of the longest and largest militarized conflicts on earth with among the highest number of security services, somewhere he had assumed he would never get to see.[33] His orders from Aabpara were: stay off the grid, bolster pro-Pakistan civilian factions, and deal with armed renegades who had switched support from Rawalpindi to Delhi.

His reports were to be encrypted and stashed at drops, where a chain of couriers, strangers to each other, would transport them to a relay point. But he planned other measures too. Uploading to the internet via comments posted on newspaper articles, leaving drafts in an email program for another user to sign into and pick up. Iftikhar's emergency plan involved letting off short bursts of signals over a portable Sky Waves UHF radio beacon, a pole, and kite-shaped wires, that were moved from hill to hill at night amid great secrecy.

At Delhi railway station the security was overwhelming. He pointedly made eye contact with the transport police. On board, he waited for the inspector's sweep through. When his turn came, his ticket was punched, and the officer strolled on. He was invisible and nine hours later he was in Jammu. Outside the station he flagged down a shared taxi and hung his head out of the window like a travel-sick dog, avoiding conversation, eventually arriving in downtown Srinagar.

Getting down at bustling Dal Gate, he bought an overpriced pouch of saffron, stuffing it into his pocket as a souvenir and a talisman. He stopped before the window of a photo studio, ogling at Hindu honeymooners swaddled in the synthetic folds of a Chinese blanket, posing in a cardboard *shikara*. He thought about how Kashmir was for most Indians a paradise of Mughal nights, while for so many in Pakistan it was a day-bright reminder of how they had been cheated by Partition.

Iftikhar flagged down an autorickshaw to take him to Ganderbal, a town on a kink of the Jhelum River, north of Srinagar, with the mountains rising behind it. His house had wooden eaves, and a green rippled roof. Behind it were stepped fields and the fast-flowing river. When dusk came, he lit a fire with kindling, as he had been told to. The smoke was a signal for his helpers. Seeing a Kashmiri *pheran* hanging on the door, he unhooked the wool cape and threw it on, while thinking of his mother who was buried in hers.[34]

A gentle knocking woke him, and a figure slipped inside. Iftikhar rose unnerved and, as his eyes adjusted, he realized it was a young woman and he recoiled, embarrassed. But she smiled and motioned for him to lie back down, as she crossed over to the hearth, where she dumped an armful of wood. "I'm sorry," he said in Urdu, feeling exposed.

She introduced herself but did not ask for his name. He was to call her Yasmeena. She was pale, with dark green eyes, and wore a rose-coloured *pheran*. She was barefoot. Perhaps she lived nearby, he thought, as he watched her bring the fire back to life. Water boiled, she made tea and they stared at each other, until she broke first, and, laughing, pulled herself away to begin cooking.

At 3 a.m., footsteps woke him. He did not remember falling asleep. Yasmeena was gone, but men with long guns pushed through the door.

~

After two wars, 1947 and 1965, Kashmir had boiled up once more in 1989, when hundreds of thousands took to the streets across the Valley to protest India's rule (and a badly rigged election).[35] Slow to act, in 1993 Aabpara had sent covert officers, via Bangladesh, to Delhi and Srinagar, to shape the unrest. Many senior I.S.I. officers we spoke to said that Pakistan wanted Kashmir, but if push came to shove, they would settle for India losing it.[36]

A young captain in the I.S.I., Nusrat Naeem, helped to form the Hurriyat (which means freedom in Urdu), a loose alliance of twenty-six organizations, that came together to fight for a separate Kashmiri state. Its leaders, Naeem told us, were glued to the I.S.I. through threats, promises, and suitcases of cash.[37] The money largely came from the C.I.A. splurge on the Pakistan military that Langley chose as its delivery mechanism in the Afghan war. A second funding stream for the I.S.I. was the sale of proscribed nuclear technology, much of it bought in grey markets in Africa and Europe and some of it manufactured in Pakistan, all of it (as well as scientific blueprints and schematics) ending up in Iran, Libya, Saudi Arabia, and North Korea.[38]

The overground political activists of the Hurriyat worked alongside an underground: a network of fighters organized in 1994 under the United Jihad Council that was led by the Hizbul Mujahideen (H.M.) – the Party of the Holy Warriors – whose insignia was two AK-47s crossed beneath a Quran.

The H.M. had been coaxed into life by the I.S.I.'s C.A.D. during the 1989 uprisings, with a chief emerging a year later in the form of fighter Mohammed Yusuf Shah, better known by his avatar Syed Salahuddin, one that he hoped evoked the historic sultanate that savaged Syria and Egypt, facing off against Western crusaders in the twelfth-century Levant.

Salahuddin became the I.S.I.'s poster boy, but after a decade a classified I.S.I. assessment, written in 2001, was excoriating, concluding that his H.M. was now an albatross "insubordinate, brutal, poorly disciplined and ineffective."[39] Iftikhar studied the report and another frank brief on the Hurriyat Conference that was staunchly defended in public in Pakistan. Some of its leaders were described as "greedy, money-minded, squabbling and pulling in many different directions." A few had "lavished crores on themselves" or were "cowards, creeping closer to India."

One leader singled out for scolding by the I.S.I. was Abdul Ghani Lone, an honest, conviction politician, who had founded the People's Conference party, and who was accused by the I.S.I. of "serious and serial betrayals." Another was Umar Farooq, the Mirwaiz, or hereditary head priest of Kashmir, the Valley's moderate spiritual leader, who was said to be campaigning "for a kind of peace that does not suit Pakistan," which the I.S.I. believed was influenced by the I.B. and the R.A.W..

Simultaneously, H.M. was being worked over by Indian intelligence who were actively surveying field commanders – powerful men with a special place in the Valley – looking to sway them to India's side. "If even one flipped," Asif Ibrahim maintained, "there was a chance R.A.W. or I.B. might capture the entire militia and wield it against the 'foreign tanzeems.'" This was the Indian security services' preferred classification for Pakistan-backed foreign fighters.

~

Down in Delhi, Monisha was moving up into the R.A.W.'s trust belt. For up to sixteen hours a day she sweated alongside her colleagues sometimes in the tower on Lodhi Road and often in satellite offices spread around the capital. None of her batch or the larger team socialized, and they were discouraged from chattering. "The conditions were clinical, the structure cellular," she explained.

She often wondered about the personal cost. Men in service were mostly married. Some had office affairs that everyone knew about but never mentioned. Bachelors made clumsy passes, which were brushed off by the many women she knew in service who remained single. To be a female spy in India seemed doubly difficult. Not only was it hard to break through the male hierarchy, but it was impossible to juggle a fulfilled private life where women was trebly restricted by custom, suspicion, and faith.

Her work was still meaningful, however, and in the summer of 2001 as Iftikhar made his way into Kashmir, Monisha reviewed India's actions regarding the Hurriyat and H.M.

The I.B.'s Ajit Doval and Asif Ibrahim were behind these machinations. Ibrahim's thinking was simple. "Why pitch soldiers from Tamil Nadu or Bihar into a bloody battle in Kashmir, when the Valley's residents could become India's hunter killers?"

The R.A.W. had studied counter-insurgency the world over, sending intelligence officers to Gaza and the West Bank, places that were steeped in containment and betrayal, and where Hamas, the Palestine Liberation Organization and its legacy organizations were deeply penetrated, forcibly divided, and eavesdropped by Israeli intelligence.

Yumnam Joykumar Singh, a young Hindu I.P.S. officer from Manipur, who would eventually become director general of Manipur Police, and then Manipur's deputy chief minister, told us that he was sent to Northern Ireland. He was hosted by the Royal Ulster Constabulary (R.U.C.), which worked with British military and its Special Forces as well as the security service MI5.

Together, these outfits influenced Protestant terror groups, blackmailed insurgents, then offered them deals and hard cash to inform, erasing their criminal records too. They sponsored hit squads that carried out killings and disappearances and encouraged punishment beatings.[40] Joykumar's Northern Ireland experiences led Indian officers to evolve new strategies in the Punjab in the early 1980s before these men were transferred to the Maoist battlefield in Andhra Pradesh.[41] There, they created the Andhra Greyhounds in the mid-1980s, a ruthless outfit, modelled on the R.U.C.'s covert work. Some of these men, including Joykumar, were transferred to Kashmir, where outfits were formed including the Special Task Force (later renamed the Special Operations Group) that used disappearance, torture, and targeted assassination to seed fear.[42] "We have to fight guns, with guns," Joykumar told us.

Ibrahim recalled how smaller armed groups in Kashmir, overwhelmed and out of cash, were seduced into mass surrenders, and then dispatched to kill their former allies. Among the most feared turncoats was Mohammed Kuka Parray. A former wedding singer, his only country was money, and he became the chief of the security-service-financed Ikhwan ul-Muslimeen or Muslim Brotherhood, in 1995, which soon gained a reputation as a death squad.[43] Obsessed by the global underworld, Kuka once told us at a gathering in his well-secured villa in Hajan, where he nibbled on sugary biscuits, ringed by men with assault rifles: "Whichever way you look at this, I'm here because of fear."[44]

In 2000, the Indian security services identified a senior Hizbul fighter to recruit. Abdul Majeed Dar had risen in north Kashmir to become the H.M. deputy commander, well loved by residents and fellow fighters. Dar had been born in Sopore, an irrepressible town on the Jhelum that was a crucible for Islamist thinkers, activists, and independence fighters and campaigners. He grew up in an era of strikes and demonstrations and told us that as a child "the sound of resistance rang in my ears."[45]

Dar worked in a dry-cleaning business but could not ignore his political yearnings. He was jailed on several occasions for public order offences and repeatedly targeted by the Jammu and Kashmir Public Safety Act, 1978, a draconian, much criticized preventive legal tool that could see people detained for crimes against the state they had not yet committed.[46] Afterwards, Dar became a figurehead for resistance, a fighting unit he led merging with the wealthier Hizbul, before he crossed into Pakistan, courting high-up contacts in the I.S.I.[47]

A deep Indian monitoring operation eavesdropped Dar talking peace in Pakistan. He worried that Islamists who were massing behind al Qaeda, and who were already blamed for the devastating suicide attacks on the U.S. embassies in East Africa in 1998, would alienate global support for the Kashmir cause too if the H.M. and others continued with an Islamic armed struggle.

But that was not what had made the case for India recruiting Dar, according to I.B.'s Ibrahim. The trigger was personal. An informer told his handler in the I.B. that Dar had taken on a second wife, Dr Shamima Badroo, a Kashmiri Muslim who was also from the Indian side, and this was a deep love match.

While Dar's first wife remained in Sopore, Dr Badroo had gone with Dar over the border to live in Muzaffarabad, the capital of Pakistan-administered Kashmir, where she worked in a military hospital. However, the informer maintained that Dr Badroo was not settled. She wanted to return. What Dar wanted, apart from an end to the killing, was for Dr Badroo to be happy.

"We had an asset reach out to Dar," said Ibrahim. He agreed to meet, telling the I.S.I. that he wanted to cross back over the LoC into the Valley and would represent Aabpara and the H.M. on the other side. The I.S.I. signed off on Dar's dangerous plan.

Back on the Indian side, while still reporting to the I.S.I., Dar secretly sat with senior Indian intelligence and military officers, as well as political figures. On July 24, 2000, a section of the H.M. allied to Abdul Majeed Dar, whose personal security was now being taken care of by I.B.–R.A.W., called for a ceasefire, causing a rupture in the H.M. and apalling Aabpara, which had assumed it owned the outfit.

~

The I.S.I. had, anyhow, spread its bets. The cornerstone of Plan B was Lashkar-e-Toiba (LeT), the Army of the Righteous. The Lashkar had announced itself in 1990 with a small attack on an Indian Air Force transport in the Valley but stepped up the pace when H.M. began fading.

However, the organization was formed years before, in the 1980s, and in the euphoria of the Afghan war, which sparked a jihad wave, with fighters who had taken down the Red Army looking for new causes, however daunting. One of these mujahids was Hafiz Saeed, a burly figure, whose family originally came from Shimla in India. They resettled after Partition among the orange orchards of Sargodha in Pakistan's Punjab, where former I.S.I. chief Hamid Gul also grew up.

An engineer who graduated from Lahore, Saeed went to university in Saudi Arabia, where, like Salahuddin, and so many others, his faith intensified. Returning to Pakistan, he served as an Islamic adviser to President Zia, and became involved in the Soviet–Afghanistan war as a cheerleader and recruiter. In 1987, he founded Lashkar with the Palestinian intellectual, fedayeen leader, and orator Abdullah Azzam, a leading figure in the mujahid landscape of Afghanistan. Azzam saw many parallels between the desperate plight of the Palestinians, who lived curtailed lives under military occupation in Israel, and Kashmiri Muslims.

Training and munitions for the new Lashkar were provided by the I.S.I., Saeed and Gen. Hamid Gul having found common ground.

Sponsorship was provided by another of Azzam's protégés, Osama bin Laden, with whom he went on to create al Qaeda in 1988. However, Azzam, an Islamist knight, was assassinated in Peshawar in 1989 before he could realize his goals for either group and Lashkar grew around the less important Hafiz Saeed, the emir becoming one of the most divisive figures in the subcontinent.

Saeed secured a fervent following all over Pakistan. Wherever we went, it was normal to hear an urbane intelligence officer, secular in his outlook and well travelled, with family in the U.K. or the U.S., referring affectionately to the Lashkar emir. Saeed, they would say, was a quietly spoken, observant strategist. He was never a disruptor, his admirers claimed, trying to blacken the military or damage the Pakistan deep state, and he called out anti-government parties and militia. He also did not leverage his influence for vast personal profit, although at its height the Lashkar was rich, powerful, and built around his kith and kin.[48] However, outside Pakistan, Saeed, who rarely gave audiences to foreigners, or interviews with Western news organizations, was regarded with suspicion and hatred, caricatured as an Islamist shrew and a cheerleader for terror in Kashmir. As far as the R.A.W. was concerned, especially officers like Rajinder Khanna, who would become the outfit's chief, Saeed and the LeT were a parasitic global menace, "growing their reach well beyond Kashmir and even India," seeding fundraisers and supporters around the world.[49] "To wage war with al Qaeda but not to attack LeT, or even tolerate it, as the West did, did not make sense," Khanna said. "Unless you looked at terror through strictly self-serving glasses."[50]

The level of state backing for Lashkar is evident as soon as you enter the campus it runs in Muridke, a market town a short drive outside Lahore. Behind a heavily guarded checkpoint patrolled by I.S.I. CAD officers, the emir, with his trademark hennaed beard and white cap, occupies an impressive villa. With its faux columns and white concrete lions, it gives the impression of belonging to a tenured professor in Georgetown.[51]

The LeT campus, when we visited,[52] had open-air lecture halls and prayer grounds that catered for thousands of students, who sat beneath a cat's cradle of fans during the summer. In winter, when we returned, studies moved inside where there were halls and tutor rooms, and even a conference centre. Posters and painted signs emphasized welfare, a healthy diet, cleanliness, discipline, and self-respect.

Saeed impressed upon these students the need for physical fitness, banning smoking, asking them to run, play football, and swim in an enormous tank he had had sunk into the grounds. When that greened over in the summer months, the undergraduates were led out to irrigation canals and taught to swim there.

According to a classified I.S.I. tally, LeT grew to 30,000 fighters, workers, fundraisers, and preachers, on both sides of the LoC, a figure that, if accurate, was almost ten times that quoted by some Western analysts.[53] But by 2001, Aabpara also worried that LeT in Kashmir had been a target of persistent Indian intelligence penetration. A classified I.S.I. briefing from February shown to us warned: "Not only are many LeT attacks thwarted by Indian security forces as a result of insider knowledge. But the LeT's internal dynamics and operational signatures have been cracked by RAW–IB that has begun manipulating the outfit's targeting, and positioning it to mount attacks that, poorly judged, hurt the Lashkar, tarnish the wider struggle – and, as a result, the security state."[54] This was one of the lessons learned by the R.A.W. when its officers studied in Northern Ireland and elsewhere: penetrate, puppet, and divide.

The I.S.I. focused on a massacre that took place on March 20, 2000 when gunmen slaughtered thirty-five members of the Sikh community in the village of Chittisinghpura. One of the worst atrocities in the history of the Kashmiri conflict, it garnered headlines around the world. The community in the southern Anantnag district was cautious about attributing blame when we visited soon after, although Delhi directly accused the LeT, taking aim at the H.M. too, accusing it of providing logistics.[55] Both made Pakistan appear complicit in heinous acts, and such was the rancour and distress after the abhorrent killings that the I.B. and the R.A.W. had a bonanza recruiting many new informers inside the LeT and H.M. from the growing pool of the disaffected, who believed the statements coming out of Delhi.[56]

Troubling questions about the Sikh massacre were raised on our visits to Chittisinghpura, by the victim families, and they persist today, as no inquiry into the assault has ever been publicized by Delhi.[57] If the atrocity was conducted by LeT, it did not serve its interest or Pakistan's, a year before or a year after. While the attack undermined peace, it also further alienated elements within H.M. disaffected with Pakistan, strengthening the hand of moderates inside that outfit, and backed by R.A.W./I.B., including Commander Abdul Majeed Dar.

An I.S.I. classified report pointed to near events too.[58] The outrage occurred the day before a high-profile visit to India by U.S. President Bill

Clinton (who was expected to advocate for Kashmir, internationalizing the crisis), and whose administration was left, afterwards, wary of being associated with the Valley or I.S.I., a development that suited India.

Indian intelligence, and especially Pakistan watchers like Rajinder Khanna, the future R.A.W. chief, frequently argues that violence has no agenda, and that political context and its timetable (often used by the I.S.I. to claim innocence) are unreliable metrics to determine the true motives or assign responsibility.[59] Asif Ibrahim said: "Outrages are tasked to a group, sometimes years before they actually happen. And after the commissioning process is completed, there is little by way of monitoring. At the launching phase of an attack there is none."

The classified I.S.I. post-mortem suggested that surrendered militants were deployed to mount the attack as "deniable Indian assets." It named a commander in the Muslim Brotherhood, the pro-India renegade outfit run by Kuka Parray who already faced multiple allegations of mass killings, rape, and torture. However, while Pakistan could be expected to wriggle, similar conclusions were drawn in classified reports authored in India, including by a military investigation team inquiring into the atrocity, that submitted its findings to the home ministry.[60]

A draft conclusion stated: "Although considerable confusion surrounds these events, it is clear to us that renegades – *Ikhwan* – likely aided or triggered it and had forewarned and/or been instructed by 7RR [Rashtriya Rifles] officers, reaching up to a sufficiently senior level for this to be regarded as a sanctioned attack. Were its consequences fully understood? We cannot say with certainty, as liaison with agencies while preparing this report has been poor."[61]

The report also suggested that the military examine events that occurred five days after the Sikh massacre. Then, 7R.R. working with the Special Task Force (S.T.F.) claimed to have killed five foreign gunmen in the forests of Pathribal, above Anantnag, in South Kashmir, all of whom were said to be involved in the Chittisinghpura outrage. So fierce had been the gunfight that the hideout used by the insurgents caught light. The dead were charred beyond recognition and their remains were buried, without post-mortems.

But when villagers in Pathribal who had reported the disappearance of five local men went to the scene and found remnants of clothing they recognized, they accused the Indian security services of staging the encounter. An army spokesman dismissed the allegations, saying at the time: "Genuine terrorists have been killed. Do not give much credence to these reports about a fake encounter. People are twisting facts."[62]

Protests churned, thousands spilling on to the streets. Only then were the bodies disinterred, and the "foreign fighters" identified as the missing locals. The C.B.I. did bring charges against five soldiers. However, the military dismissed them, as an internal inquiry could find "no prima facie case." Evading the civilian authorities was exactly what the military in Pakistan did to its elected officials too.[63]

~

When Iftikhar arrived in Kashmir in the summer of 2001, the Valley was still reeling after a turbulent year with the emergence of a new militant outfit, Jaish-e-Mohammed, the Prophet's Army, led by cleric Masood Azhar, freed in the prisoner swap after the hijacking of IC 814. The organization had made its debut packing a car with explosives that detonated outside the Indian Army's 15 Corps headquarters in Badami Bagh, Srinagar, killing six and injuring seventeen.[64]

An I.S.I. post-mortem reported "deep concerns."[65] In the run-up to his Kashmir mission, Iftikhar was told that the Jaish strategy was "poisonous" as it borrowed from al Qaeda's playbook.[66]

As Iftikhar was being briefed on enforcing peace in Kashmir, Jaish had launched two more attacks. Feeling the heat, Iftikhar pushed for a rendezvous with a Jaish commander R.A.W. referred to as Gazi Baba but whom Iftikhar and the I.S.I. knew as Shahbaz Khan. Like Masood Azhar, this man was from Bahawalpur in the southern Punjab, and he was similarly difficult to control. More worrying, according to the briefing paper, Aabpara suspected that he was either an R.A.W./I.B. asset or he had come under the influence of someone in Jaish who was, in another ploy learned by the Indian security forces in Northern Ireland and Israel.

Jaish chose a rendezvous with Iftikhar in Safapora, a village where Gazi Baba had a house as he had – secretly – married a local woman. Entering a stone cottage on the outskirts, Iftikhar waited, rehearsing his speech. When Gazi Baba slipped in, Iftikhar warned him that his lieutenant Tariq Ahmed was believed to be a double agent. Iftikhar recalled: "He did not blink. I told him that Jaish was being led by the nose and had to call a halt to operations. What they were doing was either known to, or controlled by, India." The Jaish commander left saying he understood.

Iftikhar trekked back over the fields feeling confused. He suspected that Gazi Baba was not listening, and he was starting to feel that his orders were absurd. The wrong kind of peace had broken out in Kashmir led by a faction of H.M. under Abdul Majeed Dar (and backed by I.B.– R.A.W.). And Iftikhar was to undermine it. The wrong kind of war was being waged by groups the I.S.I. had once nurtured, including Lashkar (infiltrated) and the new Jaish (penetrated). And Iftikhar was to end the fighting to make the right kind of peace, backed by Musharraf and the I.S.I.

In July 2001, back in the Ganderbal safehouse, Iftikhar, who was also still working to flush out turncoat peacemaker Abdul Majeed Dar, decided to get at his friends and family. The I.S.I. had assets inside the police, including officers working in the S.T.F., he claimed. One was tipped off about the movements of a contemporary of Dar's and his closest deputy, Abdul Hamid Tantray.[67] On July 23, Tantray, unarmed, was caught and shot dead, his body taken to an S.T.F. base, where a statement was put out claiming he had fired on the police. Iftikhar heard that Dar was devastated. "But instead of flushing out the commander, who was expected to attend the funeral, the killing provoked him to threaten revenge by blowing the cover on all I.S.I. assets in the Valley," Iftikhar recalled.

The door rattled. Iftikhar jumped. But it was only Yasmeena, and she brought fruit and bread. This time she wore no headscarf. "She got me thinking," Iftikhar recalled. "I wanted normality. And peace. She had never known it either." As she began chatting, what she wanted was to leave. "Our parents want us to get out at the very first opportunity," she said. "Leave Kashmir for the U.K. or Turkey. Thailand even. Anything but staying in this place."

He wondered if he could help. Iftikhar wanted to and he left with that thought foremost in his mind, as he hurried on his way to recover a timed drop. In a rose garden, tended by the security services, an asset had left a message in a carton of rat poison, which dissuaded curious children. It contained terrible news: Gazi Baba had not listened and he and his Jaish units were plotting more attacks. His treacherous sidekick, who the I.S.I. reported was an I.B. asset, had proposed new targets "deep inside India" and they had been green-lit by Gazi Baba.

Just a few weeks after 9/11, the outfit struck for the fourth time in Kashmir. On October 1, 2001, a vehicle was driven to the checkpoint in front of the state assembly building in Srinagar, a bomb inside it detonating, and in the firefight that followed thirty-one were killed and six injured.[68] Worse was to come.

~

New Delhi, December 13, 2001, 11.40 I.S.T.

As he watched the reports on television, I.S.I. chief General Ehsan ul-Haq felt "sickened." A white Ambassador with a security pass stuck to the windscreen had been allowed into the Indian Parliament complex, moments after both houses adjourned for the day. Constable Kamlesh Kumari pulled it over and eyed the five civilian passengers inside. Having waved them off, she changed her mind and ran to lock the gate as the travellers rolled out of the vehicle, pulling out weapons, shooting her eleven times in the stomach, killing her instantly, before charging towards the speckled Coromandel granite steps.

As grenades exploded, automatic weapons fire sent showers of sparks arcing off the Takaka marble columns. Struck by a round, an attacker appeared to explode. Believing that the gunmen were wired into suicide vests, security guards sealed off the complex as the 200 government ministers and parliamentarians inside took cover. Outside, seven guards were killed in the crossfire, which also took the life of a gardener. Within thirty minutes it was over. Nine were dead, including all five gunmen.

Barely an hour after the attack, the cable news ticker was already quoting Indian security sources blaming Pakistan. Home Minister L.K. Advani told reporters: "We have received some clues ... which show that a neighbouring country and some terrorist organizations active there are behind it."

Within days, the masterminds were exposed. "Case Cracked: Jaish behind Attack," reported the *Hindustan Times*.[69] In Rawalpindi, Gen. ul-Haq said he was "incandescent." The R.A.W. saw Rawalpindi's protestations of innocence as a diversion and reached out to the U.S. with a version of the attack, pushing, once more, to break Pakistan's "war on terror" pact.

The I.S.I. chief contemplated events. Given the rules had been rewritten post-9/11, this attack framed by the R.A.W. as an I.S.I.-backed operation would no longer be dismissed as a local tug of war. Pakistan could lose everything. "What Rawalpindi had going in its favour was the U.S. needed us," said ul-Haq. But the R.A.W., which was not going to let up, was exceptionally good at these games of seeding false trails.

Within a week, the largest Indian troop mobilization since the 1971 war, a vast phalanx of half a million men and machines, headed for the Pakistan border. The Indian government recalled its ambassador from Pakistan. Foreign embassies evacuated their staff as rumours circulated that the conflict to come might turn nuclear.[70] Even for a veteran like ul-Haq, these were knock-kneed times. Musharraf ordered all leave cancelled as he, too, sent tens of thousands of troops to the border.

The D.G.A., Lt. Gen. Javed Alam Khan, understood why Pakistan was blamed but still could not believe it. He heard from contacts in the

C.I.A. that one theory prevalent in the U.S. was that Pakistan used the Parliament attack to withdraw from a catch-and-keep operation in the White Mountains, bordering Afghanistan, a joint operation with the U.S. that was designed to mop up fleeing Taliban and al Qaeda fighters trying to escape the American air war.[71] In this version, Pakistan was colluding with al Qaeda, the Taliban or both. "But we had the most to lose," Khan protested, "and the least to gain. After a decade, we were in from the cold, a front-line state once more and a U.S. ally, sharing resources to combat al Qaeda. We had troops strung along the White Mountains to catch al Qaeda and redeploying them to defend Pakistan's eastern border against India left us vulnerable to the al Qaeda exodus. The knock-on would be al Qaeda coming through the high passes, and terror coming with them, which meant the slow destruction of our weakened economy. So, on many levels, attacking India would have been a total and absolute folly."[72] With the border glowing, Khan was reassigned from the I.S.I. to study India's offensive posture, readying troops for war.

India began describing the Parliament raid as its 9/11. "If it is not likely, or indefensible, or sometimes even undercuts the nation, then the I.S.I. will try it," said Rajinder Khanna. Officers at Lodhi Road already had a credo that enshrined Rawalpindi and that they called the Three Ds: Deny, Deflect, and Deceive. Now, Khanna added one more D, which incorporated R.A.W.'s response: Destroy. This last D had many moving parts.

A special cell of Delhi Police officers with a reputation for staging fake encounters worked in record time, recovering mobile phones, SIM cards, receipts, and scribbled-down phone numbers – apparently left lying on the ground, critical identification brought on to a clandestine raid and then left undamaged after it.[73]

On December 15, the cell arrested the alleged donnish "mastermind", Dr Syed Abdul Rehman Geelani, a Kashmiri by birth and a lecturer in Arabic studies at Zakir Husain College, in Delhi University. A telephone number allegedly recovered at the scene led the police to Afsan Guru, a philosophy major married to a Kashmiri Muslim and pregnant with their first child. They arrested her husband, Shaukat, and his cousin Mohammed Afzal Guru. The family came from the Kashmir Valley hot-bed Sopore. Afzal was a surrendered militant. It all read well. They had, allegedly, run logistics for the attack.

Police claimed Shaukat and Afzal were intercepted while, foolishly, driving back to Kashmir rather than splitting up and heading for some southern backwater. In the vehicle investigators claimed to have recovered an incriminating laptop, which had links, downloads, and search data suggesting the users had been researching Parliament and had been in touch with Lashkar and Jaish handles. On it, allegedly, were templates for the counterfeit passes to enter Parliament and fake identity cards. Also found in the vehicle were bundles of cash.

On December 20, an impromptu press call was staged at the Delhi Police Special Office, in Lodhi Colony. Two reporters were pulled in to meet a jittery Afzal Guru, who told them: "It was I who brought the terrorists to Delhi."[74] However, dates would hinder the police. Court records showed that Afzal only made a formal confession the day after. This meant that whatever he told reporters was not under oath, invalidating his statement. The computer he was said to be carrying was not sealed as evidence for more than three weeks, and even then, the hard drive showed that it was accessed again, facts not considered by any court.[75]

However, this allegation was vital as it suggested a pattern of behaviour. The same claim would be made in another case involving a Kashmiri, the well-regarded journalist Iftikhar Gilani. He was arrested on June 9, 2002, under the Official Secrets Act for possessing information on troop deployments in Kashmir. It was an arrest made in the climate of near war after the Parliament attack. Gilani argued that the report was written by a think tank and was freely available, but his computer files were edited, giving them the patina of classified, restricted documents. The backup files, however, had not been retouched, showing the original state of the documents prior to his arrest. This botched job unravelled the case. But it would take seven months for a court to release Gilani, after Military Intelligence finally admitted that the documents he possessed "were not secret."[76]

Meanwhile, Assistant Commissioner of Police (A.C.P.) Rajbir Singh, leading the Parliament case, told the High Court that the press session in Lodhi Colony had never happened, and that if it had, it was not a conference, more of a chance encounter, leaving judges, who were already worried by witness statements that looked rehearsed, to accuse the A.C.P. and his team of fabrication.

A decorated "encounter specialist," Rajbir Singh was renowned for making his own rules, although his character and trustworthiness would not be probed by any court. If lawyers had, judges would have learned that Singh had entered the force in 1982 as a blue-collar sub-inspector, rocketing up the ranks by speeding up detection rates with a series of cold-blooded killings, taking down career dons he believed the courts were too insecure to try.

He switched in 1998 to the insurgency in Kashmir, where he teamed up with the now notorious police S.T.F. Rajbir Singh engineered the death of a deputy H.M. commander and when things became too hot was transferred to Delhi in 1999, where he came to lead Delhi Range, shooting dead two alleged Lashkar gunmen near Humayun's Tomb in a bizarre operation, where few of the pieces quite fitted.

On December 21, 2001 magistrates received a sealed envelope carrying the signed statements of Afzal and Shaukat, which were leaked to the media too, revealing that, allegedly, Jaish had ordered the attack and that Tariq Ahmed (named by the I.S.I. as a Jaish turncoat, well before the Parliament attack) had arm-twisted Afzal Guru to take another man, Mohammad (named by the I.S.I. as an S.T.F. asset whom Aabpara wanted dead), to Delhi, where he became one of the raiding party killed outside Parliament.

The meeting with Tariq, Mohammad, and Afzal Guru was allegedly supervised by an S.T.F. officer, Deputy Superintendent Davinder Singh, whom Guru knew very well, as did the Indian intelligence services.

Guru had joined the insurgency back in 1990 but, changing his mind, had surrendered. From then on, he and thousands of other former militants who had given up on the endless violence were marked men.

Life could not get much worse than being a surrendered Kashmiri militant. The Indian security forces always knew where they lived and, according to numerous ongoing inquiries, had regularly used them for staged encounters or to incriminate others. Afzal Guru had allegedly been blackmailed for cash and gifts, he regularly complained to his lawyer and family.[77] And Afzal Guru's doctor found that he had been "frequently tortured," something that Davinder Singh agreed had happened at an S.T.F. camp in Budgam district, in the Valley, and that he implied was a tactic that was tolerated.[78]

Allegedly, it was Davinder Singh who had called Guru to an S.T.F. base in 2001 and introduced him to Tariq and Mohammad, compelling him to give the latter a lift to Delhi. Davinder Singh denies this.

But no court that sat for the Parliament attacks examined Davinder Singh's role, and if they had, they might have been made aware that he was already being monitored by the security services that not only doubted his honesty but also questioned his patriotism. Davinder came from Wowrigund, not far from Tral, a remote village from where the family left looking for opportunity. One of his brothers was a genetic researcher in an agricultural institute, another had a job in a medical clinic, and Davinder, a maths student who graduated from Kashmir University, became a police sub-inspector. Within months, he came across some black-market goods and tried to sell them on, getting caught, his file alleges. When, a short while later, he was cited in an extortion case, Singh was, police say, likely to have been fired. He then volunteered for a life-threatening mission, joining the new S.T.F., which back then was like enlisting in the French Foreign Legion.

In the outfit, Davinder got into trouble again. S.T.F. officers alleged that he began running with government renegades, like Kuka Parray. However, according to his S.T.F. record, he was reported for impounding weapons from Pakistan-backed insurgents to sell to renegades, who used them to commit robberies and killings that were ascribed to foreign fighters.

One of Davinder's alleged co-conspirators made the mistake of hijacking a loaded truck that belonged to a relative of the then chief minister. Another renegade unit sent to recover this load captured the driver and crew who claimed to have been armed by Davinder Singh. He denied it, but more sensitive still, Davinder was observed by the intelligence agencies cosying up to a wanted Jaish fighter, named in the file as Tariq Ahmed, the gunman also identified by the I.S.I. as a turncoat.

Davinder Singh somehow wriggled free, for now, his denials published across the media, and the Parliament attack cases reached the High Court. There, S.A.R. Geelani, whom news channels dubbed "the mastermind," was acquitted, as was Afsan, who was found to have no case to answer.[79] But for Afzal, and Shaukat, whose cases were pitted with inconsistencies, and revolved around confessions undermined by torture and extracted by cops under the scanner, there would be no escape. Their files rose to the Supreme Court of India that mulled on A.C.P. Rajbir Singh's account, that Afzal had volunteered to join the Parliament attack, supported by Tariq and Mohammad of Jaish, who ensured a shipment of arms and explosives was transported to Delhi.

In his very complete "confession" Afzal said he had helped to buy chemicals, a grinder to manufacture the explosives, a motorcycle used in reconnaissance, the white Ambassador car, and a magnetic red strobe light. He and Shaukat allegedly identified the gunman killed after the attack. They also took cops to their hideout, showing them the places where they had done their prep. Afzal stated the money the police recovered in their escape vehicle came from Jaish.

He said that he had been asked to return the computer to Commander Gazi Baba, which was why they were driving up to Kashmir when they were caught. Shaukat volunteered some background – he admired Osama bin Laden. Cops said they recovered a windscreen sticker from the Ambassador that read like a masala manifesto: "India is a very bad country, and we hate India we want to destroy India and with the grace of god we will do it god is with us and we will try our best."

In Delhi, where the police had a 26 per cent detection rate, and where courts were probing encounter killings and the framing of prisoners, A.C.P. Rajbir Singh, one of the most controversial officers of all, charged ahead with a cookie-cutter version of a complex incident.[80]

Meanwhile, several parallel inquiries into Rajbir Singh's character and connections, which were kept under wraps and never seen by the Parliament attack judges, or by defence lawyers, touched on sensitive issues, suggesting he was on the take, pathological, and, according to one highly sensitive witness (a fellow S.T.F. officer), was also "taking money from Jaish and Lashkar fighters."[81] An equally disturbing conclusion was drawn after a drugs case Rajbir Singh had triggered in 2005 collapsed at the Delhi District Court.[82] There, officers were accused of framing the defendants, portraying them as part of a global trafficking network, falsifying and planting evidence. The intelligence services were so concerned that they leaked transcripts of phone calls, which confirmed the court's suspicions but also suggested that Rajbir Singh had been in league with competing drug dealers. The A.C.P. would be shot dead in 2008, having shaken off his bodyguards to travel to the office of a property developer in Gurgaon, in a case connected to a wider alleged police–mafia bribery nexus.[83]

Davinder Singh would be arrested in January 2020. A long monitoring operation led to his car being intercepted as it headed to Jammu. Inside was an H.M. deputy commander (who had deserted the police in 2017, and was wanted for several murders), and two others allegedly connected to Hizbul, as well an AK-47, three handguns, ammunition, and explosives.[84] A charge sheet of several thousand pages filed by the National Investigation Agency in August 2020 accused Davinder Singh of "waging war against India," alleging that he had a handler in Pakistan intelligence, based at the Pakistan High Commission in Delhi. This man tasked Davinder Singh with trying to recruit an asset within the Indian Ministry of External Affairs.

Allegedly saved in Davinder Singh's phone as "Pak Bhai," or Pakistan Brother – his fieldcraft was evidently limited. This official, who left India after his asset was arrested, had sought details on the force strength in Kashmir and visits by V.I.P.s. In Kashmir, Singh had allegedly sheltered H.M. cadre, transporting them in his own car, and even, it was claimed, procured weapons for them.[85] Singh denied the charges, which have yet to be heard.

~

The presence of Rajbir Singh had worried analysts in Western intelligence too for whom – even in 2001 – he loomed like a bad lieutenant. But this was not the only alarm ringing in the West when it came to the Parliament attack inquiry. The Indian criminal investigation threw up more troubling questions than it answered, perplexing agencies outside India and colouring India's claims, analysts in London and Germany told us.

Many of the basics were missing, including the identities of the attackers. Afzal and Shaukat had allegedly named the dead gunmen as Mohammed, Rana, Raja, Hamza, and Haider. The police said they were all from Pakistan. Home Minister L.K. Advani, who claimed to have studied the faces of the dead men, said they did not look Indian to him.[86]

More worrying, a source inside the Delhi Police told Western intelligence agencies that Afzal was tortured for two days before he confessed. He was beaten, stripped, and abused, with "one senior investigator urinating in his mouth." His relatives were jailed and threatened, "making it hard for the accused to resist anything the state asked of him."[87] This kind of treatment would soon cripple U.S. attempts to try those accused of the 9/11 conspiracies, whose torture, and the obtaining of evidence under duress, saw their statements struck down, requiring new ones to be taken in 2008, delaying court proceedings so that even twenty years after the twin towers fell there has been no justice for the victim families.

Western analysts did finally come across one name in connection with the Parliament attack: Yasin Fateh Mohammed. Born in Samundri, a grain city in Pakistan's Punjab, he had signed up to the Kashmiri jihad in 1995 and trained in Pakistan-administered Kashmir, where he came to the attention of the I.S.I. He had been exfiltrated into the Valley, where he was known as Hamza but, importantly, fought for Lashkar (and not Jaish).

The I.S.I. transferred this fighter to carry out more secretive operations in mainland India. In 2000, in Thane, outside Mumbai, Hamza joined an LeT cell that was planning attacks on Indian industrial and corporate targets, mirroring similar attacks done by the R.A.W. in Pakistan's Punjab and Karachi.[88] According to transcripts and a file of photos gathered by the I.B., a dossier shown to Western intelligence, this cell was betrayed by an informer.[89]

The I.B. tipped off the Thane police, sending them verbal and written reports, including photos of the conspirators, identifying Hamza. On November 23, 2000, the police raided a house in a Muslim enclave of Mumbra, and after a battle arrested Hamza and three other gunmen. The Thane police seized a cache of AK-47s, three grenades, and some ammunition, noting everything on the arrest docket and taking photographs of the men and munitions.[90]

Hamza was formerly identified as a Lashkar cadre who had operated in the Valley and was turned over to the I.B. in Kashmir on December 8, 2000, according to these records, as he likely knew about other cells operating there. A photo of him, according to Police Commissioner S.M. Shangari, was kept on the police file too.[91] An I.B. log from that week gives a referral number for the case and then a UID or unique identifier for Hamza, a number that was a tracking reference. Here was also a two-sentence potted history of Hamza's insurgency career with the quality of sources indicated with an alphanumeric (B2 – which meant not unimpeachable but solid).

In a subsequent I.B. file, from Srinagar, the twenty-four-year-old was noted as having arrived and working for the security agencies. A second reference recorded his position as "special officer," a designation sometimes used for an asset, informer, or agent provocateur.

But the Indian intelligence community denied that the Hamza who had been caught in Mumbra was transferred to I.B. Kashmir. And then, changing their story, claimed that there was a Hamza in Kashmir but that he was not the same as the Hamza who would die in Delhi. But if the Hazma who died in Delhi was not the Hamza captured in the Mumbra shootout, where was this prisoner – and his weapons haul? And who was the Hamza attached to security services? An inquiry by the I.B. and the police could reveal answers, but none was made.

In Delhi, the criminal cases continued to progress. Shaukat's death sentence was moderated on appeal to hard labour and jail time, his release confirmed in December 2010.[92] But Afzal's Black Warrant remained.

R.A.W. officers maintained they had seen enough of the pieces to be certain of what had occurred, one senior officer telling us: "Intent is 95 per cent of the crime. If they intend to cause us harm, and that was manifested in this attack – they – the I.S.I. – and their ground forces like Jaish – are guilty."

The I.S.I., unsurprisingly, drew different conclusions. Jaish was now an enemy of the state, General ul-Haq said. Whoever in Jaish had helped prime the murky conspiracy was a problem, Iftikhar believed, and these people included Gazi Baba and Tariq.

Brigadier Azmat Hyat pondered too. What he saw was that Jaish was infiltrated by R.A.W.–I.B. "But any good intelligence agency would have done the same. More worrying for the I.S.I. was that Jaish was also cosying up to al Qaeda," Hyat warned.

Musharraf took in the broader picture. "We could not end the insurgency overnight," he told us. "We tried to make the jihad infrastructure aimed at Kashmir disappear. We would try now to crush Jaish and others. But we could not remove the instinct, the compulsion in the people, or the services. That change was generational. And there would be many, many missteps. Everyone knew there would be mistakes."

2002

Inbound was Colin Powell. During a visit to Islamabad and New Delhi, the U.S. Secretary of State wanted to refocus the two countries on the U.S. "war on terror" and douse the smouldering regional conflict. The I.S.I. wanted to use the opportunity to affirm its commitment to the U.S. pact and disown the Parliament attack in the strongest terms. R.A.W. intended to advance its case that Pakistan, a terror state, was behind the New Delhi outrage, and the U.S. should drop the pact, punish Musharraf, and cosy up to Delhi.

But on January 15, 2002, ahead of Powell's arrival in Pakistan, the C.I.A. contacted the I.S.I. A-Wing, alarmed. The details of the trip, including landing information at the Chaklala Airbase in Rawalpindi, had leaked. Al Qaeda–linked insurgents were planning to shoot down Powell's plane with a U.S.-made Stinger missile, as it approached the runway.[93]

D.G.A. Khan, still on war duties, was put in charge. The airstrip was surrounded by residential areas, most of them garrison homes for senior officers, and it was difficult to search or secure. But even before Khan reached any conclusions, the C.I.A. liaison asked him to detain the plot's supposed mastermind: Ilyas Kashmiri.

R.A.W. knew many things about the man sometimes called the "jackal of jihad." A collation in Lodhi Road that Monisha had worked on reported that Kashmiri was born in Old Mirpur, in the Samhani

Valley of Pakistan-administered Kashmir, in 1964. He had quit a mass communication degree to study at a Deobandi madrassa whose alumni included Taliban emir Mullah Omar and, more recently, Masood Azhar.

Monisha had tracked Kashmiri entering the combat zone in Afghanistan in the mid-1980s, where he lost an eye and half of an index finger. Afterwards, he was sent to run a bomb factory in Miranshah, in North Waziristan, making IEDs and shells. There he gained the soubriquet maulana. But instead of referring to his religious learning, friends were referring to his (God-gifted) ability to fall on his feet. "Kashmiri also gained his trademark look, the hennaed hair and aviator shades," Monisha said of that period.

As the Afghan war era ended, many fighters turned their attention to the closest meaningful cause. Filled with optimism at having driven the Soviets out of Kabul and determined to force India out of the Kashmir Valley, Ilyas Kashmiri took charge of a unit of fighters known as the Triple Ones – which was affiliated to the Movement for an Islamic Holy War, known by the acronym HuJI.[94] It was sponsored and mentored by the I.S.I. But there were tensions. "Ilyas Kashmiri complained that the outfit remained tethered to the I.S.I.," Monisha said. "He would never betray Kashmir. But Pakistan would, if the political pressure was insurmountable."

The R.A.W. watched the movement splinter. Kashmiri continued to fight until he was nabbed by India. "We had Kashmiri," Ibrahim recalled, referring to a brief window, in 1994, when the Indian military jailed him. "And then we lost him." After serving only a year, Kashmiri escaped back home, where he learned that his close friend Sajjad Afghani, a combat buddy from the Soviet jihad, had been captured while on escort duty with Masood Azhar in Kashmir. When Afghani died in a botched prison escape in 1999, with Azhar to blame, Kashmiri was incandescent. After Azhar was freed in 1999, following the hijacking debacle, Kashmiri refused to join the celebrations.

R.A.W. officer Rajinder Khanna watched the fallout. "In 2000, Azhar used his new-found notoriety to form Jaish-e-Mohammed, the Prophet

Mohammed's Army, but Kashmiri refused to join. The following year we heard that Jaish fighters attacked Kashmiri's camp." He survived, and formed his own fighting front, the 313 Battalion. Monisha zeroed in on the name. "It was telling as it talked to Kashmiri's psychological state."

Three hundred and thirteen was said to be the number of companions accompanying the Prophet during the decisive Battle of Al Badr, the opening foray of the wars between the Muslims of Medina and the wealthy, better armed Quraysh from Mecca. The Quraysh caravan protected by one thousand men was defeated by a far smaller force of stone throwers, who had planned strategically, filling their enemy's wells with sand, so that they came to the fight thirsty. The battle shaped the victorious Mohammed's trajectory. Ilyas Kashmiri also fancied tall odds, sharp strategy, and a righteous fight.

The 313's first foray was on February 27, 2000. Indian commandos were accused of slipping inside Pakistan-administered Kashmir and attacking Lonjot, a small village close to the LoC, killing and allegedly beheading several women, among the 14 who were said to have died.[95] This was a war crime. In revenge, Ilyas Kashmiri took the 313 into India, weaving towards the Ashok Listening Post. They stormed it, killing seven soldiers, bringing back the head of a twenty-four-year-old Indian jawan from the 17 Maratha Light Infantry, in what was also a breach of international conventions.[96]

R.A.W. monitored the fallout. "We heard that Musharraf sent a message to the 313, hailing Kashmiri," Rajinder Khanna said. "But Kashmiri maintained his distance." R.A.W. could not get inside 313 or reach its rising leader. Monisha had a plan: "What we could do was work on the volatile relationship between Ilyas Kashmiri and the I.S.I., *sensitizing* the U.S. to both." However, finding, and detaining Kashmiri in 2001 proved an unpopular mission inside the I.S.I.

~

Lt. Gen. Nusrat Naeem would, during the peak of the "war on terror" years, rise to become the director general of C-Wing, the powerful internal division. Naeem lives in Rawalpindi cantonment in a house that pays homage to martial history. A darkened hallway leading to an open staircase lined with sabres, cutlasses, scimitars, and rapiers. His ensuite snug, off a small landing, is part sports bar and part parfumier, containing a stained-glass wall of fragrance bottles instead of spirits and mixers as he is a deep believer and tea total.

Adjacent to his armchair is a flat screen TV showing clay court action. He knows all the players' rankings and foibles. Behind him are pennants and shields from the I.S.I. and elsewhere, detailing thirty-five years of service. Switching off the sound and watching the men's open final coming to a head, he explained why Ilyas Kashmiri had admirers in the I.S.I. "For some officers," he told us, "including some of those in the leadership, he was seen to be pursuing a Lesser Jihad. He was a religious insurgent fighting for freedom's cause in Kashmir." Islamic teaching placed emphasis on Greater Jihad, which was the internal battle for honesty and purity, but Lesser Jihad, the physical fight to defend Islam and its realm, had subsumed this during President's Zia ul-Haq's rule, which ushered in the Afghan war.

Kashmir's liberation was a sine qua non – the cause and the action without which there would be no I.S.I. Pakistan was, General Naeem reminded us, an acronym coined by the British in the 1930s (Punjab, Afghan, Kashmir, Indus, Sindh, and Baluchistan), where the "K" was the fulcrum.

He recalled that the I.S.I. found it hard to get any actionable intelligence on Kashmiri – because some officers had no idea where he was, while others did not believe it was in their interests to look. But the C.I.A. continued to heap pressure on Musharraf.

The I.S.I. A-Wing was asked to push too, with Lt. Gen. Javed Alam Khan in the hot seat. Finally, after several days, with S-Wing (the secretive desks that dealt with the deniable covert war and liaising invisibly with militant groups) foot-dragging, Ilyas Kashmiri was detained in Rahim Yar Khan, a town south of Bahawalpur. The C.I.A. was notified, but all U.S. requests to interrogate him were rejected.

The next morning, Secretary Powell landed without incident in Rawalpindi and attended an official dinner. But as soon as the first course was served, General Khan received a call from G.H.Q. India had opened-up on the Kashmir fault line, a barrage of shells coming down towards Sialkot, north of Lahore. Khan was forced to disturb the diners. "The chief, General ul-Haq, was pissed off," he recalled. "I suggested, 'Let Musharraf know that it's the Indians who are shelling us and do it within earshot of Colin Powell.'"

Musharraf was stunned by Powell's response. It was India and R.A.W. that had tipped off a C.I.A. liaison about the attempt on Powell's life, and R.A.W. had named Ilyas Kashmiri as the ringleader. Indian intelligence had also told the C.I.A. that Kashmiri intended to use a U.S. Stinger missile, one of those gifted to the I.S.I. by the C.I.A. and that had gone missing after the Afghan war. And now the Indian army was firing on the border.

"In our game, this is what we call a 'full flag incident,'" General Khan told us. "First, they fray everyone's nerves with an assassination plot. Then they assert that it is run by a well-known former I.S.I. asset so Aabpara looks guilty too. Finally, the firing looks like India, the victim once more, is rebuffing a massive infiltration by Pakistan, spoiling an important U.S. visit. Fair play to them! R.A.W. was getting bloody good at this game."

∽

Counterterror chief Brigadier Azmat Hyat was stuck. Building the new I.S.I. unit was, he now realized, arduous. Asking to see the files of his predecessors, he received only three dusty blue ring binders. They contained just ninety-two documents, mostly memos from the U.S. and European governments seeking answers on wanted men, and details on terror conspiracies, filing extradition requests and listing bounties. All of them were unresolved.

After the U.S. rebuffed Pakistan in October 1990 following the end of the Afghan war and when sanctions were triggered because of Pakistan's undeclared nuclear weapons programme, the I.S.I. no longer felt inclined to "go fetch." Hyat deduced: "'We will work with you,' the Americans repeatedly told us. 'We understand you.' But what we understood was that these *friends* would work with us until a better deal came into town."

Inside the binders was a thin file on Ilyas Kashmiri, who had been released as soon as Powell's plane took off for India. Here was Masood Azhar, the Jaish chief, imprisoned in India until he was exchanged for hijacked passengers from IC 814, and who was now living in Bahawalpur, while India demanded his arrest for the Parliament attack. There was Gazi Baba, the Jaish Valley Commander, who had gone missing in Kashmir, accused by India of plotting the Parliament attack and wanted by the I.S.I. as a traitor, chased by Iftikhar. Here was Tariq Ahmed – Gazi's lieutenant, who had strong-armed Afzal Guru, and who was wanted by everyone including the I.S.I. that had ordered Iftikhar to kill him as a presumed Indian asset. Also included was Omar Sheikh, the British insurgent wanted by the U.S., India, and the British authorities. He was thought to be in Lahore or Karachi, but Pakistan had reported back nothing on him at all.

Another critical file was on the sectarian insurgent Amjad Farooqi, less well known but even more important to those in the know, and wanted by India, Nepal, and the U.S. Raised in the Pakistan Punjab, Farooqi enlisted into jihad aged just seventeen, fought in the Afghan war as part of the ragtag forces that liberated Kabul, and in the early 1990s served as an outrider for the rising Taliban.

The R.A.W. knew Farooqi too, Monisha recalled. By 1994, according to a collation exercise, Farooqi was called in to handle the fallout from the capture of Omar Sheikh, when his abduction plot in Delhi had gone awry. While the British kidnapper was under guard in hospital and being interrogated by I.B.'s Asif Ibrahim, a second kidnapping was fashioned by Farooqi. In 1995, six foreign backpackers were taken in Kashmir, with a demand issued for Omar Sheikh and Masood Azhar to be freed from their Indian jail. An American escaped, a Norwegian was beheaded, and four others (an American, two Brits, and a German) were executed and buried in the hills above Anantnag.[97]

According to Monisha, in September 1996 Farooqi was spotted in the field again, among the forces backing Mullah Omar that captured Kabul and Jalalabad. Returning to Pakistan, he hung out with Lashkar-e-Jhangvi, the deadly sectarian anti-Shia militia. Occasionally, Farooqi trained Kashmir-bound fighting units – including those close to Masood Azhar.

When Musharraf began to squeeze Jaish, the LeJ, and the LeT, forbidding armed actions in India, Farooqi surfed around the jihadi breakers in Karachi, flitting from one group to another – a leg-man, driver, shooter, bomb builder, bag man. But the main reason R.A.W. wanted him was that digital and human intelligence pointed to Amjad Farooqi being integral to the 1999 hijacking of flight IC 814.

Using the legend "Mansur Hasnain," he had travelled to Nepal to train the hijack team, Monisha maintained. "At the last minute, an R.A.W. asset reported that Farooqi switched roles and boarded the flight as a hijacker, alongside Masood Azhar's older brother Ibrahim," she said.[98]

According to the I.S.I. blue binders, the whereabouts of the twenty-six-year-old Amjad Farooqi was "Unknown."

What Hyat could see from these files was that Pakistan was a nest for fratricidal minutemen from multiple sects and denominations, all of them closely watched by the I.S.I. but rarely questioned or arrested. However, what was also missing was information on the waves of Islamists heading Azmat's way, over the White Mountains, who were from Saudi, Egypt, Jordan, and Yemen, men whose arrival General Khan had predicted.

They were Gulf Arabs and Western recruits, fighting with volunteers from the Caucasus, Central Asia, and Xinjiang in China. Hyat needed lists of jihadi patronymics and pseudonyms. He wanted photographs of everyone and associated phone numbers and travel documents. He began to work on a histogram of jihad, in which Saudis were intellectuals,

Egyptians were organizers and commanders, and at the other end were the Yemenis who were knuckle draggers, while Palestinians were the also-rans, with different goals. These charts began to highlight how the religious militias were hierarchical and led by graduates, doctors, lawyers, and engineers. This was a bourgeoise revolution of professionals.

Hyat began a five-week tour, visiting the U.S., U.K., France, and Germany, seeking out the Australian intelligence officers too. He talked to Gulf powers, familiarizing himself with the set-ups in Saudi Arabia, the Emirates, and Jordan. He borrowed from their concepts of collation and analysis, paying attention to their infiltration of Islamist armed groups and their cultivation of HUMINT. On his return, he went to G.H.Q. to ask for more staff. "No one had an idea what we were supposed to do – but we divided the new outfit into three wings: Analysis, Administration, and Operations."

He knew the people he wanted, a list of officers who had impressed him when he had taught at Staff College in Quetta. "All of them were my students so I knew they would not refuse me." Soon he had eleven men, but still no overarching philosophy. "The I.S.I. Counter Terrorism Centre began in full operational mode. It was partially down to the pace of events," Brigadier Hyat said. But the lack of a cohesive counter-insurgency strategy was an age-old act of self-injury. "It should have been the other way around. Thesis. Action. But in Pakistan we always moved before we thought, whereas R.A.W. spent all its time thinking and was slow to get going."

The chief, General Ehsan ul-Haq, was bogged down fielding the U.S. intelligence community. The I.S.I. asked again for eavesdropping technology, motion detectors as well as access to satellite tracking and interception, whatever made up the U.S. "overhead grid." Concerned at what the military would do with the data, with relations between Pakistan and India tender, Washington vetoed the entire list.

The I.S.I. decided the answer was cash. "Anything the friends wanted would have a price. The I.S.I. training and administrative establishment worked on a payment process where the U.S. would deliver rewards for every al Qaeda fighter and leader captured, on a sliding scale," ul-Haq said.

If they could not trust each other, the I.S.I. would bill the Americans and make them pay in cash to deliver up notorious al Qaeda and Taliban faces required by Washington's "war on terror." The C.I.A. and U.S. Special Forces would also be charged for over-flights, transportation, leasing bases, and for accessing I.S.I. HUMINT. The dollar waterfall kick-started in November 2001 with the capture of Ibn Sheikh al-Libi.[99]

For the past six years, al-Libi had run Khaldan, a training camp in Afghanistan where two of the nineteen hijackers had allegedly stayed. The White House broadcast the arrest as an early U.S. triumph, announcing that al-Libi was an al Qaeda stalwart, and 9/11 conspirator, with knowledge of future plots.

U.S. officials wanted to give credence to a building narrative backed by C.I.A. chief George Tenet and the C.I.A.'s Counterterrorism Centre (C.T.C.) at Langley that there was no time for mercy or human rights, because a second wave of al Qaeda attacks was coming. Paranoia, grief, and a desire for vengeance meant these views were commonly held.

Men like al-Libi knew who was responsible and where the future strikes would happen, claimed C.I.A.–C.T.C. and Tenet. Harsh measures trialled by the C.I.A. in Honduras in the 1970s had been called torture by the U.S. Congress in the 1980s, leading the C.I.A. to renounce them in 1985.[100] Now the C.T.C. began scouting for a new harsh interrogation programme based on similar measures that would be rebranded and redeployed at secret C.I.A. black sites. The system would sidestep U.S. international treaty obligations and global inspection and be backed by legal opinions drafted by C.I.A. lawyers and approved by the U.S. Department of Justice.

Officers at Aabpara who served in C- and S-Wings did not recognize the al-Libi described by Washington. S-Wing knew he was the emir of Khaldan, but they also knew that Khaldan was not an al Qaeda camp. The C.I.A. detainee was unconnected to al Qaeda and had never sworn a *bayat* or oath to Osama bin Laden. Al-Libi supported defensive jihad in Palestine and elsewhere and not the wars against the U.S. and Saudis, proposed by bin Laden. He had even opposed the 9/11 conspiracy, believing it would harm civilians and bring needless death to Afghanistan.[101]

The I.S.I. knew this because for years it had protected al-Libi and his partner Abu Zubaydah in return for their help in ferrying Kashmir-bound fighters to Khaldan for training. Al-Libi saw to it that injured fighters, stretchered out of the Kashmir conflict, as well as other I.S.I. assets, were rested in Peshawar, before being escorted to a military clinic in Rawalpindi.[102]

In exchange, al-Libi was permitted to use LeT safehouses and vehicles. He, and Abu Zubaydah, remained cloaked, until the U.S. pact, when al-Libi was the first to be sacrificed, in an act that sparked dissent and caused great bitterness within Aabpara, which knew now that Abu Zubaydah would be sold too.

The first pass on al-Libi was conducted by the F.B.I. at the Bagram airbase in Afghanistan. He cooperated with interrogators and exposed the al Qaeda "shoe bomber" Richard Reid, a British Muslim convert who had passed through one of his guest houses and had hoped to bring down an airliner with a concealed explosive device. However, the C.I.A.'s C.T.C., infuriated by the F.B.I., argued al-Libi knew more, and they packed him into a coffin-sized box, shackled in a diaper and blindfolded, before transporting him to Egypt.

There al-Libi was tortured. His interrogators wanted to know about the second wave of attacks but also about Iraq's role in fomenting al Qaeda and stashing weapons of mass destruction (W.M.D.s), as this was the ground being forked by Vice President Dick Cheney, as he canvassed for a wider war in Iraq. Brutalized, al-Libi finally churned out a confession that he hoped would be lifesaving: Iraq had trained and given succour to al Qaeda, also supplying the outfit with W.M.D. technology.[103]

"Al-Libi's testimony was a desperate man's attempt at saving his life," said General Nusrat Naeem, eager to expose U.S. double standards. "And the U.S. welcomed the lie as it became *the* smoking gun for the Iraq invasion. While we in the I.S.I. were falsely accused of collaborating with al Qaeda and the Taliban, America was manufacturing intelligence or accepting leads derived from torture, to fit its political agenda. They were us and we were them."[104]

Al-Libi was not spared. After spending five years in secret C.I.A. detention, in 2006 he was rendered to his birth country of Libya, where he was sentenced to life imprisonment by a court whose proceedings, Human Rights Watch warned, did not meet international fair trial standards.[105] Committed to Abu Salim Prison in Tripoli, where more than 1200 prisoners died during the epoch of President Muammar Gaddafi, he was declared dead in 2009, in what prison authorities described as a suicide. "What we learned caused quite a commotion," Naeem said, "as al-Libi drowned in his own blood."

As predicted, al-Libi's partner at Khaldan, Zayn al-Abidine Husain Abu Zubaydah, was caught too, on March 28, 2002, at a house in Faisalabad, Pakistan, and handed over to America by the I.S.I.; a stateless Palestinian living as a refugee in Saudi Arabia, he became Washington's first "high-value detainee." The I.S.I. watched as an American fable proliferated around him, with the C.I.A. and Vice President Dick Cheney, followed by National Security Officer Condoleezza Rice, all describing the detainee as "Number Three of Four in Al Qaeda" and a "senior lieutenant to Osama bin Laden."[106]

Naeem was bemused. "The man had a brain injury and was not a combatant, instead running a guest house for mujahids in Peshawar," he said. "He was the boarding house manager for jihad, but he also opposed 9/11 and fell out with Osama bin Laden. His cause was Palestine. There was a lot of deception going on thanks to the C.I.A. and Cheney, which is fine, until the I.S.I. was accused of lying to America when it was actually defending its own national interest."

Abu Zubaydah was almost blinded during his capture, as a C.I.A.

officer attempted to scan his retina to make a positive identification.[107] As a result of gunshot injuries sustained in his capture, his leg was withered and septic. But to get the dying prisoner to talk about future attacks on America, C.I.A. contractors subjected him to eighty-three waterboarding sessions, threw him against a wall repeatedly, threatened to kill him and his family, confined him in a coffin-shaped box, and squashed him sideways into a dog crate.

To heighten the impact, these contractors, hired by Langley, added sleep deprivation, extreme cold, little or no food, the barest medical attention, anal searches, and forced nudity. During the worst seventeen-day sequence, the techniques were used on him 24/7 and Abu Zubaydah lost consciousness and almost died.[108]

The I.S.I. take home, Nusrat Naeem said, was that while the U.S. had once advocated for the Geneva Conventions, it did not believe in them any more. "Human rights are a construct used in times of peace to choke U.S. competitors," Naeem said. 'There are no values that are absolute now. Our conclusion? All of us were deep in the same foul-smelling dirt."

I.S.I. Chief General ul-Haq, a moderate who kept his own council, said he was "unnerved" by the C.I.A.'s black programme but too strategic to say anything. "If the U.S. moral authority bled out, when this black programme eventually became known, then Pakistan would be an accomplice in an unpopular, immoral, or unjust war," he warned. More crucially the old I.S.I. tactics, those quick, off-the-books fixes, covert detention, and torture, all of which undermined the courts and side-lined the cops, that Ehsan said he wanted gone, were instead validated by the C.I.A.'s course.

Ul-Haq said he worried that I.S.I. officers watching the C.I.A. would use its behaviour as justification for practices Musharraf had called out. A brigadier in the S-Wing illustrated Ehsan's concerns, telling us: "Now we were deaf to reform calls from the West. The C.I.A. was no better than us. When U.S. visitors frequented our cells, not one of them talked about human rights."[109]

It was not only the C.I.A. that amplified the backward-looking messaging post-9/11. According to the S-Wing brigadier, officers at Aabpara watched as Germany, a nation that had struggled to reconcile with its past, became an industrious European partner in the C.I.A.'s black site programme.[110] The BND, German foreign intelligence, worked hard to support it – offering transit, landing strips and logistics, as well as becoming directly involved in the rendition of at least three suspects, two of them living in Germany, with a third moved through the country, according to Naeem, who liaised with them.[111]

There were others doing the C.I.A.'s heavy lifting too. Some were obvious: Morocco, Jordan, and the Gulf countries. These were regal autocratic states facing repeated calls to pay attention to human rights. But also, in the new coalition bypassing laws and treaties were the nations that upbraided them, including Britain and France. Countries in need of a boost at the United Nations or NATO vied to join in, including Poland, Lithuania, Romania, and Thailand, all of them rewarded by the U.S. with cash or political and diplomatic advancement.[112]

Saudi Arabia was a special case. The kingdom played a deep role in the C.I.A.'s covert crackdown but also remained central to al Qaeda. One highly sensitive, top-secret I.S.I. tip-off warned that two Saudi princes, "descended from King Abdullah," were fighting with al Qaeda. They were said to have camped outside Tarnak Qila, Osama's field command, close to Kandahar.[113] When that fell in the first weeks of the US invasion, they crossed over to the tribal areas in Pakistan. "A small circle within the I.S.I. leadership was briefed, and everyone raised an eyebrow," one S-Wing general told us. "This was red hot and pressure was on us to keep it secret – and extricate the royals." The kingdom was already under scrutiny post-9/11 given the overwhelming role of Saudi citizens in the conspiracy, with fifteen of the nineteen hijackers coming from there.

But the "Saudi princes" intelligence set off alarms inside the I.S.I. because it was deeply indebted to the kingdom. Some looked to it as patrons, thankful to have a relationship with a Sunni economic superpower. They accepted gifts, hospitality, and travel. Their children received education in Islamic universities. Their private family businesses were underwritten by Saudi patronage. Some generals and their relatives took V.I.P. pilgrimage packages to Mecca. Pakistan benefited from preferential loans and some inward investment. The I.S.I. took direct covert funding from the kingdom too, bypassing Parliament.

However, other influential I.S.I. officers actively resented the Saudi money and felt diminished in their company. They privately lambasted the kingdom for steeping Pakistan in a corrosive kind of conservative Islam that was not indigenous. Many privately blamed the Saudis for the mounting levels of sectarian violence and for jihad. These days, from Rahim ki Bazar in Sindh to Bumburet in the Hindu Kush, jihad, which had come of age, trumped everything.

These I.S.I. voices had been lobbying Musharraf to back away from Riyadh and move towards its rival, Turkey. Now facing the politically explosive news that Saudi royals were fighting with al Qaeda, remnants of the Mullah Omar network that had previously resisted the Saudi writ, agreed to help the I.S.I. track the princes.[114] Taliban commanders finally lured one to a rendezvous where he was abducted, marched on to a jet and flown out of the country, although the second went to ground.

Inside the world of jihad, the C.I.A.'s brutal programme and Saudi double-dealing were propaganda gifts. In leaflets, and on posters, the Americans were portrayed as torturers and the Saudis as bigots. Pakistan and the I.S.I. too were lambasted online and in pamphlets. Its friends and collaborators (like al-Libi and Abu Zubaydah) were expendable when the bounty was big enough, Pakistanis were reminded.

The U.S. reward money for Abu Zubaydah was certainly generous. It was said to exceed $4 million and it would be invested in rebuilding a new Aabpara out of cement and marble.

In Rawalpindi, Brigadier Hyat reflected. The Kingdom of Saudi Arabia was hard to deal with. But the C.I.A. was harder. Around this time, it began lobbying for a rewiring of the I.S.I. relationship, demanding, and getting, direct access to its sensitive C-Wing, "undermining Pakistan national security," as generals Khan and Naeem saw it.

Brigadier Hyat, as chief of the I.S.I.'s counterterrorism wing, felt the changes most keenly. "I now had two bosses," Hyat recalled, grimacing. "The I.S.I. chief, General Ehsan ul-Haq, and the C.I.A.'s counterterrorism chief, Jose Rodriguez."

Every six weeks Brigadier Hyat would travel to Washington, D.C. and Langley to deliver material that was seldom good enough and receive another patronizing pep talk, as he saw it. He had a good conversation starter for American spies. "I'd tell the friends, 'Pakistan is an elephant – if you haven't seen one, I can't explain it to you.'"

∼

On January 24, 2002 the *Wall Street Journal* reporter Daniel Pearl, thirty-eight, was registered as missing in Karachi. His French wife, Mariane, pregnant with their first child, had not heard from him for almost eight hours when she contacted the U.S. consul who put her in touch with veteran detectives in Pakistan's C.I.D. and Special Branch.[115]

For foreigners working in Pakistan after 9/11, a security protocol was important. But in Karachi, a city of twenty million, where violence flicked open and shut like a switchblade, it was essential. Some of it was local but much of it was contracted through distant warlords from Baluchistan or Waziristan in the tribal area. They choreographed an underworld that lived hand in glove with corrupt sections of the security and political establishment.

Security had been on Pearl's mind too. As the paper's South Asia bureau chief, he was based in Mumbai and venturing out into Karachi as a stranger (and soon to be father), he carefully brokered a meeting with a man who said he could get him in with Sheikh Mubarak Ali Shah Gilani. He was a reclusive figure, so the promise of a sit-down was intriguing.

Little loved in Pakistan, Gilani was followed by thousands of disciples in the West, especially America, where some heralded him as a direct descendant of Prophet Mohammed. In 1999, the U.S. State Department had listed his organization, the Movement for the Impoverished, as a terrorist group, projecting its Sheikh as a kingpin.[116] The previous December, Richard Reid, the British Muslim convert, had boarded American Airlines Flight 63 from Paris to Miami, wearing shoes packed with explosives, which he unsuccessfully tried to detonate. The C.I.A. argued this was evidence of al Qaeda's next wave. Pearl was chasing an allegation that Reid had been recruited and put in contact with al Qaeda by Gilani.

Brigadier Hyat was not tasked to look at the case. Musharraf had instructed the I.S.I. to stay out, giving primary responsibility to Karachi police and the Intelligence Bureau. As the I.S.I. had more coverage and controlled the available TECHINT, this was a move that baffled Hyat and others. "That order made Pakistan appear hesitant and potentially slowed down the F.B.I.," Azmat complained.

Parsing the intelligence, regardless, the truculent brigadier concluded that Gilani's Movement for the Impoverished was insignificant in Pakistan and had also been left off the U.S. State Department list of terrorist groups back in 2000.[117] Gilani was not included in Azmat's blue files. Then there was his connection to Reid. Azmat called around Western intelligence stations in Islamabad which warned that a story linking the two, published in a U.S. newspaper, was "utter fiction." Pearl had been chasing a chimera.

On Saturday, January 26, a ransom email arrived from kidnapperguy@ hotmail.com. Attached were four photos of hostage Pearl and a subject line: "American C.I.A. officer in our custody." But in Islamabad, Musharraf faced a showdown with F.B.I. Director Robert Mueller and U.S. Ambassador Wendy Chamberlin. Mueller had arrived in Pakistan five days after Pearl was kidnapped but on a pre-existing mission.[118] Several weeks earlier an indictment was sealed in connection with Omar Sheikh's role in the abduction of a U.S. holidaymaker in Delhi in 1994. Mueller had come to deliver the message personally, hoping the U.S.–Pakistan "war on terror" pact would ensure the F.B.I. finally secured his extradition.[119]

In the meantime, the man who sent the Pearl ransom demand was captured and rolled over under interrogation, revealing himself to be a walk-on in a plot that was conceived of by Omar Sheikh.

What Azmat could see from his blue binders was that the British kidnapper, born in East London to Pakistani parents, was every bit as complicated as Ilyas Kashmiri and his presence in the Pearl plot made the I.S.I. wary.

Sheikh's father had been in the wholesale clothing business and made enough money to educate his son at the private, fee-paying Forest School in East London before he transferred him to the prestigious Aitchison College in Lahore.[120] The family back in Pakistan was influential: one of Sheikh's maternal uncles was the district and sessions judge in Muzaffargarh, southwest of Multan.[121]

Returning with his parents to the U.K., Sheikh was clever enough to get into the London School of Economics (L.S.E.), and sufficiently iron-willed to be selected for the U.K. arm wrestling team. Like others in the British–Pakistani jet stream, he straddled two worlds and could express himself in two continents but remained an outsider in both. This provenance placed him in a similar orbit to Osama bin Laden and Khalid Sheikh Mohammad – all of them well-born, well-funded, and well-educated black sheep.

Sheikh's childhood suggested darker traits. He rarely acceded to the rules of any institution, and former classmates and L.S.E. contemporaries recalled how he frequently got into fights. He tried directing his aggression into boxing but in 1992 he quit the L.S.E., having been deeply affected by a documentary about the persecution of Bosnian Muslims. He told friends he was going to become an aid worker.[122] The I.S.I. noted that Sheikh came into contact with the Hizb ut-Tahrir (Party of Liberation), a preaching group, working in Europe and Pakistan, where it aimed to build a global Caliphate and undo the secular state. Hizb followers told the I.S.I that Sheikh volunteered for the Convoy of Mercy, driving provisions to Bosnia in 1993. In 1994, he headed for Lahore and then Afghanistan, the I.S.I. monitoring his arrival at Khaldan, where he came under the thrall of its emir, Ibn Sheikh al-Libi.

While there, Sheikh began contemplating an idea to free Pakistani Islamists in Indian jails by swapping them for captured Western backpackers. In 1994, he travelled to Delhi using his British passport and fronted with his British background to befriend a forty-three-year-old tourist from San Francisco, two Britons, and an Australian, luring them from their guest houses in Paharganj, the travellers' quarter of Central Delhi, and into captivity. Held hostage outside the capital and chained-up for eleven days, they were accidentally found by cops probing an unrelated break-in. Sheikh was shot trying to flee and was admitted to the same hospital as the hostages, where he was, by chance, identified as the kidnapper by sharp-eyed I.B. thinker Asif Ibrahim. Sheikh then joined those like Masood Azhar he had been seeking to free in Tihar Jail, until the notorious IC 814 hostage swap.

Hyat's blue binders showed how the I.S.I. tracked Sheikh as he made his way back to Lahore from Kandahar. A year after his release he married Saadia Rauf, a graduate with a master's in English and became a father. Prior to 9/11, they visited his family in Britain. However much the family hoped that this change of life, and his new responsibilities, would settle him, they did not. Incandescent at Musharraf for backing the U.S., Sheikh went back to war.

Hyat pieced together the rest. In January 2002, when Sheikh came across Daniel Pearl casting his reporter's net, his mind wandered back to the failed 1994 plan. The F.B.I. maintained that Sheikh allegedly set a trap hoping to capture the reporter and use him as a bargaining chip to free mujahids jailed in Afghanistan and Guantanamo Bay, Cuba, writing his demands with the vaulted grammar and Victorian cadences of a person who was educated in the UK but conversed with family and friends in Pakistan.

Hyat wondered what could be done. He knew that even if the I.S.I. caught Sheikh, Musharraf would never give him up to the Americans. Not only did he have far too many connections to groups that the I.S.I.

observed, but his choice of the Spartan mujahid life over his decadent Western one made him a hero if not a role model for many. An unruly man made gallant by jihad was a hard person to hang in Pakistan. If punishment was meted out, and Omar Sheikh was found to be guilty, it would be by the Islamic Republic rather than the U.S. or the U.K. "Sending a man like him to the West would be seen as capitulation," Hyat recalled.

~

In Delhi, Monisha was looking at the Pearl case too, and its connections to Masood Azhar via the protagonist Omar Sheikh – two of India's evergreen enemies.

She examined the wider hinterland of jihad that seemed to be changing rapidly. She generated concept hierarchies, with data classified into meaningful nodes, looking for common characteristics and constant characters. These methods that she had studied meant that a sheet of words became maps that were live with possibilities. Extraction, creation, and classification – these were the tools of an analyst. "A.K. Verma would have been proud," she hoped.

For R.A.W., in Lodhi Road, what leapt out was a picture of the Pakistan security establishment being riven by its own, as old affiliations were abandoned. One name in the Pearl saga that intrigued her was Mohammed Adil. He was only a courier who had organized the delivery of the ransom demand. But Adil was also a Special Branch cop, with access to urban intelligence files.

He too had trained in the Khaldan camp, and had moonlit as a member of a Kashmir-bound insurgent group before going rogue.

Another focus was the hijacker and insurgent Amjad Farooqi, whom India had long wanted and now heard was also possibly involved in the Pearl abduction. Monisha proposed reframing the Pearl kidnapping around Farooqi, Sheikh, and Adil, all men who had slipped the I.S.I. leash Lodhi Road wanted to project them as hard men enabled by the

Pakistan state and mobilized for a secret bloodletting, leaving Aabpara also in the frame – by insinuation – for Daniel Pearl and enhancing India's ongoing attempts to get more traction with Washington.

When the R.A.W. story gained attention in Western newspapers, the I.S.I., furious, flat-out denied it was implicated. The C.I.A. also wanted to be clear, issuing a statement denying that Pearl was an American asset. Feeling the heat, more than thirty Pakistani police officers were dispatched to scale the three-metre wall around a bungalow belonging to an aunt of Omar Sheikh's, forcing her to call him.

Teams were also dispatched to Sheikh's ancestral village of Nankana Sahib in the Punjab and at his wife Saadia's home in Lahore, putting the family under pressure. Throwing smoke, Musharraf described Sheikh as an MI6 asset recruited in Bosnia, who went rogue. I.S.I. chief Ehsan was, privately, livid with his boss and shortly after lost control of Pakistan's narrative – as Musharraf brought in old allies to clumsily finesse a story.

On February 12, the U.S. intelligence community learned that Omar Sheikh had handed himself in to the police in Lahore. Government lawyers insisted that he was arrested on February 13 "near the outer signal of Karachi Airport."[123] Omar Sheikh's family disagreed. They revealed that fearing an extrajudicial killing or torture, Omar was taken by them to the police on February 5, when they had sought out the deputy inspector general of Punjab Police, whom the family knew. To protect himself, the nervous D.I.G. contacted the intelligence services. Brigadier Ijaz Shah, a Punjabi bruiser who had fixed a deal with religious minority parties to come together and back Musharraf to ensure his rule, and whose reward was to be elevated to the home secretary of Pakistani Punjab, received a request to "take control."[124]

Shah's starched white kurta concealed an uncharted world of secrets. Born in Nankana Sahib, a provincial Punjabi town that was most famous for being the birthplace of Guru Nanak, the founder of Sikhism, the brigadier was a blunt force. Haughty, he liked to be hands-on, which meant he always left a messy trail that R.A.W. followed closely. Shah's modus operandi was complex. He balanced terror with amity, strong-arming insurgents, playing them off one another, without ever becoming the target. He also had a flair for political management, impressing Musharraf.[125]

Monisha believed that this prehistory created an interesting crosscurrent. While Musharraf needed Shah for his own political survival, many in the I.S.I. regarded him sceptically, which gave the R.A.W. something else to play with. Ul-Haq and Hyat regarded him as an underperformer who should have been retired. However, he had a significant advantage in the kidnapping case: he knew Omar Sheikh. Shah understood his political and religious gestation and was familiar with his armed affiliations. And there was even a suggestion that the Sheikhs and Shahs had converging antecedence in the Punjab via blood and real estate, or as older Jews called it in Middle Europe: *lockshen pudding*.

According to an I.S.I. Punjab classified file, Shah was given seventy-two hours to debrief Omar Sheikh while the I.S.I. "sanitized" the area and detained everyone connected. Only then was Shah to make public Sheikh's detention. I.S.I. Punjab believed that seventy-two hours was generous, officers told us, as a typical I.S.I. deep clean could be done in two days. But Shah ignored the brief, he conceded.

Three days became eight, much to ul-Haq's indignation, time in which a kidnapped man's life hung in the balance. The news created a furore inside the intelligence world and suspicion outside it. What had happened to Omar Sheikh in those missing days, the U.S. demanded to know. "Even when we are winning, we appear to lose," Hyat reflected, dolefully. Ul-Haq fumed. "We have capable officers, and we have stone heads," he said. For R.A.W. it was grist to the mill. A senior I.S.I. officer would now be projected as having interfered in the case by concealing the main suspect, and seriously hindering the F.B.I.'s ability to find Pearl.

By February 11, Shah claimed he finally provided the I.S.I. with a list of names, some of which were already known and that reached into Masood Azhar's faction, as well as the rancid LeJ that was melding with al Qaeda. Insurgents had escaped the bounds of their outfits for the first time and moved to where the fight was.

Shah also claimed Daniel Pearl was now in the care of "Arabs in Karachi." On February 21, 2002, a video was released showing the sadistic murder of Daniel Pearl. On May 16, Karachi police were led to a makeshift grave in a north-eastern suburb, where they finally dug up Pearl's decomposing remains. After being decapitated, his body had been cut up into ten pieces. The tip-off came from someone secretly stashed in an I.S.I. holding cell. This prisoner also claimed that "Baloch people were behind Danny Pearl's beheading," which the I.S.I. decided could mean Khalid Sheikh Mohammad (K.S.M.), the 9/11 planner, whose Balochi parents had migrated to Kuwait before he was born and whose family had been on the I.S.I.'s radar since the 1980s when he and several brothers had relocated to Peshawar to join the Afghan jihad.

The authorities in Pakistan were now in a bind since Omar Sheikh had already been charged with Pearl's kidnapping and his murder. The new intelligence could allow Sheikh to overturn the murder conviction on appeal, assuming one was lodged by his wife, Saadia. Knowing Pearl's family, they would attack the kidnapping conviction too.

But whether Omar Sheikh was guilty of the killing or not, he would not be getting out of jail. Musharraf told the I.S.I.: "[Omar] will never be extradited. He will never go free."[126] Just as the C.I.A. and its contractors who tortured Abu Zubaydah had obtained advance pledges from senior C.I.A. officials and the Justice Department that the detainee would never be released, Omar Sheikh was to become Pakistan's first "forever prisoner."[127]

~

Daniel Pearl's death was a wake-up call for the I.S.I. It was failing to control Karachi and even Islamabad was fraying. The pressure intensified after Khalid Sheikh Mohammad invited Al Jazeera correspondent Yosri Fouda to a Karachi safehouse where he appeared assured, before giving a frank and detailed interview.[128]

On March 20, 2002, two men with shopping bags strolled into Islamabad's secure zone, a short distance from the Presidency. They entered the Protestant International Church and tossed Russian grenades. Eight blasts ripped into the congregation, killing five people, including Barbara Green, a secretary at the U.S. embassy, and Kristen, her seventeen-year-old daughter. Kristen's father, Milton, an air force veteran, suffered shrapnel injuries to his legs and stomach as he curled around his ten-year-old son, Zachary. Hyat's men learned that Amjad Farooqi, the LeJ, and Jaish were all involved in the attack which demonstrated the deadly formation of a terror front.

The I.S.I. went on the offensive making many high-profile arrests – some of whom were sent by the C.I.A. to Guantanamo Bay. While these netted millions of dollars in rewards that filled the military's coffers, subsequent investigations raised new questions about the ongoing stability of the security establishment.

Abu Zubaydah had been seized in a house that belonged to a Jamaat e-Islami leader, while another of the safehouses had been facilitated by the LeT. More so-called high-value detainees seized by the I.S.I. in Rawalpindi were found in homes within military enclaves that were owned by a Jamaat activist. Both the LeT and the Jamaat had long and complex relationships with the I.S.I., and since Jamaat also played a leading role in Musharraf's political coalition, it remained fireproof. Discreetly, Hyat added Jamaati leaders to his database, preparing for a time when he could make real inquiries.

Brigadier Hyat's six-weekly cycle in and out of Langley and Washington had turned him into a C.I.A. trustee, a status that made enemies in Aabpara, where whisperers warned his loyalties were divided and pressed for his removal. He clung on, trying to understand many of the baffling conspiracies the C.I.A. was chasing.

"No one ever asked us to untangle the knots," said Hyat defensively. "We just went along with the Agency and the I.S.I. got paid. Worse, perhaps, the U.S. was endorsing shortcuts, vengeance, and the heavy hand. Everyone knows that these are not things you tell an outfit like the I.S.I."

The gusher of HUMINT continued. It led Hyat to Quetta where a source was certain Khalid Sheikh Mohammad was hiding. "We arrived one hour late," Azmat recalled wearily. Khalid Sheikh Mohammad had left in a hurry, leaving the brigadier to wonder if the I.S.I. had a mole.

~

In the spring of 2002, Major Iftikhar was back in action having taken a break with his family. This time he had been routed into Kashmir via Kathmandu, then Delhi, and by road from Jammu to Ganderbal and the green, ripple-roofed house. His mission was to "eliminate R.A.W./I.B. assets" and reassert I.S.I. operations, while keeping the peace. "What did any of that mean?" he asked himself.

Aabpara still wanted to throttle the renegades, Kashmiri fighters like Kuka Parray, and was still after the turncoat H.M. commander Abdul Majeed Dar. Rawalpindi wanted revenge for the complex Parliament attack which no one was investigating. Who was behind it remained unclear. However, Pakistan continued to be blamed in Washington. Jaish traitors Gazi Baba and Tariq Ahmed had to be brought to book – which Iftikhar took to mean "death."

Iftikhar was told to massage the Hurriyat faction that – like Abdul Majeed Dar – was tilting towards Delhi. He was to use "loving kindness," to get the liberal wing of Hurriyat to come back into the pro-Pakistan fold. Iftikhar was not sure Aabpara, or he, any longer knew what *kindness* was but he read his way into the problem.

In April 2002, the Hurriyat leader Abdul Ghani Lone had visited Dubai on his way to Pakistan. He met with allies there including the mirwaiz Umar Farooq, and debated Pakistan calling for all armed fighters to quit.

Lone had had a quiet tête-à-tête with the intelligence chief General ul-Haq also, during which Lone complained bitterly about the I.S.I. insensitivity in handling Hurriyat, attacking one of Iftikhar's superiors for bullying, an officer whose legend was "Brigadier Abdullah."

General ul-Haq had listened, irritated too. Lone was a client and required deft handling, even as he worried that Lone's pacifism was inadvertently playing into R.A.W.–I.B. hands.[129]

Pakistan needed peace in the Valley to keep its U.S. pact, but if Pakistan assets backed an Indian truce, it looked like surrender, something the I.S.I. could not stomach. Shortly after Lone's visit, an "Abdullah" was shunted off the Kashmir desk, but Iftikhar heard that the sacking of his former boss pricked anger inside the I.S.I. Lone had no idea, and even if he had, he might not have cared. Having spent a life in struggle, he believed he had earned the right to speak freely.

But in Kashmir Iftikhar soon saw how difficult his mission was. He read in the Kashmiri newspapers how three insurgents dressed as Indian soldiers boarded a bus, travelling from the Kullu valley to Jammu, and opened fire on passengers. The driver and six civilians, four of them women, were killed, many injured. The militants would go on to kill twenty-three more in the family quarters of the 196 Artillery camp.[130]

The Indian prime minister described the scene as "carnage" and Asif Ibrahim was called in to probe the I.S.I.'s involvement. At the R.A.W., Monisha also dug. Iftikhar, bewildered, did the same, reassured by Aabpara that the attack was not sanctioned from Rawalpindi.

The answers that came back were daunting: Ilyas Kashmiri – in R.A.W.'s sights and now running from the I.S.I., where his file in those blue binders was growing – had returned to the Valley, as a freewheeling commander, intent on smashing the Indian truce, and undermining Musharraf's call for peace. Iftikhar felt torn. He was bound to uphold I.S.I. orders. However, his heart was with the unfiltered mujahids.

He pressed on, guiltily, striking new ground on his quest to find Abdul Majeed Dar, the H.M. commander. In Kashmir, poverty, lack of opportunity, and death were triple pressures that tested loyalty. There had been a fallout between some of Dar's household who blamed his activism for their woes. These relatives took I.S.I. cash and in return located the well-concealed commander who was in Muzaffarabad with his wife, Dr Shamima Badroo. To lure him back to the Valley, Dar was warned by a confidante that his mother was in grave danger.

But as Iftikhar waited to see if Dar took the bait, he was thrown a curveball. On May 20, 2002 veteran Abdul Ghani Lone was shot dead at an open-air rally in Srinagar. R.A.W.–I.B. blamed the LeT. Lone's son blamed the I.S.I. Monisha was staggered, as Lone was an elder statesman. The killing was also a body blow for Indian intelligence. Prime Minister Atal Bihari Vajpayee was expected in the Valley to crown a peace movement that R.A.W.–I.B. had spent two years slowly crafting. Monisha, who watched the fallout from Lodhi Road, recalled thinking: "Soon there will be nothing worth saving, and no one to win over."

In Ganderbal, Iftikhar felt sick. Killing Lone was not good for the I.S.I. He assured his assets that Aabpara had not sanctioned the hit. But a life of deceit made truth hard to know. Finally, visiting every source he could, he arrived at a terrible version that rang true. The planner was the vengeful I.S.I. Brigadier "Abdullah," whom Lone had got fired. He had recruited three ex-LeT fighters, paying them from a slush fund to carry out the hit, before vanishing.

Iftikhar, furious, could not sleep. The bodies were piling up.

2003

On February 28, 2003, Azmat Hyat's men were asked to support another C.I.A. operation, based on a highly classified tip-off that Langley declined to define as was becoming the way. He sympathized with the Agency as he too worried about the integrity of secrets at Aabpara. All Hyat's team knew was that the suspect they were gunning for was an H.V.T., or high-value target, and there were three dozen names he could think of that fitted the bill. He found these power dynamics gruelling.

The C.I.A. did not care about the ways in which Pakistan would have to deal with the consequences of mistakes being made up and down the country. Washington was preoccupied with the here and now. But the I.S.I. was hoping for a marriage. The mismatch of intentions and outcomes led to a toxic relationship. Pakistan was being paid handsomely, U.S. officials argued, when they were accused of riding roughshod over Rawalpindi. Musharraf mostly was preoccupied with his own political survival. Brigadier Hyat was losing faith.

The I.S.I. noted the address the C.I.A. gave them: 18A Nisar Road, in the Westridge district of Rawalpindi. The information came so late there was no time to check its affiliations. After 2 a.m., on March 1, the raid team pulled down their balaclavas and strapped themselves into their body armour, ready to blast into the two-storey grey villa, which was situated behind a military dog training centre.

The I.S.I.'s Counter Terrorism Centre did what the C.I.A. asked of them, advancing on what was an affluent property, a five-minute drive from military G.H.Q., something that made all of them pause. Whoever was inside had solid connections of a sort that explained the C.I.A.'s reluctance to share intelligence with the I.S.I. and the chainsaw tension that I.S.I. officers felt entering that grey house, fearing whom they would encounter.

The front door went in. First down the hallway was a colonel who remembered feeling as if the ghost of his career raced by, as he prayed not to come across a Pakistani general asleep in one of the rooms who would court-martial him. Now all the I.S.I. operators were inside, and they marched through, upstairs and down, waking up sleeping residents, who were shooed into a back room.

In the last bedroom, they found an unmistakable figure: Khalid Sheikh Mohammad, fast asleep. On the bedside table was a bottle of pills and it took some effort to rouse him. When they did, he scrutinized their faces, and immediately offered them cash for his freedom. When that failed, he ran through his contingencies, suggesting they join his religious and ideological struggle. There were no tears or protests. Just indignation.

The 9/11 planner was led from the house hooded like a hawk. One more H.V.D. followed Mohammad out, a diminutive Saudi accountant who the C.I.A. believed had managed 9/11 cash flows.[131] His laptop allegedly contained messages to the 9/11 hijackers. Here was also an email address and possibly a phone number for Abu Ahmad al-Kuwaiti, a man whose contact details had also appeared in Abu Zubaydah's address book. Al-Kuwaiti was Osama bin Laden's guardian and so finding him would bring the search closer to the world's most wanted man.

Hyat began digging into the raid detritus and grew worried. Every lead pointed him towards former or serving members of the security services and a circle of untouchables surrounding Musharraf's political camp. The new state had signed up to the U.S. pact, but it was chafing against the old.

Hyat researched the grey villa. It was owned by Dr Abdul Quddus Khan, a seventy-eight-year-old microbiologist with the Food and Agriculture Organization. Dr Quddus and his wife, Mahlaqa, who were away at a wedding in Lahore, were prominent members of the Jamaat.[132] Of the two, Mahlaqa was the more active. This did not make them al Qaeda shills, but did raise the prospect that another hideaway used by al Qaeda was linked to this party that was integral to Musharraf's survival.[133]

Other family members were in Pakistan. The Quddus had a son, Adil, who was an army major, serving in the 45-Signals Regiment, Kohat, south of Peshawar. Hyat had him picked up and transferred to Islamabad. An intelligence triage of that cantonment home began, taking in the larger area.

A call's origin could trigger a line tap. And someone ringing from Afghanistan to a monitored grid – populated by military families, for example – alerted the I.S.I. Just such a call from Afghanistan lit up Colonel Khalid Abbasi from the Kohat Army Signals Centre.

He was also a Jamaati and the caller from over the Durand Line asked him to accommodate two men. Their names were on an Islamist watchlist.[134] Abbasi's arrest and questioning led I.S.I. deeper, and to Rawalpindi, arriving at the door of Lt. Col. Abdul Ghaffar of the Army Aviation Command, who was suspected of conspiring in a plot to crash a light aircraft into the U.S. consul in Karachi. Ghaffar led operators to yet another Jamaati. He was Major Ataullah Khan from the Judge Advocate General branch that ran legal services for the armed forces. As they pulled on it, Hyat's men wondered where this *azaband* ended.

The next place it took them was the Strike Corps, stationed in Multan, a vital and strategic command that Lt. Gen. Javed Alam Khan ran after his service in I.S.I.-A. There Major Rohail Sarfraz was accused of having links to the Islamist cell, which led the I.S.I. to Capt. Dr Usman Zafar. He was serving in the Mujahid Force, a territorial reserve in Pakistan-administered Kashmir.[135]

A brigadier assigned to the case file told us: "There were another 165 suspects whose records we marked. The impact on morale was grim."

How many more officers and men, raised in Jamaati ideas, steeped in stories of the mujahid wars, were turning? How many, like Iftikhar, had been stirred by Ilyas Kashmiri and his 313?

In classified reports compiled by the C-Wing, the I.S.I. concluded that just prior to his arrest, Khalid Sheikh Mohammad had been in Kohat and stayed with Adil Quddus.[136] Also at the gathering, according to multiple accounts, was Osama bin Laden. The I.S.I. had narrowly missed them all by a few hours. But how to investigate the Pakistan military's links to Mohammad and ultimately Osama bin Laden?

Incredibly, the I.S.I. did not have a specialist detachment, or in I.S.I. speak "a Det," for Osama and his family. There was no "bin Laden unit" let alone a "conceal bin Laden" unit, Hyat complained. "There was no entity in Pakistan scouting for Osama at all."

~

In Ganderbal, in March 2003, Yasmeena had come to visit but Iftikhar did not feel like talking. He sat, sipping tea, and brooding, hating himself a little more, he recalled. Many things were left to do, and much of what he had been tasked with was going nowhere.

Outside, a three-hour drive south, in Nadimarg, in a village in Pulwama district, a military patrol arrived, the soldiers rousting Hindu families. Villagers were marched out of their homes, unsure of whether this was an official cordon and search. The security services came often, and people knew what to do. They never resisted or talked back. Then the soldiers began shooting and executed eleven men, eleven women, and two children, with at least twenty others wounded in the frenzy of killing.[137] Delhi accused the LeT, so that Rawalpindi was made to hurt. Iftikhar, appalled, contacted the Lashkar and it denied it, pointing the finger at Jaish, another of "the uncontrollables."

Iftikhar went into a frenzied deep dive, poking around for clues, and confirmed that Jaish had carried out the murderous raid. Masood Azhar's cells were back in the Valley, and, like Ilyas Kashmiri's 313

Brigade, they were pressing the Clausewitz button, calling for total war, hoping to ruin any chance of a lasting ceasefire and to permanently damage Musharraf. The man behind the slaughter was Gazi Baba, the absconding commander played by Indian intelligence and wanted dead by the I.S.I.

One task that did get some traction was the Abdul Majeed Dar case. A message recovered from a dead drop by Iftikhar suggested that Dar had taken the bait and was going to come home to Sopore with Dr Badroo. Dar went against everyone's advice and his plan was supposedly secret. I.B.'s Asif Ibrahim recalled hearing and feeling conflicted. "Dar had survived Pakistan, where we thought he would die, and he should, theoretically, have been safer in India, although every trip, anywhere, was a risk for a man like him," he reasoned.

Before travelling across the LoC, Dar took some basic precautions. He cut his hair and clipped his beard, hoping to throw people off the trail, as he arrived at the family home that was being rebuilt.[138] The construction work was being supervised by his brother Fayaz. Dar's mother, Shah Begum, and sister, Rehana, were stunned to see him. Fayaz rushed to the market to buy some meat for a feast.

News travelled fast. Shortly after, two young callers came. They greeted Shah Begum, asking to see "Abdul," requesting help from the commander. The elderly woman shooed them away, turned to re-enter the house, and they followed behind her. Glimpsing Dar sitting in a carpeted room, they opened-up with handguns. Hearing the first rounds, Shah Begum ran back and threw herself between the boys and her stricken son. Rehana heard the *pop-pop-pop* and ran into the line of fire too.

The young gunmen, staring at the fallen women, and the bleeding man, finally recognized him as a hero of the Valley. No one had told them to shoot the women and they had never imagined their target was the famed Abdul Majeed Dar. Horrified, they ran, leaving the weapons behind them.

Asif Ibrahim, depressed, watched the fallout. "This was a dark day," he said. The Indian security services attributed the killing to the H.M.

But the direction was Iftikhar's and the killers were procured from an orphanage. Distraught, the two young men caught a ride to a safehouse, wondering how to explain the missing firearms. Stepping inside, they were hooded and bundled into a minivan, before being walked into the woods and shot in the head. Back in Sopore, Dar's mother and sister were rushed to hospital and stabilized. But Commander Dar was dead.

Fear was the cruellest master, Iftikhar thought. In the exhausted Valley, that evening at six, barely a thousand mourners came to see off the Commander, who was buried at the martyrs' graveyard, behind the Girls' Higher Secondary School. For a towering figure, many tens of thousands had been expected. But in the Valley another calculus was at play. If a man like Abdul Majeed Dar could be assassinated in broad daylight, what hope was there for the average resident? Instead, they remained indoors at their TVs, watching the cricket World Cup final between India and Australia, willing the power to stay on and the signal to remain uninterrupted, and praying that the Aussies smashed it out of the park, as a tribute to another dead son of Kashmir.

Iftikhar now focused on Ajit Doval's man, the renegade Kuka Parray. The wedding singer had informers everywhere and no fixed routine. When he travelled, he was flanked by a small army that liaised with the Indian security services. But Parray, a killer many times over, had become a stone in everybody's boot. His crimes were so numerous and he incriminated so many that even the Indian security services wanted him gone. An informer emerged from the S.T.F. who presented Iftikhar with an opportunity in September 2003, when Parray agreed to inaugurate a cricket match. Iftikhar's men lay in wait until, finally, his SUV approached, without its usual entourage. They flung grenades and then let loose with semi-automatics, pumping rounds into the vehicle.

Parray was fatally wounded and died on his way to Srinagar hospital. The chief minister of Kashmir described his death as a setback to the peace process. Monisha thought otherwise. It was, she said, a perfect example of the Pareto *optimality* – described by the eighteenth-century Italian thinker and engineer as a state where resources were distributed in an efficient manner, meaning an effective one. Under these conditions, one side's situation could not be improved without making the other's worse, striking a natural balance. "A measure of overall efficiency in Kashmir was when one outcome was no better than any other," she said.

The Valley was a zero-sum game in which everyone remained in the same state – *hurting*.

~

Iftikhar needed to finish up and get out. He contacted a veteran gunslinger. This I.S.I. asset was now, like many of his kind, a taxi driver, as the trade gave him licence to rove the Valley. The driver couriered a message to a drop used by Jaish between Chattergam and the Marvel irrigation canal. All of these were one-way trips. To prevent ambush, he collected replies from different spots.

Iftikhar had practised for many weeks, setting and checking dead drops. A closet inside a home – pulling down the horizontal pole and stuffing a note inside it. An office door – pealing back the laminate on the top edge to hang a message inside the cavity. Vermin traps and electrical junction boxes – both of which came with hazard warnings that kept children away.

The note left for Jaish was sufficiently enticing, reporting a windfall, suggesting their fighters should come and collect. It was a cache once used by Abdul Majeed Dar. There was ammunition and some money, as well as military and police IDs. He proposed a rendezvous for Jaish in Srinagar. Then Iftikhar tipped off his contact in the police's S.T.F.

Soon after, sections of the 60 and 193 Battalions of the Border Security Force (B.S.F.) rolled into Dana Mazar. At around 4 a.m. a cordon and search began, a clickety-clack of splintering doors and smashing windows, hauling out families into a humid night. It made just enough noise to alert a drowsy gang holed up inside a three-storey building, who had arrived the night before. They panicked, firing down on to the troops, from the upper floor. When the firing stopped, the S.T.F. climbed upstairs.

In a bedroom, blackened by a grenade, lay a corpse with a smooth, beardless face, and a clipped military moustache. He was, the S.T.F. confirmed, Gazi Baba. And things had become so tangled and there was so much Gazi Baba could expose that there was no one left who wanted him alive.

Iftikhar was done, he said. He wondered if Musharraf had bought himself the time he needed to secure the U.S. pact. And he asked himself if he could any longer reconcile these missions with his deeper beliefs as a Muslim and a patriot. Iftikhar felt sick to the stomach.

~

Ijaz Shah's report into the Daniel Pearl tragedy had warned that the massing Islamist forces, many of which were previously with the I.S.I., were overcoming sectarian and organizational barriers, uniting to target the Pakistan state. The amalgam of former I.S.I. assets, of radicals and insurgents, was growing more deadly and hard to control.

Briton Omar Sheikh continued to plot from his prison cell. Jaish fighters were on the run, while the quixotic Masood Azhar remained influential, and in hiding. The sectarians of the LeJ had splintered and were being hunted down all over Pakistan by I.S.I. death squads. Amjad Farooqi, hijacker and soldier, was winning followers who all went underground, as did his mentor in the 313 Brigade, Commander Ilyas Kashmiri, the jackal of jihad.

Clamping down on these killers was a full-time mission that was freighted with political difficulties that Musharraf struggled to overcome. He banned some more armed outfits, while leaving others in place, saying that Pakistan did not have the resources to "stand down 250,000 armed mujahids or possibly more."[139] Instead, the I.S.I. did what British intelligence and the C.I.A. had done in the past, in Northern Ireland and Latin America. It would enable one group and, upon it becoming infamous or ineffective, split it into several smaller versions, killing off some of those and leaving behind the kernel of another, like jihad matryoshka dolls.

General Ehsan ul-Haq saw this as pragmatism. "It was not possible to fight everyone simultaneously without paralysing the country," he said. But a D.D.G. in C-Wing was more circumspect. "We don't want them. But we need them. We dispose of them. They come back. And then we love them, as it starts over again."

The R.A.W. had zero sympathy. Instead, analysts like Monisha were ordered to go hard showing Pakistan as "playing all sides," while Pakistan's American *friends* rolled their eyes. U.S. Ambassador to Pakistan Nancy Powell visited Karachi and told reporters: "We are particularly concerned that these banned organizations are re-establishing themselves with new names."[140] But even though Washington was worried, keeping Musharraf in place was America's best hope for a cooperative Pakistan.

Some at Aabpara still regarded terror as a tool. I.S.I. officers in Sindh, for example, revealed how while gunning for the LeJ, they gingerly allowed another armed group to come into being that would continue the sectarian work against Shia leaders, who were regarded as dupes for Iran, one of Pakistan's most challenging neighbours, and despised by Rawalpindi's sponsors in Saudi.

The new outfit was called Jundullah (Army of Allah) and led by a Karachi University statistics student well known to the I.S.I. As an undergraduate, Atta ur-Rehman had been a leader of the Jamaat-e-Islami student wing.[141] This was the first point of contact with Aabpara. In 1991, Rehman and others travelled to Afghanistan, undergoing training at a camp used by Kashmir insurgents where Masood Azhar had briefly turned up. This was the second point of contact.

Rehman in 2003 recruited two dozen members to work with him to form the Jundullah, most of them graduates from Karachi University, including engineers and medics. They began with a fundraiser, robbing a branch of the Habib Bank in Karachi on November 18, stealing $70,000, which they accounted for in the group's ledger, meticulously kept by a man who had a good head for numbers.

While the I.S.I. monitored Jundullah, Rehman began secretly looking beyond his military connections to Wazir militias in South Waziristan, where the Pakistan Army, Special Forces, and I.S.I. paramilitaries were targeting al Qaeda fighters in an operation that was enraging local tribes. In a matter of months, Rehman found a sponsor, a young, disgruntled hardhead from Wana, the bustling hub of South Waziristan.

Handsome, and sporting a lavish beard, Nek Mohammed Wazir had fought with the Taliban against the U.S., afterwards winning a following. Crossing back into Pakistan with thousands of al Qaeda and Taliban fleeing the Americans post-9/11, Nek, who had come of age, decided that Musharraf and his American pact was the problem. When the two met, Nek had a way of reaching right into Karachi and Rehman had all the weapons he needed.[142]

~

President Musharraf's security had to be rethought. His movements began each day before dawn when he drove from Rawalpindi to Islamabad, a forty-minute journey some of which passed through narrow, congested streets. Options considered included felling the trees or installing cameras in them. The airspace over the president's secretariat and the G.H.Q. was locked down to commercial traffic whenever he set off and a helicopter carrying secondary surveillance radar sometimes flew overhead. Internet and phone signals were suspended along his route.

The I.S.I. briefly considered body doubles – a survival technique favoured by Saddam Hussein – but instead it purchased identical Mercedes sedans that were reinforced with armour capable of repelling high velocity rifle rounds travelling at twice the speed of that from a sidearm. The cars' toughened glass windows were coated in a polycarbonate to prevent glass shattering, their run-flat tyres enabling them to keep rolling on their rims if the rubber was shredded.

Each vehicle carried U.S.-supplied body armour and the President, who habitually carried a sidearm, chose which to ride in at the last minute. A rapid reaction force of twenty commandos from the Special

Service Group (S.S.G.), Pakistan's elite Special Forces, and Musharraf's former unit, accompanied his convoy, along with an ambulance.

On December 14, 2003, General Ehsan ul-Haq heard a snarling boom and mouthed the word "bomb." Glancing at his watch, and seeing it was 7 p.m., he called Musharraf as he was due in from Karachi and should have been heading home. The President had landed at the Chaklala Airbase just as the U.S. revealed it had finally captured Saddam Hussein, the story fizzing around the world.

Musharraf climbed into one of the armoured Mercedes debating the news with his military secretary, Major General Nadeem Taj. Just after setting off, they both had heard a muffled blast. The thick glass deadened the sound, but they were flipped from their seats as a pressure wave spun the vehicle. Musharraf recalled feeling melancholic as he landed in the footwell. "Some leaders get to visit the scenes of tragedy and pass on condolences. Instead, it was me who continually received commiserations," he reflected.

Their driver put his foot down and the Mercedes clanked on its rims to Army House, half a kilometre away. Musharraf's phone came back online, and Lieutenant Colonel Asim Bajwa, also in the motorcade, told him that the I.S.I. had eavesdropped chatter about the bridge having been wired with explosives. As Musharraf entered the house, and saw his mother sitting with his wife, Sehba, he took the latter to one side, to tell her, in his own words, what had gone down, before the TV news told it in theirs.

Musharraf had to be surrounded by loyalists even if they were not the best men. On December 18, he promoted his inexpert military secretary, Nadeem Taj, to become head of Military Intelligence, in a mismatch that rankled many in Rawalpindi. A week later, on December 25, the President left the Islamabad Convention Centre for Army House at 1.15 p.m. A chopper went up. The S.S.G. was deployed. The ambulance went out.

Ba-Boom.

His car was aerial again. And he was in freefall. Through the smoke, and cascade of debris that drummed on the roof, Musharraf thought he could see body parts raining past the windows. The powerful high explosives shredded vehicles and bystanders. "It turned dark," Musharraf said. His ears ringing, guts shaking, he clawed himself back into the seat and unholstered his sidearm. Jan Mohammad, his driver, came to, and drove on, reaching the next petrol pump.

Ba–Boom.

A howl barrelled in at them with such force that even the armoured sedan with its 3000-kilo chassis skittered. In the darkness again. In the footwell again. Musharraf searched for his sidearm again. He hauled himself out, *again.* And he listened to the pitter-patter of debris falling, imagining it was the end of days. And then something gigantic crashed on to the windscreen. The toughened glass did not give, and Jan Mohammad gassed the wrecked Mercedes, lurching forward on its rims.

Arriving at Army House, Musharraf recalled hearing screaming – again. He foresaw a nightmarish scenario. The attack had been a diversion and his family was dead. But the noise was coming from Sehba. He jumped out of the sedan and rushed to his wife. She pointed at something behind him. He turned to see his Mercedes, buckled and baked, a patchwork of human flesh.

Brigadier Hyat's men got to work amid the twisted metal and smashed concrete. More than 200 kilos of C4 had been installed in panels across the span of the bridge. It required military-level ordnance and engineering skills that suggested martial minds, like those of Ilyas Kashmiri and soldier Amjad Farooqi. There had to be inside help from the security services as the blast area was under constant observation. An inquiry zeroed in on officers responsible for the President's security detail. All of them had clearances, which meant they had had background checks and ongoing monitoring, the effectiveness of which was now in doubt as well as their loyalty. "What else was compromised?" Hyat asked.

When they identified one of the bombers, they learned he was only twenty-three, and a Jaish man. He had been guided to an al Qaeda training camp and fought in the battle for Kabul in November 2001. Taken prisoner by the U.S., he had been handed back to Pakistan, where he was jailed, and released in the spring of 2002. But he had gone back to Jaish and volunteered for a suicide mission.

A second identity was fished from the wreckage and he too was in Hyat's blue binder. This man had joined Ilyas Kashmiri's outfit, ending up in South Waziristan harrying the Pakistan military in its first operations in Wana. He had moved to Rawalpindi a few days before the twin attacks.

Musharraf said his instincts were to go towards the sound of gunfire, which troops appreciated but planners resented. He ordered the arrest of Masood Azhar, but he was in hiding, as was Ibrahim, his older brother. An I.S.I. general told us: "We snatched the younger brother, Abdul Rauf, and took him in and gave him a beating."[143] I.S.I. S-Wing operators, the covert ops men, were sent to find Ilyas Kashmiri.

Both S- and C-Wings were ordered to eradicate what was left of the LeJ and kill Amjad Farooqi.[144] Hyat's C.T.C. was tasked with calculating how many suicide cells were still out there. They were tracking five and learned that a hundred ex-servicemen had defected, including officers, loosely gathering around Ilyas Kashmiri, swearing on a Quran in May 2002 to eliminate General Musharraf "at any cost."

Among them, alarmingly, was a core group from the 1st Commando Battalion of the S.S.G.[145] Many homes and hideouts were raided but the commandos were gone, leaving behind four huge Chinese-made 107mm rockets, an improvised launching device, 30 detonators, crates of C4 explosives, det cord, and Russian-made 50m launchers and grenades.

More investigators were needed, and one of those called up was Iftikhar, who had recently returned from Kashmir, jaded and angry. He recalled how he was sent on a catch-and-kill mission after one of the bomb makers, who was also thought to have served with the S.S.G. But Iftikhar was not giving the mission his full attention. "More blue-on-blue," was how he characterized it, chasing military men or mujahids whom he had begun to regard as patriots, but whom the state, which he increasingly mistrusted, classed as rogue.

Iftikhar's team got on the trail of one of the key suspects. An IMEI sniffer picked up a phone. A spotter was dispatched and got a visual on a man who vanished into a Rawalpindi store. To make certain, the spotter contacted Iftikhar, who was outside in the street and dialled the phone number. It rang inside the shop.

"We've laid down a cordon. You're going nowhere. Give yourself up, bhai," Iftikhar urged.

The I.S.I. spotter watched as the bomb maker emerged, clasping the phone to his ear. The spotter radioed Iftikhar, worried. "We've got him, but he's looking bulkier than in the mugshots. Is this the *right* guy?"

Iftikhar was certain and approached the suspect. "Hand yourself in and we'll spare you." They had been chasing him for weeks. "Look, we've already got your brother and his kids."

"Pull back," the nervous spotter pleaded with Iftikhar.

When Iftikhar came to, he was lying in a military cot. A medical orderly explained he was in intensive care and that a coin-sized piece of shrapnel had drilled a hole in his mouth. If he was feeling addled it was because he had concussion injuries and was likely suffering from an internal bleed, triggered by a fast-moving blast wave. The bomb maker had been wearing a vest and he had detonated it, releasing a wave of compressed, high-pressure air, moving at supersonic speed, that had thrown Iftikhar into the air, narrowly avoiding the shrapnel plume. But it had scythed through the spotter, killing him instantly.

~

Ilyas Kashmiri was finally tracked down by I.S.I. S-Wing in the dying days of 2003. But S-Wing complained about the mission, and Musharraf (facing a revolt) ordered C-Wing, I.S.I.'s internal department, to handle the interrogation. One C-Wing officer told us: "They said, 'hammer Kashmiri.' Most of us felt bad about it." Beaten, starved, and hung upside down, and then dangled from a single wrist, Kashmiri was kicked, whipped, and slapped, his kidneys punched, his legs carved with cuts. "We were told to let him live and tell him that this was Musharraf's gift."[146]

An S-Wing general intervened, contacting Sayed Salahuddin, the emir of H.M. Moustachioed Salahuddin, who commuted between Muzaffarabad and Islamabad, was like a moose's head over the mantle. At one stage, he had been a beast. But now he was a moth-eaten trophy that the I.S.I. appeased. And what Salahuddin wanted was to act as Ilyas Kashmiri's guarantor, ensuring he retired, in exchange for his freedom.[147] Battered Kashmiri was released.

But Musharraf was no longer paying close attention. The President was looking north and east. U.S. pressure, and his own recent near-death experiences, had persuaded him to finally go hard in the tribal areas, a region where the Pakistan military held little sway. War was inevitable but only if he could bring the politicians and military with him, something that the U.S. assumed would happen, but that was a formidable hurdle. Intelligence chief ul-Haq had had another tangential thought that he shared with the President.

When Pakistan was vulnerable, the R.A.W. took advantage. The I.S.I. suggested Musharraf do something counter-intuitive to break the cycle, like courting India. Confidential talks with the senior U.S. State Department officials had led ul-Haq to believe that Pakistan's hit-and-miss efforts that were finally throttling I.S.I.-backed conflict in Kashmir might win Islamabad talks with Delhi. The President liked the idea. It also offered him a legacy. And he had been kicking a similar plan around G.H.Q. with favourable results: *talk to the enemy*.

There would be two stages. Pakistan was hosting a South Asian summit in January 2004, with India's prime minister A.B. Vajpayee coming over. Musharraf planned a private huddle. The thirty-minute off-camera chat, the first since the Kargil betrayal, set Vajpayee on a new course. He responded with a generous communication, declaring that nations must move from "mistrust to trust, from discord to concord and from tension to peace."[148] He said: "Mutual suspicions and petty rivalries have continued to haunt us. History can remind us, guide us, teach us, or warn us. It should not shackle us."

Musharraf built on the statement, pledging that he would "not permit any territory under Pakistan's control to be used to support terrorism in any manner." The details would be hammered out secretly, and Musharraf had a man in mind, Tariq Aziz, his former college mate, and a preferred trustee.

Aziz, the son of a sessions judge from Sargodha, in Pakistan's Punjab, where the family owned a lucrative farm, had joined the civil service in 1967. He became an income tax inspector at the Central Board of Revenue. However, as part of the powerful Warraich clan that traced their descendants back to the Persian empire, he was also well connected and independently wealthy. Reconnecting with Musharraf ten months after the 1999 coup, Aziz, who was retiring from the revenue board, offered to bring money and block votes to his political cause.

Appointed Musharraf's Principal Secretary, he had orchestrated the sensitive issue of exiling the family of deposed prime minister Nawaz Sharif to Saudi Arabia, before skilfully neutering what was left of their Pakistan Muslim League (P.M.L.) and taking over its financiers and power players. Now the President asked Aziz to reach out to New Delhi and offer face-to-face meetings, preferably in the Gulf or Thailand.

"Making peace with India is child's play compared to politics in Pakistan," Musharraf joked with Aziz.[149] He set out to win over Brajesh Mishra, India's insightful and lateral N.S.A., one of the very few officials who did not fear running into a headwind.[150] Mishra had cut his teeth in China, courting Chairman Mao's inner circle in the 1970s, believing that India should hedge against the Soviets as allies.[151] He had used this connection in the 1980s to create an earlier backchannel into Pakistan. A maverick, who became Vajpayee's political secretary in 1998, a tenure that saw India best the C.I.A. and test its nuclear bomb, Mishra once told us he went for the Musharraf deal because he could see "the utility in Aziz." Mishra added: "Even as others in the [Ministry of External Affairs] lambasted Musharraf's man as 'a fop who loved horses more than his family,' I sensed that he had the President's real trust, which made him invaluable to me. If Aziz cared then Musharraf did too."

The foreign offices of both countries created their own Gavrilov line, fax numbers to where a steady to and fro of handshaking messages were sent prior to the secret face-to-face sessions in Thailand, London, and the Gulf. "Everything was on the table: Sir Creek, Kashmir, headwaters, LoC, you name it," Musharraf recalled he told Aziz. "Feel your way. I hope I'm still here when you're done."

Mishra sensed the urgency: "This was a once-in-a-lifetime convergence where the U.S. might do good for India, inadvertently, by bolstering Pakistan and its I.S.I."

2004–05

In Lodhi Road, a deep crisis was unfolding. The R.A.W. was losing faith. However hard it tried to gain Washington's attention, having begun talking to Pakistan at great political risk, Langley remained largely indifferent to India, beyond keeping an eye on regional peace and a possible nuclear showdown. "It felt as if there was no place for India back then," said Rajinder Khanna.

Over the border, the "war on terror" had moved north, into the Federal Autonomous Tribal Areas between Afghanistan and Pakistan, a colossal and alienated province consisting of seven tribal agencies and six frontier regions, occupied 27,224 square kilometres (about the size of the U.S. state of Massachusetts).

To the west and north, it bordered Afghanistan's Kunar, Nangarhar, Paktia, Khost and Paktika provinces, so instability there sent shockwaves crashing over the Durand Line. Inside FATA there lived between 5 and 15 million people, depending on which census you believe, as population maths becomes a complex discipline when numbers translate into (per capita) funding.[152]

One of Pakistan's poorest regions, FATA recorded a 69 per cent unemployment rate and its residents were governed by the British-era Frontier Crimes Regulations (F.C.R.). More than 190 million people outside FATA lived by the reformed Pakistan penal code that melded sharia with case law. Inside FATA there were no jury trials, collective punishment was the norm, as was the confiscation of assets for those convicted by jirgas – a council of worthies that was a court and a jury – that prohibited appeals. Residents were denied the power to contest the F.C.R. or reform them. A criminal system designed by desperate British imperators to quash endless Pashtun uprisings had been adopted by independent Pakistan too.

The Pakistan army and the I.S.I. had not had much luck in FATA until now. Since withdrawing from the White Mountains after the Parliament attack, there was still no counter-insurgency strategy and the raids that were sanctioned were piecemeal and relied on Google Maps and World War II flight charts.

Ever resourceful, G.H.Q. devised a kitchen-cupboard solution, strapping GoPro cameras to transporters that flew over FATA. But engine vibration and low light meant the picture quality was appalling, with disastrous consequences on the ground. In one ill-fated operation, troops attacking a suspected al Qaeda compound were left defenceless and cut down, with a dozen fatalities.[153]

India, meanwhile, had entered a secretive $1.1 billion deal with Israeli and Russian defence manufacturers to transform three Ilyushin 76 transporters into state-of-the-art Airborne Early Warning and Control (A.W.A.C.) aircraft to conduct 360-degree surveillance deep inside Pakistan and China – an aerial command for future wars.[154]

The Pakistan military also faced a philosophical question in FATA. "Pakistan soldiers going after Pakistan citizens was a serious thing," recalled Lt. Gen. Masood Aslam, then commander of the 23rd Infantry, who would go on to lead XI Corps, the main Pakistani formation fighting in the North-West Frontier Province and the Northern Areas.

Masood believed the military had forgotten about FATA. Tactical and historic problems would be hard to overcome, and harder still to explain to the U.S. that could not conceive of an ungovernable country within a country. Even more difficult was finding a way to deliver a clear message throughout the province, via political agents, or the I.S.I.'s assets like clan elders or maulvis, as well as traders running transport routes.

"Communicating our aims was complex," said General Khalid Rabbani, who would take over XI Corps in 2011.[155] When the Soviets invaded Afghanistan, the C.I.A., I.S.I., and mujahids came to FATA in droves with money and weapons. The local tribes who had spent centuries sparring, family on family, village on village, were galvanized, recruited, paid, and motivated to become mujahideen or to care for them. "Back then the villagers would come out and escort the mujahideen, carrying their ammo boxes, shouldering their bags, and cooking for them as if this was a noble cause," Rabbani said.

After 9/11, a new mujahideen had risen to fight the U.S. and defend the Islamic Republic of Afghanistan. General Masood pondered this: "How to explain why these insurgents, also religious and engaged in a David and Goliath struggle, were now bad mujahids?" He reflected: "Without a plan, the military began moving into an area about which they had very little hard knowledge. Really the army had no idea what FATA had become. What *was* tribal culture? What were the strategic challenges: the terrain, culture, needs on ground?"

Pre-Partition, the British Indian Army had maintained training grounds in Waziristan where soldiers learned frontier warfare in preparation for forays into Afghanistan. "Every second lieutenant's desire was to get posted in Waziristan so that they would experience actual field combat," said General Masood. The British had cantonments in Wana and Razmak, which was known as "*chotta* [little] London." There were small landing strips, a major airfield in Miranshah, and a railway line that reached all the way to Bannu. Everything was abandoned after 1947. "The focus drifted east, to war with India. And the Pakistan Army never bothered with FATA again."

With Tariq Aziz distracted by his secret peace mission with Indian N.S.A. Brajesh Mishra, the coalition of right-wing religious parties that Aziz had wrangled into the pro-Musharraf United Council for Action began to chafe.[156] It demanded a withdrawal from FATA.

XI Corps Commander Lt. Gen. Safda Hussain mooted a face-saving plan. An amnesty was offered to warlord Nek Mohammed and others, brokered by local clerics close to the Council. They organized a *jirga* at Shakai, an expanse of apple and apricot orchards. But within hours of the general leaving, Nek Mohammed gathered local reporters. "Since my teachers came to *me*, I have no option but to accept this accord," he told them. "But they are all old people and when you grow old, your legs are weak." The I.S.I. was incandescent. A classified report, shown to us, concluded: "Expect aftershocks."[157]

At 9 a.m., on June 10, 2004, a convoy emerged from V Corps H.Q. in Karachi and drove down Abdullah Haroon Road towards Clifton Bridge, a high security zone. In it was Lt. Gen. Ahsan Saleem Hayat, the V Corps commander, and a close Musharraf ally. Accompanying his flag car were two security detachments and two motorcycle outriders. Heavy, hot streams of rounds from automatics thudded in from three directions before an explosion sent the vehicles skidding. The corps commander recalled screaming at his driver to "pick up speed," but he was slumped on the wheel. He had been struck by several rounds and General Saleem Hayat's uniform was sprayed with his driver's blood. He crawled out, unholstering his sidearm, with more rounds clattering in.

The last place to hide in an ambush was inside a vehicle. Bullets bored through glass and door panels and then rattled around inside the cab, creating ricochet and shrapnel injuries, shredding metal and fabric, hot metal forcing fibres along channels in human flesh, infecting wounds that would never heal. When the firing began, a soldier was trained to run for solid cover. But when the general looked, the rear vehicle remained stationary, its troops still on board. He screamed at his men to "wake up" but six of them were already dead. The change in air pressure, the aroma of explosive charges, the sweat and grit, the ferrous churning, had cowed the survivors. Finally, they came to their senses, slipping out of the vehicle and pressing forward. When the firing stopped, eleven had been killed, of whom seven were military, and three were police, two of whom, according to eyewitnesses, were caught in friendly fire. More than a dozen people were injured but remarkably the commander, fifty-seven years old, survived unscathed.

The attack had relied on classified details about the movements of senior military leaders, and the intelligence pointed, yet again, to hijacker-insurgent Amjad Farooqi.

What followed was tit-for-tat assassinations, as a sectarian war roiled Karachi. Musharraf deployed 20,000 more police and paramilitary rangers, as the I.S.I. stepped up its hunt for Farooqi's fighters, Brig. Hyat reporting back that another state asset had gone rogue plotting this attack. It was the statistician Rehman who had started Jundullah.

He was picked up, and was unrepentant, shouting from the dock of the anti-terrorism court: "I have done nothing wrong."[158]

Digging into Rehman's computer and phone, the I.S.I. fished out two deleted numbers that they traced to Akmal Waheed and his younger brother Arshad. A cardiologist and an orthopaedic surgeon, the Waheeds were active Jamaatis, who were now jailed by an anti-terror court that convened inside Karachi's Central Prison.[159]

Elements of the Jamaat were still plotting, and remained untouchable as part of Musharraf's council. But what to do about Rehman's sponsor in Wana, youthful warlord Nek Mohammed who had mocked the military?

~

In the spring of 2004, a blistering internal report by the C.I.A. Inspector General John L. Helgerson highlighted serious abuses of detainees in the Agency's covert prisons.[160] He focused on operations by the C.I.A.'s C.T.C. that often worked closely with Brigadier Hyat's unit. The report triggered a rethink in Langley.[161]

Instead of being jailers and interrogators, the Agency decided to outsource harsh interrogations to contractors and, where possible, to kill "enemy combatants" in the field. The I.S.I. was pulled in its wake. "In Pakistan, the judicial system was hardly working, the I.S.I. reasoned. We need the enemy dead, and not in the dock," said General Nusrat Naeem, who would become the C-Wing director general in 2006.

Intelligence chief ul-Haq was visited by a C.I.A. liaison who explained the new thinking. The Agency would fly unmanned aerial drones to hunt and kill the enemies of Pakistan if the I.S.I. opened its airspace over FATA. Ul-Haq insisted that Pakistan approve the "kill list." He restricted the Agency to narrow air corridors that avoided sensitive military and civil installations.

The U.S. had to keep away from Pakistan's nuclear sites, given Rawalpindi had had to detain the metallurgist A.Q. Khan at the behest of Washington, after he was accused of running a one-stop sales shop for proscribed nuclear know-how. Following that humiliation, A.Q. Khan, who was regarded as a hero in Pakistan, was forced to take the fall, so that the Pakistan military, that had participated in the network, could escape censure. That dance – the lengths to which the U.S. went to shore up Pakistan – made the R.A.W. seethe.

Pakistan asked for more cash. "The U.S. would pay to lease and secure landing and hangar space for drones at some of Pakistan's airbases," ul-Haq recalled. G.H.Q. suggested they use the Shamsi airfield in Baluchistan, 320 kilometres south-west of Quetta, which already had a foreign presence as it was rented to Abu Dhabi.

After 9/11, Musharraf had proposed U.S. Special Forces operate from the Shahbaz airfield in Jacobabad in Sindh, and it was also now earmarked for drone operations. Chaklala Airbase in Rawalpindi had been utilized by the C.I.A. and U.S. Special Forces in the 1980s. It was also to be a drone site. So was Peshawar's Air Station. Finally, Tarbela Ghazi was also selected. This was super-sensitive, as it was the headquarters for the 3rd and 8th Commando battalions, a training centre for the S.S.G. officer corps but also an H.Q. for the S.S.G.'s Zarra Company, the anti-terrorist specialists (from where the faction targeting Musharraf had broken away).

In the summer of 2004, the I.S.I. handed the C.I.A. the first set of coordinates. The target was in South Waziristan. At 10 p.m. on June 18, six men were sitting inside a compound eating. One lay on a day bed, chatting on a satellite phone. Within seconds, all that remained was a two-metre-wide crater. Nek Mohammed was dead.[162]

General ul-Haq was unapologetic: "The Shakai accord was absolutely wrong. It was poor thinking. No one cared about Nek. He was a small man in a hurry. We are the military. The elders understand that Pakistan always comes first."

~

By 2004 Pakistan was awash with U.S. aid. Looking at combined programmes, the increase in U.S. military assistance in just the three years after 9/11 was a stunning 50,000 per cent, growing from just $9 million in the three years before the attacks to nearly $4.7 billion in the three years after. These numbers made Pakistan the third highest recipient of U.S. military training and assistance in the world, trailing only long-time leaders Israel and Egypt.[163]

But in India, the C.I.A. was accused of shoplifting what it needed from R.A.W. classified resources, taking advantage of ragtag operational security to buy-off select senior officers inside Lodhi Road and affiliated agencies, who had access to sensitive information. These files were uploaded using encrypted file transfer protocols that were not picked up in Delhi because of the inconsistent enforcement of security protocols, according to one Counter-intelligence Service audit.[164] Betrayal, break-ins, eavesdropping – India became a target even as it sought to be an ally.

By 2004, paranoia inside Lodhi Road was palpable, recalled Monisha, who was injured by it. Instead of lobbying for more funding, better training, stronger internal security, and a strategic rethink, R.A.W. turned on itself. Acting on a tip-off, the C.I.S. began looking for traitors but also intimidating officers with clean sheets in what became a punitive environment. Even the C.I.S. became a leaky ship and Monisha heard from a source inside it that the focus in the spring of 2004 was a Joint Secretary, the third highest non-political executive rank in Lodhi Road.

On May 7, 2004, Rabinder Singh failed to come to work and when the C.I.S. went to his home in Defence Colony it found that he and his wife, Parminder Kaur, had run. Scouring borders and airports, the C.I.S. discovered that the couple had crossed into Nepal. But in Kathmandu, they had obtained new passports in the names of Rajpal Prasad Sharma and Deepa Kumar and flown to Virginia in the U.S., always several steps ahead. One mistake by the C.I.A. gave the R.A.W. a lead. Further digging revealed that the air tickets and a hotel in Kathmandu had been purchased by an American, known to be in the Agency.

On and off, throughout her career, Monisha had come into Singh's orbit. An army major, he was already deputed to R.A.W. when she joined and was later inducted into the counter-intelligence unit CIT-J, a partitioned section that raised proxies to hit Sikh insurgents inside Pakistan's Punjab.

Monisha recalled that the first warning signs came during the 1990s, when Singh was serving at the Indian embassy in Damascus, trying to procure canopies and other parts for MiG fighter jets. On one occasion, the Syrian Air Force had flown Singh to its Al Dumayr air force base, at Ghoutra, outside Damascus. At an embassy function soon after, the major told an Indian journalist about his trip there and his missions. When the same reporter was later asked by a U.S. official at the function if he knew that the Syrians had an airbase in Ghoutra called Al Dumayr, he became suspicious. After a little digging, the journalist learned that the American had heard about the base from "an Indian diplomat buying parts for MiG fighters." Singh was reported. But no action was taken in Delhi.

Over the next decade Singh amassed influence inside Lodhi Road and travelled surprisingly frequently, requesting more leave than Monisha. He repeatedly went to Nepal, where he said he was trekking. Monisha doubted that. The C.I.A. had an active station there too. In 2002, she was startled to hear that Singh had dispatched himself to the U.S. on a counter-hijacking course. As he was then on the Southeast Asian desk, where hijacking was low priority, this jarred. Singh was reported again to the C.I.S. by Monisha and others. "It felt like setting fire to my career," she recollected, "but Singh was either profligate or a traitor."

When Singh returned, she heard from her C.I.S. colleague that his accounts of his time in America were not credible and suspicions mounted about his wealth. Government employees like Monisha earned a pittance and stayed in official apartments, while Major Singh seemed to have access to substantial cash reserves. He ate out at five-star hotels, kept a large staff to cook, drive, and clean for him at his home in upmarket Defence Colony. His children attended foreign schools, with at least one of them studying in the U.S.

The C.I.S. inquiry deepened but was hobbled by seniors who did not want a scandal. A colleague told her that the major had been soliciting information from R.A.W.'s Science and Technology (S&T) desk. It was super-sensitive, having been established by the nuclear scientist Krishnamurthy Santhanam, who had worked on the Pokhran-II bomb tests of 1998 that had blindsided the Americans, making India the first of the two South Asian neighbours to declare its nuclear arsenal. S&T had also beaten the U.S. in pinpointing A.Q. Khan's top-secret centrifuge park at Kahuta, where the feedstuff for Rawalpindi's n-bomb programme came from.

In early 2003, the major pressed a little too hard for information from S&T: his line of questioning was about Iraq. *What did R.A.W. think about Saddam's W.M.D. programme?* He asked if Indian intelligence was going to corroborate the Bush Administration's contested claim that Saddam was concealing W.M.D. and sponsoring al Qaeda. India's position on this was clear. Delhi opposed a war with Iraq and did not believe in the W.M.D. claim. Singh's line of questioning now set off alarms. Finally, another mid-ranking R.A.W. officer, senior to Monisha, reported him as a suspected C.I.A. asset.

But there was more foot-dragging. Incredulous, Monisha recalled: "The C.I.S. inquiry was stalled again – and this time by R.A.W. senior executive officers who said they were wary of impacting the Lok Sabha elections, a decision that created deeper suspicions of a wider network that was protecting Singh inside Lodhi Road."

It was not until later in 2004 that a surveillance operation began and right away it was holed. Monisha said: "The C.I.S. learned that one of its own had tipped off the target Singh, and he ran. The post-mortem concluded that the major had likely been groomed by a female C.I.A. officer in The Hague, a classic honeytrap." One estimate she saw suggested 5200 pages were uploaded to his C.I.A. handler and that a circle of fifty-seven officers were implicated, R.A.W. officials who had been subcontracted by the major and paid with C.I.A. cash.

Monisha was called into the C.I.S., and attended her interviews willingly, cooperating fully with the inquiry, and then watched as officers who had known Singh were transferred into dead zones, while her career iced over.

The National Security Adviser M.K. Narayanan, mentor to Ajit Doval, tried to settle the intelligence community by appointing a new R.A.W. chief, Hormis Tharakan, a Kerala straight shooter from the I.P.S., early the following year. But more fissures emerged, with Monisha and some of her seniors convinced the C.I.A. was to blame.

In 2006, the Delhi Police, wielding draconian secrecy laws, claimed to have uncovered an espionage ring inside the National Security Council Secretariat (N.S.C.S.) and arrested R.A.W.'s computer chief, an information security specialist at the N.S.C.S. who was a commander on deputation from the navy, as well as a third man, who was a systems officer at the secretariat. Monisha heard that these officials were targeted in a C.I.A. influence operation, a slow-moving attempt by an American officer to gain the trust of three specialists, who later would be manoeuvred into divulging highly classified materials. But the three had resisted. Loyal, the only files they shared were publicly available briefings, authored by the Bharatiya Janata Party (B.J.P.) in 1999, and two files that had no classification at all.

"The three officers made a strong case for having done everything by the book," Monisha said. She heard the police were pressed into action by I.B. and she worried the insecure services were eating themselves. No one went after Rosanna Minchew, the American at the epicentre of the scandal, who was listed as a third secretary at the U.S. embassy in Delhi.

It described her as a junior diplomat who was registered to participate in an India–U.S. cybersecurity forum.

Minchew left India but in 2019 she outed herself, joining Atlas Obscura, a "global community of explorers" that staged a walking tour of Georgetown, in Washington, D.C., whose theme was espionage. "Get the inside scoop behind the city thought to be home to more than 10,000 spies from a veteran of one of the most secretive agencies in the United States," a press release announced. The host "for an evening of spy games and an espionage-themed walking tour" was a "C.I.A. veteran, D.C. native Rosanna Minchew," who would share "(cleared) insider tales from her 15 years with the intelligence agency." She led walkers to the homes of the C.I.A.'s "father," "Wild Bill" Donovan, and that of a former F.B.I. agent who allegedly spied for Russia, and former C.I.A. director William Colby and pointed out notorious spots "where Cold War–era games of smoke and mirrors played out between the United States and the Soviets."[165] She did not mention her service in India, where three workers attached to the R.A.W. had been contaminated and cast into Tihar Jail, where they would remain for more than three years.[166]

The discontent deepened when rumours spread of a break-in at a classified site in North Delhi. Metcalfe House was used by the Defence Research and Development Organisation's Science Analysis Group and by the Institute for Systems Studies and Analysis, two sensitive outfits. They worked on communications encryption for the security forces, and they evaluated war games, weapons tests, and threat analysis data. They were an easy back door into critical systems. Despite security audits that had proposed higher walls, barbed wire, checkpoints, and many more patrols, as well as electronic surveillance, no changes were made and I.B. reported that dozens of hard drives and C.D.s were stolen. Monisha learned that the C.I.A. was once again the prime suspect.[167]

No one went after the Agency. The police repackaged the incident at the behest of I.B. as a break-in, but Tharakan at the R.A.W. was advised that encryption on all secure communications and databases had to be overwritten because of the thefts. The official who failed to secure

Metcalfe House escaped censure, as he had powerful sponsors. Monisha concluded: "Our op-sec was just terrible and when we failed, we covered up or lashed out. This was not what I had in mind when I signed up."

Inside Lodhi Road, the Major Rabinder Singh affair continued to work like sepsis. Even though she had only been in his outer circle, the office was a vengeful place and the failure to rout him caused officers who should have done better to blame others who were powerless to stop him. Monisha suspected that being a woman did not help within a service that "smelled strongly of tobacco smoke."

One of the R.A.W.'s least attractive qualities was its male chauvinism. But strategy wonks in Washington, D.C. threw India a lifeline. They began lobbying to recast the republic as the last best choice for building a bulwark in Asia. Geopolitical fault lines had made Pakistan a necessity in 2001, but as Islamabad's economy collapsed and its institutions crumbled, overcome by the terror war, so India began to shine by virtue of not succumbing, emerging as a bulwark to emerging superpower China.

In January 2004, the U.S. and India signed the "Next Steps in Strategic Partnership," a sinewy document that opened the way for Delhi to receive assistance with its civilian space programmes, high-technology trade, missile defence efforts, and civilian nuclear activities. A by-product was bringing the U.S. and Indian militaries closer together, even the intelligence services, much further down the line, creating an alliance that would immediately concern Beijing.[168]

Philip Zelikow, counsellor to U.S. Secretary of State Condoleezza Rice, pointed towards this without saying it, briefing reporters that the partnership's "goal is to help India become a major world power in the 21st century ... We understand fully the implications, including military implications, of that statement."[169] It would soon be bolstered by the US–India Defence Relationship Agreement, which the U.S. Ambassador Robert Blackwill described as enabling "democratic India to stand up to Beijing, with its aspirations to gain regional dominance."[170]

Within a month, U.S. hedging against Pakistan and China took off in a real way, under Zelikow's supervision, with the unveiling of an unrivalled deal: the US–India nuclear pact. In a single strike, Washington demolished a three-decade U.S. moratorium on nuclear trade with India, which had surreptitiously acquired nuclear weapons know-how, while leaving a bar in place for Pakistan, where righteous indignation further soured U.S. relations. Non-proliferation specialists everywhere were also astonished.[171] However, for Prime Minister Manmohan Singh it was a victory, as India's civilian nuclear energy programme could now apply for international assistance, while Delhi hived off its military fissile programme in secret sites that remained beyond international inspection.[172]

~

In Rawalpindi, Major Iftikhar was at a loose end. Discharged from a military clinic, he was expected to report for service. Instead, he headed home to Jhang, without permission, feeling exhausted and irritable. Entering the city, he picked up a newspaper. Scanning the front page, his eyes locked on a single column.

Nawabshah, September 26, 2004: A house in Ghulam Hyder Shah Colony, northeast of Karachi, was surrounded. Police ordered everyone out. Residents opened fire. I.S.I. paramilitaries lobbed in tear gas and flash bangs. Two women and three children emerged with their hands up. A man made a run for it, shooting at officers, who returned fire, killing him. The deceased was formally identified as Amjad Farooqi.[173]

A charismatic, dangerous, uncontrollable, fighting man who had started off life as teenage bodyguard for Masood Azhar and who had played a critical role in numerous outrages from the 1995 kidnapping of Western backpackers to the IC 814 hijacking, the killing of Daniel Pearl, and many attempts on Musharraf's life, not to mention the bombings of diplomatic missions and their places of worship, had finally been run to ground.

Iftikhar was shocked. "Farooqi was in many ways a hate-filled, dogmatic hard-liner. But while I despised his sectarianism, the Sunni supremacy, Farooqi was also a passionate Pakistani." Why were these faithful, committed mujahids the enemy? He wondered about the cause of Kashmir that Aabpara had bartered and thought about Yasmeena who was desperate to quit the Valley. The combat between the I.S.I. and the R.A.W. had become mechanical, the people caught like sugar cane in the gears of a juicer.

Iftikhar could not shake a growing feeling of doom that tinged everything including his memories of Yasmeena, whom he missed. He decided to call, wondering if their lives might ever converge. For the first time, despite their age difference, he wanted to make that happen. But ringing a number over the LoC raised suspicions. Instead, he tried Yasmeena's A.O.L. messenger account. Nothing came back. He pinged a neighbour in Ganderbal who could be trusted. "Adaab . . ." he wrote in Kashmiri, asking after her family. "Khuda hafiz . . ."

No reply.

Starving, he went in search of food, and ran into a face he recognized, although the name escaped him. In need of some friendly banter, he sat and chatted over snacks, both men spooning down plates of gol gappas. As they munched, Iftikhar tried to extract his companion's identity without letting on.

Finally, it dawned on him. This man was Major Abdul Rehman Hashim Syed, better known as "Pasha." He had served in Musharraf's maroon berets of the S.S.G., but then slipped out to join the LeT and become a bagman for Ilyas Kashmiri and his 313 Brigade. Pasha was an opaque and deadly bomb builder and assassin who had turned against the state.

He travelled openly, staying in officers' messes, without ever being rumbled, because his support network within the military was plush. Iftikhar knew the retired soldier's face because he had studied it for many months when he was ordered to kill him. Now, they were eating together, and he could reach over the table and kill the major before he had even dropped his spoon. Iftikhar laughed to himself. Nowadays he felt more affinity for this killer than anyone in Aabpara.

Pasha stopped eating. "Care to share the joke?" he asked.

Iftikhar realized that he had been grinning wildly. He knew that some things could not be said. Instead, he asked: "How's the maulvi?"

"Which one?" Pasha countered, his face a mask.

Iftikhar touched a finger, and then touched his eye, marking Ilyas Kashmiri's war wounds.

"Bismillah! Didn't you hear?" Pasha wiped his fingers on a cotton square. "Kashmiri got out. And he's joined the Arabs in Waziristan. I will go there too."

Iftikhar shook his head. But it was not in consternation. It was a feeling of wonder.

Pasha rose. "Hand me your phone."

Iftikhar reached into his pocket and placed the handset on the table. Luckily it was off and so did not arouse suspicion. Pasha powered it up, typed in a number, saving it to the handset.

"Call me – whenever you are ready Major *Iftikhar*." He strode off, leaving Iftikhar stunned. It was Pasha who had been hunting him.

2006–07

In Pakistan the war on terror bored into FATA. The I.S.I. continued to send detainees the C.I.A.'s way. Nabbing an al Qaeda courier, Salahuddin, officers worked him over and used him to lure out of hiding the super-cautious Abu Faraj al-Libi, who had taken over as al Qaeda's operational chief for Afghanistan and Pakistan.[174] Musharraf could barely contain himself. "Al Qaeda's Number Three. We've got him," he told General John Abizaid, the U.S. CENTCOM commander.[175] Bush heralded the capture as "a critical victory in the war on terror" and the I.S.I. received a cash bounty thought to be around $10 million.[176]

But Abu Faraj was steely and had prepared for this moment with layers of stories, sending officers off on leads that sucked up time, including a long surveillance operation of a suspect who turned out to be an Osama bin Laden impersonator.[177] Frustrated, the C.I.A. rendered Abu Faraj to Afghanistan, where he was brutalized using Enhanced Interrogation techniques, before he was rendered again, to another secret facility in Romania, ending up at Guantanamo Bay.[178]

However, money (and strategic differences) made C.I.A. officers and White House officials impatient with Pakistan. "In five years, we were taking on so many groups, reconditioning others, rehabilitating militias, and levies, keeping steady," ul-Haq said. "But in the West, they pointed to U.S. dollars, as if to say, 'we are paying, you move faster.'"

A brigadier in A-Wing told us: "The West examined its tinder box cities – Paris, Liège and Charleroi – and appealed to be given generations for changes to kick in, transformations that would separate out racism, exclusion, and petty criminality that produced violent, urban mujahids. Pakistan was given months and then the U.S. and Europe complained we were 'too slow' or 'failing.'"

Over time, Brigadier Hyat noticed how Pakistan started withholding intelligence from the C.I.A. The U.S. felt the chill. "I have a good relationship with Azmat Hyat," Jose Rodriguez, deputy director of operations for clandestine services and the number three in the C.I.A., told us.

"After 9/11 General Musharraf decided to do a total turn of the wheel of the ship and throw in his lot with us and everything worked very well for a fair few years, because a lot of these al Qaeda people were hiding in the settled areas and we worked very effectively with I.S.I. But once the fighting and intelligence war shifted into the tribal areas, it became harder," said Rodriguez, recognizing the difficulty, while the White House was less inclined to do so. "They themselves didn't reach into FATA. And for many years the service had cooperated with the Taliban and a lot of these people were still serving. They had created the Taliban and their loyalties were still with them. It was *out of sight out of mind*. They had their own thing going on."[179]

Drones were expedient for the C.I.A. and Pakistan but they were deepening hatred and dissent. In January 2006, after four more divisive aerial attacks, with villagers protesting that scores of civilians had been killed and none were from al Qaeda, I.S.I. analysts were asked to review a C.I.A. overhead.

It was a black-and-white silent surveillance clip of a compound in Damadola, a remote community cupped by mountains in Bajaur, north of Peshawar. A senior I.S.I. officer who attended the briefing told us: "The village was well known to the I.S.I. and C.I.A. Some residents followed an Islamist outfit banned by Musharraf in 2002. But what could be determined from the footage? Not much at all."

I.S.I. officers claimed that C.I.A. analysts told them it showed mujahids mingling with Taliban fighters. "They pointed to other figures, who, given their dress and weapons, could be al Qaeda Arabs or Uzbeks. The C.I.A. was vehement, pointing out the proximity to the Afghanistan border – over which attackers came striking U.S. forces. The allegations were supported with chatter from ground units, they said."

But the footage was insufficient and the C.I.A. request was rejected. The pressure on the I.S.I. increased when U.S. briefers suggested that Ayman al-Zawahiri, the al Qaeda number two, was there. "It was now a 'go.' And the I.S.I. took the cash."

As daylight broke, residents hearing explosions ran to a large compound that contained three or four homes. Now there was only a crater and rubble. Eighteen people died, fourteen from one family, including many women and children. None of the dead, local reporters claimed, were al Qaeda or Taliban.[180]

But even if a handful had affiliations, the killings – a blunt force packaged as a high-tech solution – pricked anger and it spread throughout Pakistan, as a debate began around the world with human rights organizations and lawyers asking who weighed the evidence and who passed the death sentence, in acts that circumvented national laws and collided with international conventions.[181]

Inter Services Public Relations (I.S.P.R.), the Pakistan military's publicity machine, fogged the news. The drones were U.S. fighter jets that had taken off from 50 kilometres inside Afghanistan. Pakistan sovereignty had been disregarded, it was claimed, weakly. But rallies swelled, the largest in Karachi where tens of thousands marched chanting "Death to America."[182]

Musharraf took to TV to address the nation. "If we kept sheltering foreign terrorists here . . . our future will not be good," he pleaded. Professor Ghafoor Ahmed, a senior member of the untouchable Jamaat, turned on Musharraf, telling the massing crowds: "The army cannot defend the country. The President has to go."

But Musharraf was not ready to quit and would not stop the U.S. drone programme because the C.I.A. was lobbying hard, he said. On

October 30, 2006, a deal was struck by the Pakistan government for peace in Waziristan, despite advice from the I.S.I. that it would delay an inevitable war. The military reasoned that talks had to be given another chance, given that so many in Pakistan did not support fighting in FATA. The signing ceremony was to be staged in a village called Chinagai, where the red earth ran into green hills. To mark the occasion, the students, who had returned from Eid ul Fitr holidays and were excited to be hosting such a historic event, decorated their local seminary.

Daylight glimmered in a purple helix on the horizon. Missiles slammed into the madrassa. As the dust cleared, a few survivors, buried or bleeding, began to scream, villagers running to them, hauling from the rubble the dead, wrapping 55 of them in winding sheets. Twenty-six more residents vanished altogether, eviscerated by a fire-and-forget twin strike, launched from a U.S. drone. From the 81 recorded fatalities, 69 were under the age of seventeen.

As the U.S. denied involvement, the protests in Pakistan boiled. Musharraf recalled feeling "dumbfounded." He had sanctioned Cobra gunships to attend the scene and strafe the hills, ascribing the raid to Pakistan. Now he had to eat the political pain.[183]

Hyat brooded. A full-bore war in FATA and N.W.F.P. had still not been sold to officers, politicians, and the people. Tensions were growing within the judiciary, as investigations began into the cases of enforced disappearances and street killings by the I.S.I. in their fight against the enemy within, which had been encouraged and enabled by the C.I.A.[184] Langley, which had encouraged street justice for Islamists, did not foresee the consequences. Activists, lawyers, and journalists were also swept up in the nightly I.S.I. roundups, one classified I.S.I.-C. report putting the figure at an extraordinary number: 6200 detentions.[185]

Musharraf's grip on the country was loosening and the U.S. began to spread its bets, wooing his primary civilian enemies, former prime ministers Benazir Bhutto and Nawaz Sharif.

She was a Harvard and Oxford graduate. Sharif was a mercantile Punjabi from a conservative family of wealthy pragmatists, who graduated from Government College University and Punjab University. She was spiritual but secular, punishing herself on her running machine, and eating mainly carrots. He was cunning, occasionally Islamist, girthsome with a taste for oily nihari. His palace in Raiwind was filled with zebra stripe prints and gold faucets and hosted a petting zoo with a menagerie of wild animals who were a study in behavioural despair. Hers was filled with good copies of old masters.

As a woman, Bhutto had been forced into a marriage with the playboy Asif Ali Zardari to better her political trajectory among socially conservative Pakistanis. But her counsel came from Eastern and Western male consiglieri who felt they were the *one*, men strung like piano wire in a court of frustrations. Sharif married a linguist and philosopher, who was not just a First Lady but also president of the P.M.L. (N.) and a member of the National Assembly – but he still came on strong to female war reporters, offering one, Kim Barker, an iPhone to secure her place at his court.[186]

A report generated by the I.S.I.'s C-Wing highlighted Bhutto's powerful sponsors, including the U.S. and British intelligence services, as well as former and serving U.S. State Department officials. I.S.I.-B reported that Sharif's main support base was the Kingdom of Saudi Arabia. "We do not yet know what the K.S.A. will do but they are preparing to launch Sharif at us," the classified brief warned.[187]

In January 2007, Musharraf flew to Abu Dhabi to secretly meet Bhutto. They held a second meeting later in the year. General Naeem said: "He was egged on by the U.S. and Britain that now saw democracy as a glue that might hold Pakistan together long enough for America to wage its war in FATA. But not because those Western powers preferred democracy."

When Musharraf returned, he told the I.S.I. he was planning to offer legal amnesties in return for Bhutto and Sharif supporting an extension to his presidency. The I.S.I. sent a warning brief: "You lose, only slower. They will erode the military in the end while giving you a few more months."[188]

But Musharraf had yet to play his hand. What only a handful of people knew was that Tariq Aziz, outwardly a dilettante, but privately dependable and unstinting, had almost locked down a blueprint for an unlikely and comprehensive deal with India that took in Kashmir and other disputed territories. From the outside Musharraf looked vulnerable but he felt secretly confident. "Appearing to lose, we were actually winning," Musharraf told us. "This *is* Pakistan."

~

The country simmered with bomb blasts and drive-by assassinations, plotted by faces pinned inside Azmat's blue binders, assisted by an entire section of the elite Zarra Company of the S.S.G., that also planned to besiege the presidency, and kill Musharraf and his supporters.[189]

Into this cauldron came U.S. Vice President Dick Cheney. His historic visit on February 26, 2007 should have been a fillip, with Musharraf pushing back against the U.S. Bhutto plan, while spilling the news of his unprecedented India deal. He had even put the clashes between the C.I.A. and I.S.I. behind him and readied a report on Hyat's significant successes.

But instead, Cheney, whose Iraq project was mired in bloodshed, and who was on his way to Afghanistan, where too there were no gains, was in a foul mood. He complained about Iran meddling in the former and the Taliban's resurgence in the latter. And where was Osama bin Laden? Cheney told Musharraf that the U.S. wanted his head. It also needed to see a broad military campaign against insurgents in FATA. The time for peace was well and truly over. "We have never known peace," Musharraf noted sourly.[190]

He had been staring over the border into southern Afghanistan and the British military in Musa Qala, where the International Security Assistance Force (ISAF) had rebuffed 100 attacks in just 40 days.[191] First came a ceasefire that held. Then there was a town meeting, and finally Musharraf was advised by the I.S.I. of a controversial shura in the desert, where British officers and U.K. Foreign Office officials met with Musa Qala leaders. Taliban commanders were also in attendance. "British troops from the Royal Irish Regiment were then evacuated in Jinga trucks secured by 3 Commando, but with the Taliban in the background overseeing proceedings from a distance," the I.S.I. noted, furious.[192]

The I.S.I. brief concluded: "The British Army (and ISAF) has effectively recognized the Taliban to prevent a demoralising defeat or untenable casualities. Elsewhere, we hear ISAF members are doing the same, paying Taliban commanders for transport passes so that their lorries are not attacked. In Sarobi, we understand that the Italian contingent is paying *not to be attacked*."[193] This information was verified by the British and German intelligence services.

There were still so many reasons for Pakistan not to fight a full-on war, Musharraf argued. In G.H.Q., and at Aabpara, the Campaign Plan was to "take care of both borders," the Durand Line and the east. This meant that more than half of all forces were committed to facing India or in cantonments, until the peace talks emulsified. Only a small portion of the army could be sent to FATA and Swat anyhow, which left the military "unable to conduct a regionwide clearance, whatever Cheney wanted."[194]

The military could clear one agency at a time, XI Corps recommended. The I.S.I. brief concluded: "The ISAF cannot afford an Afghan-wide operation, or even a military campaign that spans the Durand Line. They told us it was impossible. So, how can we?"

This frustrating Cheney visit also seeded a highly sensitive plan, which all sides now publicly deny. Iraq was finally being described in a U.S. National Intelligence Estimate as resembling a civil war, between Sunni tribes and Shia militia, some of which were backed by Iran.[195] "We were asked to tighten the ligature on Iran and one way was via proxies on the Pakistan side of the Iranian border that could be boosted, to attack," an I.S.I. general who attended the briefing maintained.

C.I.A. officers we interviewed declined to comment, but the I.S.I. general's recollections were backed by two other senior executive officers, one of whom, a D.D.G., maintained: "We had been active on the Iran border for four years, as had the C.I.A., so it was a case of reheating relationships between us and cells of minority Sunni rebels fighting the Iranian Shia security forces." The rebels belonged to Iranian Jundullah, the Soldiers of God, an outfit that had strong links to the outfit of the same name in Pakistan, that I.S.I. enabled to pressurize Shias in Karachi. The Karachi iteration had viciously turned on the I.S.I. once already, trying to kill the V Corps commander. But now the I.S.I. was asked to approach the Iranian arm of Jundullah again. The general claimed the outfit was "useful but murderous." He added: "We had done worse. And for less."

The Sunni-dominated armed forces of Pakistan were paranoid about Shias. But Pakistan was also investing heavily in Gwadar port, in Baluchistan, and it was only 70-odd kilometres from Iran's Chabahar port – both harbours competing to take goods transported from Central Asia and Afghanistan out into the Gulf of Oman, a lucrative and strategically vital business. The I.S.I. had long wanted to penetrate Chabahar, just as the Iranians tried repeatedly to do the same in Gwadar.

While China was a principal sponsor of Gwadar, it was India that was a potential client in Chabahar, where by 2016 it would invest up to $500 million in the port and an industrial park.[196] The I.S.I. complained: "R.A.W. is constantly operating remotely in Gwadar, sponsoring Baluch separatists to ambush vehicles carrying Chinese engineers, kidnapping them and blowing up their depots."[197] Pakistan planned a double tap to serve its own interests and those of Washington: strike R.A.W. and its Iranian hosts, using deadly Jundullah.

In Karachi, where Jundullah was formed in 2003 by the I.S.I. asset Rehman, the assassination bid on the corps commander caused most of its members to flee to Baluchistan and FATA. There, Iranian Jundullah mopped them up. Set up by Abdolmalek Rigi, a pathological teenager, jailed in Iran for fatal stabbing, Rigi had learned while incarcerated with Baluch nationalists, who were part of the Iranian minority Sunni community, about their hardships. Upon his release, he decided to deepen his religious education and hopped over the border and to a Sunni seminary in Binori Town, Karachi, that hot-housed Masood Azhar. There, Abdolmalek caught the attention of the I.S.I. as he allied with Jaish.

Issued with a Pakistan identity card in the name of Saeed Ahmed, he set up shop along one of the world's busiest heroin smuggling highways, the border road heading west of Quetta to Taftan in Baluchistan and beyond that Iran. Jundullah was soon a politico-criminal cartel and crossed into Iran to carry out its first assault, a brazen attack on the motorcade of Iran's President, Mahmoud Ahmadinejad.[198]

Jundullah Iran was sheltered in Pakistan by the I.S.I., where it built a base, officers claimed. It was beefed up by taking in the stragglers from the Karachi Jundullah operation and other sharpshooters and bomb makers holed up around Quetta and FATA. It was also given a publicity platform. One outlet was Baloch Voice radio, in Stockholm, Sweden, but the I.S.I. also connected it to the Al Arabiya network, based in Dubai, owned by the brother-in-law of the late King Fahd of Saudi Arabia.[199]

They struck in February 2007: one attack killed eighteen members of the Islamic Revolutionary Guard Corps (I.R.G.C.) while the second was a bombing in a girls' school which injured thirty.[200] In August, Jundullah cells re-formed to strike near the Iranian port of Chabahar, with I.S.I. backing. More than thirty gunmen manned a roadblock, set alight ten trucks and trailers, hauling drivers and their mates out, and then took others watching from nearby cabs. In all twenty-one Iranians were taken prisoner and escorted over the border into Pakistan.[201]

After a major attack the following year, where three police hostages were shot, and Jundullah demanded the release of 200 prisoners, Iran publicly blamed Pakistan and the U.S. However, in Iraq, Moqtada Al Sadr, the powerful Shia cleric, and militia leader, offered the U.S. a six-month truce.[202] I.S.I. officers claimed the same U.S. officials who had asked them to activate Jundullah now pressurized them to shut it down.

I.S.I. paramilitaries traced the abducted police and drivers to the flinty hills of the Pakistan–Baluchistan border. In a two-hour gun battle, one kidnapper was killed, and two others injured. However, sixteen Jundullah cadre were taken alive. Under interrogation, the I.S.I. realized that one of them was Abdolhamid Rigi, the elder brother of the Jundullah founder, and I.S.I. asset. But this was war, and to improve relations with Iran, Aabpara ordered that Abdolhamid Rigi be taken to the Taftan border crossing and secretly handed to the I.R.G.C., unsettling the S-Wing of the I.S.I. that deals in covert conflict.

Abdolhamid was compelled to make a televised confession. He blamed the C.I.A., remaining quiet about the I.S.I., claiming America alone had paid him $100,000 to wage war in Iran.[203] A blunt classified I.S.I. report delivered a warning: "We have now made an enemy of Jundullah. It is reaching out to al Qaeda. If they join forces, we will not be spared."[204] Once more, the need to keep its Washington paymasters on-side, risked terrible injury to Pakistan.

~

The Islamist uprising finally reached the capital, Islamabad, in 2007. An I.S.I. file produced by Brigadier Azmat Hyat's C.T.C. warned that two brothers running a religious complex known as the Lal Masjid or Red Mosque (because of the colour of its walls) were a Trojan horse for irregulars from FATA and the Swat valley.

Their family had once been in the heart of the military establishment, their father a veteran of the Afghan war and an I.S.I. chaplain. President Zia bestowed favours on him, granting funds to build a mosque complex in upmarket Islamabad G6/4, close to Aabpara, so that spies and soldiers who had shared a bond from a golden age of licensed jihad could pray together.

A decade later, new policies were in play, and the father had been assassinated by the I.S.I.[205] From the pulpit, Maulana Abdul Aziz and

Abdul Rasheed Ghazi, who never forgave the security services, offered prayers for the Taliban and called on clerics not to bury fallen troops during the Pakistan army's first Waziristan campaign. They demanded Pakistan be ruled by sharia, called for the banning of music and D.V.D. shops in the capital, and their supporters mounted morality patrols (in the style of the Taliban), armed with staves and slogans, laying siege to hair salons that they maintained were covers for brothels. They abducted Chinese women accused of prostitution – causing Beijing to rear up.[206]

General Nusrat Naeem, then the C-Wing chief, rang the alarm at the I.S.I. as surveillance was stepped up and assets inside the Lal Masjid were recruited, including the brothers' two chief bodyguards. "They reported that guns, ammunition and explosives were being offloaded inside Lal Masjid from the Swat Valley," an I.S.I.-C "sit-rep" concluded, warning that in the capital a millenarian cult was armed to the teeth and ready to explode.

The I.S.I. dug deeper and in a highly sensitive operation claimed to have recruited one of the two brothers, Abdul Aziz, who began informing on the other, Abdul Rasheed, giving the I.S.I. a bird's-eye view into the mosque. Lal Masjid was looking a little more like Waco every day.[207]

I.S.I.-C got messages from inside. "Abdul Aziz wants to quit and demands I.S.I. help." He claimed that hardcore fighters from the N.W.F.P. and FATA were in complete control and had "hijacked the protest that they aimed to turn into a bloodbath." He warned that his brother Abdul Rasheed "had realized too late and was a prisoner too." The I.S.I. briefed Musharraf: "The brothers have lost control. We cannot wait."

Naeem's men suggested that Abdul Aziz "disguise himself and quit the complex, when the next batch of female students surrendered." The I.S.I. arranged a rendezvous point and grabbed their asset who was dressed in a burqa.

The S.S.G. and 111 Brigade blew holes into the mosque walls and darted in and out, mapping the fortifications. Armoured cars ringed the building. Two students were shot as they ran. Ten more were wounded – four critically.

Now even the weather conspired against Musharraf. A cyclone lashed the country. In Baluchistan, 60 per cent of the landmass was under water and only accessible by helicopter. Two million people were homeless, and hundreds were dead.[208] Musharraf decided to fly into the heart of the relief operation. But as the President's plane took off, hot rounds came pulsing towards it, forcing the pilot to make sharp, evasive manoeuvres. Musharraf radioed it in, continuing his journey.

The I.S.I., which recovered an abandoned 12.7mm anti-aircraft gun, two 7.62mm machine guns, and two shoulder-launched missiles, concluded: "The weapons jammed which saved Musharraf. Pakistan Air Force officers connected to the Chaklala airbase, working with SSG defectors, are behind it, steered by fighters in FATA."[209] The al Qaeda hive mind was churning.

In July 2007, the army surrounded the Lal Masjid. After ten days of talks, holes were blasted into the mosque walls and 150 S.S.G. commandos clambered inside, triggering volleys of gunfire from above and below. By the following day the main perpetrator was dead, and the mosque was secured. But instead of allowing in reporters to see the military-style build-up and the arms dumps, as well as verifying the number of dead and injured, which the I.S.I. put at ninety, Islamabad police were ordered to purge the scene. A classified I.S.I. report from C-Wing's Naeem was indignant: "Army and police have lost control of this story, which will spin out of control."

Former XI Corps Commander General Masood Aslam watched the eruption that followed: "Every funeral for the siege dead was like a match thrown on kerosene, especially in Swat and Peshawar." Al Qaeda's deputy Ayman al-Zawahiri attacked Musharraf and told Pakistanis to join the jihad and seek revenge on the Pakistan army. In South Waziristan a small masjid known as Green Mosque was renamed Lal Masjid overnight, as G.H.Q. pulled the trigger on a military operation and troops were finally ordered into FATA and Swat.

The R.A.W. was watching too, as the violence inched south. "It was mind-dumbing. Harrowing," Monisha recalled, as the reports landed in Lodhi Road. "Seeing so much bloodshed in Pakistan had left many people in R.A.W. thankful that India was not indebted to the United States after all." They also pondered the mooted Pakistan–India strategic deal. "Would Musharraf be around long enough to see it through?" I.S.I. officers like General Naeem wondered the same.

His team continued to write the unthinkable. One such extraordinary missive came in a top-secret I.S.I. briefing: "Is Musharraf a Liability for Pakistan?" This classified exploratory note, signed by Musharraf showing he had read it, concluded that as a commander Musharraf was still respected, but in his present role, he was losing friends and allies. He led from the front, not collectively, the report suggested, but was surrounded by officials and politicians who were far less anchored to his goals. Unable to stabilize Pakistan, he was making enemies of the judiciary and the religious right. And he had enabled the return of Benazir Bhutto and Nawaz Sharif.

India, however, was rising, and already ahead, thanks to its ground-breaking civilian nuclear deal signed in 2006, in Washington, by President Bush and Manmohan Singh.[210] Taking all of this in, the controversial I.S.I. report concluded: "The question of Musharraf's successor has to be raised." He was in the endgame – and there was a strong case to be made that if the military was to be saved, Musharraf had to go. In November, having suspended the chief justice, bypassing the courts, declaring a state of Emergency, upending the constitution, he unwittingly began that work.[211]

~

Major Iftikhar, still in Pakistan, was A.W.O.L., having decided not to report back to duty. He logged on in an internet cafe, using a V.P.N. which placed him in Nepal and – safe from trackers – checked his A.O.L. account. There was still nothing from Yasmeena in Kashmir. He had been thinking about her daily, and wondered why she had not got back in touch. But for the first time, a neighbour in Ganderbal was online. He pinged a message to her: "As-Salamu-Alaykum."

After a moment, a reply came in Kashmiri. *"Vaaray chivaa?"* How *was* he doing? His correspondent continued typing, the words, barely believable, streaming across his screen. The neighbour was glad he had got in touch after so long. She had too much news. The hit on wedding singer Kuka Parray had triggered chaos in the Valley. The I.S.I. was blamed, and a manhunt had begun after Iftikhar's cover name was leaked to the renegades by Iftikhar's asset in the police S.T.F., who had switched sides, for cash. Armed with that information, Parray's fighters had gone berserk. The gunmen got smashed on rum and arrived, mob handed, in Ganderbal, where the S.T.F. mole revealed the I.S.I. operator had last been seen. They had kicked in doors, finally coming to the green, ripple-roofed house. Finding it empty, they had crashed into a nearby home and found Yasmeena. Neighbours heard screams and scuffles before a convoy of jeeps tore off.

After a while, the neighbours crept out and entered the house. It had been turned upside down. Yasmeena was missing and when she did not turn up the family went to the gatehouses of every nearby military camp, showing her photo, in the sad pilgrimage of mercy made by many Kashmiris. A week before, newspapers had reported a body pulled from a ditch on the edges of Kuka Parray's territory. The family had travelled to a nearby hospital and were shown the corpse of a woman, which a nurse, shaken, whispered had been tortured and raped. Beside the gurney was a small tray laid out with a few personal possessions. They could not bring themselves to pull the shroud back but they did inspect the keepsakes. One bracelet was familiar, a birthday gift for Yasmeena, that she had treasured.

Iftikhar slumped. Yasmeena had been kidnapped, assaulted, and slowly killed. He recalled slinking out of the cafe, filled with a deep self-loathing. "Everything was collateral for men like me," he told us. The system he was part of was corrosive. "We were like U.S. smart bombs that we were told were precise but that in reality shredded entire communities."

He knew what to do. He reached for his phone and dialled; the call was picked up right away.

"As-Salamu-Alaykum – *Iftikhar!*" It was Major Pasha, and it was as if he had been waiting. Pasha proposed a meeting. But not with him. He asked Iftikhar to see a thinker he trusted and who acted as a gatekeeper "for their little organization." *Someone who would straighten him out.* Iftikhar memorized the address and caught a lift on an empty military bus returning from wherever the front was nowadays. The driver was a Pashtun boy who sat on a box grappling with a wheel so big it could have steered a galleon, singing all the way: "*Sta da Mahfil na Wasgma /* Despairing for you, I am leaving."

Dropped off at a security checkpoint at the entrance to an unfinished gated community on the outskirts of the upmarket Bahria Town, Rawalpindi, Iftikhar walked the rest of the way to a sand-coloured villa, standing alone among plots allotted to military officers that had yet to be developed. Guards, without name patches, dressed in fatigues, interrogated him with the softly spoken manners of veterans who had seen death often. He was let into a living room whose windows looked out towards the brown Margalla Hills.

Dr Wahid entered and introduced himself. He was a preacher for Hizb ut-Tahrir, the Party of Liberation, that was working to implement sharia law and overthrow the secular state. Iftikhar knew his face. This man featured in Brigadier Azmat Hyat's blue binders as a fire-starter and agent provocateur who had engineered the split in the Pakistan Special Forces, especially the Zarrar Company of the S.S.G. An intelligence bulletin reported that Wahid had lectured operators inside one of their bases about a fatwa supposedly issued in Saudi to kill Musharraf. And Wahid had done the same at the Pakistan Air Force. The results were multiple assassination plots and bomb attacks.

This conversation with Wahid and its unsettling setting left such a deep impression on Iftikhar that he recounted it without interruption.

"*Al amr bil Ma'ruf wa Nahy an al Munkar,*" Dr Wahid said to Iftikhar, who realized after a second that it was not a greeting but a Quranic stanza that he had last heard as a child: "Muslims should command good and forbid evil."

Dr Wahid produced a slim pamphlet, the chapters on *Zuhd*, which, he said, was an important word in Islam that referred to contemplation: a pious existence. He leafed through to Hadith 2317 and picked out a stanza: "Whoever among you sees an evil action, let him change it with his hand. And if they cannot change with a hand, only then with his tongue." Iftikhar was not a God-less man, and this was workaday Islam, the pillow-talk between a father and his child, he told the doctor. In Islam every kid learned that what they did was more important than what they thought.

"Action," the preacher continued. "This verse calls for every Muslim to do something for *hisba*," he said, invoking the Islamic concept of accountability. "The collective duty of Muslims is to *stop* wrong."

A shoeless Pashtun boy appeared at the frosted glass door, bringing glasses of warm water. Wahid raised his and tipped it into his mouth making a sound like a fish gasping. Iftikhar recalled becoming distracted by shadows that flickered behind the frosted glass. He wondered who the unseen houseowner was. Someone wealthy who was against the present order. Iftikhar resented these elites who played being pious at home and sinned abroad. Growing irritable, he interrupted the lesson, telling Wahid: "But life cannot be a free for all. There are always orders."

Dr Wahid nodded, smiling. "We know from other scholars, like al Nawawai, that hisba is not the responsibility of the authorities. It is directed by God. Let Him command us to act."

This was a piece of rudimentary gymnastics, Iftikhar thought. It was not *absolutely true* that all action predicated on faith was legitimate. Religious men did bad things all day long. But it was undeniably right that, as Pakistan collapsed, action was called for. Iftikhar wanted to do good and to resist evil. Being diverted from these simple rules had led to mindless carnage in Kashmir and elsewhere, he believed. Innocents like Yasmeena were the victims. Iftikhar recalled that he said something like this: "How do we choose what to endorse and what to disparage? Not all of us are trustworthy. Without rules or instruction, there will be chaos. Demagogues already terrorize us." He thought of the Lal Masjid.

The sound of diesel engines gurgled outside, as a pickup arrived, and Iftikhar could make out the slapping of chappals on dry gravel, as men jumped down. There were murmured conversations. These were the noises of insurrection.

Iftikhar tried again, looking directly at the doctor. "Men brought up believing in democracy are being asked to set this aside by preachers like you so that we invest in . . . a religious autocracy?" It was important to be good, but he could not invest in a leaderless world. It was hard for a spy whose life was dedicated to trespass, to accept a future without guidelines.

Dr Wahid shook his head. "All of us are governed by *tawhid al-rubibyya*. The rightness of the Almighty. *Hakimiyya:* this is the *recognition* that only Allah is empowered to pass laws. We should embrace 'legal domination' by the Almighty and rise-up in revolt against manmade laws. Bad men cannot rule people of the book."

Iftikhar recalled thinking hard. He told us: "Wahid had at last said something which I thought was absolutely true."

Wahid sensed his moment, the give in the conversation. And he pressed home. "We ask you to denounce Muslim societies and governments that mimic the Western ones ruled by manmade laws," Wahid continued. He picked up his Quran and flicked to 4:140: "When you hear the Verses of Allah being denied and mocked, then sit not with *them*." Wahid looked up: "To do nothing to counter the activities of kafir [heretics] is to become kafir."

Wahid pulled out a piece of paper. He read from it. "Who Are We and What Do We Want?" Then, his finger trailing the words written below, he continued: "No doubt that he who prefers manmade laws to those of God is a kafir . . . as it is not allowed for a kafir to rule over

Muslims, it is our duty to depose the rulers of our country." Wahid then added: "This comes from a different time. Do you know *who* wrote it?"

Dr Wahid folded up the paper and handed it to Iftikhar.

"*Shahids* from Egypt penned it as their *declaration*. They secretly shared copies with others. All of them were in the Egyptian Special Forces in Cairo who deserted and then plotted against President Anwar Sadat in 1981 and shot him dead for pursuing peace with Israel."

It occurred to Iftikhar the present crisis was not current at all. These were timeless problems, for every soldier to solve, in ways that he saw fit.

Tarbela Ghazi, North-Western Pakistan, 70 kilometres from the capital,
8 p.m. After prayers at the high-security Special Forces base, in a
campus now sublet to the U.S. for clandestine drone operations, S.S.G.
commandos and other members of the Special Operations Task Force,
which was created with American mentoring, sat for dinner in the
canteen.

A Pashtun Special Forces operator from the elite Zarrar Company
strolled in and detonated an explosive vest. When the debris was cleared,
twenty corpses were pulled out of the rubble, mostly S.S.G. operators,
support staff, and canteen workers. Thirty wounded, six of them critical,
were driven to Attock and military hospitals in Rawalpindi, where a fifth
column of operators no longer loyal to the state was heading too.

Qasim Market, Rawalpindi, 6 a.m. A watchman sat in the gallery of a
shop and scanned the busy junction. The minivans came and went. His
phone buzzed with a missed call. They called this a "Hello Number," a
burst that could not be tracked and that said, "everything was on time."
Thirty minutes later, his phone buzzed again – the "passengers" were
moving into place.

A 7 a.m. an unmarked bus passed by. The driver opened the door
to let in three men. As the last stepped inside, one detonated his vest
that was packed with ten kilos of explosives, studded with ball bearings,
nuts, and nails. A roar: windows and doors of nearby apartments rattled,
an eruption of flames expanded and then contracted, enveloping the

vehicle. Pavement slabs lifted off the ground. Drain covers flew into the air, and a whistle, sharp as a cut grass, had everyone holding their ears. The blast wave came next, throwing bodies out of the shattered windows, limbs and debris landing on the road in a drizzle of blood, bone, and ash. The bus was twisted, smoke and flames licking around its chassis, and eighteen I.S.I. workers and officers were dead, dozens more injured. So powerful was the fireball that it streamed out of the bus door and punched through an adjacent brick wall. This attack was designed with the kind of charnel engineering that evolved from practice. The young bomber had in his hand a mechanical striking pin that could not be electronically jammed. Once the safety was pulled, there was no way to stop the striker hitting the charging cap. Even the elevated position of the bomber had been calculated. The blast wave was not absorbed by the tarmac. Instead, it was human bodies that felt its full force, as well as the whirling metal. The detonation mechanism was later found, its factory code, lot, and batch intact, enabling investigators to link this blast to several others, including those at the Kohat Army Mosque and the Police Training Academy in Hangu, all of these the work of Ilyas Kashmiri, the Jaish, and the S.S.G. break-away, with al Qaeda in the background.

A police picket near the district courts in the cantonment area of Rawalpindi. A place cops gathered at and chatted; I.S.I. had men here too because of the sensitive location – close to G.H.Q. and to military homes and bases. Now, a cyclist popped off his bike and detonated a vest.

Woomph.

The pressure wave and then the flames engulfed everyone: eight died on the spot, including three police officers, while fourteen were ferried to hospital.

A checkpoint 100 metres from the main gates to G.H.Q. Soldiers massed, spies too, but they failed to detect a car that tried to get through, and detonated, slicing up three soldiers, two dying. The vehicle had been stuffed with mortar rounds and packed with potassium chlorate, the spaces in between filled with hand grenades.

A bus carrying I.S.I. officers and workers, turning into Hamza Camp, Faizabad: Inside was a walled enclave with a residential section used by I.S.I. and M.I. officers. A car rammed the bus. This time the bomb maker used military grade RDX, pierced with sticks of dynamite, the explosives mounted on a mattress of ball bearings, nails, and screws.

They never stopped innovating, poaching knowledge from Afghanistan and Iraq. When the fireball was finally doused, thirty corpses were removed from the wreckage. The same kind of device that was trialled here would be used in an attack on the Danish embassy in Islamabad.[212]

Was Iftikhar connected to all these bloody attacks, we wondered. They all occurred after his meet with Dr Wahid, and an officer like him knew where to strike at the I.S.I. in Lahore and Rawalpindi, in Islamabad and Karachi. At some point, we had to confront him.

~

I.S.I.-C, General Nusrat Naeem's section, continued to Red Hat the administration, testing its defences, writing the unconscionable.

A report: "What if Benazir Bhutto is assassinated in Pakistan?" The General Intelligence Directorate (G.I.D.), Saudi's spy agency, had directly warned Aabpara that the kingdom "is not happy at all" with Musharraf's dialogue with Bhutto, his team reported. The K.S.A. was "incensed by the idea that she might become Prime Minister again."

The I.S.I. report warned: "KSA is absolutely clear that it will not tolerate Bhutto becoming the head of state. KSA will disrupt Pakistan if we ignore them." Naeem said the I.S.I. had already picked up calls and messages from FATA where insurgents openly chatted about "killing Bhutto." C-Wing speculated that the noises-off from FATA might have been provoked by Pashtun agents working for the G.I.D., as well as the renegade forces in Hyat's blue binders.

The report did not acknowledge that the I.S.I. was also playing a role in fomenting tensions about Bhutto's possible return, or Musharraf's falling out with her. It did brazenly contemplate the consequences if she was killed, and its conclusion was striking. "Such an event would be ruinous for Pakistan. The real instigators will remain cloaked, and the blame will fall on I.S.I. and GHQ." The military's popularity would plummet. "Musharraf would be fatally wounded," it suggested.[213]

On October 18, Benazir Bhutto returned into this bewildering chaos, ending eight years of exile. Her homecoming was bookended by the footage of her climbing down to the tarmac in Karachi airport, pausing, tearful, on the bottom step to pray and, afterwards, the devastating explosion at the tomb of Pakistan's founder Muhammad Ali Jinnah, where tens of thousands came to welcome her.

Turkish-made bomb jammers were supposed to have radiated a bubble of dead airwaves around her vehicle. If they ever worked, their batteries had likely run down.[214] Mobile phone towers were switched off to thwart spotters for an attack or remote controllers. But in the end the bomb or bombs were manually triggered. Live television footage caught the kettledrum strike and showed furious and terrified onlookers running towards Bhutto's vehicle, when a second eruption cut them down. It was the twenty-eighth suicide attack of the year.[215]

Bhutto told us she was aware of the dangers. She had been issued with warnings in London and Washington, where officials also willed her to take the risk, as Musharraf was now widely seen in the West as a stumbling block, just as the I.S.I. thought the same.[216] As she took in the mutilated bodies through columns of black smoke she wondered if it was worth it, she told us later. More than a hundred corpses were laid out and four hundred wounded taken to hospital, while she sought refuge at Bilawal House, her family home in Clifton.[217]

Brigadier Azmat Hyat was not one of those who wanted Bhutto dead. He wanted answers. But no one at the I.S.I. seemed able or wanted to get to the bottom of the Karachi blast, even though, according to the investigation report, the faces of the bombers – their skin masks – were found, "one 26.6 feet away from the point of detonation and the other 78 feet away."[218]

Hyat, who worried that Musharraf had declined to bolster Bhutto's security, in a petty, self-defeating act that incriminated him, latched on to a single find: an MUV-2. It was a detonator, 12.5 centimetres long and 11 centimetres in diameter. Resembling a cartridge, it had a metal sleeve that encased a bolt. When a safety pin was pulled with the force of a kilogram, a spring was released, pushing the striker down against a percussion cap, starting the chain reaction that culminated in a blast.

This model was identical to those found at the scene of eleven bombings, including recent ones in Rawalpindi where the I.S.I. was targeted. All of them were linked to Baitullah Mehsud, a Waziri warlord, who strategized with the 313 chief, Ilyas Kashmiri, and al Qaeda, using Jaish and Lashkar cadres and teenage bombers from FATA to pull the pin. Whoever was trying to kill Bhutto was also hunting the security state, Hyat worried. But this kind of thinking was never brought into the open – even though it supported Musharraf's case.

Because the I.S.I. suppressed details of insider attacks and kept a tight hold on investigation results from the first attempt on Bhutto's life, these linkages would remain obscure, in another own goal that was like those scored during the Pearl inquiry. What emerged from these C.T.C. documents was that one of Musharraf's weaknesses was indecisiveness towards his enemies, and indifference towards Bhutto's security, whereas the I.S.I. was exhausted, dealing with an existential threat, fanned by rogue insiders, sectarians, and proven terror cells.

With Bhutto readying herself for a massive rally in Rawalpindi, the Kingdom of Saudi Arabia sent Nawaz Sharif to Lahore, as they had warned the I.S.I. they would. Sharif was picked up airside by an armoured sedan supplied by the K.S.A. that was on diplomatic plates.[219]

On December 27, while Bhutto took her campaign to Liaquat Bagh in Rawalpindi where a crowd of tens of thousands massed, a Pashtun teenager, wearing sunglasses and a dark shirt pushed forward. He may have discharged a gun three times. Perhaps he also detonated a suicide jacket. Or possibly an explosive belt was triggered, and no gun was fired. All three versions were backed by different sides, but whichever was right, Benazir Bhutto slumped back into her armoured Toyota Land Cruiser. She might have bumped her head on the way down, or been killed outright, or even died in-transit from a bleed.

The Pakistan military lurched, miscommunicating and misdirecting, again. Confronted by chaotic scenes, with a crowd of hysterical mourners painting themselves in the blood of the dead, the deputy inspector general of police ordered a clean-up with high-pressure hoses. It looked like he was sluicing the scene of crime, but he insisted that the action was on his head alone. Two anonymous sources disagreed, telling a U.N. inquiry – that lambasted federal and local authorities for "fatally insufficient and ineffective" security – that his order came from above.[220] Bhutto's car got the same treatment. Her widower, Asif Ali Zardari, declined permission for a post-mortem. Everyone, for different reasons, obscured, diluted, or misdirected the truth, especially the Pakistan military and the I.S.I.

The writer and broadcaster Owen Bennett Jones observed: "Liaquat Park was named after the first prime minister of Pakistan, Liaquat Ali Khan, who was assassinated there in 1951. In what many believe was a cover-up, the police shot his killer on the spot. One of the doctors who tried to revive him at Rawalpindi General Hospital was Dr Khan. Not an uncommon name in Pakistan, Dr Khan treated Benazir too, a Mussadiq Khan, the son of the original doctor, who was unable to revive Bhutto at the same hospital where Liaquat died."

Pakistan was home to circularities and this one was a helix.

~

In Aabpara, a panic set in. I.S.I.-C released the script of an eavesdropped call, hoping, General Naeem recalled, that "it would act as a pressure valve." As part of Ehsan ul-Haq's root and branch reorganization of the

I.S.I., a desk was observing the warlord Baitullah Mehsud, in North Waziristan. The matrix captured Baitullah crowing over the murder, in a chat in Pashtun with an unknown cleric. Azmat's men got to work, finally identifying him as Maulvi Azizullah, who ran his own madrassa in South Waziristan. But after the Lal Masjid raid, Azizullah had turned his students into human bombs that struck at the Pakistan military, I.S.I., and now Bhutto.

More classified reports confirmed what was in Azmat's blue binders. Baitullah Mehsud had financed the plot and Ilyas Kashmiri had assembled it, while Jaish fighters procured and concealed the weapons and explosives in a Rawalpindi safehouse in Shah Jayyona Colony. The men involved had been mentored by the hijacker Amjad Farooqi, before his death. Everyone reported back to al Qaeda. The military had failed to protect Bhutto, and whitewashed subsequent inquiries. However, a failure to release detailed and timely internal reporting enabled far more serious charges to be levelled: that the military was also complicit in her death.

Two months on, in February 2008, Zardari and the P.P.P. crashed into power in an election fuelled by grief, the widower brandishing what he described as his wife's will in which she supposedly asked him to lead her Pakistan People's Party and described him as "a man of courage and honour."[221] However confused P.P.P. supporters felt about Zardari's stunning claims, they begrudgingly backed him as he became President of Pakistan in August that year. It was an act as unforeseen as Musharraf's stone-in-a-well fall, the general plummeting into a dark, airless exile.

∼

In Delhi, Ajit Doval, who had retired from I.B. in January 2005, after serving as its chief and having doubted the backchannel peace mission between India and Pakistan, felt vindicated. He told us: "This is our neighbour. Whatever they say and however *they* sell it, I.S.I., and the military, are culpable for the Bhutto assassination. We can dress it up and come up with caveats, which is what I.S.I. count on, but the combination of a terror state and its savage proxies did this deed. The killers are killing again."[222]

In Lodhi Road, Monisha and her circle wondered about the overspill, trying to calculate where the al Qaeda amalgam of turncoats and former state assets would strike next. "It genuinely felt as if the forces of darkness were gathering for a final push," she recalled. "Whatever they all said in public, about building a wall with our neighbour, we could not afford a failed state next door."

On January 8, 2007, Prime Minister Manmohan Singh, having endorsed the backchannel with Pakistan and invested heavily in the U.S.-backed administration in Afghanistan, daydreamed out loud of a time "while retaining our respective national identities, one can have breakfast in Amritsar, lunch in Lahore, and dinner in Kabul." However, now there would be no "paradigm shift" as Singh (and Musharraf) had once hoped for.

Instead, that Pakistan peace deal was gasping, and within the Indian intelligence community and among political hawks there was hardening against Rawalpindi, even though the military there had delivered on many things, for the U.S., but also India. The insurgency in Kashmir was turned down to a simmer. By 2008, the total number of deaths in the Valley had slumped to 541, compared to the 4500 who died in 2001.[223]

Rajinder Khanna, at Lodhi Road, saw a different kind of opportunity. "We hoped the U.S. would slam the door on Rawalpindi and move towards India." Senior R.A.W. officers waited to hear from the C.I.A. liaison, sensing that both sides were ready to put aside their doubts and fears.

But even now, the I.S.I.'s covert world was far from dormant. Instead, proxies were working frantically elsewhere, and Monisha, in Lodhi Road, picked up on it. R.A.W. had been following LeT clerics, fundraisers, and fighters around the globe. They flew to Bangkok and popped up in northern Thailand. They were spotted in Bangladesh, Sri Lanka, the Maldives, and Myanmar, movements that commonly mirrored natural disasters. The earthquake around Gujarat and Kutch of 2001 had seen 20,000 die and the one that devastated Kashmir in 2005 killed almost 90,000. The tsunami of 2004 claimed 200,000 lives, while cyclones in Bangladesh in 2007 and in Myanmar in 2008 took 142,000 lives. Wherever there was mayhem, LeT recruiters did what impoverished governments could not, and clambered through the driftwood of people's lives to offer aid, an ear to listen, and a helping hand. Sometimes, LeT activists swiped genuine foreign assistance, relabelling U.N. aid cartons as their own. All the time they were seeding supporters and potential sources of future funding.

In 2005 when the magnitude 7.6 earthquake shook the Kashmir region, leaving four million homeless, Western intelligence agencies semi-seriously joked about the upside – that it would wreck the mujahid world. However, in a classified cable from the U.S. embassy in New Delhi, the political counsel Geoff Pyatt relayed how R.A.W. sensed the opposite: "The quake did not, in fact, wipe out these [armed groups in Kashmir]. Rather, it may have strengthened the terrorists and weakened Indian defensive perimeters. Proof of this . . . is that police have seized 1,600 kilos of explosives since the quake, while only 140 kilos had been intercepted in the nine previous months."[224]

As the Rohingyas were hounded in pogroms overseen by the military in Myanmar, survivors heading for refugee camps in Bangladesh, LeT struck out for Cox's Bazaar and Chittagong. R.A.W.'s Khanna, when stationed in Myanmar, reported that the outfit tried recruiting and piggybacking the Rohingya armed wing, unsuccessfully.[225] They also worked with anti-Indian non-Islamic groups, including the Khalistan movement, hosting warfare courses on Thailand's forested north-western border.[226]

Some LeT funding came from Britain, where the security services had exposed a *hawala* or black-market transfer operation, run out of a convenience store in King's Cross, London. What made this 24/7 wire service stand out was the volume of trades, with the British estimating that it had guaranteed "many millions of dollars" in payments to the

LeT and other Pakistan-based Islamist groups, money raised from the diaspora but also through crimes committed in the U.K. including counterfeiting, credit card cloning, and fraud.[227]

The LeT also sourced bomb-making materials via the U.K. and U.S. using, in one case, a thirty-one-year-old father of two from Coventry, Mohammed Ajmal Khan.[228] Working with British counterterrorism detectives, the R.A.W. learned Khan had undergone basic weapons training at Muridke and at an LeT combat camp in Muzaffarabad. Later, he flew to the U.S., where the F.B.I. trailed him to a meeting with a schoolteacher from Maryland, whom the I.S.I. had first spotted at LeT camps and, despite backing the Lashkar, tipped off the C.I.A., as the presence of all foreign fighters was now an own-goal.[229]

Both men tried to buy weapons, drone technology, thermal imaging, and night vision equipment, as well as large quantities of Kevlar, the F.B.I. would allege. Both would be jailed, protesting they were entrapped.

R.A.W.'s LeT case files suggested that the outfit was a global Islamist threat and not a regional irritant. But the U.S. intelligence community, privately, did not buy it. Most knew next to nothing about the grinding Kashmir conflict and did not care to learn. All Lodhi Road got back from the intelligence liaison at the U.S. embassy in Delhi was a mundane information exchange. Anodyne summaries were swapped, and an annual conference staged. Occasionally, the R.A.W.'s counterterrorism chief met with the N.S.A.'s SIGINT liaison officer, but according to Monisha, who prepared materials for these sessions, "nothing was shared and nothing was learned."

2008–09

The al Qaeda amalgam – led by the jackal Ilyas Kashmiri, with Jaish and the protégés of hijacker Amjad Farooqi, steered by al Qaeda – did not give the P.P.P. civilian government time to settle in. A colossal truck bomb devastated Islamabad's Marriott Hotel, an American chain where visiting U.S. officials often stayed. Rescuers recovered fifty-seven bodies, with 266 casualties taken to hospitals. Among the fatalities were the newly arrived Czech Republic's ambassador and two American military personnel. Scores of Pakistani staff and guests died. The Marriott was only a few hundred yards from the prime minister's house, where President Zardari was sitting down to eat, having just made his maiden speech. He emerged shaken, and, with a trembling voice, promised: "We will get rid of this cancer."

The I.S.I. reeled, the A-Wing arguing that the West only saw Pakistan as the incubator of terror. But more than 27,000 lives were lost between 2007 and 2009. In the middle year alone, in FATA, 3067 people were killed. And from two years before this, and until three years after it, in the Swat Valley 11,862 more were dead.[230] The mind-numbing volume of incidents was rending the country: places and names flashing by, a zoetrope of bone-shattering images.

A Band Aid–style Pakistani supergroup produced an anti-terror anthem, "*Ye Hum Naheen*" (This is Not Us), which went viral, and a petition opposing terrorism was signed by more than sixty-three million people.

But what men like Major Pasha knew was that he was not them and he did not need their consent. The Caliphate he and his kind were hoping to declare, propelled by the Hizb and the Jamaat and supported by everyone else in Brigadier Hyat's blue binders, would be imposed and not elected. This parallel state had unleashed a barrage of terror that was in many ways far more deadly than a regular army: sacrificial in its objectives, pattern-less in its deployment, lateral in its methods, predicated on loss, feeding off rage and self-hatred, to occupy liminal spaces that the government or its mosques struggled to reach.

As Rajinder Khanna had predicted, Pakistan's continuing entropy brought the American intelligence community, begrudgingly, to Delhi. In March 2008, the R.A.W. received an invite. Lodhi Road was asked by the U.S. National Security Agency (N.S.A.) to join a regional body known as S.S.P.A.C. (Signals Intelligence Senior Pacific), which was a step up. Its members included the so-called Five Eyes Countries – Australia, Canada, New Zealand, Britain – but also South Korea, Singapore, and Thailand, whose entry was a reward by President Bush for playing a leading role in the C.I.A.'s secret black site programme and helping to shut down al Qaeda's Southeast Asia wing.[231]

The S.S.P.A.C. was a platform for sharing technical intelligence, and here countries pooled their signals, gathered through eavesdropping, but also built trust and learned new surveillance techniques from the world's most powerful spy agencies. Senior N.S.A. officials flew into Delhi for high-level meetings. Finally, the R.A.W. began breaking through and winning N.S.A. plaudits, as much for submitting "the highest volume of reports" as their quality, U.S. analysts added in a snarky tone.[232]

R.A.W. officers were now "read into" some highly classified reports and introduced to data produced by cutting-edge technology and coding that bored into Islamist hotspots.[233] Monisha's sources shared tantalizing morsels, while other, highly classified insights only made sense to her after she studied the secrets data dumps created by N.S.A. whistle-blower Edward Snowden in 2013, files that unveiled the extent of powerful, invasive U.S. mass surveillance programmes for the first time.

Some of these advances came about because of a tragic failure in Britain. After the 7/7 attacks, when bombers detonated devices inside the London Transport network, killing 52 people and injuring hundreds more, the British security services were lambasted for losing sight of the four attackers as most of them were already known to the police. What had been missing was their relationships with each other.

To find suspects and describe their associations – panning out to even wider friendship circles – involved pooling colossal amounts of sensitive metadata from an enormous volume of calls and messages in Five Eyes members states and (surreptitiously) beyond.

This meant the sender and recipient details for emails, or the phone numbers someone called from, and to, as well as time stamps for when these messages, emails, and calls were sent and made. All of it would be funnelled into a new reference repository, known as SMAC, or the Sensitive Metadata Analytic Collaboration programme. By October 2007, each partner state within an acronym that Ian Fleming would have been proud of sent an analyst to the N.S.A.'s H.Q., a black glass cube in Fort Meade, Maryland, where they trawled the haul.[234]

Many of the most significant advances came from "contact chaining," a method used by British technical intelligence at G.C.H.Q. in Cheltenham, to describe entire networks linked to a single exposed phone. Analysts examined calls, messages, and emails from one suspect and derived from them lists of others and their associates, building a matrix of association in top-secret projects, code-named CLASP and Prime Time.

But then they made it smarter by experimenting with algorithms that could automate the system, activating alarms when suspicious keywords were used by a caller or a writer, triggering a chat, or alert for an analyst working in a highly classified project code-named Salty Otter. The trigger terms included "wedding," "birthday," "a date," "engagement," and "marriage," or "shopping". It was like school kids mugging on the phone to their teenage friends over weekend drug deals, only these codes potentially indicated a slaughter.

With the sifting beginning, the work widened to look at the places where insurgents and planners spoke to each other and the devices they used. One of these was the Thuraya satellite phone: lightweight and affordable, it was as likely to be needed in remote areas like the Durand Line as it was by funders and cheerleaders in Western cities.

The top-secret Menwith Hill surveillance station, in North Yorkshire, with its white golf-ball antennae array, began fishing for Thuraya signals using a program called VoiceSail. It liaised with G.C.H.Q.'s International Terrorism Team, which focused on nine British cities, where some callers and receivers lived and were now mapped.

Mobile phones were another study area but even more relevant to the Indian experience, Monisha found, were the tools that G.C.H.Q. and the N.S.A. were developing to counter the *burner phone*: disposable, prepaid mobiles. The bane of security services the world over was a boon to the insurgent, suicide bomber, and street corner drug dealer, leaving them invisible. Men like majors Pasha and Iftikhar thrived on disposable, unregistered handsets. Iftikhar's getaway from Aabpara had been concealed because of them. And his survival afterwards ensured by them.

G.C.H.Q. described a gang or cell using burners as a "closed loop" that was extremely difficult to spot. This was one reason why the 7/7 conspirators were not stopped, as while each was visible their relationship to each other was not. A burner phone might only light up if a conspirator mistakenly dialled out of the closed loop. Occasionally, spooks got lucky if a handset was recovered in a police raid or one was dropped in a pursuit or left in a car.

But now, G.C.H.Q. was experimenting with identifying a closed loop by looking for its shadow pattern. The highly classified program homed in on the most basic Nokia models, preferred by conspirators everywhere, searching for a window of time when the low-cost handsets were switched on. Analysts then plotted the usage of these devices over time and geography.

These ingenious collection methods that ploughed through everyone's

right to privacy helped shape the linkages between callers using burners
in the U.K. talking to insurgents in Iraq. But, more interesting for
Monisha, G.C.H.Q. identified several hotspots of callers and receivers
inside Pakistan.

One was linked to Rashid Rauf, a British baker who had fled a murder
inquiry in the U.K. and enlisted with al Qaeda in Pakistan, where he had
mentored the 7/7 cell, shoe bomber Richard Reid, and many more plots
beside. In November 2008, Rashid Rauf, who had been captured but
slipped away, was killed, the I.S.I. claimed, in a U.S. drone strike whose
targeting came out of this operation.

However, a second circle of burners radiated from a hub glowing with
comms in Pakistan-administered Kashmir. Menwith Hill zeroed in on a
compound, before handing off to G.C.H.Q. and a specialist team within
the N.S.A., known as Geo-Cell 2SL. It called in specialists from the
National Geospatial-Intelligence Agency who read data and analysed
images from spy satellites in their offices in Bethesda, Maryland. At
G.C.H.Q. technicians called on the European Security Centre, in
Darmstadt, that assisted in fleshing out the connections.

Monisha learned that a storm was brewing in Pakistan-administered
Kashmir and its landfall would be in India. The burgeoning conspiracy
began in Muzaffarabad devised by Lashkar blowhards. Regional
mercenaries were massing at a training centre there before being
transferred to a safehouse in Karachi. One of them was identified by his
nom de guerre, Zarrar Shah. The R.A.W. believed his real identity was
Abdul Wajid, and that he was from Sheikhpura, in Pakistan's Punjab.
Another was Abu Al Qama, real name Mazhar Iqbal, from the Mandi
Tehsil area of Punjab. He was a combat trainer who was working with
a team of retired Pakistan soldiers and former Special Forces, running
their physical training.

Finally, out of the static came an identity Monisha had not heard of
before, a retired major in the Pakistan army with the codename "Pasha."
German intelligence advised he was a rogue operator, who had quit the
Pakistan military, and that his real name was Major Abdur Rehman

Hashim Syed. This was Iftikhar's new mentor, who was wanted by the I.S.I. for savage attacks on the security services in Pakistan, in which, we believed, Iftikhar had played a critical role.

If Pasha was the lead, Monisha was advised, there was a high degree of probability that Ilyas Kashmiri would be there too, as they had overlapping interests. If Pasha was at the helm, we reasoned, Iftikhar would also take a seat, suggesting that Monisha was tracking Iftikhar too.

She reported her findings up the line. LeT was training recruits for a marine assault on a major Indian city. The 313 was involved and a cell of military operators who likely had retired from the Pakistan military. Chatter and maps concluded, with reasonable certainty, that the target was Mumbai. She asked two questions. Was the I.S.I., which was also being bloodied by these elements, in the know? Or was it a target too?

~

To escape the heat of downtown Dubai, Iftikhar took us for a drive to the border with Oman, where red earth folds into the black Hatta Hills. We were unusually quiet, burdened by the difficult questions we intended to ask, and he sensed our discomfort. When he stopped for a bite at the Bukhari, ordering Afghani tikka and Qabuli pulao, we began to try to flesh out the fraught past, cautiously probing the scope of his collusion in the savaging of the security state in Pakistan, even the Marriott Hotel suicide attack, which the I.S.I. believed he had worked on. Most difficult of all we mentioned the crossover between some of these attacks – protagonists, equipment, bomb-signatures, and logistics – and the murder of Benazir Bhutto. And we were about to raise the attack on Mumbai too.

Iftikhar looked volcanic. "I had nothing to do with Bhutto," he glowered. "I was – and I am – absolutely against corrupting of our faith and my country. A corrupt state is illegal in the eyes of God. Bhutto was no President Sadat. Her killing was murder. That's that. And it left

Pakistan worse off. Simple." For the first time since we met, Iftikhar seemed shaken. "I stood against chaos." His face reddened, his eyes moist. The only time before we had seen him tear up was when he recounted the death of Yasmeena. "But these . . . thugs . . . Pasha, etc. brought it on."

The attacks on the I.S.I. and Special Forces: was Iftikhar central to all of them? Shaking his head, he blurted out something that was akin to a map of his limits rather than a denial: "Major Pasha . . . I began to see him differently. As a psychopath. He was pushing Pakistan into an abyss. They became frenzied, sacrificing their own people to strike in Afghanistan, where they killed so many civilians." He was not answering the question but was raising doubts about Pasha and his crew. After Bhutto's death they had tried and failed to kill Afghan President Hamid Karzai, twice. "Then when Pasha and Co. came back to Pakistan, the red mist came over all of them. Nothing short of an apocalypse was good enough for those guys."

When had he last seen Pasha, we asked, trying to focus in on details?

"He called me to Lahore." Iftikhar shifted uneasily in his chair. Pasha said he had been watching the LeT with building frustration. "He said the Lashkar in Pakistan was bent out of shape as its chief, Hafiz Saeed, remained wedded to the I.S.I., even though his Kashmir project had been wrecked when they turned off the violence over there." Rooting around, Pasha said he came across a plan from 2001 that the I.S.I. had forced Lashkar to shelve. "Pasha said he was going to revive it," Iftikhar said. "And I should play a role. But he seemed manic. Deaf to everything. He saw himself as Ilyas Kashmiri. The new jackal."

The plot Pasha was reviving stemmed from when a cell of Lashkar fighters and trainers migrated down to Makli, a town east of Karachi, not far from Keti Bandar, a silted coast of inlets, from which small boats could reach India via the Sir Creek estuary. Iftikhar said: "Back then, as Kashmir had become a no-go, LeT observed that India's coastguard was massively underfunded."

The Lashkar boats easily evaded the few coastguard vessels. "They started running military explosives and guns into India. They considered landing teams of trainers to recruit local gunmen who could mount hit-

and-run attacks," Iftikhar said. "Then it occurred to them that instead of sending recruits over the mountains in Kashmir to get into India, this sea route was wide open. They began to think of a sea raid on India. This was the plan that Pasha decided to revive."

In Mumbai, there was every nationality and faith. "A marine attack on that city would be hard to repel and difficult to detect. Afterwards, foreigners would fear coming and India, its image, and economy would suffer like Pakistan's had."

Pasha sold the plan hard. "The Pakistan army is mobilizing, he warned. They are finally getting ready to hammer North Waziristan and everywhere else in FATA. We have to stop them, or we will be forced out." President Zardari was reaching out to India again trying to reheat the Musharraf peace deal.

There was a macabre logic, we said, and did Iftikhar go along with it? "I saw something different," Iftikhar countered, bitterly. He did not want to know our opinion or reveal his motives and actions. "With Pasha's raid on Mumbai he wanted to trigger a war between India and Pakistan which meant he was gambling with the lives of millions of people. It was completely reckless."

Iftikhar's head hung low. We looked around for the first time. The diners had finished, and the staff were smoking out back. Iftikhar's face was a puzzle of hurt and rage. "I turned Pasha down," he insisted. "I just kept thinking that I did not sign up for chaos and slaughter. I had told Dr Wahid this, in our fireside chat. I believed in order, and in justice."

So, what did Iftikhar do with his information on the impending Mumbai raid, we asked. He had a way of writing himself out of the worst incidents while laying blame on others. Iftikhar was slippery. He turned, grimly, and packed away his notebooks. We followed after him, irritated by how he cherry-picked our sessions, avoiding our most difficult questions, and we wondered if this would be our last meeting.

Our plane back left in two days. And his patience was worn thin.

~

On 26/11, ten gunmen landed in Mumbai in the dead of night and held the city hostage for 68 hours, wreaking havoc, laying siege to hotels, torturing the Jewish residents of an Israeli counselling centre, striking down Indian commuters and pedestrians, culling guests drinking in a cafe, setting fires and bombs as a paralysing fear gripped India. And the world watched, open-mouthed.

It was one of the most brazen attacks on the country. More worrying, it was remotely controlled from inside Pakistan, with gunmen directed, goaded, and groomed over leased internet phone lines, with handlers watching the results on 24/7 cable TV, in actions that combined all that the terror amalgam had learned since its first sorties in 2002.

Monisha – who reviewed all available intelligence – saw Major Pasha's hand, along with the other Lashkar diehards named in the Western intelligence bulletins. She focused on Ilyas Kashmiri who seemed to float behind the conspiracy, like he had on so many others. But she could not decide if the I.S.I. was the driver or if the raid was a high-water mark for the rebellion inside Pakistan that was as anti the state as it was opposed to India.

A critical collation exercise by R.A.W. concluded that Pasha was the synthesis of all that had gone wrong inside Pakistan. His father was Major Abdul Ghani, a Lahori who served in the sixth battalion of the Baloch Regiment. Pasha followed in his footsteps, graduating from the prestigious Pakistan Military Academy in Kakul. In 2002, he had been sent to the Afghan border to mop up al Qaeda but refused to fight, placing his faith before country.

Pasha was demoted, and he reacted by going A.W.O.L. The I.S.I. caught sight of him in the company of Lashkar fighters, but he ran from them too, because of Aabpara's oversight of that outfit and instead enlisted with Kashmiri's 313 Brigade, which would have no truck with Musharraf or the I.S.I.

Beneath them was intelligence on two brothers whose trajectory solidified Lodhi Road's highly sensitive internal view, which would be significantly more nuanced than the political pasting Pakistan came in for. They were majors Haroon and Khurram Ashiq, who were also born into a military family from Panjeri village in Pakistan-administered Kashmir. Khurram was selected for the S.S.G.'s elite Zarrar Company and became an assault commander in the army's anti-terrorist force, before being deployed on a U.N. peacekeeping mission in Africa.

But he and Haroon retired from service, as it edged towards the U.S., and joined LeT to fight for Kashmir. When operations there were quashed by Musharraf, the brothers travelled to North Waziristan, where they trained with the 313 Brigade that attacked inside Kashmir but also harassed ISAF forces, especially the British army in southern Afghanistan.

I.S.I.-S officers approached both in 2004 and asked them to cooperate. They also, according to Azmat's blue binders, identified Major Pasha, and approached him. All three rejected the deal. In Azmat's binders Major Khurram was recorded as Killed in Action – dying in a strike on a British position in Helmand in 2007. Grieving, Major Haroon teamed up with Pasha to take their revenge. According to reporting in the R.A.W. and the I.S.I., seen by us, Pasha had recruited Major Iftikhar and the three veterans – Iftikhar, Pasha, and Haroon – had been responsible for attacks on the I.S.I. and military quarters, vehicles, personnel, and checkpoints inside Pakistan, something that Iftikhar had refused to address or concede to. But here it was in writing.

Iftikhar was adamant he had broken away from Pasha and Haroon when the plans for what would become 26/11 were first raised. But these two retired officers had, nevertheless, continued with the deadly Mumbai raid, alongside Lashkar, Kashmiri, the 313, and al Qaeda.

Monisha said she despaired. What unfolded on 26/11 was so close to the intelligence excavated by Western agencies. Insight hadn't just come from the S.S.P.C.A. The C.I.A., Monisha noted, had an undeclared, high-value source inside the plot, who had sent 18 detailed briefs, including likely targets in Mumbai, the number of attackers, their route, and method, all of which had been passed on to R.A.W.–I.B. That source she knew was called David Headley, born Daood Syed Gilani, an American of Pakistani descent, who some analysts inside India intelligence believed was a quadruple agent, serving the U.S., I.S.I., Lashkar and – mostly – himself.

The son of a Pakistani poet-cum-diplomat who wed a Philadelphia heiress, Headley was a rich-kid-turned-drug-dealer, a fantasist who as soon as he was caught dealing drugs in Pakistan, and then in the U.S., had turned on his erstwhile trafficking partners and worked as an asset for U.S. law enforcement and American intelligence agencies until 9/11. Then, he had also dabbled in another fantasy, to become a mujahid. Daood had approached LeT, where he had been befriended by Major Pasha, who saw utility in this man who, due to his age and lack of fitness, would never have survived as a fighter.

Headley, who did fail the physical try-out for Lashkar, as Pasha knew he would, was turned into a reconnaissance agent for the 26/11 plot instead. Changing his name to David Headley, donning his Western self to recce Mumbai for the attack, he went unnoticed by security agencies looking for Islamic terror tropes and not Western businessmen. Monisha was certain Headley's reports not only went to the Lashkar but also to American intelligence, which fed them back to her.

Subsequently the LeT also suspected Headley was a C.I.A. asset and froze him out.[235] The I.S.I. too gave David a wide birth, believing he was a double or triple agent, answering to the C.I.A.[236] What was certain was that Headley, a man who attempted to befriend everyone, returned to Lahore, from where he watched 26/11 unfold on the TV, furious and comforted by a triumphant Pasha. What he saw play out on the small screen were attacks on targets Indian intelligence had been told to safeguard by the U.S. and others – intelligence that was largely ignored.

"Something went terribly wrong," Monisha reasoned. "I was unable to get traction in Lodhi Road. But that was not the real issue either. It was not about *me*. Or my effectiveness. What mattered was whether India bothered to develop the intelligence from G.C.H.Q. and the N.S.A. before the raid. Or did we fail, through laziness, or – worse still – by intent?"

R.A.W.–I.B. had been hunting LeT for so long in Kashmir and had penetrated it so successfully that many officers believed the outfit was a pushover. "I began to ask myself a question," Monisha said, "and imagined a case being made in the R.A.W. that this 26/11 plot would be a trifling matter. I could believe that the hawks in Lodhi Road thought it might not happen at all, and even if it did, Pakistan would be shown to be the originator and a failed terror state."

She pondered: "Things were also changing in the intelligence community. I was starting to hear arguments from officers who were far more ideological and far less empirical. Some were also openly religious in a secular agency. Energy was being wasted on blackening Pakistan, rather than working to safeguard India. Intelligence was being shaped to tell chauvinist Hindu-centric stories – about the majority – that excoriated minorities like Muslims and helped sectarian politicians rather than the secular vision of our country. We were supposed to produce a product that went to consumers who made decisions for India. But now we were manufacturers and consumers, conspiring with politicians and this is a deadly combination. For some of the intelligence officers who went down this path, the Mumbai raid might have loomed like a potential victory, one in which they gambled with a city to injure Pakistan, catastrophically, and finally killed off the C.I.A.–I.S.I. pact. Was this their goal?"

At the very least, a trust deficit had opened-up in Lodhi Road where analysts like Monisha could contemplate both a total failure and a deep conspiracy within the R.A.W. In the weeks following 26/11 while international mediators worked to keep India and Pakistan apart, global condemnations focused on the LeT and the Islamist levies assisting them.

Diplomats were careful not to overtly blame the Pakistan military or the I.S.I., although they were accused of being – still – a launch-pad for terror. Inside Lodhi Road, as Monisha and some of her colleagues went over the build-up repeatedly, she decided that her future lay outside an outfit she had once lived for.

In Rawalpindi, the attack provoked dread and disbelief.[237] Ajmal
Kasab was the sole survivor of the LeT raiding party, a young man caught
by plucky Indian detectives and who told them he was dragooned by the
LeT that lifted him from miserable poverty in Faridkot, in Pakistan's
Punjab. But battle-drunk senior officers in the military and I.S.I. insisted
that Kasab was an Indian impostor, from Uttar Pradesh.[238] These were
clever, well-informed people but they still viewed the calamity in
Mumbai, in which 166 died, as a conspiracy rather than conceding that
Pakistan's Islamist levies were behind it.

In the West, these musings appeared madcap. But inside Pakistan so
many unresolved events from the past were steeped in intrigue, including
the death of President Zia in the mid-air explosion of 1988, that citizens
schooled in the improbable embraced the impossible.

It would take many weeks for officials in Islamabad and Rawalpindi
to finally accept that the LeT was the driving force behind 26/11, but
so were sectarians like the LeJ, jihad fronts like Masood Azhar's Jaish,
al Qaeda, and former Special Forces, retired I.S.I. officers, and former
members of the armed forces, who had turned on the security state. It
was clear that 26/11 was the embodiment of the cannibalistic rebellion
that could – unless action was taken – collapse Pakistan.

~

The 26/11 raid broke the Pakistan–U.S. relationship. The Indian
intelligence community finally had American attention, only to drop
the ball. The N.S.A. had begun passing counterparts in India selected
top-secret material, such as interrogation reports and recordings of
intercepted phone calls. In the weeks following 26/11, some of these
were leaked to the media. "At times it seemed a daily occurrence," the
N.S.A.'s country desk officer complained.[239]

Accused of "poor tradecraft," R.A.W.–I.B. was told to double-
down on security – or nothing more was coming. To make their point,
N.S.A. officials flew to Delhi in May 2009 with new protocols limiting

the supply of top-secret information, until new systems were in place, officers carrying with them a letter from the N.S.A. director underlining "the seriousness of the leaks."[240] Embarrassing though the episode was, it was manageable.

Over the border, 26/11 caused an axe to fall on the I.S.I. The Leviathan of C-Wing was smashed up. The C.I.A. had made the case that C had too much power and too many responsibilities: counterterror, political management, counter-espionage and counter-insurgency, organized criminal networks and information warfare, the disappearances and secret prisons, inspired, in part, by the C.I.A. Brigadier Azmat Hyat's C.T.C. became semi-autonomous, leaning towards the Analysis Wing and tilting to U.S. intelligence, which now drove it.

Hyat was hustled out of his own operation, which he had begun with eleven officers and now had more than 450 working for it. A spurious whispering campaign suggested that he had flown too close to Western spy agencies. He was confined to his home in Islamabad and occasionally allowed to travel to the Gulf, where he tried to remake a living as a guest officer working inside a Gulf intelligence service, until he returned, instructed by Aabpara to keep to himself. "We built something real," he said, "that broke apart as the U.S. and Pakistan diverged. Both sides lost out."

The C-Wing chief, Nusrat Naeem, who had come through the Lal Masjid siege, the political crises leading to Musharraf's ouster, Bhutto's assassination, and the Mumbai raid, bore the brunt. The S-Wing director, Lt. General Asif Akhtar, was also shunted for failing to control the LeT and squash Jaish and the sectarians of the LeJ. Akhtar's parting gesture was to refuse his last mission: to punish the LeT emir Hafiz Saeed. "I said no," Akhtar told us.[241]

General Naeem recounted how he took on the assignment that cemented his exile from Aabpara. "Asif Akhtar made a case that S-Wing 'could not get its hands dirty' or it would never be trusted again. I said I would go to Faisalabad, where the LeT emir Hafiz Saeed was lying low." Naeem, who always thought of himself as the last man standing, headed out and began a day of uncomfortable talking, describing to Hafiz Saeed how the country was being crushed in the post-26/11 vice, with diplomatic and economic pressure, while its western and eastern borders remained precarious. The groundwork was laid for Saeed to propose his own solution.

"We could not tell him," Naeem recalled, "but we could encourage him to reach a point of view." Here was a clear demonstration of just how difficult it was for the I.S.I. to manage Lashkar. There was a huge debt of gratitude owed Saeed for his dedication to the Kashmir cause. "Finally, he suggested that perhaps he had become an obstacle to Pakistan's recovery." The LeT chief solemnly decided to place himself under house arrest, suggesting that he withdraw from public life – for now.

A sportsman, Naeem was cast since childhood as a winner, which sometimes was interpreted by batchmates as a cruel streak. It led to rough play. In 2004, after multiple attempts were made to kill Musharraf, he put together a plan to capture and kill Jaish and LeJ fighters all over Karachi and Punjab, even contemplating a rigged jail break in which inmates would be slaughtered.

In 2006, incensed by what he saw as negative reporting by the *New York Times* from sensitive Quetta, he ordered the Det there to deal with it. Rough men in plain clothes broke into correspondent Carlotta Gall's hotel room and seized her notebooks, computer, and cell phone. The *New York Times* wrote: "[Gall] protested when one of the agents grabbed her handbag, and he promptly punched her twice in the face, knocking her down. The officer in charge accused her of trying to interview Taliban members, which he said was forbidden."[242]

Now Naeem was losing – to the insurgency, and to the C.I.A. (which had issued a pink ticket against him, a traditional diplomatic complaint that coloured a relationship as unworkable) – and also to his intelligence chief, General Ashfaq Parvez Kayani. His studied, silent deliberations Naeem read as wavering, but Kayani actually loathed back-seat drivers and preferred the counsel of officers other than Naeem. As did his successor, General Ahmad Shuja Pasha.

The C-Wing chief also caused the I.S.I. establishment to speak its mind, which Aabpara detested, the D.G.C. officially opposing a C.I.A. station chief in 2006–07, an officer Naeem argued was hurting Pakistan's security services. The C.I.A. replaced him but with someone far more hawkish, veteran Frank Archibald who would later become the director of the National Clandestine Service.[243]

Naeem lobbed one last grenade, before he shifted from Aabpara altogether, a complex whose business and rebuilding he had overseen, using U.S. reward money, which by the end of his tenure totalled more than $450 million. He wrote a classified report noting that there was still no Osama bin Laden Det. No Det either for Dr Ayman al-Zawahiri, the al Qaeda second-in-command. "There was always action but seldom a plan," he complained, dispatching the written brief with a striking title: What happens if Osama bin Laden is found in Pakistan?

The I.S.I. and military would look guilty if Osama was found in Pakistan, or even near one of its bases, Naeem argued. But if Aabpara insisted it had not concealed Osama, or looked for him, it would also appear incompetent. The leadership was asked to consider what Pakistan should do if asked to arrest Osama and family on behalf of the U.S.

Would it be able to weather the backlash domestically and internationally, or resist the request? Should Pakistan lead such an operation on its own, or with Western partners? And if it did, would it provide more ammunition for those claiming that the Islamic republic served the Christian West? Alternatively, Pakistan might not be trusted to participate in such a sensitive U.S.-led mission, which, if it was successful – without Pakistan's aid – would undermine the Pakistan military. He reached his own conclusion. "Better to seem stupid or weak, than treacherous," the bin Laden report concluded.

Like so many things the I.S.I. was asked to consider in this terrifying epoch, this was the best worst result.

The I.S.I. began a silent, top-secret crackdown on the 26/11 masterminds and the captains of the murderous domestic rebellion over the next twelve months. It began with a tip-off, from a caller who gave "precise intelligence," after which Major Haroon was intercepted by Pakistan's motorway police while he was driving through Rawalpindi interchange. Inside his vehicle, the police found a kidnapped businessman from Karachi, blindfolded and trussed up in the back. Haroon would be taken by helicopter to Adiala Prison in Rawalpindi, but would likely never be convicted, becoming another I.S.I. forever prisoner like Omar Sheikh.

A week later, on March 3, 2009, twelve gunmen ambushed a bus carrying the Sri Lankan cricket team on its way to play in Lahore. Some of the attackers escaped, while six police officers and two civilians were killed. Seven members of the team were injured. An I.S.I. internal investigation concluded that the insurgents were seeking hostages to barter for Major Haroon – and the planner was his friend Major Pasha. Then the I.S.I. received another call-in, with a similarly detailed tip-off, and finally in the summer of 2009 they caught Pasha too, who, like Haroon, struck a deal.

A man who bragged that he would never surrender, who had come close to killing Musharraf (many times) and Hamid Karzai (twice), was implicated in the Bhutto assassination and was responsible for slaughter in Rawalpindi, Lahore, and Karachi, who had helped set Mumbai on fire and picked off U.S. forces in Afghanistan, and assisted in the flattening of the Marriott Hotel, revealed that he was now planning the same across Europe. But he agreed to roll over and set traps on behalf of the I.S.I., the outfit he had scorned.

His first move was to clear up a messy conspiracy that stretched out to the West and involved one of his long-term collaborators: David Headley. After 26/11, he had remained in touch, introducing Headley to Ilyas Kashmiri. He was just the kind of American chameleon that the 313 Brigade chief wanted, a convincing, invisible asset, with a passport, the look, and lingo. He could help Kashmiri's outfit grow, by casing targets in Europe including a Copenhagen-based newspaper, where in 2005 inflammatory cartoons of the Prophet had been published. The 313 sought to behead its editor and was also weighing up targets in France and Britain. Then there was a possible broadside on the National Defence College in Delhi but also a secretive Indian nuclear research site on India's west coast. Drawn into Ilyas Kashmiri's circle, Headley travelled to Denmark, London, and Paris, updating Pasha, who passed news on to Kashmiri. After Headley finally met with Kashmiri face to face, he won his backing for full-bore operations all over Europe.

However, now Major Pasha gave the I.S.I. all of Headley's contact details that were passed to a C.I.A. liaison. Langley was forced to hand the information to the F.B.I. In October 2009, David Headley was arrested at Chicago O'Hare airport. He would be sentenced to thirty-five years in prison in the U.S. for his multiple plots, while still sticking to his operational strategy of betraying everyone around him. In 2016, he told an Indian court by video link that the I.S.I. had orchestrated 26/11, going against much of the available evidence seen by Western intelligence. Bidding to get himself released early and into witness protection as a Confidential Informant, he humoured his American interrogators by agreeing to talk to India's investigators, telling them what he thought they wanted to hear.[244]

The I.S.I. heavily promoted its role in the murky capture of Headley, hoping to bury the lingering suspicions over its connections to 26/11, but the U.S.–Pakistan pact was frozen as India's relationship with American intelligence warmed.

There was, according to Brigadier Azmat Hyat, a clash of heads and goals. "Cooperation continued between the I.S.I. and C.I.A. over al Qaeda, but there was outright hostility over Afghanistan and the Durand Line," said Hyat. "Many of Rawalpindi's strategic aims conflicted with Washington's. Neither side would budge."

There was another factor: already mired in the chaos of Iraq, incoming U.S. President Barack Obama had ordered the C.I.A. to end its torture programme, close all black sites and revamp its stalled Osama bin Laden hunt. For all the close cooperation between the C.I.A. and the I.S.I., the Agency still suspected that Pakistan was protecting the al Qaeda leader or not hunting him.

To placate America, Zardari offered India, without consulting his security services, a "no first strike" policy, tethering Pakistan's nuclear assets by committing to not using them unless the country was attacked, riling the military, which controlled these assets and worried their deterrent value was fading.

The jarring disconnects fed a deep and building paranoia between the I.S.I. and the civilian politicians, but also between India and Pakistan, as well as Aabpara and Langley. Hyat's old friend Jose Rodriguez had retired and was under investigation for his role in what Obama described as the Agency's torture programme. The days of cash rewards and overlooking the I.S.I.'s domestic black programmes, many modelled on the C.I.A.'s, were over.

As Brigadier Hyat saw it, America's failure to understand Pakistan, and Pakistan's inability to explain itself, was matched by Rawalpindi's growing fear of India's intentions in the region and the R.A.W.'s warming relationship with the C.I.A. The failure to capitalize on Musharraf's backchannel, which could have resolved Kashmir (among many other issues), impacted the Afghan crisis too, where the U.S. was looking to bolster a regime committed to Washington and friendly to Delhi, that Rawalpindi loathed.

The American intelligence community watched the fallout, while sieving thousands of hours of cross-border chatter that described a resurgent Taliban switching between hideaways on both sides of the Durand Line to strike at international forces, facilitated by I.S.I.-backed networks, and by I.S.I. Dets. Indian consuls, trade missions, and companies also became targets, as well as Afghan intelligence centres, safehouses, and military facilities, addresses supplied by the I.S.I. too, the C.I.A. argued.

General ul-Haq, who maintained that the Taliban would have sprung back regardless of Pakistan, recalled: "The I.S.I. could not contemplate a pro-Indian government in Kabul that was hostile to Rawalpindi, but it seemed like this was something the U.S. could buy into." He saw India's Afghanistan ambitions, and its overtures to Langley, as intolerable. "The Durand Line is our forever border," he complained. "Imagine waking up in the U.K. and finding that Russia had installed a government in France! Naturally you would be concerned." India pressed its case that it had every right to invest in Afghanistan as it had been doing for many years, and officials in Delhi emphasized that they asked for nothing in exchange.

Taliban sponsorship was not a focus for this book, but what many veteran spies and intelligence analysts highlighted was that it had become clear to them by 2010 that U.S. political resolve was slipping in Afghanistan. Veteran ul-Haq agreed: "Washington had failed to remake that country but still would not accept a government of national reconciliation that includes the Taliban, a plan we had first mooted in 2001, backed by Saudi and even the U.K. We said then that the Taliban won't evaporate but feint and come again. No one wanted to hear this then, and pointless violence followed with the waste of trillions of dollars."

The Taliban of now was not the same as the movement of the 1990s. General Naeem maintained: "Once they had been austere students. But they were now settled in compounds, marrying and travelling." Indian intelligence watched, horrified. As of 2012, Delhi had invested $3 billion overtly in a nation without the Taliban and spent considerable

amounts on covert assistance and welfare projects, hoping the movement
had been crushed for good.

~

In Pakistan, General Masood Aslam, XI Corps Commander, repeatedly
warned that the hardest thing for a national army was to fight its own
people. But in 2009 the military finally began a push in deadly Bajaur,
in FATA, through the lines of the Pakistan Taliban, known as the T.T.P.,
an umbrella of prickly dissidents, religious ultras, and sectarians, which
formed after the Red Mosque siege.

The T.T.P. struck back at the Manawan police cadet school in Lahore,
slaughtering 18 and injuring 95 during a gruelling eight-hour battle.
The military leveraged public opinion to launch Operation Black
Thunderstorm to take back the Swat Valley. By June, the G.H.Q. had
dispatched more than 30,000 soldiers to a place where thousands had
died, and more than two million residents had fled. The military also
launched operations in South Waziristan, where warlord Baitullah
Mehsud, a key player in the Bhutto conspiracy, had his stronghold.

General Khalid Rabbani, who was a general officer commanding a
division in South Waziristan and would go on to become XI Corps
Commander in 2011, recalled: "We received intelligence that there
was also a strong al Qaeda presence along with the T.T.P. within the
Mehsud belt." Three prior operations had been halted by talks or deals
that collapsed. G.H.Q. scattered letters from planes, signed by General
Ashfaq Parvez Kayani, who had moved from I.S.I. to G.H.Q. as army
chief, and described the Mehsud tribes as courageous and loyal. General
Rabbani reflected: "The peace process failed because there was no trust.
We thought we could charm them with cash and threats. We also made
outright mistakes like the drone mass deaths."

The birthplace of warlord Baitullah Mehsud was Kotkai. The
Pakistan army finally took control, but on the fourth day of ground
operations a wave of T.T.P. fighters galvanized, pounding the exposed

Pakistan positions, and reclaimed the town. S.S.G. commandos had to be air dropped to take the high ground, covered by jets and helicopter gunships.

Military Intelligence now reported that 12,000 Pakistan Taliban, bolstered by Uzbeks, Uighurs, and others, were bedded in. Rabbani said: "The detritus left behind in camps suggested they had received training from another national military." Officers were stunned to find field hospitals and professional entrenchments. They also stumbled into morale-sapping ambushes. I.E.D.s were strung in the trees that fell on to withdrawing forces like explosive webs, killing 14 soldiers in a strike. Officers reported to G.H.Q. that they suspected "India had played a distanced role, in logistics, training and supply."[245]

Finally, they found drums of chemicals. Rabbani called in the Defence Science and Technical Organisation (DESTO) that took samples, before burying the supply in situ. DESTO concluded that some contained precursors to manufacture high-grade explosives, while others stored super-concentrated hydrogen peroxide. They recovered Pakistan military training manuals, some translated, and an alcohol cache, that pointed to the presence of non-Muslim trainers or mercenaries, as mujahids mostly remained teetotal on the battlefield. Inside abandoned tents they recovered hard drives and notebooks containing the names of haulage companies in Afghanistan. Working on these, an I.S.I. Afghan desk report claimed these trucks serviced Indian fronts associated with R.A.W. operations in Afghanistan. "It was as much as any intelligence service could hope to glimpse its rival in action," said General Rabbani.

The trucks and routes led the I.S.I. to what it claimed were R.A.W. safehouses that were photographed and filmed. They also followed couriers in Kandahar and Jalalabad. These men worked the Durand Line and two were seen entering a compound used by the R.A.W. in Spin Boldak. From there a religious pilgrim was allegedly followed "carrying a jute sack filled with U.S. dollars into Pakistan." Some of it ended up with Mehsud chieftains fighting the Pakistan army, the I.S.I. claimed in another field intelligence report. Some cash, they wrote, went to clerics in North Waziristan, who distributed it to fighting groups allied to the T.T.P. Some went into Baluchistan where a nationalist insurgency permanently simmered, Aabpara would complain, and that India kept alive in revenge for Kashmir and the Punjab.

The I.S.I. also reported that it caught sight of R.A.W. operating in Karachi, infiltrating the Mujahir Qaumi Movement (M.Q.M.), the political party founded by Muslims who migrated from India after Partition. In the 1990s, the M.Q.M. leadership, facing multiple murder and extortion allegations, fled into exile in the U.K. and South Africa. In both places the British security services and the R.A.W. went to work recruiting, including the R.A.W. chief Samant Kumar Goel, seen by the I.S.I. as the most aggressive and capable Indian conduit in the Karachi operation.

A window into this world opened-up after a brutal murder in Edgware, in North London, in 2010. Dr Imran Farooq, 50, an M.Q.M. leader, was ambushed walking home, and repeatedly stabbed and bludgeoned with a brick. During the inquiry that followed Scotland Yard detectives were told in sworn witness statements that millions of dollars was delivered by the R.A.W. to the M.Q.M. via diplomatic missions in Vienna and Johannesburg.[246] When India required chaos in Karachi, M.Q.M. was paid by Lodhi Road to make it happen in a mirror of B. Raman's equivalence operations.

~

On August 5, 2009, a U.S. drone cruised above Zangara, a village in South Waziristan, and fired twice, killing the T.T.P. bulwark Baitullah Mehsud, who the I.S.I. insisted had commissioned the death of Benazir Bhutto. The T.T.P. hit back on October 10, when gunmen dressed in camouflage attacked G.H.Q. in Rawalpindi. After a 45-minute battle, four attackers and six soldiers were dead. While Pakistanis watched broadcasts on tenterhooks, more gunshots and explosions rang out from inside the vast G.H.Q. campus. Wearing suicide vests, attackers roamed the epicentre of Pakistan's military operations, killing officers and taking hostages. Whoever was behind this attack knew the layout of the complex that was classified.

One of the hostage takers was Aqeel Ahmed, sometimes known as "Dr Usman," and whose aliases were detailed in Brigadier Hyat's blue binders. He had come to this moment along a well-worn path. Ahmed was a soldier who had run from the Army Medical Corps in 2006 in protest at the drone mass deaths and joined the "Amjad Farooqi" unit of the T.T.P., a guerrilla formation created in honour of the dead hijacker of IC 814. It was coached by Ilyas Kashmiri's 313 and Ahmed had led the team that had fired at Musharraf's plane, narrowly missing the President in 2007 as he headed for the floods. It was Ahmed again who led the attack on the Sri Lankan cricket team in Lahore, demanding freedom for Major Haroon and Briton Omar Sheikh. At 6 a.m. on October 11, the S.S.G. raided G.H.Q., recovered the hostages, and captured Ahmed, who was injured. Like Pasha and Haroon before him, Ahmed rolled over, and led the I.S.I. to his safehouse where they found a cache of weapons sourced from a Pakistan military arsenal. Ahmed did not resist. "It does not matter what you do to me," he told his interrogator, "Ilyas Kashmiri is coming."[247]

Soon after, four gunmen from the 313 Brigade ran into Rawalpindi's Parade Lane Colony during Friday prayers and stormed a mosque used by military officers. Two men detonated vests while another two fired into the congregation, killing 40, including 10 children. "They took people by their hair, and shot each of them in the head," recalled a retired officer, Ahmed Sharif. By the time it was over nine senior officers were dead.

Also killed was Hashim, the only son of the XI Corps Commander, General Masood Aslam. He would not talk about it. Like General Khalid Rabbani, whose son Saad was serving in the Pakistan military, the older generation of officers kept family suffering to themselves. Soldiers were dying all over Swat and FATA.

2010–11

There was almost no blowback in India from the rise of al Qaeda, as the I.B. veteran Asif Ibrahim had predicted. However, Monisha registered a domestic reaction to Rawalpindi's stridency, where officials and activists allied to the religious right were becoming sectarian and politicized, in a mirror of the forces that were corroding Pakistan.

There, the security services faced a loyalty crisis, with officers in the I.S.I. and all wings of the military asserting their Islamic credentials and peeling away from Rawalpindi to savage the U.S. pact. In India, an as yet unknown number of police officers, spies, and soldiers began to elevate their Hindu values over those of the secular Indian republic. They began to brazenly promote a Hindu land, whose neighbour was an Islamic one, to where India's Muslim should go, questioning whether a secular nation could ever be a united and powerful one, suggesting a Hindu land would be prouder, overcoming colonial lag faster, and as a less apologetic, assertive state it would also be harder to ignore. When Monisha picked up on this sea change, she began, actively, speeding her way out.

For years, the I.B. had highlighted attacks across India by Islamist cells, which were occasionally home-grown and mostly foreign, which meant nurtured by Pakistan. Between 2008 and 2011, in Maharashtra alone, there had been more than 500 deaths in explosions that were said to lead back to Pakistan-based outfits, some of whom, like the 313 and Jaish, were also savaging the Pakistan military and the I.S.I.

But in 2010, the home minster, P. Chidambaram, switched track and spoke about "saffron terror," a phrase that provoked the ire of those for whom the colour represents faith.[248] This semantic row failed to divert the home minister from the facts, as he saw them – which had little to do with political differences, he claimed, and a lot to do with existential questions.[249] Some terrorist incidents, according to files shared with him, had been reinvestigated and were now considered insider operations, or false flags, carried out by Hindu militias, amateurs, and provocateurs, who intended to drag down Pakistan and Islam, rending multi-faith India too.

Chidambaram's statement was ground-breaking as most states refuse to entertain their darkest inclinations. The British security services in Northern Ireland would not concede that they supported death squads, collaborating with banned, armed Loyalist outfits, mentoring their gunmen, some of whom were creatures of a secretive British Army unit, and stalked and killed Republicans, including a prominent lawyer, shot dead in front of his wife and three children.[250]

The Indian home minister who was ready to confront the worst was fuelled by a classified I.B. briefing that was based on a wide-ranging review of cases and intelligence.[251] It suggested there was official collusion by members of the security services with Hindu militias. Some I.B. officers were suspected, but also those from the S.T.F. in Kashmir and some in the armed forces, with enablers appearing in the brand-new National Investigation Agency, India's prestigious counterterror task force that was created after the 26/11 raids.[252] In a tandem inquiry, a number of R.A.W. officers were accused by the C.I.S. of distorting intelligence, according to Monisha. The conspirators, nationally, were thought to be in the hundreds, and represented a small but powerful clique, playing to a far wider Hindu audience of citizens exhausted by what they saw as endless Pakistan aggression.

Inside the R.A.W., Monisha registered the impact and said her instructors and some of her superiors were increasingly openly hostile to non-Hindus, and unable or unwilling to distinguish between terrorists who were Muslim and Islam in its entirety. This made missions inside Islamic nations doubly dangerous as non-Muslims posing as Muslims risked far more. Until 2011, the R.A.W. required some male Hindu operators working in Muslim countries to undergo circumcisions, so they could better conceal their identities. Senior R.A.W. officers told us how there were attempts to break this deadlock, with the selection of two high-flying Muslim I.P.S. candidates, only for them to be flatly turned down. Monisha concluded: "Lodhi Road was dominated by the I.P.S. and constricted by I.P.S. thinking that Muslims were duplicitous."

Not only were Hindu militias allegedly launching attacks that were blamed on home-grown and foreign Muslim levies, but officials were conniving to conceal the protagonists and misdirect blame.[253] "Communalism has entered the nation's polity," mused Lt. Gen. V.R. Raghavan, a former director general of military operations. He wanted to know how deep the "politicization" of the security forces went.[254] The I.B. report prepared for the home minister referenced other inquiries by the Bureau that had never before been acknowledged and suggested these phoney attacks began in Kashmir in the 1990s, and were manifest in the Parliament raid in 2001, about which "there were many unanswered questions, especially regarding the role of the S.T.F. as agent provocateurs."[255]

Anti-Terrorism Squad (A.T.S.) cops came under the scanner too because of inquiries conducted in 2008 by Hemant Karkare, then chief of Maharashtra's A.T.S., who detailed in multiple interviews how he came across evidence that matched the I.B.'s concerns, adding the A.T.S. to a list of organizations that were now under the scanner.[256] Karkare, a forthright and capable officer, was an establishment trustee and that was why his insight mattered. He had served in the R.A.W. for nine years, stationed in Austria, among other places, where he liaised with the U.N. and the International Atomic Energy Agency (I.A.E.A.), and investigated money laundering and gems smuggling, before, for personal reasons, returning to the police force in Mumbai.

Shortly before 26/11, he told us how he began investigating twin bomb blasts in Malegaon, a textile hub in the north of Maharashtra, incidents from 2006 and 2008, in which 47 were killed and hundreds were injured. In 2008, blasts in Modasa, in Gujarat, in which a teenager died, and a similar explosion in Delhi, were also scrutinized by him.[257] In I.B. and A.T.S. reports, these events had been described as the work of Pakistan-mentored Indian terrorists.[258] Many Indian Muslims were arrested, and alleged they were tortured before being jailed, pending inquiries that never concluded.[259] However, digging back into these cases, Karkare settled on 11 Hindu suspects with links to a Hindu armed militia formed in 2006: the Abhinav Bharat (A.B.), named after a turn-of-the century anti-colonial movement.[260]

The A.B.'s alleged organizers included an Indian army veteran and a serving Military Intelligence officer. There was also a connection to a military school in Nashik where facilities were used for training A.B. cadres. Another military campus in Nagpur had hosted military-style Hindu training camps as far back as 2001. Both these institutions insisted they had only leased out their facilities and did not condone or even know about the activities carried out there.[261]

The Karkare inquiry pulled from the blast wreckage the registration of a motorbike connected to a former state secretary of a right-wing student outfit affiliated to the Rashtriya Swayamsevak Sangh (R.S.S.), the parent organization of the B.J.P.[262] Now he had to be careful. Digging some more, his men excavated the role played by a science-graduate-turned-fire-and-brimstone-Hindu-swami, whose bully pulpit was accused of having triggered communal unrest in Gujarat.[263]

Pernicious sectarians were bloodying Pakistan, but they were also gathering momentum in India. Some of Karkare's most disturbing conclusions, however, were only shared within the I.B., as they were deemed too incendiary to publicize. We were asked not to write about them, until he retired, or, worse still, died in service.

Above the ranks of the A.B., Karkare had glimpsed a far broader right-wing web. Primed and assisted by intelligence officers and military men, boosted by Hindu activists, these fellow travellers were, he believed, responsible for attacks on mosques and shrines in Hyderabad and Ajmer, and killings and bombings all over India that for years had been misattributed to the LeT, to Jaish and even to Ilyas Kashmiri, as well as home-grown outfits with names like Indian Mujahideen (I.M.) and the Student Islamic Movement of India (SIMI). These last two groups existed – and had carried out multiple bloody terror attacks in India, sponsored by the I.S.I. However, Karkare also deduced that they were mimicked and puppeteered, their names used by Hindu plotters. Elsewhere, I.M. and SIMI cells were entrapped into acts, just as happened to the Jaish in 2001, and Lashkar before them. This was also a preferred method of renegades in Kashmir, like the wedding singer Parray. "Outfits that carried the imprimatur of the I.S.I. were also a vehicle for I.B.–R.A.W.," Karkare told us. "Some of this reflected the mentoring of Indian intelligence by foreign outfits in Israel and the U.S."

Forensics analysed by Karkare's team connected the Malegaon attacks to a cache of unexploded devices recovered in Ahmedabad, in Gujarat. He also zoomed in on a Hindu group active in Goa. A list of two dozen incidents which he considered "contrived" was sent to the home ministry and to I.B. Bomb factories were springing up in several locations, Karkare warned, calling up the files from an inquiry in 2006, when explosions were reported in the houses of Hindu activists linked to the R.S.S., and other Hindu nationalists, where several R.S.S. members were killed by their own unstable I.E.D.s that were a long way from the sophisticated mines and bombs produced by the 313's munitions factory in FATA.[264]

"Paperwork and maps recovered at the scene suggested the IEDs were intended for several mosques," a report suggested. "False beards and Muslim clothing found by police showed how the Hindu protagonists had planned to sow a phoney Islamist trail."[265]

Karkare's most contentious line of inquiry was that "the investigation into the Parliament attack of December 2001 should be audited with a focus on the identity of the attackers, and an emphasis on falsified or misleading evidence."[266] However, he would never get to push this through as he was killed in service, during 26/11, while trying to trap the Lashkar gunmen, a faulty armoured vest letting him down, as did an overworked police control room that could not send backup fast enough.

After Karkare's killing a chowk was named after him in Malegaon and the inquiry into the internal war briefly widened, with the new N.I.A. taking a deeper interest. It filed a charge sheet in a court in Panaji, Goa, accusing eight members of the right-wing Sanatan Sanstha of plotting blasts which killed two of their members, as they transported devices to a festival in Margao.[267] The N.I.A. also began reinvestigating historic bombings in Pune and elsewhere where the Muslim accused were now presumed innocent or investigators were looking for Hindu protagonists.

Confronted by Karkare's evidence, the swami who ran an ashram in Hardwar was arrested and confessed that Hindu militants belonging to A.B. had been involved in blasts at Muslim centres in Hyderabad and Ajmer but, also, allegedly, were connected to an attack on the India–Pakistan train, the Samjhauta [friendship] Express, that had killed sixty-eight people. Up to this point the R.A.W. and certain officers in the I.B. had blamed the LeT and the I.S.I.[268]

The I.B. leadership pushed back against the sectarians. In 2011, a special director warned regional police chiefs at a private briefing that at least 16 bombing conspiracies had been linked to suspected Hindu militants, and that new intelligence detachments would have to be created to probe the far right-wing threat in India, just as Israel was doing with its home-grown Jewish right-wing chauvinists.[269]

However, when the B.J.P. was swept into government in 2014, and Ajit Doval was elevated to the job of National Security Adviser, the painful soul-searching was curtailed. A public prosecutor in the 2008 Malegaon case, Rohini Sailan, claimed officers in the N.I.A. told her to "go soft" on cases of "saffron terror," later filing a claim in court that named a superintendent from the N.I.A.'s Mumbai office who "acted as the delivery man for a political appointee." She also warned that the N.I.A. had been taken over by some officers who placed their faith before their duty, Hindus who tried to prevent her dropping Muslim from the charge sheet.[270]

In 2018, a court acquitted all 11 men accused in the 2007 Mecca Masjid blast, with the victims' families having no right to press the case any further.[271] An investigating officer in the N.I.A. told us: "We were squashed; told to end it or quit the service."[272] The following year, the Samjhauta Express case also collapsed, with the four accused, all connected to the A.B., freed by a special court.[273] The N.I.A. declined to appeal, and instead the LeT was once more blamed, alongside the I.S.I., even though the evidence points in a different direction.[274] The B.J.P. home minister Rajnath Singh addressed reporters, saying he was speaking in a personal capacity, when he concluded: "Pakistan is always responsible for such terrorist attacks."[275] In this climate of impunity, the swami in Hardwar was next, recanting his confession, claiming he had been tortured.

However, inside I.B. discontent deepened. One veteran officer told us: "Make no mistake, there is the enemy outside India. Pakistan will always be there. But like Pakistan, we in India now have to tackle the hyper-religious, para-nationalists who are trying to dismantle the secular state."

~

On May 2, 2011, Pakistan woke to the news that U.S. Special Forces had killed Osama bin Laden, his guardians, and one of his sons, in a compound close to the Pakistan Military Academy at Kakul, Abbottabad. It was hard to find a senior officer in the R.A.W. who believed the I.S.I. insistence that it had no knowledge of Osama's presence. Rajinder Khanna told us: "There are no coincidences in Pakistan. There never was a pact with the U.S., just leverage and lies."

The I.S.I. followed Lt. Gen. Naeem's suggestion and chose the "incompetence defence." Pakistan–U.S. relations were at their nadir. As Pakistan struggled, Ilyas Kashmiri seized his moment, and three weeks after Abbottabad, he sent 15 fighters from the 313 to attack the Mehran naval air station in Karachi.[276] The government claimed the raiding party cut through barbed wire around the perimeter where there were no C.C.T.V. cameras. But the I.S.I. reported, in a classified briefing, that the insurgents were dressed as officers and knew the base's security protocol, as they had with the G.H.Q. attack.[277] "Traitors on the outside, and collaborators helped them inside," a brigadier in the I.S.I.'s Sindh division told us.

The attackers used rocket propelled grenades and RDX to destroy two U.S.-supplied multimillion-dollar marine surveillance aircraft and took 42 hostages. Commandos from the S.S.G. reclaimed the base after 16 long hours, by which time 14 people were dead, including three hostages. When global arms control analysts asked if some of the country's nuclear arsenal was locked down nearby, as many believed was the case, there were renewed calls for the resignation of army chief General Kayani and his I.S.I. chief General Pasha.[278]

Well versed in proxy plays, R.A.W. officers told a C.I.A. liaison that the I.S.I. had staged the daring raid itself, to distract from the bin Laden fallout and to broadcast the continuing threat to Pakistan posed by al Qaeda. Rajinder Khanna said: "The Osama operation threatened to curtail all Pakistan aid. The C.I.A. had already had enough of the I.S.I. boosting the Taliban. Rawalpindi had to demonstrate its case – that Pakistan was too dangerous to abandon. The cost to the West would be, for example, its W.M.D. programme falling into Islamist hands. And sure enough, Mehran happened, and ensured that allies in the West, although exhausted, came back to Rawalpindi offering help. A paid P.R. in Washington could not have done a better job."

Inside Aabpara, a complex, and far more disturbing, story was emerging. A brigadier in C-Wing stationed in Karachi told us: "We learned that there had been multiple prior warnings about plans for just such an operation on Mehran, but the intelligence went nowhere and was not developed, which was either incompetence or the work of collaborators."

The first was recorded in January when a marine was detained for colluding with the T.T.P. and the 313, the prisoner divulging that the

naval base was a target and that he was part of a larger group. The second
came when a naval rating aligned to the 313 was nabbed inside Mehran
in March with the same story.

Amid the tumult, on May 27, 2011, the Pakistani scoop-getting
reporter Saleem Shahzad wrote a sensational story for Asia Times.[279]
He was the first to tell us that nine more were nabbed inside the navy,
all of them part of "a service network of al Qaeda sympathizers." An
al Qaeda intermediary (who came from Kashmiri's 313) contacted the
I.S.I. and suggested a pact, the release of the men in exchange for a
pause in attacks on the security services. The I.S.I. mulled the deal but
decided against it, given Pakistan looked complicit with hiding bin
Laden. Ilyas Kashmiri gave the go-ahead for the devastating raid.[280]

It was not Shahzad's first swipe at the military and intelligence elite,
but it would be his last. Shahzad's golden breaks – which included
interviewing the publicity-shy Ilyas Kashmiri and Major Pasha – were
occasionally alloyed with sensationalism, and he was not above some
wild speculation. But he was also one of only a few investigative writers
from Pakistan, in a land that discourages private inspection, and where,
since 9/11, 80 journalists have been murdered, and hundreds detained in
I.S.I. roundups.[281] Shahzad was regularly threatened, but thrived on the
pressure, getting inside the mujahid world.

From FATA to Karachi, he had filed hundreds of reports for the
Asia Times portal, delivering insights that Western reporters could only
dream of getting. On May 28, he told friends the I.S.I. had threatened
him again, and shortly after, on May 29, he disappeared while driving
through Islamabad to a television debate. The following morning, his
body was pulled from a canal 161 kilometres south-east of the capital.
The post-mortem showed 17 lacerations and his liver was ruptured. He
had two broken ribs and had died from a beating. He had clearly been
tortured.[282]

In a first, Obama administration officials briefed *New York Times*
reporters that they believed the I.S.I. was responsible for an act that was
"barbaric." Forsaking the usual vagaries, the official said the I.S.I. had

"directed the attack…in an effort to silence criticism."[283] Admiral Mike Mullen, chairman of the joint chiefs of staff, issued a rare public rebuke to the Pakistan government "for having sanctioned" Shahzad's killing.[284]

I.S.I. officers declined to talk to us about the murder, although most we met expressed a deep loathing for Shahzad, believing that Pakistan was too volatile to be scrutinized, and, depressingly, that the process of accountability only benefited the country's enemies. "We are at war and some things can be known but should not be said," Nusrat Naeem told us, summing up the attitude of many. "In Britain during World War II, traitors were arrested too, and shot. Is that not true?"

The Pakistan government recoiled, while making weak pledges to investigate the murder. But generals Kayani and Pasha kept their jobs and no one inside Aabpara was sacked as in this system of perpetual military motion the regulators were Kayani and Pasha. However, a C-Wing brigadier told us that the I.S.I. turned a corner, deciding to go even harder against the al Qaeda amalgam, galvanizing new and super-sensitive sources.

Several were, the brigadier said, "former military and intelligence officers who had had a change of heart and having defected to al Qaeda turned back to the military." Now we were sure that one of those was Iftikhar, who had already given up majors Haroon and Pasha, who had been jailed.

The next tip-off came from a caller who contacted the I.S.I. duty officer to deliver, we were told, "precise and actionable" intelligence on a high value target. He identified compounds in South Waziristan, 20 kilometres south of Wana at a place called Ghwa Khwa. "The intelligence was handed to the C.I.A., which prepped a drone," a brigadier told us, doing away with the fig leaf that the U.S. acted unilaterally. "It hovered above an apple orchard and focused on a small group of men sitting beneath a tree, sipping tea." The following day the local political agent emerged to reveal that one of the dead had been identified as Ilyas Kashmiri, who had a $5 million bounty on his head.

After burying him in Karikot, south-west of Wana, Kashmiri's fighters issued a statement, mourning his loss and heralding the lives of eight others who were killed in the attack and who between them had waged jihad for 160 years.[285] "We lost our hero," said one. But until DNA evidence was recovered from the scene the R.A.W. would not accept that the forty-seven-year-old was gone. "A deadly man like Ilyas Kashmiri is hard to kill," Rajinder Khanna warned.

~

On a cool evening, Iftikhar surprised us. We were packed and ready to leave for London, when he loomed, awkward and sullen, like a teenager coming home with a bad school report. He asked us to join him on a drive, and as he motored and the palms zoomed by, he mawkishly recalled the start of his I.S.I. career.

Shortly after he was inducted, he was called to headquarters, and popping out for a smoke, he had met a gardener. They shared a cigarette, and the man told Iftikhar he was also new. The man expressed surprise that an I.S.I. security officer had turned up at his place to take photos of his wife and children.

"The gardener asked me, 'Why was that?'" Iftikhar decided it was too tricky to explain that the gardener's family were now collateral and would be used to enforce the silence rule. If the man blabbed, his family would be punished. A few months later, Iftikhar took a weekend off and returned to Jhang. "My father got me on my own."

"Mash'allah." His father winked at him.

What was he talking about?

"Oh, these fellows came around," the old man replied. "Said they were your batchmates. Me and your mother invited them in."

"But what did they *want*?" Iftikhar pressed.

"They said you'd asked them to photograph us all. What have you won, son? Is it for a yearbook? Are you getting married, boy?"

Iftikhar said nothing.

He knew the risk he took in choosing his path. The enormity of his decision to enlist was eclipsed, later, by his dangerous decision to break with the I.S.I. And when Iftikhar said he fell out with Major Pasha, in disgust at the way the rebellion had become pathological, even darker forces were stacked against him, consigning him to a solitary life, forever in exile, looking over his shoulder. Iftikhar never returned to Jhang, but his parents were still living there, mourning a missing son.

This fact prompted a harder question about sacrifice. We had to try to ask it. Had Iftikhar, who had evidently turned in majors Pasha and Haroon, also guided the I.S.I. to Ilyas Kashmiri? Did Iftikhar play a role in ending the life of the man he most admired?

He rubbed his brow. And stared, shoulders hunched, at the long, dark road ahead. Finally, he said, quietly: "When a person, even a great leader, no longer cares about the future, we have a duty to let go of their past."

Part 3

Back to the Future

FATA

In Pakistan, the fight against the enemy within had reached a remote and verdant cul-de-sac in the mountains that the military had seldom patrolled. Historically, people entered the Tirah only to disappear. Local inhabitants were said to be fierce and in the nineteenth century this remote valley, which was filled with walnut and mulberry trees and two-storey mud and timber houses, had been the scene of a bloody year-long campaign fought by the British army. Smugglers, arms traffickers, drug runners, and outlaws, all regarded the Tirah as a tunnel between Pakistan and Afghanistan. The al Qaeda–T.T.P. amalgam too.

Khalid Rabbani (well before he was promoted to lieutenant general) had helicoptered once into the Tirah in 2001 to help close the back door for al Qaeda and Taliban fighters escaping the U.S. dragnet. Now it was the turn of Rabbani's son, Saad, a young captain in the 8 Punjab, who was being sent in to rout the fighters allied to the Pakistan Taliban, even though he had only two years of service.

The commanding officer contacted General Rabbani confiding that he had decided on extra security measures. Saad's uniform patch now stated that he was Captain Bilal. Memories of the killing of General Masood Aslam's son, Hashim, at the Rawalpindi Parade Lane mosque massacre were still raw.[1]

Saad's unit climbed to a steep ridge between Shersali Sar and Inzergul Markaz, where the firing began almost immediately, coming in at a rate no one expected. On another ridgeline, the T.T.P. had installed 12.7mm-calibre heavy machine guns. Down below was a small village. Escaping to the village was perilous. But there was no cover in the heights. The only way out of a killing ground was to fight.

The first man down was Captain Wasim-uddin Razi, the twenty-four-year-old company commander of 3 Commando. Almost no one would publish his name or the circumstances of his death because in Pakistan, individual, daily sacrifice was never commemorated and instead was drowned out by the cacophony of the continual mayhem. But by the end of that first day, there were thirteen casualties. At the end of day two, thirty-seven infantrymen were down and twenty or more from 3 Commando. The S.S.G. had lost fourteen highly trained operators. The survivors climbed higher to get out of range of the 12.7mm guns but there was no cover from the long-range snipers.

Soon the ridgeline and slopes were littered with hundreds of bodies from both sides. As night fell, the counterattacks began, and by the time dawn broke, there had been five T.T.P. surges. Aerial cover arrived in the morning, but the altitude was too much for the Cobra gunships, which were unable to fly high enough to be safe from ground fire. The soldiers watched horrified and helpless as one army chopper was shot down, through its rotors, killing everyone on board.

The troops were running out of ammunition. All that 8 Punjab had left were small arms and support from medium mortars. Within hours, even that was gone, and the dark was coming, which meant the counterattacks would begin. The only way to survive would be to gather ammunition from dead T.T.P. fighters. Volunteers, organized by Saad, crawled down the mountain in the dark. Several hours later they re-emerged, weighed down with belts, rounds, and clips. Then, their radios died. No one could call in or out. There was no backup, or aerial support.

General Rabbani was in the ops room when he heard his son was missing presumed dead. "We had likely lost the entire unit. That's what I was advised. I wondered how to break it to my wife." Rabbani refused to make a fuss. "A commanding officer cannot grieve for his own son,"

Rabbani said, "and we knew of fifty-one dead on the ridgeline." When Rabbani's wife entered, he saw from her face that she already had an inkling. The wife of the chief of staff had called to warn her. The tight-knit family of command was leaning in.

More bad news filtered down from the Tirah. "The 8 Punjab was totally overrun. The brigade commander requested D.F.O.L." This was a termination order that every commander dreaded, and it stood for Defensive Fire Own Location, which was a barrage by Pakistan artillery or aircover on Pakistan positions to prevent their weapons, paperwork, and kit falling into insurgent hands – but also the bodies of the dead, which would otherwise be mutilated, or carved up into trophies.

"Should I give the go-ahead?" Rabbani pondered. "I picked up the phone and talked to the brigade commander. 'How many stragglers have returned?' The commander said, 'Not one, sir.'" Rabbani was stunned. "I had never seen a unit annihilated. I told him: 'You are out of contact. You have to get out and search for them. No one just vanishes. What if they have comms problems?'" Rabbani played for time. "I said: 'No permission for D.F.O.L.'"

Rabbani was woken at 5.30 a.m. "In truth I had barely slept." A call had come in from 8 Punjab. "The adjutant said some of them were alive and the fighting was still on." Rabbani was, for the first time, hopeful. One day later, the survivors, somehow, escaped the Tirah, carrying nothing. Three battered and bleeding *jawans* led by Captain Saad Rabbani, found their way to a command post. Saad was stunned by their losses, and his own good fortune. "I said, 'economy of fire,' and all that, you know, 'go slow and conserve the rounds,'" Saad told us. "That order stayed good on paper. But once they came at us, again and again, never getting tired, it's quite another thing. We gave them what we had – and then we had nothing left."

~

But that was not the end of it. After the Islamists allied to the T.T.P. alliance lost the Tirah, the baton passed back to the new Jundullah, an outfit whose story embodies Pakistan's backfiring wars, stoked also by the C.I.A. The group with that name in Karachi was facilitated by I.S.I. assets. Another was encouraged by I.S.I. to spy and kill inside Iran. The former went rogue and ran to the tribal areas, where the latter had been courted by the I.S.I. under instruction from U.S. officials, Aabpara claimed, encouraging Jundullah to carry out savage hit-and-run attacks inside Iran, hoping to push back whenever Iranian-backed militia in Iraq killed U.S. troops.

But when the Shia insurgents in Iraq called a halt, the C.I.A. asked the I.S.I. to close down Jundullah, again, Aabpara maintained. I.S.I. paramilitaries who had already captured the brother of the outfit's founder and secretly turned him over to Iran now captured the outfit's founder, Abdolmalek Rigi, an asset, trained and funded by Aabpara. Abdolmalek was also secretly handed to the Revolutionary Guards, who put him on death row in Tehran, from where he was made to denounce his C.I.A. paymaster, staying quiet about I.S.I., as per the agreement between Rawalpindi and Tehran.

The remnants of both Jundullahs, incandescent and looking for revenge against the I.S.I., pooled in FATA and approached al Qaeda commanders, according to an I.S.I. briefing note.[2] Jundullah offered its foot soldiers as well as its formidable arsenal of weapons and I.E.D.s. Al Qaeda set the outfit a test. It asked for assistance in shaking free Osama bin Laden's family members who had secretly sheltered inside Iran in 2002 and were now stuck there.[3]

An I.S.I. report noted that Jundullah kidnapped Heshmatollah Attarzadeh, an Iranian diplomat, who lived and worked at the Iranian consulate in Peshawar and spirited him away to South Waziristan.[4] "In March 2010, after one year in captivity, the diplomat was set free in exchange for a promise from Tehran that bin Laden's older wife [Khairiah] and her son [Hamzah bin Laden], would be released," the report concluded.

In June 2010, Iran exacted its revenge by hanging the Rigi brothers and Jundullah, now accepted by the al Qaeda amalgam, unleashed volleys of hellish violence, playing an undeclared but central role in the Mehran attack of 2011 and the 2014 slaughter at an army-run cadet school in Peshawar, where gunmen killed 141 people, 132 of whom were children.

In June 2014, they helped the al Qaeda amalgam attack Karachi International Airport, where heavily armed gunmen disguised as security forces stormed a freight terminal, with at least 23 people killed and 18 wounded, as flights were grounded.

Army chief General Kayani immediately ordered the army into North Waziristan – tens of thousands of troops marching, a force that took more than a year to gain traction, while one million refugees were displaced. The military losses were recorded (conservatively) at 900 troops with 3500 insurgents killed in air strikes and the ground offensive. In 2012, more than 3000 deaths in Pakistan had been caused by terror, whereas after the North Waziristan campaign took hold, the figures plummeted to 600.[5]

The fighting was still not over. And as it had done in 2001 and on 26/11, the al Qaeda amalgam looked for a lifeline by striking sensitive locations inside India. A region in freefall provided shelter and bought them time to mend. The I.S.I. (through indecision) and the Indian security services (through muscle memory) played into their hands.

Kashmir and Burhan Wani

The Pakistan-backed insurgent apparatus directed at Kashmir was largely dismantled by 2010, according to reports from the Defence Intelligence Agency (D.I.A.) in India.[6] Jaish lingered on, but hounded by the I.S.I., its membership was whittled away, hunted down, and shot dead, jailed, or driven out of Pakistan. Its training camps were depleted and pushed over the Durand Line, while the upper echelons that ran the franchise were divided. But Aabpara was still undecided about what to do with cleric Masood Azhar.

The Jaish chief and orator remained in Punjab, closely monitored and occasionally used by the I.S.I. as an emissary, carrying peace missives and communiques to two troubling groups – Jundullah and the ETIM, an armed Islamist group from Xinjiang that China wanted Rawalpindi's help in crushing.

The LeT's emir, Hafiz Saeed, remained in very public self-isolation, as more of his bank accounts were shut down, leaving him impoverished and making a desperate appeal to old friends in the I.S.I. and the Ministry of External Affairs, who lobbied on his behalf at the U.N. to remove him from an al Qaeda sanctions list to which he was added in 2008.[7]

Foreign fighters in Kashmir, according to India's D.I.A., would soon dwindle into "double digits," but the Valley, nevertheless, erupted.

~

One evening in April 2010, an officer from the 4 Rajputana Rifles arrived at a remote police post outside Kupwara, near the LoC Major Opinder Singh "seemed in a hurry," a duty policeman recalled. Up in the heights of the Pir Panjal range, through which Singh had descended, it was snowing, and his boots leaked, he complained.

"The officer reported that the previous night his men had killed three Pakistani terrorists who had crossed over into our Machil sector," the policeman recalled. "Where are the bodies?" he asked, filling in a first information report that started a criminal inquiry. "They were buried where they were shot," Singh replied, and this had happened many times before, so the policeman thought nothing of it.[8]

On April 30, 2010, an armed forces spokesman in Srinagar confirmed Singh's story, announcing a counter-infiltration operation.[9] Three AK-47s, one Pakistani pistol, ammunition, cigarettes, chocolates, dates, two water bottles, a Kenwood radio, and 1000 Pakistani rupees had been recovered. It was the standard-issue infiltration kit. The corpse-less the triple-death inquiry was an open-and-shut case.

A few days later, three troubled Kashmiri families turned up at the Panzalla police post to report the disappearance of their sons: Mohammad, 19, Riyaz, 20, and Shahzad, 27. They had not seen them since April 28. A fieldworker for a non-political civil society group, the Jammu and Kashmir Coalition of Civil Society, told us how he travelled to the village and found an eyewitness, who claimed the Indian army had offered the three Kashmiri men jobs, in a deal brokered by a Special Police Officer (S.P.O.), Bashir Lone.[10] He had given each of them about Rs 1000, "as a show of good will," before taking them to a remote army camp in Machil.[11]

When S.P.O. Lone was approached, he broke down, claiming that nine soldiers had shot the three innocent Kashmiris so they could claim reward money. The army routinely gave bonuses to soldiers who killed infiltrators. It had begun as a morale-boosting prize. But in a militarized bubble in which soldiers were immune from prosecution, protected by the Armed Forces Special Powers Act (A.F.S.P.A.), 1990, troops, lethally, abused the system.[12]

In May, three bodies were exhumed from graves close to the army camp. The families identified Shahzad, Riyaz, and Mohammad by articles of their clothing. Wielding A.F.S.P.A., the military pushed back, announcing it alone could investigate. However, the cash-for-killings story coincided with disturbing findings from the State Human Rights Commission that confirmed there were more than 2080 unidentified corpses in unmarked graves in 38 sites across Kashmir, with another 4958 bodies being investigated elsewhere, and dozens more sites identified that had yet to be fully excavated and mapped.[13]

The security services brushed off the reports, saying the dead were all armed, Pakistan-bound combatants, illegally crossing the LoC from India, or returning. Or they were foreigners. Human rights lawyers pointed out that without an investigation no one knew who they were.[14] However, since 1989, thousands of Kashmiri civilians had disappeared, and their habeas corpus cases were backlogged in the courts, with the U.N. High Commissioner for Human Rights, Zeid Ra'ad al-Hussein, a cousin of the King of Jordan, warning: "There is almost total impunity for enforced disappearances with little movement towards credibly investigating complaints, including into alleged mass graves sites."[15] Whoever was right, what was certain was that fields of largely paperless deaths, with some graves stacked three-deep, had been uncovered.

Unrest exploded across the Kashmir Valley. Crowds of youths armed with stones faced off soldiers, police, and paramilitaries, who returned fire with gas canisters and live rounds. The security services bore a heavy toll, the state recording that 5188 members were badly injured, but so were 5300 civilians, many of them children and teenagers. Thousands were arrested, most under the Jammu & Kashmir Public Safety Act (P.S.A.), 1978, which requires no evidence before detaining someone for a crime that they might commit in the future and from which there is no clear exit point – a preventive jailing law, long criticized by lawyers in India.[16]

In the southern subdistrict of Tral, fifteen-year-old Burhan Wani was out with his elder brother Khalid when the security forces stopped them and beat them, the family claimed. Their father, Muzaffar, a well-regarded head teacher from Shareefabad, recalled he counselled his sons to put it behind them. They were a family of learning and Burhan was due to attend Aligarh Muslim University. In secret, Muzaffar made plans to take him away to relatives in Britain. However, by the autumn Burhan Wani had vanished and the next time Muzaffar saw him he was cradling an AK-47. "We prayed for our lost son," he said.[17]

~

By 2010, the grid in Kashmir had become a formidable tool. A matrix made of every kind of intelligence, compiled by multiple Indian agencies, and refined with U.S. assistance and Israeli hardware and software, and driven by indigenous persistence. It was fuelled by brothers, sisters, fathers, and mothers, a legion of human sources, many of them children, who were marked with the army codes for reliability, a source referred to by an alphanumeric that indicated their provenance but also the likelihood that their information was good.

If you were an A1 you were certain and co-confirmed by different sources, and your information was solid, whereas an F6 was unknown (unevaluated) peddling information about which no one could vouch. The HUMINT network was built, as in Israel, the U.S., and the U.K., painstakingly, and it counted on fatigue, outrage, and blackmail.

After a horrendous attack, officers from the I.B. and the S.T.F. went out recruiting, focusing on those who were jaded or appalled. After riots or a funeral when hundreds or thousands were hauled in, deals were made to have charges dropped. Some high-up individuals, stellar names at the apex of movements or political parties, were *bumped*, which meant an intelligence officer engineered a meeting – at court, in the hospital, or at a car accident or bike crash.

And here they would broach the sensitive subject of what a target might need. Different kinds of offers were made. Some wanted a suitcase of cash, others were scared and would talk for free, while some liked the juice of being a friend of the intelligence community. A few, like commander Abdul Majeed Dar, had political goals.

The HUMINT was bolstered with SIGINT, technical intelligence processed by the R.A.W. and specialist agencies including the National Technical Research Organisation (N.T.R.O.) but also by M.I. and the D.I.A., as well as the B.S.F. They listened to phones, mobiles, satellite, and copper-lines. They intercepted emails, Twitter feeds, Facebook, WhatsApp, and all other social media.

In power since 2004 and for all but eighteen of the last sixty-seven years, the Congress party had embraced the backchannel to President Musharraf, walked the country back from war after 26/11, and, with its allies, constructed the grid.

But welded to its dynastic aetiology, blamed for conceding to the worst elements of the status quo, including corruption, stagnation, and bureaucracy, Congress, come 2014, faced #NaMo – Narendra Modi leading the B.J.P. – and the kind of social media campaign India had not seen before, bankrolled and configured by corporates who hoped for full-bore modernization. It worked. Congress was hammered in the general elections, and reduced to holding only 44 out of a possible 543 seats in India's Lok Sabha, the lower house of Parliament, giving the B.J.P. a record victory.

Prime Minister Modi weighed his new constituency. "Brothers, sisters, you have faith in me, and I have faith in you," Modi, 63, told voters. "The people of this country have given their verdict. This verdict says we have to make the dreams of 1.25 billion people come true. I must work hard."[18]

Commentators wondered how much of Modi's past would colour the future. He had been the head of the B.J.P. in Surat when communal riots broke out in 1992 and 1994, leaving anywhere between 20 and 200 dead. And he was chief minister of Gujarat in 2002 when more than a thousand died and 2500 were injured, the majority Muslim, in another round of pogroms.[19] A judge-led commission in December 2019 subsequently cleared Modi of complicity.[20]

The new prime minister, described by his close advisers as a "studious, deep listener," but who was kept away from all free-flowing interviews and TV inquisitions, envisaged a kinetic and assertive government that required a new national security set-up that would assume control of the grid. He recruited "can-do" Ajit Doval as his N.S.A., the I.B. officer and former chief who had spent some of the years since his retirement running a powerful conservative think tank in Delhi, peopled with members of the security services and a few diplomats.

Like most spies, Doval encourages conversation but says very little. Instead, stories are told about him by loyalists and admirers.[21] Those circulating after his appointment described a seven-year period Doval spent undercover in Pakistan as India's "James Bond" when he zeroed in on insurgent groups and sought out the mafia don Dawood Ibrahim.[22]

Doval was said to have had a close shave in Lahore, when a genial white beard watching him at a mausoleum took him to one side to warn that he was recognizable as a Hindu because of his pierced ears. A small surgical procedure enabled him to be put back in the field, where he answered India's questions about the growth of Pakistan's top-secret fissile programme by finding a barber who cut the hair of nuclear scientists. Sweepings he stole from the shop were tested back in India for exposure to uranium, so the story goes.

All of these are good tales, which are also hard to track and difficult to counter, the kind of stories that have become Doval's signature. At the time of his alleged barbershop visit, he was stationed at the Indian High Commission in Islamabad, from where almost no clandestine work is done as it remains one of the mostly highly observed posts in the world. Instead, R.A.W. active operations aimed at Pakistan are handled thousands of kilometres away at the Indian High Commission in London.

According to his contemporaries, Doval, while in Islamabad, ran internal security, a high pressure posting requiring rigour but without the sizzle. He deepened relations with ambitious future Pakistani statesmen, and within Sharif's P.M.L. and Zardari's P.P.P., prescient work he was exceptionally good at. As for Dawood – he was beyond everyone's reach, ensconced in a Karachi villa ringed by I.S.I. C.A.D. operators. Even stepping on the block triggered an alert, as a friend from *Time* found out when a swarm of security officials nabbed him and kept him in a dark cell for days.[23]

It was in domestic intelligence where Doval made his name, wading into brutal Pakistan-magnified insurgencies in the North-East, the Punjab, and Kashmir, countering D-Company and the gang's manifestations in Gujarat, Maharashtra, and U.P., forcing through extradition pacts with Muslim states that had snubbed India, and if those failed prompting splits in the syndicate, sending rivals to kill each other. He offered homesick gangsters deals that divided their families, who headed home, only to find the reassurances evaporated while jail-time loomed.

But even here were self-seeded fables, one of which credited Doval with preventing a massacre in 1988 when he slipped inside the Golden Temple in Amritsar posing as a rickshaw puller, telling Sikh insurgents holed up inside that he was from Pakistan intelligence. He reported back that there were 200 fighters and not the presumed 40, and an intended raid was called off, preventing another "Blue Star." However, some of those leading the I.B. operation told us another version – where water was cut on a sweltering day, and deception and thirst ended the siege, the key moments painstakingly negotiated over a phone by junior I.B. officers in the field.

The past is not a passive tense for spies. It is the most kinetic of realms where war is waged, events re-contextualized, facts challenged, new ones inserted, partisan versions of history produced, and – most importantly – narratives shaped. The future is unknowable but the past was malleable.

~

The new N.S.A. began by bolting together a National Security Advisory Board to lead the republic's strategic interests. It was a rocket ship channelling security, diplomacy, the internal and external threat, technical, diplomatic, military, and human intelligence, as well as, most ambiguously, the positive *projection* of India.

Moving into Sardar Patel Bhavan and an office on the third floor, Doval, as captain of the N.S.A.B., became, arguably, the republic's most powerful unelected official and R.A.W. officers said it felt as if he reached down into their lunchboxes. Doval, who answered only to Modi, handpicked N.S.A.B. members. Many of his top team were in their 60s and 70s, with 35-plus years of service, among them the capable Rajinder Khanna, the former R.A.W. chief, and dogged Asif Ibrahim, who rose to be a director in I.B., as well as perceptive Pakistan watchers including Lt. Gen. Vinod Kandhare from the D.I.A. and the former Lodhi Road veteran Tilak Devasher, who rose to become a Special Secretary in the R.A.W.[24]

~

By January 2011, the grid in Kashmir caught up with Burhan Wani who had slipped out of the family home at the age of 15. Wani was on his way to becoming the Valley's most wanted man thanks to his prolific use of social media, rallying others to the cause.[25] Following his emergence on Instagram and Twitter, in Facebook posts and on YouTube, thousands were following the Kashmiri pin-up's feed. Burhan, who had planned to become a doctor, romanticized the mujahid movement, and young Kashmiris, confined to their homes by crackdowns, curfews, and closed-down schools, were drawn to his words and pictures.

Wani posted photographs of himself in battle gear wielding an AK-47 and wrote emotional speeches about the day he would unfurl the flag of Islam over Delhi's Red Fort. His movements, words, images, and contacts, in and around Pulwama, 25 kilometres south of Srinagar, were monitored by tech-savvy intelligence officers there and in New

Delhi, who scrubbed the images for hints about his hideouts and his accomplices. For Wani, it was a high-risk strategy, but it worked in his favour, especially after false reports of his death in 2013 went viral and he emerged, unscathed, like the Prophet and his 313 followers who out-fought a larger army at the battle of Al Badr.

Every few days, from approximately October 14 to February 15, different I.B. officers reported in, using their numeric references, plotting Burhan's journey including his meeting with a veteran LeT commander, whom I.B. knew well. Abu Qasim a.k.a. Abdul Rahman was, according to a thumbnail sketch input into the grid, from Bahawalpur, in Pakistan's Punjab, where Masood Azhar came from. He had been in service for five years and, the previous August, had organized a murderous assault on a bus full of B.S.F. officers that left two dead.

Before then, in 2013, Rahman was involved in an attack on an army bus on the outskirts of Srinagar that killed eight soldiers. Between those two dates, he had come and gone, accompanied by 15 bodyguards. But the LeT was not trying to recruit Burhan, the grid recorded. It was the other way around. He was offering his men and guns. However, Rahman, under constant surveillance, would be dead by October.[26]

On January 7, 2015, Burhan Wani was in Arigom, and seven days later he was still there. But there was no raid; no cops to call in at the two-storey stone house he stayed in. The I.B. was puzzled. One source for these sightings was inside Burhan's circle, which was an intelligence coup. Still no move was made and when the S.T.F. was sent, it reported back that it had "narrowly missed" Burhan.

I.B. officers began asking questions about the grid's management and the overarching Burhan strategy. However deep their reporting on him, and however regular the production of HUMINT, whenever they got close, they encountered resistance from other parts of the security services.

In Shareefabad, where Wani's father lived and taught, the I.B. identified a safehouse used by Burhan. Finding anyone to snitch on the new hero was a struggle but by February 2015, they had recruited a tout living close to his maternal uncle in Dadasur. On February 9, at 9.30 p.m., Burhan returned to Tral, visiting Gamiraz village.

An I.B. asset who greeted Burhan personally reported that he was in the company of a local schoolteacher and an "overground worker" or O/G, security parlance for a sympathizer, rather than a fighter, who was U/G or underground.

And it went on, with multiple reports posted each day: hamlet, town, timing, company kept – subjects discussed, with notes added by units working for the D.G.M.I. that had an observation post close to Masjid Kirmani in Pulwama. These military sources confirmed that Burhan had become a lightning rod, bringing people together and receiving from them deep support and favours. The lethal risk of being seen or photographed with him was eclipsed by the chance of obtaining the ultimate selfie.

If the HUMINT was overwhelming, the SIGINT was also powerful. While Burhan understood his public profile was growing, from the likes and follows, he and his small gang seem not to have known they were also being tracked in real time. The combination of HUMINT and SIGINT told the I.B. something significant.

Burhan had not yet carried out a single operation, but he had galvanized militiamen who frequently distrusted each other. A senior LeT commander was considering defecting, attracted by Burhan's fresh style, untainted by affiliations and debts to Pakistan. Men came to Wani from the Jaish too, their names jotted down by the I.B., including "Shari" and "Saqib" from Noorpora, and "Aqib" from Hayun. They would all be dead soon.[27]

He charmed civilians. The Kashmir armed struggle had run out of steam until the Machil killings and those grim fields of paperless corpses. But Burhan began shaking things up. When he first unmasked himself on social media, he was positioned as a Kashmir-raised insurgent, of a kind that had not emerged since the late Abdul Majeed Dar.[28]

Some photographs were posed, others were verité: Burhan and his cadre playing cricket, or lounging in forests; standing on outcrops, evoking the young Fidel Castro and his five captains or the Long March to Havana.[29] The grid locked on to the photographer, identifying him as "Younas." In another month, Younas would be dead.[30]

The I.B. was startled to learn that one raid – on a remote village in Tral – had come close to Burhan in March 2015, but, again, somehow he slipped through the net. Was this intentional, they wondered? When I.B. Srinagar heard that Burhan was injured and being treated in a friend's house in Tang Mohalla, near the Higher Secondary School, the address was put forward for another raid, but it took an age to organize and by the time security forces reached there Burhan was gone, again. Fearless, he admitted himself to S.M.H.S., the main hospital in Srinagar, and under the noses of the security establishment he was bandaged up by nurses who knew who he was and took the risk anyhow.

A party sent to intercept him at the hospital arrived too late and he escaped to his cousin's house in Rajbagh. The grid knew. It was solid, accurate, and expansive. The I.B. deduced that the supervising instruction from Delhi was to slow local operations to achieve a deeper strategic goal. A senior I.B. officer who served in Srinagar called it narrative control. "Delhi was building stories, especially in the Valley," he said, pointing to the N.S.A. Ajit Doval. "But we could not figure out yet what they had planned for Burhan Wani or how the story was supposed to end."

On March 18, Burhan was spotted with "Ayatollah Bhat," as the Jaish commander was called, a fighter who had been active since 2010, snatching weapons from police and killing local officials, sometimes going by the name "Khomeini." He and Burhan were in Dadasur, in Tral. But Burhan slipped away. Ayatollah Bhat would be dead soon.[31]

By April, I.B. Srinagar was following yet more recruits running to Burhan, five or six at a time. They listened in as one of them, Nisar Ahmed Wani, arranged his rendezvous. Nisar would die soon.[32]

That month, Burhan Wani's elder brother, Khalid, stepped into the grid. He took food and friends into the forest. An ill-advised trip, it ended in a grove, with a surreal picnic, Khalid kicking back with Burhan and company, who were annoyed with him for taking unnecessary risks.

As if to prove Burhan's point, a routine army patrol passed by and saw them. Burhan fled, but soldiers caught Khalid and handed him over to the S.T.F. who reported that he died. Khalid's family, when they received the body, claimed he had been tortured and beaten to death in custody, triggering a deep mourning across Tral, where Burhan blamed himself for making wild moves and many mistakes, while still not firing a single round.[33]

The I.B. and the D.I.A. picked up on Burhan's grief right away, feeding inputs into the grid, reporting on "his mood."[34] They warned on April 17 that Burhan's men were intending to snatch weapons from the security forces by way of revenge. More snippets came. But before Burhan could mount a mission, he was injured again, having still not discharged his gun. As a passing patrol spotted men with guns in the woods, they fired and a bullet struck his left leg.

By now, everyone in the freedom struggle wanted a piece of Burhan. Old-timers, spent forces, burnt-out brigades, activists, and fighters. Shabir Shah, campaigner, politician, and separatist showman with a trademark bouffant, a man who had spent thirty-two of his sixty-seven years in prison, was watched visiting Burhan's home town seeking a meeting with the family.

On May 15, the deputy commander of H.M., Amir Khan, telephoned at dawn to offer condolences to Burhan's father, who had not been expecting the call. The D.I.A. was listening in, stunned by H.M.'s blasé attitude, and its lack of understanding of how they compromised the Wani family.[35]

Burhan kept moving. He was seen at the Darul Uloom in Tral, meeting supporters. The D.G. of the M.I. and the B.S.F. reported that some of them suggested that as revenge for Khalid's death Burhan target patrols, convoys, and a Road Opening Party – the survey group that heads out before a convoy checking for I.E.D.s and boobytraps. His followers finally mounted their first attack on May 11, in Anantnag, although Burhan Wani stayed back with the core group of younger men. Two members of the security forces were killed. When Burhan arrived at a safehouse in Shahbad Bala, it was already under surveillance and identified with a code number. It was owned by a female friend, also registered as an O/G, who had long been under surveillance too. No raid was called in again, but this woman would be detained under the P.S.A. soon.

The support Burhan Wani was receiving caught the attention of H.M. Central, listing in its offices in Muzaffarabad, the capital of Pakistan-administered Kashmir. It had never recovered from the Abdul Majeed Dar killing, which had split its command.

The D.I.A. recorded H.M. calling Burhan in May, offering to promote him to "operational commander South Kashmir." Voters in the Valley looking to break the impasse elected the B.J.P., unexpectedly, as the minority partner in the state's government, the party forming a counter-intuitive administration with a pro-Kashmir group, the People's Democratic Party (P.D.P.). Bemused B.J.P. party workers in Batagund now were monitored as they deserted their posts to seek the rebel out too.

In June, Burhan Wani, who had still not discharged his weapon, was wounded again by a patrol. Followers came to help, the D.I.A. eavesdropping as they celebrated "Naseer Pandit joining H.M." Pandit was a former Kashmiri cop who had left his job to enlist in Burhan's new group, which was known as Hizbul Mujahideen-W. But Naseer Pandit would be dead soon.[36]

Sclerotic H.M. Central began showering Burhan with gifts, sending a courier with a Thuraya sat phone, unaware that the N.T.R.O., like G.C.H.Q. before it, were all over these, thanks to highly classified programs like VoiceSail, with tech and know-how, some of it shared by Israel, Britain, and the U.S., post the S.S.P.A.C. agreement. Burhan was asked to call H.M. command in Rawalpindi and the Thuraya turned him into a walking G.P.S. coordinate, followed intently in Delhi and Srinagar. The N.T.R.O. tracked back and zeroed in on the caller in Pakistan, reporting the identity as "Khurshid Aamir, HM Commander."

H.M. Central projected Burhan as their folk hero and even suggested operations, offering to boost his unit's profile. Around the young commander were now at least 20 young fighters, their photos uploaded to social media, with defectors from different outfits arriving every day. R.A.W.–I.B. tracked LeT men who risked crossing into Kashmir from Pakistan to try to find him. They monitored social media and followed all of those who swapped his videos or downloaded them, later arresting them under the P.S.A.

This was how they zeroed in on "19 yr old boy, Mohd Ishaq Parrey, who lived in Laribal, in Tral, whose cousin brother was a terrorist (killed)." Parrey was a bright scholar who had scored 98.4 per cent in his Class X exams and was hoping to become a doctor, until the Machil encounter had set the Valley alight. Ishaq is Arabic for Isaac, which (together with his smarts) had led to the nickname *Newton*. Aged 19, he abandoned his studies and found Burhan Wani, by when, via his social media, he was being tracked in real time. Newton, too, would be dead soon.[37]

In July, Burhan's gifted Thuraya lit him up in Shopian, south of Srinagar. Meanwhile, the monitoring operation inside social media channels yielded more names and addresses, with a slew of arrests following under the P.S.A. The grid gave summaries. "Suspect B on 13 Jul 2015 revealed that suspect A had a video of HM terrorist Burhan, which he sent to suspect B on WhatsApp," said an I.B. officer involved, recalling a log. "And then another was caught on Twitter. And another using Gmail." Intelligence created contacts chains, just as G.C.H.Q. and the American N.S.A. had done after the 7/7 London attacks. The Burhan Wani videos were broadcast on TV channels on July 13, 2015 and marked his international debut.

More people of every kind wanted in. Veterans risked the LoC crossing into India, without knowing that the N.T.R.O. and R.A.W. were constantly monitoring them, Burhan Wani acting like flypaper for the Indian intelligence community. One H.M. cell made the long and dangerous journey from Kahuta, where Pakistan's uranium enrichment facilities were based. The R.A.W. tracked them, referring to the infiltrators with an alphanumeric code. It also eavesdropped a cloaked mujahid station in Pakistan-administered Kashmir phoning fighters dotted around Pakistan, asking "for news about Burhan Wani," including a cell connected to Al Badr or the New Moon group, labelled D9, while others, including a Lashkar break-away unit, was labelled C8.

Men located in Rawalpindi and Muzaffarabad were preparing to come over too, single fighters, or pairs, amateurs, and veterans, leaving from Maharaj Gund in Pakistan-administered Kashmir and entering India to the south of Tangdhar in Kashmir. They would try to find Wani "whose unit now included Khurshid, Imtiaz, Hassan, Majid and Jansahab." The security services hunkered down. All of these fighters from Pakistan would be dead soon, "as well as the infiltrators gathering in Tangdhar."

By August, the Indian intelligence community had recruited a second asset inside Burhan's group, and he led them to the village of Wachi on the Shopian Road, north of Anantnag. Burhan was now working on recruiting surrendered fighters, telling them to re-enlist in a Kashmir unit run by Kashmiris. A new struggle was underway. Burhan hopped to the birthplace of the Sufi saint Noor-ud-Din Noorani, then trekked to Lurgam. By the middle of August, he had enough weapons and fighters to finally launch a real attack.

The R.A.W. eavesdropped as H.M. Commander Syed Salahuddin came on the line. A man who did not make calls, Salahuddin now "wanted to speak to Burhan Wani personally."[38] Salahuddin had a plan, he said, and he rattled off potential missions. But Burhan Wani did not bite.

The monitoring deepened, watching and listening as Burhan was propelled forward by his own anger and desire, feeding off the love and encouragement of the teachers, clerics, shopkeepers, and pharmacists, in hospitals, school buildings, clinics, homes, and masjids across the southern part of the Valley, for whom he seemed to be the youth of Kashmir, no longer disconsolate, fearful, or compromised, not a dupe, a collaborator, or a useful idiot. For some of them, Burhan Wani was an irresistible martyr, walking as a free man towards his death, without firing a single shot.

~

In the summer of 2016, the grid picked up Burhan Wani trekking with Pervaiz Lashkari, another H.M. fighter in his twenties. They walked the backwoods and criss-crossed the streams. They skirted around the super-orchards of Bamdora, a tin-and-brick village south of Anantnag. There, they met another young H.M. fighter, Sartaj Sheikh, whose uncle welcomed them into his house, delighted to host such a celebrity.

Fussing about, Uncle Farooq instructed his daughters to make the three young men a special dinner, before they fell asleep on the floor, exhausted. The next day, Wani and his companions, sore and tired, could not rise. Uncle Farooq insisted they stay put, fetching salt tea and hot bread, while he ordered in more supplies.

Outside the Valley, in New Delhi, something had shifted: 19 R.R., a counter-insurgency force, that was facing mounting accusations of human rights abuses in Kashmir, received a tip-off. An officer we interviewed about the operation recalled the snippet he received: "H.M. fighter Sartaj Sheikh is visiting his maternal uncle Farooq."[39] The 19 R.R. contacted its liaison in the police S.T.F., which made remote inquiries in Bamdora, although Sheikh was a minnow and they wondered what the fuss was about.

Someone was sent to speak to the village butcher who reported that the forester Farooq had bought meat for special guests and his daughters were cooking a *dawat*, or homecoming feast. The S.T.F. did not want to alert Farooq but they had something on a neighbour. He was facing police charges and was quietly offered an amnesty and he coughed up. H.M. fighter Sartaj Sheikh had brought home someone who was "trouble," the neighbour said.

The 19 R.R. radioed back to headquarters, asking for orders. "An operation was sanctioned and Bamdora was sealed off," the officer told us. A neighbour saw the uniforms and ran to Farooq's home to warn the family, as the cordon was gathered in. Burhan Wani told the women to run, and slipped out with the others, as he had done so many times before. "Do not worry," he whispered, heading for the trees. "We will be fine." But as Burhan Wani and company sprinted away, 19 R.R. soldiers gave chase. They had been given orders to fire on sight and Burhan Wani fell in the first volley, only a few metres from the house, bleeding to death, along with his two deputies.

A senior I.B. officer in Srinagar pulled the news from the grid. "Wani's death was shattering for the Kashmiris, a morale-crushing kill," he said, describing how a young man, who seemed impervious, had fallen. Within hours, graffiti went up. At one intersection, a billboard renamed it "Burhan Chowk."[40] His funeral in Shareefabad attracted over 200,000 people from all over the Valley and 22 sets of prayers were said, as waves of mourners kept coming.[41] Burhan was interred beside his brother, Khalid, in a small walled graveyard in Tral that became a shrine.

Afterwards, gangs of young men clashed with the security forces, day and night. They bombarded soldiers and paramilitaries with stones. Live fire came back at them and volleys of metal pellets or birdshot, later chilli grenades.[42] Within the first four days of the worst upheavals seen since the Machil cold killings, fifty were dead. Each new case was another trigger. When fourteen-year-old Insha Mushtaq was blinded after being struck by more than a hundred pellets on July 12, the security services blaming her parents for allowing a teenager to be out on the streets, protesters went wild.[43]

A policeman was murdered, his vehicle pushed into a river, and more teenagers came out from their homes. Within three months, Kashmir endured one of its longest ever lockdowns, internet services were turned off and the national highway linking the Valley to the rest of India was closed, more than 150 civilians were dead, 17,000 children and adults were injured, as were 100 members of the security forces. According to records at the S.M.H.S. hospital in Srinagar, 782 people sought treatment for eyes ruptured by metal pellets.[44]

A state where armed insurrection had been stifled, where endgame talks almost succeeded, where Pakistani infiltration had slowed to a silken thread of men traipsing into India through the snow, was on fire again. More than 200 were killed during the government's "Operation All-Out" response.[45] I.B. officers, plainly dismayed, talked to us about "a ham-fisted overreaction from Delhi" but wondered also "if this was part of a wider plan."[46]

~

Peace was not on anyone's mind. In November 2016, amid the chaos, gunmen came to settle an old, festering score in the Bagh-e-Islam area of Srinagar. They barged into the home of a paralysed widow and shot her three times. Wheelchair-bound, she ran an NGO for people like her, and orphans. She was rushed to S.M.H.S., where doctors could not save her. Staff there knew her well. She was Dr Shamima Badroo, head of the Majeed Dar Foundation, and the widow of Abdul Majeed Dar, the H.M. commander who had been killed in a hit organized by Major Iftikhar.

Dar had been suing for an Indian peace, and now the woman he loved, who had only narrowly survived an earlier shooting in 2006, was claimed by a war with a long memory.[47] Gunmen, according to an I.B. report, connected to H.M. Central still wanted to erase everything to do with a popular leader who had betrayed Commander Salahuddin.[48]

In 2017, with the Kashmir Valley lurching into its deepest crisis for a decade, an Armed Forces Tribunal freed the soldiers accused of the Machil killings, claiming there was insufficient evidence to convict them.[49] The unrest deepened, roads were blockaded, and despite curfews in ten districts, stone-throwing crowds massed. Pellet guns and the P.S.A. were used to disperse the population. Nine thousand people were detained, 15,000 hospitalized, and 4000 members of the security forces were injured. As the state writhed, one of Kashmir's most capable journalists, Shujaat Bukhari, a local with a global profile, was shot dead near his office in Srinagar's Press Enclave in June 2018.[50]

Bukhari had been engaged in peace talks, a citizens' movement seeking a solution, a process that created enemies. He had already received death threats and had bodyguards, who were also murdered by the assassins who came heavily armed on a motorbike, riding freely through a closely observed, high security zone.

At H.M. Central, facing yet another crisis of popularity, Salahuddin was forced to deny his fighters were responsible, but made no mention of Adil Dar's dead widow. The Kashmir government pledged to find Bukhari's killers at a time when it had failed to prevent 130 deaths in the recent clashes. An excoriating U.N. report, the first on Kashmir by the Human Rights Commission, described a "conflict that has robbed millions of their basic human rights and continues to this day to inflict untold suffering."[51] The U.N. Commissioner for Human Rights called for a "comprehensive independent international investigation" into human rights violations. Delhi, furious at international interference in what it saw as a domestic conflict stoked by Pakistan, rejected the entire report, colouring it as politically motivated and arguing, gnomically, that it undermined the global consensus on "zero-tolerance for terrorism."[52]

Soon Kashmir would have no government at all.

Pathankot to Balakot

On January 2, 2016, a team of gunmen wearing Indian army fatigues waded through a branch of the Ravi River on the India–Pakistan Punjab border. Arriving on the Indian side, the men hijacked vehicles and drove towards the sprawling Pathankot Air Force base.

Scaling a perimeter wall, they recovered in the long grass and then ran towards a residential compound where the first gun battle crackled. Four attackers were killed and three members of the Indian security forces. Four more Indians died the following day in an I.E.D. blast. It would take three days for security forces to be certain they were back in control, ending a strike that embarrassed and enraged India, which responded by heaping pressure on battle-weary Pakistan, threatening war.

But internal reporting by combined intelligence was coruscating and painfully honest. It acknowledged that several key pieces of protection were missing, "despite constant warnings."[53] More than 91 kilometres of the Punjab border was not fenced. At least four reports had suggested that rivers (and dry creaks) were vulnerable spots, but no nets were pegged across them. There were no extra patrols, despite six written requests.[54] Surveillance technology and movement trackers had not been deployed. The B.S.F. was thin on the ground because it concentrated its activities in Kashmir, and its requests for more men had been ignored, repeatedly, a B.S.F. officer told us.

The security services also teased apart complex evidence that suggested that several insurgent forces were operating together in the lead-up to this attack, including the Jaish, H.M., Sikh fighters, and a combination of criminal cartels from all over India, who were linked to global narco-traffickers. A significant player on the Pakistan side was an Indian national, Harmeet Singh, who travelled under many aliases. He was known by the nickname "PhD" as he had once worked in the religious studies department at Guru Nanak Dev University, in Amritsar, where he had grown up and where his parents remained. Singh, who secretly headed an armed Khalistan faction, had been sheltered by the I.S.I. for many years.[55]

His partner in crime was a Dubai-based drug smuggler and money launderer called Jasmeet Hakimzada, a man whom agencies in the West were tracking for allegedly shipping opioids and heroin to America, Canada, and Britain. He would soon face sanctions imposed by the U.S. Treasury.[56] Their international network was profit-driven but it also acted as a clearing house for anti-India terror and money laundering. At the far end of this consortium were entrepreneurial Taliban commanders from Jalalabad who concealed heroin and opium in shipments of rock salt that were dispatched to Kashmir.[57]

They were allegedly received by two brothers, Farookh and Tariq Lone, whom R.A.W.–I.B. had under surveillance.[58] They allegedly delivered the haul to a man whose alias I.B. had down as "Shoe Mallet." He supervised the salt shipment down to Delhi, it was claimed, from where the haul was redistributed globally via Dubai. The proceeds trickled back through Kashmir, carried by couriers, or shifted using a hawala-style token system that was hard to track. One of the benefactors, the I.B. believed, was the Hizb-ul-Mujahideen in Kashmir, which these days was starved of I.S.I. cash.

Jaish had paid for the 350 kilos of explosives but they had been procured in India and the haul was waiting for the raiding party on the Indian side. Indian allies, including corrupt local police officers, were suspected of scouting the airbase. One of these dirty cops had found an area where there were multiple vulnerabilities: the floodlights were down, and the C.C.T.V. cameras had no coverage. There was no surveillance equipment of any kind and a large tree grew beside the perimeter wall that one written report identified as a security hazard. "The police officer or one of his collaborators had climbed up and attached a rope. The raiders had used it "to heave over 50 kilos of ammunition, and 30 kilos of grenades, mortars, and AK-47s," an I.B. officer who investigated told us.

A combined services triage in India – which saw all available inputs gathered in one place – reached subtle conclusions that were not made public. It dismissed direct connection to the I.S.I., instead highlighting recidivist "elements within the Jaish that is deeply divided through a combination of external pressures and actions by Pak-Mil." It also warned: "Border security and organized narco-terror in India should be an operational focus here." Publicly, however, politicians and the security services in India double-downed on Rawalpindi, with the Pakistan state directly blamed for the raid.

There was one solid outcome, fished using an age-old method. Someone tracked down Harmeet Singh to his bolthole in Pakistan's Punjab and shot him in the head. The Lahore I.S.I. detachment, an officer there told us, accused the R.A.W. of Singh's killing.[59]

~

Five years on from Osama bin Laden's death in Abbottabad, U.S.– Pakistan relations were sub-zero. India's friendship with the U.S., however, had overcome leaks, traitors, deep penetration, double-dealing, fishing, and deception ops, as well as break-ins.

China and its growing economic and military influence, its cyber aggression that plundered Western engineering and biomedical research, its billowing debt diplomacy, where it lent billions of dollars for infrastructural development in South and Central Asia, Latin America, and Africa, its cultivation of a "string of pearls" from the Gulf to Gwadar in Pakistan, the special relationship between G.H.Q. in Rawalpindi and the Communist Party of China that was also tilting to Iran, was causing the U.S. to accept a thesis long made on K Street.[60] India could be a biddable buffer in the newly re-emerged "Indo-Pacific," a coupling in a multi-polar region that would favour Washington.[61] This was, as B. Raman long predicted, not a love marriage.

The I.S.I. did what the R.A.W. had done in a similar situation. It relied on the covert world to push back, pulling the trigger on complex, tangled operations that aimed to put Lodhi Road on the back foot.

~

On March 3, 2016, the I.S.I. announced it had detained a man just inside the Iran–Pakistan border at Mashkel, south of the official crossing point between the two nations, at Taftan. Claiming he had been caught during a counter-intelligence raid, the prisoner was being investigated for espionage and terrorism. There are no black swans in the spy world. Nothing happens without a reason.

At a press conference in Quetta, the capital of Pakistani Baluchistan, reporters were told that the prisoner was travelling on an Indian passport that identified him as Hussein Mubarak Patel, a Muslim citizen. But under interrogation, he had admitted that his real identity was Kulbhushan Jadhav, a Hindu who was a serving commander in the Indian navy, his military number 41558Z. The son of a Mumbai police officer, he had a wife, Chetankul, and two children waiting for him at their home, in Powai, north-east Mumbai.[62]

The Pakistani press reported that Jadhav was an R.A.W. officer and had been in contact with outlaws and banned groups, fuelling sectarian violence in Baluchistan but also in Karachi. Reporters also recalled how, the previous September, Pakistan had handed to the U.N. three dossiers prepared with utmost "diligence and care" containing "hard and irrefutable . . . proof of Indian involvement in terrorist activities" in Karachi and Baluchistan.[63] The work had been compiled by Lt. Gen. Asif Yasin Malik, former XI Corps commander and director general

Joint Intelligence, a facility created as part of the Ehsan ul-Haq reforms. But none of the allegations about funding of the Pakistan Taliban, arms shipments to the M.Q.M., and fomenting terror in Baluchistan had gained international traction in the West – until now.

Because there were so many inconsistencies in the Jadhav story, we decided to venture back to a relationship we had closed down. Even though we had said our goodbyes, and left him brooding, we tried, once more, to engage Iftikhar in the puzzle.

We left a flurry of messages, and finally received his usual emoji-bouquet in return. We sent back a summary of the Jadhav case, knowing that his first love was data, his second, for a conspiracy. He replied in an hour. But the tone was new and it suggested a panicked man in flight.

There would be no face-to-face meeting, he warned. Iftikhar, drowning in memories, kept awake by corrosive dreams, hunted by skilled trappers in the pay of intelligence and jihad, had had to quit Dubai in a hurry. He was now somewhere in Turkey, "working with refugees from Daesh." We wondered which parts of this were true.

A day later, he pinged us on Signal, and by the tone and volume of his messages he seemed to have escaped the doldrums, biting on the story. "All facts will be hotly contested," he wrote, "each side is throwing out chaff, to prevent anyone locking on." Projecting India as the permanent victim of Pakistan and Muslim aggression was the R.A.W.'s gambit, while foreign operations run by Lodhi Road went unseen and unspoken of. This we knew.

But Iftikhar had an add: "The I.S.I. is trying to re-wire the narrative too, exposing the R.A.W.'s rough play." He struck a note of caution. "But that does not make Jadhav what the I.S.I. says he is, and the R.A.W.'s version will be a piece of work too." In the spy wars, everyone had a position.

Indian intelligence sources emerged to tell the media in Delhi that Jadhav had served with the Indian navy but "prematurely retired."[64] Since then, the ex-serviceman had been an unsuccessful maritime scrap merchant and courier, who had never worked for the R.A.W. In this version, Jadhav scraped a living in Iran, and was kidnapped in bandit country on the Iran–Pakistan border and framed by I.S.I. All this came as a surprise to his family.

The abduction, an Indian security source told reporters, was carried out by "a little-known group, Jaish ul-Adil," whom they described as "an extremist Sunni radical outfit that owes its allegiance to the al Qaeda" with "500 or so fighters."[65] The story R.A.W. was headlining was about a downtrodden Indian entrepreneur held hostage by an al Qaeda front, managed by the I.S.I. inside the Pakistan "badlands."

But this version had problems. One of them was Jaish ul-Adil that was formerly Jundullah, the group drawn from Iran combined with fighters from Karachi and elsewhere that had been enabled and betrayed by I.S.I. (and purportedly by the C.I.A, which denied it), and subsequently ripped into the Pakistan security forces as well as towns and villages, slaughtering hundreds. It was a battering ram wielded against the Pakistan military. To complicate matters, Western intelligence was trying to verify claims, made by multiple sources in the region, that an R.A.W. asset was observed reaching out to this murderous outfit, encouraging it to hit more security targets deep inside Pakistan, while asking the outfit to procure sensitive intelligence on Pakistan troop movements and military base security.[66] An R.A.W. officer we put this to said it was "far too sensitive to comment on" but then called back to "absolutely deny" that it was true.

More I.S.I. prompts found their way into Pakistan newspapers. Jadhav was said to "have revealed during preliminary investigations that his main agenda was working for R.A.W. to sabotage CPEC [the China–Pakistan Economic Corridor] through propaganda and create disharmony among the Baluch nationalist political parties."[67]

CPEC was a $62 billion economic corridor of titanic infrastructure projects underwritten by China.[68] It included the prestigious deep-water port at Gwadar, in the far south of Baluchistan, which was a constant target for insurgents and saboteurs that Pakistan insisted were primed by the R.A.W.

According to the I.S.I. version, Jadhav had crossed back and forth between Iran, Pakistan, and Afghanistan. When he was arrested, he had been on the fifteenth day of a mission to "contact various Baluch nationalist leaders and insurgents."[69] Jadhav had been monitored for eight months "distributing millions of rupees among the nationalists and insurgents in the troubled province." The security services had "arrested him after collecting ample evidence," finding on him "Afghan and Pakistani SIM cards as well as maps."

Having laid the groundwork, Pakistan now presented what they said were extracts from Jadhav's confession. He claimed he had converted to Islam for cover in his long-term mission "to destabilize Pakistan since 2013." This element of the story – potentially a forced confession extracted from a terrified man – did, however, chime with complaints by Lodhi Road veterans about R.A.W.'s decision to deploy non-Muslims in dangerous foreign operations.

Jadhav allegedly confirmed he had been tasked with "strengthening the separatist movement in Baluchistan and Karachi." From Iran, he had crossed into Pakistan Baluchistan where he travelled to rebellious Wadh, a six-hour drive north-west of Karachi, and it was here that he met with rebels from Jaish ul-Adil, who back then were mauling the Pakistan security state.

More I.S.I. prompts followed. Jadhav claimed to have travelled to Karachi "many times" where he was planning attacks, an important theme for Aabpara and one that Lodhi Road had to rebut, as the Scotland Yard inquiry into the Farooq murder in Edgware had turned up detailed allegations about R.A.W. funding and weapons trafficking to the M.Q.M. in Karachi.

A single, twisting case, of a man whose life hung in the balance, was being used by rival spy agencies to ruthlessly prosecute their long-standing regional agendas and grievances, exploiting each other's weaknesses.

Smatterings from Jadhav's career emerged that did not help Lodhi Road: he had joined India's National Defence Academy in 1987 and enlisted in the navy's engineering branch in 1991, which meant he would remain in service until 2022, so when Jadhav was captured, he was, theoretically, still a commander in the navy.[70] In India, reporters searched for Jadhav's service record, as did we, but the hard copy had vanished.[71] The R.A.W. countered that an Indian prisoner was being abused and Delhi might pursue war crimes charges. This last claim hinted too at Jadhav's torture at the hands of the Pakistan military. Although possible, even probable, this was equally problematic for India, given the well-publicized tactics of Indian security services, especially the S.T.F. in Kashmir.[72]

One month later, the Pakistan military made a surprise announcement. "The spy had been tried at a Field General Court Martial (F.G.C.M.) under the Pakistan Army Act (P.A.A.)." He had been "provided with a defending officer" but had been found guilty and sentenced to death.[73]

Iftikhar got in touch, stunned. Even this jaded warhorse could not believe what he was reading. "If I were to guess," he messaged us, "this black warrant is revenge for Afzal Guru." The alleged Parliament attacker had finally been hanged in 2013, provoking furious protests outside India. Iftikhar had described that execution as a "body blow." Now there was a potential hanging in Rawalpindi too.

In Delhi, where Afzal's death sentence had been passed without forensic or corroborative evidence, to sate, according to the Supreme Court, the "collective conscience of the entire nation," Jadhav's death sentence was positioned as "premeditated murder."[74] Delhi warned the Jadhav verdict voided the "basic norms of law and justice." No "credible evidence" was lodged, it argued.

India began a blizzard of briefings about an ordinary man that consular staff had requested to see in Pakistan thirteen times between March 25, 2016 and March 31, 2017, applications that had, allegedly, been ignored.[75]

$\sim$

We called around. I.S.I. officers gave us more context on what we were seeing play out. Iftikhar chimed in too. They described how Aabpara had canvassed to operate deeper in their strategic western border region, because the Iranian port of Chabahar vied with Pakistan's deep-water docks of Gwadar to become a pre-eminent marine staging post. Located only 72 kilometres apart, these two harbours in neighbouring countries influenced the strategic balance of the region.

Gwadar – in the Gulf of Oman, close to the Strait of Hormuz – gave China (Pakistan's patron) access to the Indian Ocean, and the ability to monitor U.S. and Indian naval activity in the Persian Gulf and Arabian Sea. Chabahar, backed by India and a station for R.A.W., enabled India to observe Pakistani and Chinese naval activity, and sought to make Iran the gateway to Afghanistan, Central Asia, Russia, and beyond.

Former chief of C-Wing, Lt. Gen. Naeem told us: "Progress in the Chabahar region was painfully slow because I.S.I. fouled its network." The handing over to Iran of the Rigi brothers, the Jundullah founders, who were hanged, set Iranian Sunni fighters against the I.S.I.. "We had not much left."

Iftikhar learned from officers in the Karachi Det that I.S.I. had found a solution in that city. "Aabpara latched on to a home-grown Karachi bandit with deep connections into Iranian Baluchistan." This man was a landlord, trader, thug, local hero, robber, and philanthropist. His name was Uzair Baloch, and he ran a profitable syndicate in the tenements of Lyari, one of Karachi's oldest neighbourhoods, where dense lanes were home to duelling gangs.

Uzair Baloch had an irresistible provenance. He was the cousin of the former kingpin of Lyari, a legendary gangster-philanthropist whose death in a police shootout in 2009 had triggered political and criminal vendettas. To assert his thug empire, Uzair had abducted his main competitor, Arshad Pappu, his brother, and a friend. They were driven to Lyari and tortured, before being publicly decapitated. Pappu's head was used as a football, while his body was dragged behind a donkey cart, set on fire, and thrown into a sewer.[76]

The entire sequence had been filmed and uploaded to social media. When paramilitary Karachi Rangers stormed Lyari looking to arrest Uzair and restore the reputational damage done to Pakistan, he fled to Muscat where he was not welcome. When he crossed the border into the U.A.E., the National Electronic Security Authority (NESA), which did not want him either, tipped off the I.S.I. "Uzair was told that his old life was gone forever," Iftikhar said. "And now he had to decide what he wanted to become."

Uzair had travel documents that enabled him to cross the Pakistan–Iran border freely, and a nephew, who still lived in Lyari, had a deep network that ran from Karachi to Baluchistan and into Iran. A brigadier in the I.S.I. Baluchistan Det confirmed the story. "Aabpara made an offer to keep him out of the Pakistan courts, so long as he signed up to the I.S.I.'s counter-intelligence operation that aimed to snag India and make headway in Iran," he said.

I.S.I. officers in Karachi described how after Uzair agreed to have his network spy inside Chabahar, he was flown back to Pakistan in 2014 and "moved into a safe house guarded by the army's V Corps and Covert Action Division operators."[77] After some months, Uzair's network, suborned by the I.S.I., zeroed in on one compound in Chabahar secured by the Revolutionary Guard.

Soon they identified men they believed to be R.A.W. officers and they puzzled over one repeat visitor they did not know. This stranger was followed back to the nearby port city of Bandar Abbas. "He was not an Iranian. But he appeared to be running a marine freight business from there," an I.S.I. officer claimed. This "ferryman" was watched as he travelled into Pakistan, heading for Karachi, where the Baloch family was waiting.

Acting for I.S.I., it reached out to the ferryman, and obtained a copy of his travel document, number E6934766, issued in Pune in India, in the name of Hussein Mubarak Patel. It stated he was a Muslim and, according to one I.S.I. briefing note, "inside were seven entry and exit stamps for India and two visas for Iran, issued in India." He moved in

Muslim circles in Iran, washing, praying, and eating with them. However, according to the I.S.I., Baloch's network finally spotted something jarring – the Muslim ferryman was uncircumcised. Whatever he was, he was not a Muslim.

Iftikhar messaged. He had the bit between his teeth. "Officers I talked to claim they photographed the ferryman making contact in Baluchistan and Sindh with individuals and groups who belonged to outlawed groups." Iftikhar added a caveat. He could not decide if this information was real or if the I.S.I. had found a way of manipulating a naive Indian trader, travelling incognito. He preferred the latter theory – that a hapless man had walked into an I.S.I. trap. Iftikhar vanished, saying he was going to explore this avenue.

We got in touch with I.S.I. officers in Karachi, who claimed that the next time the Baloch brothers got to look at Jadhav's papers, they found he had a second travel passport. Its number was L9630722, issued in 2014, expiring on May 11, 2024. This one came from Thane and gave Jadhav's place of birth as Sangli in Maharashtra, which was a slip as this was where the real Jadhav was born on April 16, 1970.

"It was a lucky strike," the I.S.I. officer told us. The document was registered to a home in Mumbai – C-11, Jasdanwala Complex. This place belonged to Avanti Jadhav, the wife of an assistant commissioner of police, Sudhir Jadhav, Kulbhushan's parents.

Iftikhar was incredulous: "A real birthplace and home address; living, reachable people. The game was up. Even if Jadhav had done nothing, he was an Indian serviceman, travelling with two sets of papers, issued under an assumed identity, with a religion that was not his, but with official visas, issued in India. And one of these passports was linked to the man's real family. Tradecraft is everything," he sniffed. "But in this case, there was none. And Jadhav was now the I.S.I.'s mark."

The Indian sailor was small fry and the I.S.I. intended to turn him into an enormous trophy, a C-Wing brigadier told us. A colonel in B-Wing, external intelligence, based in Europe, agreed. "The I.S.I. waited patiently, hoping to grow Jadhav into something special and then when he was big enough, as a target, the I.S.I. would pull him in," he claimed.

Iftikhar sent a message that evening. It was not about Jadhav. He was going dark again, and quitting Turkey. "Doing you a favour," was how he put it. His Signal account had been compromised, he suspected, which meant they were looking for all of his correspondents too. He did not say who *they* were or how this had happened. But so many people were furious with Iftikhar that that list was long, featuring, among many others, the I.S.I., R.A.W., al Qaeda, and the Pakistan Taliban.

We imagined Iftikhar commencing with his S.O.P.: phones charged, and one placed into a padded envelope, which he couriered to another Gulf state. Switching on his V.P.N. to shield his I.P. and then logging on from another country to cancel his email accounts. Burning his laptop and driving around recovering go-bags, with currencies, ID cards and clothes. Cramming everything into a small holdall, he would become his own launch commander, scrambling into another country. Was this the last we would hear from him?

～

By 2016, Monisha had given up grappling with the taint of the Major Singh affair and still felt a lingering dismay over the 26/11 fiasco, and the tincture of chauvinism that she worried coloured everything. Unwilling to serve in a sectarian service, she had left Lodhi Road.

"I could not get over the fact that as we drew closer to the U.S., we, as a service, became less invested in secular democracy and far more sectarian, while telling everyone this was assertive behaviour," she said. "This was what had happened to the I.S.I. as it became wrapped up in the C.I.A. terror wars – that service endorsing or encouraging all of its worst proclivities, as far as I could see, or tolerating them so as to maintain the relationship. The I.S.I. used the C.I.A. as cover to become its worst self. The R.A.W. seemed to be doing the same, knowing that Langley, which needed Lodhi Road, would not sanction it."

Some senior officers in the C.I.A. told us frankly they preferred the military in Pakistan, whatever the U.S. State Department said about democracy. Multiparty politics Pakistan-style was too short-lived and messy. Pakistan frustrated Western agencies. Monisha said: "In practice India was becoming a lot like Pakistan in that our services became weighed down with religion and our analysis was bent out of shape. Spies are conspiring with politicians to create events or misconstrue them. This is not my vision of India or the R.A.W." Other senior officers in the R.A.W. vehemently disagreed with this view, they told us, but conceded the services were polarized, "like many others, in any country. Take the C.I.A. – it's a city and in it are many neighbourhoods with different political constituencies."

Monisha made it to the U.S. West Coast, and it was from there that she mined down into Kulbhushan Jadhav's story for us, while we continued to stress test the I.S.I. material on the security services in India. "A starting point is the Parliament attack of 2001," Monisha maintained, when she finally got back in touch. "After that, many officers lobbied for harder operations inside Pakistan – a return to the B. Raman quid pro quo."

As Musharraf slowly shut down Kashmir operations, the Indian Navy spotted cells of LeT fighters shifting down to Karachi. The Indian Navy and the R.A.W. feared the LeT might try to create a marine force. Monisha's contacts suggested that Commander Jadhav, who was outraged by the Parliament attack, offered to assist although nothing was official. She believed that he had first travelled to Iran and Karachi in 2003 using, for the first time, the Hussein Mubarak Patel passport.

After forming a trading company, Kaminda, he shuttled between Chabahar and Bandar Abbas. But if he was a spy, which no one would comment on, his training was terrible, or perhaps he had undergone none. Kaminda's foundation document stated it repaired marine engines and carried loads, but it only had one asset, a boat leased from another company. When we asked contacts in Chabahar to check it out, they found it was in a dry dock. Published tax filings were available, and they revealed that the business was idling, with no turnover.

"Two passports, a broken boat, and a brass plaque company, it looks like an amateur show," Monisha said. "This was a cover with no depth. The R.A.W. would never have done this if it was tasking an officer." What Jadhav did have was access, and while R.A.W. officers insisted they did not recruit him, Monisha's contacts maintained that senior officers suggested Jadhav "stay in touch."

This was opportunistic, Monisha believed, with some officers in Lodhi Road regarding Jadhav as an asset rather than an officer, without the naval commander, who was inducted into the engineering cadre, understanding the difference between the two. An asset gave information as a self-employed informer, and an officer was trained to serve the state, potentially under cover, and received its protection.

But Jadhav survived, and idled, until 26/11. Monisha said: "Suddenly he was an asset that every service wanted: an Indian inside Pakistan who could move around Karachi unhindered and dip into Iran too."

A senior I.B. officer told us that after 26/11 the service lobbied to have access to more communications intelligence and to develop its own sources in foreign countries where conspiracies were plotted to attack Punjab, Kashmir, and the North-East. "There was a debate about loosening R.A.W.'s monopoly, and that of technical intelligence agencies," the officer said. Monisha believed that the I.B.'s desire for a foreign asset dovetailed with Jadhav's availability, and the Bureau had encouraged him to prove his worth, just as the Indian Navy and the R.A.W. did too. Serving I.B. officers declined to comment on this. R.A.W. officers denied it.

By 2010, Jadhav was, according to I.B. officers and Monisha, sought after by the I.B., the R.A.W., and the Navy, operating without training in a lethal environment, weaving between Quds Force, I.S.I., Jaish ul-Adil, al Qaeda, regional separatists, and Baluch kingpins. Two years later, still alive, Jadhav reported something that was too good to be true. Monisha said: "He told the people he was speaking to in India that he had managed to work his way into the Baloch family of Lyari. His contact was a nephew of Uzair Baloch."

Jadhav, who thought he had struck gold, had been ensnared by the

I.S.I. which had been dangling the Baloch family, hoping he would bite. I.S.I. C-Wing, which argued that they should grow Jadhav, had caught him red-handed with something incriminating. The Baloch family was told to provide a lure. A report from C-Wing we were shown claims that Uzair's men asked Jadhav to join them on an ambitious strike on an airbase inside Pakistan, an operation supposedly supported by Iran.

The Uzair family claimed to have a source in the Pakistan Air Force who had blueprints that showed security vulnerabilities at a base. They offered to give Jadhav the plans and in return he would have to arrange men and weapons.

Monisha concluded: "Jadhav probably had very few contacts – possibly none – but if he took the military blueprints for the base, given him by the Uzairs, he would now appear to be a fully-fledged Indian spy – when he was really a fall guy."

The game was on, an asset who wanted to be an officer; Indian services that wanted deniable information; a Karachi crime family serving the I.S.I. to buy their freedom; the I.S.I. that wanted to manufacture a big, fat Indian catch.

I.S.I. surveillance teams claimed they watched Jadhav trying to recruit fighters and shopping for weapons in Baluchistan. But no evidence to back this up was shown to us. Whatever the truth, Jadhav got cold feet in 2016, although by then, the I.S.I. maintains, he had taken the Air Force blueprints, and possession of these, by an Indian serviceman travelling incognito, with a false identity, was deadly.

The Baloch network that was selling the Pakistan Air Force base attack to Jadhav warned the I.S.I. its mark was "scared and losing interest," an I.S.I. colonel in Karachi told us. "Jadhav told us he felt as if his luck was running out. Jittery, he complained that he was unable to sleep. He was certain he was being watched. He wanted to go home to his family in India."

The Baloch network pushed, and persuaded Jadhav to agree to meet in March 2016 and together they headed for the Pakistan border, the I.S.I. officer in Karachi told us. But here Jadhav had second thoughts again, even as an I.S.I. trap was sprung. Jadhav insisted that the Baloch network's outrider go on ahead, arguing they should not be seen together. The Baloch man crossed on his own, telling the I.S.I. he had failed. But after many hours of cogitating, Jadhav gathered himself, and crossed over into Pakistan too, the I.S.I colonel told us.

Finally, in the desert chill of a dark night, both men greeted each other in Mashkel, where the I.S.I. emerged from the shadows and grabbed their manufactured "Indian spy." Jadhav did not resist, a C-Wing brigadier told us. He had no Plan B. No counter-interrogation training. No back stories. He was winging it, until he was caught. And then, inhaling the stale sweat of a dark Pakistani cell, Jadhav broke down. The I.S.I. could make him into whatever they needed. Jadhav's dubious confessions were leaked as Prime Minister Modi visited Iran in May 2016, signing a memorandum to allow India access to Afghanistan via the port of Chabahar. In the background, loose ends in Pakistan were tidied away. The Baloch network was rolled up, Uzair, emerging from nowhere, was taken into military custody, and a hasty trial began, where he was accused of being a traitor, collaborating with an Indian spy.[78] But – maintaining their deal – he was kept alive, for now.

A local incident – Jadhav's detention – spiralled into a regional tug of war that sublimated into the international courts, where India went petitioning that due process had not been followed. The courts agreed that international treaties were flouted by Pakistan in Jadhav's case, as he was denied a proper defence or consular access, but the International Court of Justice had no power to try the case or free the prisoner.[79]

Pakistan and India took their arguments to Europe and North America, where nervous allies declined to get involved. As Jadhav languished in a windowless cell, the spy war was transported back to the old, vascular theatre of Kashmir.

~

The unlikely coalition in Kashmir between the B.J.P. and the P.D.P., a party which canvassed for autonomy, a pact that came together in 2015, had governed over chronic disorder. The period had many profound lows: the missing, the murdered, and the mass stoning of security forces, to an extraordinary video of an Indian army major, Leetul Gogoi, of the Rashtriya Rifles, who had been posted to 53 Sector, driving a vehicle through Budgam with a Kashmiri shawl maker tied to its fender. Farooq Ahmad, accused of throwing stones, was used to shield the R.R. officers.[80] The army chief, reacting to howls of protest, awarded Gogoi the C.O.A.S. Commendation Card "for sustained efforts in Counter Insurgency operations."[81] But almost two years later, the major was out of the Valley, after a court martial heard how he was arrested by police for fighting with staff at the Grand Mumtaz Hotel, who had refused him entry along with a Kashmiri woman he had met on Facebook and talked into a triste, his crime, as far as the military saw it, deserting his post.[82]

In June 2018, the minority B.J.P. withdrew from the political pact, collapsing it. Two of the I.B. officers on the Burhan Wani operation said they finally understood the long game played in Delhi by Ajit Doval's team: "Build Burhan Wani. Kill Burhan Wani. Destroy the morale of the Kashmiris. And when people go wild, and law and order crumbles in the Valley, politics will become gridlocked too which is when Delhi can step in and break the state."

Much of this was "open source," R.A.W. and I.B. officers told us. Modi's election manifesto pledged to remove Kashmir's special status, enshrined in Article 370 of the Constitution, as a state that could formulate some of its own laws with limited autonomy, where landownership was a birthright – small but significant details that highlighted Kashmir's bitterly contested nature.

The matter was now settled – for the B.J.P., but also for the many voters, who backed the party's manifesto pledges on Kashmir, and for the majority of parliamentarians who voted, overwhelmingly, in support. Constitutional reformers argued that Article 370 elevated the will of a long defunct maharaja's assembly, over a contemporary, elected parliament. Likewise, the vast will of the voters, 171,660,230 of whom backed Modi, was being undercut by the slim writ of residents in the Valley (pop: 12.55 million).[83] Article 370 was, they maintained, a pontoon bridge built in 1949 to get around Kashmir's block on integrating India, post-Independence, rather than the permanent engineering of the republic's relationship to an outlying state.[84] Many supporters argued that what Article 370 had enabled was "30 years of terrorism and ethnic cleansing."[85]

In these versions, Kashmir was seen as Pakistan's failure, as an amplifier of dissent and terror in the Valley. The profound grievances and desires of many residents, the kinetic, brutal role played by India and its security services in re-animating the crisis, the building international outcry over wholesale abuses and the bypassing of international conventions and norms – the rules of war and peace – were ignored by R.A.W.–I.B., just as the C.I.A. ignored them too in creating its enhanced interrogation programme, black sites, renditions, and Guantanamo Bay.

Some in the B.J.P. cut to the chase and pressed the ethno-nationalist button. In August 2019, when Union Home Minister Amit Shah announced the scrapping of Article 370, a B.J.P. spokesperson described the move as a "befitting reply to separatists and Pakistan who are supporting and nourishing terrorism in the state," an action that would "bring the people of the Valley into the national mainstream."[86] Any chance of an agreement on contested Kashmir with Pakistan – like those dangled before Zia and Musharraf and that had come so close to emulsifying – were now ruled out.

However, the next move from the muscle state in Delhi that was played in December further clarified the agenda, moving it even further away from constitutional reform, or even counter-terror. Parliament passed the Citizenship (Amendment) Act, which allowed immigrants from Hindu, Christian, Buddhist, Sikh, and Zoroastrian communities from Afghanistan, Bangladesh, and Pakistan to become citizens. The eligible would be fast-tracked to citizenship and could apply within five years for these rights – all of which Delhi argued showed the philanthropic state at work, an essential feature of a developing nation becoming a regional and global power. But opponents pointed out that Muslims, including those under threat, like the Rohingya refugees or the Ahmadiyya sect (that was seen as heretical by some Sunnis), were excluded. B.J.P. president Amit Shah's words compounded these concerns. "There is a fundamental difference between a refugee and an infiltrator," he said, drawing a line between Christians in flight as opposed to persecuted Muslims from Bangladesh or the Rohingya. "This bill is for refugees."[87]

Non-Muslims deserved a haven, but Muslims were undesirable law breakers, a burden to be thwarted or removed. This was another election pledge, and when Shah addressed a rally in Delhi in 2018 he told supporters: "Illegal immigrants are like termites and they are eating the food that should go to our poor and they are taking our jobs. They carry out blasts in our country and so many of our people die."[88] A senior R.A.W. officer told us: "India first. Why not? We are being honest here, in recognizing that the Muslims that India lets in have sometimes become enemies of the state, so why should we continue with these acts of self-injury. Let the West do that. Britain, France, and Germany, all have been attacked by people it describes as migrants."

India was now fully in sync with America, where in the run-up to his successful presidential campaign the candidate Donald Trump claimed – wrongly – that "thousands and thousands" of Muslims cheered in New Jersey as the 9/11 conspiracies unfolded.[89] In one of his first acts as President, eight days after his inauguration, on January 28, 2017, President Trump issued an executive order banning people from six Muslim-majority countries from entering the U.S.A., shutting out refugees.

The Spy Exchange

The I.S.I.'s "espionage" ploy was almost overcooked by 2017, when officers involved in the Kulbhushan Jadhav operation began trying to auction in the U.S. and the U.K. "top secret interrogation transcripts."[90] Using a well-regarded London-based consultancy that rinses reputations, the I.S.I. had them pitch the file to publishers in India and Europe, and writers and TV stations, the documents coming with provenances as gossamer as the claims made in them. One was the mind-boggling suggestion that Jadhav had confessed to the I.S.I. that 26/11 was carried out by the R.A.W.

The I.S.I. was also in a profound quandary over Kashmir, and despite some heated rhetoric, military and civilian leaders told us they knew they could do nothing. The situation was made worse by India's new-found proximity to the U.S.

The I.S.I., hoping to elevate Aabpara, began mulling a jailbreak. Its Peshawar Det had picked up a rumour about a planned prison conspiracy at the city's Central Jail, an overcrowded colonial legacy of whitewashed brick and blue piping where al Qaeda suspects had been tortured, using methods similar to those deployed by the C.I.A. When the I.S.I. probed the gang that was plotting the break-in, they concluded that it was a ruse concealing the real masterminds. But the roster of convicts that could have escaped was far more revealing. Among them was Shakil

Afridi, whose presence made this escape bid an act of international brinkmanship.

Afridi had trained as a medical doctor at Khyber Medical College in Peshawar and worked as a health official in the North West Frontier Province, where he was abducted by an Islamic levy in 2008, the same militia young Captain Saad Rabbani would narrowly survive in the Tirah Valley bloodbath. The militia chief claimed Afridi was a molester and chiselled poor families for cash. Afridi's family denied everything but paid a fine of $11,100, after which the doctor and his family fled to California. But in the U.S. Afridi grew worried about his children's secular upbringing. He returned to Pakistan and appeared on the radar of C.I.A. talent spotters in November 2009, when he was contacted by "Kate," a Pakistan-based American Save the Children charity worker, who asked him to supervise a new hepatitis B vaccination campaign.

The money offered was more than ample. Kate and her project were green-lit the following year and in early February 2011 Afridi turned up at Ayub Medical College, Abbottabad, recruiting female nurses to knock on doors and carry out blood tests.

After the U.S. Seal Team raid on Abbottabad in May 2011, Afridi was exposed as having worked, unwittingly or otherwise, on a C.I.A. operation to secure DNA proof that the bin Ladens were in residence. Two weeks after bin Laden's death, Afridi was arrested as Pakistan hunted for U.S. collaborators. Charged and convicted of anti-national activities, he was locked up.[91]

Now, a C.I.A. asset was safely ensconced in Peshawar Central Jail, and an I.S.I. major, working in B-Wing, told us that this was when they contacted Washington: what would the U.S. give for their "accidental agent" Afridi?

Nothing happened for three years until Donald Trump, looking to gain some traction in the presidential race of 2016, talked up the fate of the jailed doctor, using his plight to lambast President Obama for turning his back on an American hero. It was a refrain similar to

Benghazi where the Republicans claimed that Hillary Clinton and her officials had turned their backs on U.S. Ambassador Chris Stevens, leading to his avoidable murder when a diplomatic outpost in Libya was overrun and torched.

Candidate Trump pledged to win Afridi's freedom, a promise that would take "two minutes" to fulfil. He told Fox News: "I would tell them, 'Let him out,' and I'm sure they would let him out."[92] During the first weeks of Trump's administration, in February, Afridi's family was optimistic. His brother told the *Washington Post*: "[Trump] is a man of action who does what he says."[93]

But a dysfunctional White House was pulling in many different directions, and the Trump–Afridi gambit clashed with another plan for Pakistan that was being debated at the National Security Council.[94] The Trump administration was intent on withdrawing U.S. troops from Afghanistan, which was only possible if there was peace. That could only happen if the I.S.I. was coerced into strong-arming the Taliban into talks.

First came the stick, with Washington announcing it was crashing out of its pact with Rawalpindi, colouring the relationship as double-dealing, with the U.S. fighting the Taliban while the I.S.I. propped it up. All military aid would be severed, Rawalpindi heard. Then the I.S.I. was contacted by a European intelligence liaison who suggested a way back. Aabpara accepted the challenge, hooking in the Taliban, as its role in any future administration in Kabul would ensure that Afghanistan remained Pakistan's ally, whereas right now, the government in Kabul was closer to India.

Pakistan hosted many backchannel meetings between British, Gulf, and American intelligence services before the Taliban talks began. The I.S.I. kept Afridi locked up, still hoping for a trade if the right one could be found. When the I.S.I. uncovered the U.S. plot to snatch their bargaining chip, Afridi, from jail, in the first month of the Trump administration, an operation that would leave the new U.S. President winning without paying, the I.S.I. toyed with exposing it.

Worried about the backlash, and eager to use the Taliban talks to warm relations with Washington, I.S.I. B-Wing instead inserted a cryptic article in an English-language Russian news portal watched by both sides, signalling that it knew about the jailbreak plan, while Afridi was transferred twenty hours south, to a high security prison in Hyderabad, where he was stashed with the forever prisoners including Omar Sheikh and majors Pasha and Haroon.[95]

As the Taliban talks picked up pace and looked to be gaining traction, the I.S.I. claimed it was contacted by the White House which suggested a prisoner swap: a doctor for a doctor. Afridi could be exchanged for Aafia Siddiqui, who was a cause célèbre in Pakistan. She was a doctor's daughter from Karachi, who had won a place at M.I.T. from where she had graduated in cognitive neuroscience. But in 2010, Siddiqui had been convicted by a New York court of trying to kill American military personnel in Afghanistan and sentenced to eighty-six years, starting a new life as prisoner 90279-054 at the Federal Medical Centre, in Carswell, Texas.[96]

However, Siddiqui had a dangerous back story. The U.S. maintained that she had been transformed by 9/11, and angered by the invasion of Afghanistan, quitting her American life as a capable scientist, abandoning a husband, and marrying Ammar al-Baluchi, the nephew of the 9/11 planner Khalid Sheikh Mohammad. Siddiqui, whose family insist that the marriage was not consummated, vanished in 2003, when Khalid Sheikh Mohammad was caught in Rawalpindi. The U.S. alleged she had joined al Qaeda and was caught after a tip-off in Afghanistan, where she grabbed a weapon from a U.S. serviceman and tried to kill him.

Aafia's family scorned these stories. They told us the I.S.I. abducted Aafia along with her three children, on her way to Islamabad. Her uncle was certain that she was confined in an I.S.I. holding centre, where they threatened to kill her children unless she infiltrated al Qaeda. After she refused, the family believed the I.S.I. handed her over to the C.I.A. in a staged encounter in Afghanistan and she spent months as a ghost prisoner in Bagram air force base – which Langley strenuously denies – before being extradited to the U.S., where she was charged and convicted.[97]

Whatever the truth there were many unanswered questions, and even more about Aafia's three children. The Afghan government handed over Ahmed, Siddiqui's son, to her sister in Karachi in 2010, although her uncle told us he was "not the same boy" he had known before she was kidnapped but that they accepted this child like a surrogate. After Siddiqui's daughter, Maryam, mysteriously appeared outside the family home, no one in the family wanted to talk about the incident or Aafia. They had been warned by Aabpara. Siddiqui's third child, Suleiman, who was six months old at the time of her disappearance, remains missing, presumed dead. Since her conviction, Siddiqui declined contact with her lawyer and terminated her own appeal, although her sister Fowzia insisted this decision was also conditioned, describing Aafia as a political prisoner.[98]

Afridi and Aafia stayed locked up. On paper in the West Wing, the Bridge of Spies prisoner swap must have looked like a stunning win-win for Trump (and the G.H.Q.): another grand gesture. But what it really was, was an allegory for the covert underbelly of the "war on terror," a bundle of loose ends (lies, claims. and unknowable allegations) that engendered profound discomfort in Aabpara and at Langley. Both camps preferred a "no deal" (even for a Muslim woman whose treatment had transformed her into a fable of Islamophobia) rather than exposing the dirty machinations of the spy wars.

Pulwama

Although erratic, the India and U.S. pact that saw bilateral trade in goods and services rise to $142 billion was publicly feted.[99] In June 2017, Trump hosted Modi at the White House, taking him on a guided tour of the President's quarters including the Lincoln bedroom. Modi presented the First Lady Melania Trump with, among other things, handwoven shawls from Kashmir, signalling the emotional and political pulls on the divided state.

Pakistan too – finally – was back in America's field of vision, working hard on fluffing the Taliban. The I.S.I. received props from the C.I.A. and the U.S. interlocutor Zalmay Khalilzad.[100]

However, whenever there was a convergence, and the last time was in 2007, when the India–Pakistan backchannel achieved traction, the al Qaeda amalgam attacked, pushing for a regional war.

~

14 February 2019, 15.10, Pulwama, Kashmir. A Scorpio SUV was driven the wrong way down the national highway and into a paramilitary convoy. The procession of coaches, armoured trucks, and troop carriers, delayed in Jammu for days by heavy snowfall, was ferrying thousands of men to relieve the forces in Srinagar. Now in the mulch of a sloppy thaw, the Scorpio exploded, sending a fireball into a bus carrying thirty-nine paramilitaries from the Central Reserve Police Force 76 Battalion, burning them to death.

Thirty minutes later, a martyrdom tape was uploaded on to social media. "By the time this video reaches you, I will be in Heaven," said a slight, round-faced young man, his eyes trained on a script held up by unseen hands. He was not the usual cannon fodder from the lowlands of Pakistan's Punjab but twenty-year-old Adil Dar, who lived locally and had volunteered for a death squad run by Jaish-e-Mohammed. "Don't fall in love," the clean-shaven Dar advised Kashmiris. Perhaps this was his anti-Valentine's message, a young man telling his peers that romance in a time of war was a luxury none of them could afford. It was also, Kashmiri newspapers maintained, a reference to the grid that arm-twisted girlfriends and wives to inform on the lovers and husbands.[101]

By 16.30, the cops called on Ghulam Dar, in Gundibagh, in South Kashmir's Pulwama district, seven kilometres away from the blast scene. Adil's father, a door-to-door cloth salesman, was told that all that was left of his son was shreds caught on the branches of roadside trees. Ghulam, a thin-faced man, with a closely cropped greying beard, had been half expecting this day. In 2015, a cousin, Manzoor Dar, had been killed in an encounter with Indian security forces. A relative, Touseef Rashid Dar, had left home to join the insurgency the previous year, but changed his mind and returned after fourteen days, only to be jailed under the P.S.A.

Ghulam revealed that Adil had dropped out of school, becoming a part-time carpenter and labourer but he had wanted to become a cleric. However, in a state of interrupted lives, having only managed to memorize eight chapters of the Quran, Adil vanished. The family lodged a report with the police in March 2018, as an insurance policy, Ghulam said, parents in a dystopian state taking actions to protect themselves against their children. And from that day, unable to collaborate in his son's presumed life, a father began mourning. One year later, Adil Dar's books were buried in place of a body.

On the surface what followed was white-hot anger from India whose responses were coloured with some divisive, communal language, while

Pakistan, seemingly stunned, was defensive. Prime Minister Modi told the nation that he knew its "blood was boiling" and that "the government has given full freedom to the security forces to act as they see fit."[102] India was portrayed as being at breaking point rather than at the end of a long road in which peace had been squandered and conflict fanned.

The next day, as global condemnation of Pulwama mounted, demonstrations erupted across India, with strikes and riots directed at Pakistan, Muslims, and Kashmiris in India. Broadcasters pulled out of telecasting Pakistan cricket. Pakistani actors were barred from Bollywood sound stages. Kashmiri students in colleges all over India were evicted, beaten, and intimidated. A Kashmiri trader was bludgeoned to death in Kolkata. A Pakistani prisoner, charged with spying, was stabbed to death in Jaipur. Shops began selling Pakistani flags and cigarette lighters. In Mumbai, where organized crime is communal, fearful Muslims marched down Mohammed Ali Road carrying the Indian tricolour.

But beneath the hood of this rapidly developing crisis lay as many uncertainties as there were opportunities. The I.S.I., bolstered by the Taliban talks, began to push back. Indian intelligence was far more muscular and unforgiving since the B.J.P. took charge and rehired Ajit Doval. Spies from both sides of the hot border made frantic outreaches, calling politicians, policymakers, and Western liaisons, road testing "hot takes," trying out arguments on an audience beyond the subcontinent, whose influence might prove crucial in global forums, while the domestic market was primed with anonymous briefings: a source, an officer, a member of the security services.

Within six hours of the Pulwama outrage, we were talking to Lt. Gen. Nusrat Naeem, the I.S.I.'s former C-Wing chief. "People are describing this as a callous act," he said. "How does it look to you? What is R.A.W. saying?"

Photographs of the scene showed the tarmac in Pulwama strewn with swatches of flesh and strips of rubber and metal. A blue coach, with its standard-issue luggage rack, had been reduced to a blackened cube. And Pakistan-backed Jaish was in the frame.

"Who is the winner here?" General Naeem asked, sounding exasperated. He pointed out that blacklisting hung over Islamabad at the Financial Action Task Force (F.A.T.F.) in Paris.[103] It threatened to sanction Pakistan for failing to curtail fundraising by jihad fronts including Lashkar and Jaish.[104] Pakistan was accused of delaying the upgrading of surveillance to track the funding of banned Islamist groups, and still allowing them to adopt new names to outpace banning orders. Another misdemeanour would push Pakistan over the edge – from greylist to blacklist – and in India, before any evidence was gathered, Pulwama was being portrayed as just that.

Two days after the bomb blast, the Jaish chief Masood Azhar uploaded a speech. If India did not surrender Kashmir, the flames of jihad would burn the subcontinent. Azhar, initially the I.S.I.'s fellow traveller, became its nemesis in 2002, repeatedly cheering on fighters who harried the deep state, killing spies and soldiers, before becoming a fugitive. "However, now, inexplicably, he was a free-floating maulvi once again," said Rajinder Khanna.

Naeem remained unflinching. "A Kashmiri set off this bomb," the general interjected. "Adil Dar was not launched from Pakistan. F.A.T.F. sanctions would hole us. What are *they* saying?"

We told him that the R.A.W. was certain the Jaish had armed Dar. Even though Jaish had been banned in 2003 in Pakistan, it was still collecting funds. When we last checked, the website for Jaish remained active using local servers. However, the Jaish was also now working under a new name in Pakistan, and it had a third identity in Kashmir.[105] We pointed out that Indian intelligence repeatedly told us that when Pakistan was imperilled, the I.S.I. lashed out, and that Pakistan always struck India when it was least expected. General Naeem was unbending. "We are fighting, diluting, and smothering these right-wing fanatics. Stop listening to *them*," he suggested, ringing off.

Lt. Gen. Vinod Khandare, a senior officer serving at the heights of the D.I.A., had a long, deep take for us. "See how our neighbours behave?

How does it look?" He was a careful hawk, his ear tuned to the static, painstaking in his choice of words. "What's the feeling over there? Is our anger understood?"

People we spoke to were shaken by Pulwama. But if the bomber was from Kashmir, and even if the Jaish was behind him, why was Pakistan blamed? The Jaish was a siren luring everyone to war. We repeated the I.S.I. concern about the F.A.T.F. blacklisting, as one forceful reason for Pakistan having no direct involvement. While we were on the call, messages arrived from an I.S.I. officer in its A-Wing, the analysis section, that stressed that Jaish remained an I.S.I. target and was on its "kill list." We read one of these out to Khandare: "For the last sixteen years, after Jaish tried to repeatedly kill Musharraf and many other officers, the ISI has been hunting down its fighters and striking them. They are in our crosshairs – do not forget."

Khandare disagreed. "You know, terror has no reason or season," he said. "Plans are seeded and then gestate. They go off like rockets on short fuses. Do not judge an atrocity by its timing. Judge Pakistan on its record. Pulwama bomber Adil Dar was a Kashmiri. True. But he was in the thrall of an outfit that has its bases inside Pakistan. Anyhow, what else is Aabpara saying?"

In the West, we said, there was a belief that Pakistan was still riddled with militia that could turn up terror at a moment's notice. But the I.S.I. was arguing that it had declared war on those outfits, denuded them, and suffered more than any other nation. What had happened in the Valley was also a facet of Indian mismanagement. Brutal crackdowns in Kashmir had seen thousands detained, maimed, and killed. Adil Dar was from the beaten youth, who for the first time in twenty years, were joining insurgent groups in large numbers, inspired by Burhan Wani's managed decline. Adil had abandoned his studies to choose death with Jaish. This did not excuse his actions, but it did explain them. Many Kashmir observers in India, including spies and soldiers, were now filled with dread.

Still, Khandare refused to accept India had any responsibility or that this context was vital. "If violence spikes, Pakistan funds it. A stone is thrown, Pakistan pays for it. These insurgent groups need backers. The rolling paper you all place between the banned outfits and the Pakistan state, we burned a long while back. I am sure Pakistan gets hurt too by radicals. The smoker and passive inhaler both get cancer. What else are *they* saying?"

We came back to timing. We suggested that Pakistan was driving the Taliban talks, alongside the C.I.A. interlocutor Zalmay Khalilzad, Gulf intelligence services, the British and others. Why would the I.S.I. spoil these overtures, and lose out on military aid, which Trump was talking about reinstating? India, however, was opposed to these Taliban talks, and given its colossal investment in Afghanistan, where the government it backed might now fade, Delhi had the most to gain from Pakistan being lambasted. R.A.W. wanted to keep the C.I.A. to itself, and to do so always portrayed the I.S.I. as rogue, conflating Aabpara with Islamists – it was an age-old game.

Khandare was not impressed: "The I.S.I. employs arsonists and then complains when they burn down their house." Similar ideas appeared in Indian newspapers the next day.

Facts about Pulwama were still low on the ground and, whatever the R.A.W. suggested, this attack was finely dialled into events, local and global, just like 26/11 had been. Pakistan was vulnerable and India was red hot. The Indian general election was set to take place, with Modi hoping to win a second term. Security and Pakistan were key campaigning issues in an India where the B.J.P. was strident, as were the security services.

Pragya Singh Thakur, one of those accused by the A.T.S. chief Hemant Karkare of participating in the 2008 Malegaon blasts, a Hindu attack that framed Islamists, was standing for the B.J.P. in Bhopal. Endorsing Thakur, Modi described her as a saint and said she was an answer to those who tried to portray 5000 years of Hindu culture as terrorism.[106] Elsewhere, Yogi Adityanath, chief minister of Uttar Pradesh, portrayed the opposition Congress party as infected by a "green virus," projecting its Muslim supporters as an unwanted, untreatable sickness.[107]

Vigilantes had lynched Muslim men for allegedly killing cows. Social media was filled with incendiary propaganda about the forced conversion of Hindu girls by Muslim boys under the hashtag #love-jihad. Critics of the B.J.P. were branded as anti-nationals. Party officers proposed erasing or downplaying key personages and episodes in India's history that foregrounded Islam – even the Mughals.[108] India was becoming Hindu-stan, with an argument emerging that Muslims in India should migrate to the Islamic Republic of Pakistan next door – or elsewhere.[109]

In this incendiary atmosphere, Modi galvanized support from Indian voters who were exhausted by proxy wars and covert bombings – many of which were genuine terror, carried out despite the I.S.I. or in its sight, while some were ambiguous attacks, magnified or managed by elements in R.A.W.–I.B.

Lt. Gen. Asif Yasin Malik, who had spent many years inside the I.S.I., told us: "I just don't get it." Pakistan was engaging in generational restructuring, he said. "Change now, they insist."

Maybe so, we said, but until Pakistan addressed worrying inconsistencies, Rawalpindi and Aabpara would never see their ideas gain traction. After Pulwama, there had been Jaish roundups inside Pakistan, with almost fifty organizers and fighters arrested, but Masood Azhar remained a free man, albeit under dialysis in a military clinic in Pakistan's Punjab, which felt like a metaphor. Azhar was part amulet, part-time gofer, emissary, and Aabpara whipping boy, but he was not in jail. This meant that many outside Pakistan continued to believe that facing a far larger army next door, Pakistan refused to strip insurgent culture back to the boards, as proxies remained Rawalpindi's force multiplier. Or, we asked, was it that the state was too weak to exorcize massing right-wing insurrectionists like the Jaish, Lashkar, and other talibans?

Asif Yasin Malik was not a man to publicly entertain faults or weaknesses, which to him were the companions of defeat. However, Major General Ghulam Qamar messaged next. A soldier-thinker, working on a doctorate in Britain, he was moving to the highly sensitive division that looked after Pakistan's nuclear policy. But before Qamar disappeared into that dark box, he was developing new counter-insurgency strategies for the Pakistan security forces. "Imagine for a moment," he told us, "that the U.K. had an army of 250,000 Islamic minutemen who were battle hardened and needed to be stood down. How would the U.K. do it without collapsing the state? That is our quandary. Mainstreaming, killing, intimidating, bribing, cajoling, empowering, diminishing? You name it we are trying it – without signposting it – but with so much religion and armour knocking around Pakistan it's incredibly hard and we are nowhere near as robust as the U.K. Even you with your wealth and old institutions were ground down by the Irish Republican Army." The I.R.A. had fought the heavily armed British security forces to a standstill in England and Northern Ireland, with perhaps only a few hundred hard-core fighters, armed with Semtex and AK-47s.[110]

A call came in from an I.S.I. station chief in Europe. A Punjabi I.S.I. officer, he suggested something extraordinary. Pulwama was a false flag operation conducted by New Delhi, he claimed. "Look hard at the bomber," he said, "check the Kashmiri newspapers and you will see this Dar was arrested in Shopian in 2017 and tortured by Indian security forces, after which these types become assets of Indian intelligence. Pulwama means we get sanctioned, lose the new Trump pact, and Modi wins a landslide victory."

Some truth was bound with pernicious fiction. The next morning this story was running on Pakistan news portals and an Indian intelligence contact, who had been involved in I.B.'s Kashmir policy, called us. "Does anyone believe this crap?" he complained, exasperated, explaining that the man arrested in Shopian in 2017 was Adil *Hussein* Dar, a completely different Dar, with a different middle name. The Pulwama bomber was Adil *Ahmed* Dar, who had not been arrested before and was not an I.B. asset.[111]

Several South Asian online portals told us that stories on this older encounter had, over the last twenty-four hours, been edited by unseen hands. Internet versions were revised so that the Pulwama bomber's name was inserted in the older Shopian stories, so that he seemed to be an I.B. asset. Spy games were at play by seasoned officers on both sides of the border who knew that once the past was edited the future remained clouded.

Deputy N.S.A. Rajinder Khanna was worried. "They're trying to wriggle out of this again," Khanna told us. "Don't you think? We *know* them. The I.S.I. is reaching out to you and selling you spoiled goods and imbedding doubt, so you think it's not them. This is their modus. Our troops are dead."

We had many questions for Khanna. If the grid in Kashmir was so all-seeing, how did Pulwama happen at all? Explosives, sourced in India, had been transported across the Valley and given to a young man reported missing by his parents in March 2018, who appeared on multiple lists compiled by I.B. and the state police as a likely insurgent, who was "under surveillance." There had been at least four warnings about a Pulwama-style attack, we had been told by an I.B. officer. Pakistan missed the bomb plot, but India did too. The Jaish was in the frame but not the I.S.I. Khanna did not agree: "India is not infallible, but Pakistan chooses not to look," he said. "And when Pakistan 'slips up' by not preventing an attack, it is Indian blood that is spilled." Could we see the forensics for Pulwama, we asked? "They will come," Khanna assured us.

Twelve days after the Pulwama attack, Indian Air Force jets struck a hillside in Balakot, a town north of Muzaffarabad, in Pakistan. India reporters claimed that three precision munitions, bought from Israel, known as Spice 2000, a variant of the U.S. J.D.A.M. used in Afghanistan – a 2000-pound dumb bomb strapped into a GPS or electro-optically guided cradle – had destroyed a Jaish base, with up to 350 fighters killed.[112]

As the Pakistan press exploded, fighter jets from there entered Indian airspace, dropped a few bombs, and left for home, having chosen to hit nothing. However, during a dog fight, the theatre of this skirmish turned lethal, with an Indian MiG-21 brought down, its pilot captured.

India immediately re-nosed the event, claiming that as Wing Commander Abhinandan Varthaman crashed, he managed to shoot down a Pakistan F16 jet, packing this claim with radar images, electronic signatures, and transcripts.[113] All of this was roundly rejected by Pakistan, whose gesture of returning the wing commander, live on TV, won the optics battle, and plaudits from fearful peacemakers at home and around the world.

Washington, some of whose F16s Pakistan's Air Force had flown into India, stayed out of it. European, Australian, and American intelligence officers and analysts – with less to lose – said they had yet to see any evidence to back the fatality figures, warning that the Balakot camp was defunct, three missiles failed to hit, through a targeting error or by choice, and no Pakistani F16 was missing.[114] Ambiguity and circumstantial evidence ruled the day. What was brought down, certainly, was an Indian military helicopter, struck by friendly fire, with six crew members tragically dying.[115]

We talked to Ajit Doval. A report on Pulwama was coming, Doval assured us, and it would lay bare the I.S.I.'s involvement. Balakot, he said, was pivotal for India. "What really matters is the operation itself, that India has changed its strategic calculations." A new escalatory codex was written. The threat of nuclear weapons, deployed by both sides, no longer prevented tactical strikes. Covert attacks by Islamabad-backed forces would now draw conventional responses from Delhi. "This India will not sit on its hands or differentiate between Pakistan and its proxies," he said.

This was clear, but what about the proactive operations that got India here, like sculpting the life and death of Burhan Wani, we asked, and pitching Kashmir into chaos out of which the revoking of Article 370 was realized, but so was Pulwama? Intelligence agencies creating the conditions for legislators to implement policy switches, was, after all, a standard ploy of the C.I.A. and others. R.A.W.–I.B. were now doing what outfits around the world had done for years. Ajit Doval, who headed off to a meeting with the Saudis, did not agree – or disagree.

Three months after Pulwama, Narendra Modi and the B.J.P. won a landslide election, in which there was one of the highest-ever turnouts. That the persuasive spectacle of the Balakot strike had been on Modi's mind, and Ajit Doval's, was accidentally revealed when police in Mumbai began investigating tampering in TV viewing data, where statistics that purport to show audience share for TV channels and against which advertising revenues are raised, were said to be being manipulated. A charge sheet filed carried an appendix that contained a transcript of WhatsApp chats between Partho Dasgupta, the former chief of the Broadcast Audience Research Council, and Arnab Goswami, of Republic TV.

Goswami wrote to Dasgupta about the impending top-secret Balakot strikes, three days before they happened, a source telling him that people would be "elated," which was good for the "big man" in "this season."[116]

After Balakot, the feverish work continued in all theatres. At the U.N., persistent and convincing Indian lobbying paid off. Escapologist Masood Azhar, despite mounting allegations, had never been proscribed by the United Nations. China, which held a veto, used it, in deference to Pakistan. Beijing did not want Islamabad to be tarnished in international forums. Until Pulwama. Now, after some black-belt diplomacy by Doval's team, and others in the Indian Ministry of External Affairs, China defaulted, and the cleric was finally sanctioned as an affiliate of al Qaeda, a milestone that was also surreal, given the classified reporting by the I.S.I. that back in 2002 secretly categorized Azhar as an al Qaeda shill.[117] Here, yet again, was proof of the harmful disparity between private strategizing and the management of public truths in Pakistan.

Finally, in the spring of 2020, as the world was first gripped by Covid-19 and the subcontinent became immobilized, the Pulwama inquiry got traction. Investigators who were probing a Jaish bomb maker, Umar Farooq, who was killed by the security forces in Kashmir in March 2019, after Pulwama, had recovered his Samsung Galaxy Note 9 and sent it to a lab.

Many barren months of form filling followed, and waiting, with a court order taking an age to bake, before the phone was handed to technicians. Finally, they fished from it sixteen hours of voice messages, videos, photographs, and call records that revealed an extraordinary disregard for operational security, and an unexpected connection between Umar Farooq and Pulwama, but also clues that would make this bomb maker and his missions emblematic of the age.[118]

Umar Farooq was not an ordinary man. He was born in August 1996, in Bahawalpur, where Masood Azhar, soldier Amjad Farooqi, Jaish turncoat Gazi Baba, and British insurgent Rashid Rauf either hailed from or went to ground, and so many others in Brigadier Azmat's blue binders that if this city in Pakistan's southern Punjab was moved to France, it would be entitled to apply for a jihad *appellation*.

Umar's father was Ibrahim Athar Alvi, the older brother of Masood Azhar (Alvi), who, the R.A.W. was certain, had played a central role in the hijacking of IC 814, another of the seminal creation stories for the epoch of terror. That hijacking happened when Umar was only three years old. This lineage meant that when he was sixteen, Umar was also inducted into the family business.

In the spring of 2016, by the time Umar was twenty years old, he was sent to be indentured in guns and bombs by his uncle Ammar Alvi, who was a launch pad commander, a man whose job it was to exfiltrate fighters into neighbouring countries, especially India. But Pakistan was changing, and Umar did not go to a camp in-country, like Balakot. It had been shuttered by the I.S.I. – before Pulwama. Instead, the phone data reveals that the Pakistani crackdown inside the country meant that Umar headed for Jaish's new and improvised training facility in Sangin, in Helmand province, Afghanistan, where he was billeted with fighters and instructors allied to foreign jihad fronts, including diehards from al Qaeda, who were all opposed to the I.S.I. and the Pakistan deep state.

Returning to Bahawalpur in 2017, Umar married Afeera Bibi (eight months his junior) in 2018. A wedding never augured well. In these circles it was solely designed to create progeny for a wife who would raise them, as – likely fatherless – future fighters and schemers. Umar, married off, soon joined his uncle Masood Azhar to celebrate another departure. They said goodbye to his brother Usman Ibrahim Alvi, who had also trained in Sangin, as a sniper. And in 2018, he was infiltrated into Jammu via Shakar Garh, north-east of Lahore, not far from where the Pakistan Rangers have their headquarters.

Umar's turn came in April 2018, when he left pregnant Afeera behind and, with two others, scrambled over the border, popping up close to Hiranagar, south-east of Jammu. Indian intelligence believed they brought along some explosives, possibly as much as 30 kilos. However, reports from the D.I.A. and I.B. concluded that at least 165 kilos more was obtained in Kashmir, which was mixed with aluminium powder, in similar proportions to the device that destroyed the Marriott Hotel in Islamabad. The design and components for this bomb that was being constructed in Kashmir are telling. It shared the engineering hallmarks of 313 Brigade, and those devices built by the school of Amjad Farooqi, Ilyas Kashmiri, and Majors Pasha and Haroon – all of whom led the harrying of the Pakistan security state too. These forensic details implied that Pulwama was another of those operations intended to canvas for a regional, end-of-days war, by the forces that had turned on Rawalpindi, and the U.S. pact, back in 2002.

Nothing happened until October 2018, when Umar received news that his brother, the sniper, had been shot dead in the Valley. A call to, and messages from, Jaish leaders suggested a revenge strike was impending, devised by Umar: a brother honouring a brother.

A house in Kakapora, in the Valley, was taken over to assemble two I.E.D.s, with extraordinary selfies taken in January 2019 by Umar and Adil Ahmed Dar, the local-boy-turned-bomber, their faces smothered in metallic powder, like tinmen from Oz.

An accomplice finished off the shopping they required using his Amazon online account. They procured a car and waited. Messages and voice notes exchanged between Jaish leaders then explicitly called on targetters to trigger a war between India and Pakistan. They suggested a repeat of 26/11, with a massive strike in Kashmir that would "inflame India" and push it to attack Pakistan.

Finally, the target was chosen, and a day, all of which was signed off in calls and messages to Jaish, where Ammar and another Alvi brother, Rauf, the military commander, gave the green light. According to Western intelligence services, scanning the Durand Line, both were using their Pakistan-purchased mobile phones, that were triangulated to an area around the Sangin compound, in Helmand, where Umar trained.

The inner workings of the conspiracy revealed complexities that the I.S.I. and Indian intelligence did not want to highlight to the public at large.

Jaish was still deadly, but now in the way that al Qaeda was. It had sublimated from a Pakistan entity, rooted in Punjab, with I.S.I. care, into a regional and even global terror front that blended with al Qaeda, Pakistan talibans and elements of the Islamic State. Its strategists were in Afghanistan, along with key members of the Alvi family. Its propaganda wing – as well as the ailing Masood Azhar – remained in Punjab. The outfit detested Pakistan as much as it did India, both of which it viewed as "heretical states."

The unedited data was not what Delhi projected, after Pulwama, instead preferring to humiliate the Pakistan military. And the uncomfortable truth for the I.S.I. was that after two decades of gnarly bloodshed, the security services were still confounded by armed Islamist groups whose members were too numerous to defeat with bullets and bombs. Their dispersed operations – melding men from the Jaish, the Pakistan Taliban, the LeJ, Jundullah (Jaish ul-Adl), and Islamic State – remained deadly, and many of them now trained and planned in Afghanistan and other out-of-the-way places. Inside Pakistan, there was also a nagging concern that an old guard of spies and soldiers who were *lifers* – colonels in their sixties and seventies – continued to hold sway over the portfolios for Afghanistan, Kashmir and elsewhere, officers who resisted change and, according to junior I.S.I. officers, were reluctant to jettison their strategy of proxies as force multipliers, despite the havoc that wrought.

The I.S.I. needed to address these questions, the legacy of barbarism and the state's lack of transparency, as well as its covert side deals with other nations, something they were reminded of when in February 2021 the Pakistan Supreme Court called for the freeing of "forever prisoner" Omar Sheikh, as the Briton had served time for the kidnapping of Daniel Pearl, and insisted he was not guilty of the journalist's brutal murder after all.[119]

The action upset Pearl's family, understandably, and triggered the new Biden administration, which indicated that despite "Howdy Modi," that 2019 rally in Texas, and "Namaste Trump," the return match in 2020 in Gujarat, and the frequent snipes by Indian officials at Democrat lawmakers who spoke out against communal violence in Delhi and the resurgent conflict in Kashmir, he would continue building the figurative Indo-Pacific pact.[120] The Biden administration also reopened negotiations to extradite Omar Sheikh to the U.S., ostensibly for the abduction in Delhi of the American backpacker in 1994.[121]

However, this story has a coda. I.S.I. officers who worked the original Pearl case insist that Omar Sheikh was charged with murder, even though there was insufficient evidence to proceed at the time, because Musharraf demanded closure, as he was being pressurized by the White House, the C.I.A., the State Department, as well as the F.B.I. Once Omar Sheikh was jailed, and convicted, despite insisting that he played a role in Pearl's abduction only, the Briton wrote a note accusing an LeJ commander, Atta ur-Rehman, of Pearl's murder.

But this was also problematic for the I.S.I. Rehman, since 2002, had been wanted by Aabpara as he was a conduit between al Qaeda and Pakistan sectarian groups, like Ilyas Kashmiri and soldier Amjad Farooqi, who mentored him to attack the state. Rehman appeared as a deadly, hate figure in Azmat's blue binders, which detailed how he was sent by Farooqi to Afghanistan for military training in the Khost area, before he began operating back in Pakistan, where he never used a mobile or couriers, and relied on public pay phones and family messengers, which kept him out of earshot.

However, Rehman was "betrayed by a family member," and secretly arrested in June 2002 in a northern suburb of Karachi. The I.S.I. then secretly concluded that Rehman was central to the abduction and death of Pearl, but his capture and connections were suppressed for five years, with Rehman vanishing into a black site, as the I.S.I. knew that this intelligence undermined the case against Omar Sheikh.[122]

The Briton was charged with the murder and abduction of Pearl three days after the secret detention of Rehman, who would be held, off the grid, until 2007, when the police in northern Sindh announced his "arrest." Two years later, in 2009, Rehman appeared in court, but over the seven years he was in secret custody, the police was incapable of building a case and had amassed so little prosecutable evidence that only a single charge of weapons possession was proffered. Even this collapsed, and Rehman was back out on the streets, slotting into a cell controlled by the al Qaeda amalgam that was behind the lethal attacks on the Mehran naval base, the Kamra airbase, I.S.I. H.Q. in Lahore, Karachi airport, and many others.

In March 2007, another would-be Pearl murderer emerged. This diversion was triggered by the C.I.A. – eager to prove its notorious Enhanced Interrogation programme was working – that claimed that Khalid Sheikh Mohammad, the alleged 9/11 architect, who vanished into C.I.A. black sites after his capture in Rawalpindi in March 2003, confessed also to Pearl's killing. The F.B.I. then weighed in claiming it was able to match the video of Pearl's killer, circulated after his murder, with the veins on Mohammad's hands.[123] However, Mohammad's confession was inadmissible in court, because of the brutal tactics used by the Agency in coercing it and he later retracted it completely, claiming he had made it up to stop the torture.

In 2015, the I.S.I. pounced on LeJ commander Rehman again, and stashed him in a holding cell, even as the Sindh home ministry announced a bounty of $125,000 on his head. Rehman was turned over to the courts in 2016, which convicted him in 2020, when he was executed, without him ever being publicly challenged over the murder of Pearl, which he had admitted.

The politicized, partisan, and incomplete investigation into Omar Sheikh by the I.S.I., the secret detention of Rehman and his execution, all coloured the Pearl inquiry just as the mauling of Mohammad by the C.I.A. – and others put through the Enhanced Interrogation programme – prevented justice being served for the victim families of 9/11. Twenty years after that catastrophe, no one has gone on trial.

In the Pulwama inquiry, however, there were many new facts that also chafed with earlier versions of the outrage sold by R.A.W.–I.B., and that had taken India to the brink of war with Pakistan, prior to the election. While the forensic evidence convincingly nailed Jaish for the outrage, it did not incriminate Rawalpindi, as the perpetrators of the appalling convoy bombing also canvassed to collapse the Pakistan state.

A message came through from an I.S.I. C-Wing brigadier, asking us for news. We used the opportunity to request for Pakistan's Balakot report that we had been promised by the I.S.I. many months before and that never materialized. He said that it would be ready soon but, in the meantime, he wanted to tell us that he was "delighted" with the optics post the Pulwama skirmishes. Pakistan had fended off the F.A.T.F. blacklist threat again, remaining on the grey list. "I think we are reaching you people," he said. "And that is so important these days. Getting our story out there. Getting it straight. We had a respectable war over Balakot. A good war."

We confronted him with the intelligence from Umer's phone that showed how Jaish had survived the I.S.I. cull and remained deadly, in Afghanistan, but with Masood Azhar still talking up war inside Pakistan. We mentioned Omar Sheikh and the unresolved Pearl case, about how despite the billions invested in Pakistan, criminal justice remained fragile, even as the military bristled with new capabilities.

The general weighed the information. "Ask our Indian cousins over the border. These days, in everything, facts come second to perception," he said. "What is the difference between a good lawyer and a great lawyer?" he asked us. "The former knows the law. But the latter knows the judge."

Two colossal rivals, Aabpara and Lodhi Road, would continue to trade versions and allegations, while the Pulwama families remained inconsolable and Kashmir festered, its resentment flowing beneath a brittle crust, glowing and deadly.

~

Pakistan Air Force Asghar Khan Academy, Khyber Pakhtunkhwa, February 3, 2021: a surprise announcement. "Pakistan and India must resolve the long-standing issue of Jammu and Kashmir in a dignified and peaceful manner as per the aspirations of the people of Jammu and Kashmir," General Qamar Javed Bajwa, army chief, told reporters. At the LoC, where India and Pakistan had been murderously shelling one another, with Pakistan alleging there had been 3000 violations of a 2003 ceasefire, during which dozens of civilians had died and scores were injured, the big guns fell quiet.

Outside the region, hope swelled as news leaked of a backchannel, instigated by the Saudis and shepherded by another Gulf monarchy, who were praised for having pulled this rabbit out of a hat.[124] But in Aabpara and Lodhi Road senior officers were looking towards Ajit Doval. His scorched earth policy in Kashmir, and elsewhere, had forcibly removed from the table issues that had been up for grabs under Musharraf – including Kashmir, which was now assimilated.

"Thanks to Doval's blitzkrieg, we can, at last, afford to negotiate, pleasing our new best friends in the U.S. because we have little to give," a senior R.A.W. officer told us, echoing the conclusions drawn by Doval after the IC 814 debacle, all those years ago. Talking was useless, unless the outcome was predictable. India could now put the onus on Pakistan to respond, knowing that the military there had not forked the ground, domestically, for a deal.

Winning the peace in new India required that Pakistan tacitly accepted defeat, while critics in-country (from climate activists to lawyers and even fact-checkers) were jailed, indicted, or cable-whipped on social media. Over the border, agreeing to talk ensured legacy for Pakistan's military leaders, while at home some of their civilian critics were being similarly beaten and vanished.

And on both sides of the border, an entire disbelieving class of citizens shrugged their shoulders. Or opposed the dangled talks as a sideshow.

Long promised development – education, robust healthcare, and real, salaried jobs – were in peril, as a decade's worth of economic and social advances were undone by a cruel and inexhaustible pandemic.

Its real cost was being manipulated and concealed in a region where now brute power – disguised as patriotism – trumped individual rights but also facts.

Notes

Prologue

1. "The C.I.A. in Hollywood: How the Agency Shapes Film and Television," Tricia Jenkins, University of Texas Press, March 2013.
2. "Alleged Assassination Plots Involving Foreign Leaders," Senate Select Committee to Study Government Operations with Respect to Intelligence Activities, November 20, 1975, see https://www.intelligence.senate.gov/sites/default/files/94465.pdf.
3. The so-called Kubark interrogation manual was first produced in 1963 and then revised in 1983 and used in Latin America until 1987, see https://nsarchive2.gwu.edu//NSAEBB/NSAEBB27/02-01.htm.
4. "The Caring, Sharing CIA," John Patterson, *The Guardian*, October 5, 2001, https://www.theguardian.com/film/2001/oct/05/artsfeatures.
5. "Tequila, Painted Pearls, and Prada: How the CIA Helped Produce 'Zero Dark Thirty'," Jason Leopold and Ky Henderson, Vice, https://www.vice.com/en/article/xw3ypa/tequila-painted-pearls-and-prada-how-the-cia-helped-produce-zero-dark-thirty.
6. "Artists Write 'Homeland Is Racist' Graffiti on Set," BBC News, https://www.bbc.co.uk/news/world-us-canada-34536434.
7. "New Delhi Office Vacant as RAW Not Willing to Share," Saikat Datta, *Hindustan Times*, November 10, 2013, https://www.hindustantimes.com/india/new-delhi-office-vacant-as-raw-not-willing-to-share/story-c3eKjgHPD8ZfNDAcnmvtbI.html; and "Government Looking for Tenants for Research and Analysis Wing Building in Delhi," M.K. Tikku, *India Today*, March 31, 1978, https://www.indiatoday.in/magazine/indiascope/story/19780331-government-looking-for-tenants-for-

research-and-analysis-wing-building-in-delhi-823333-2014-12-22.

8. "CBI Raids ex-RAW Officer Who Wrote Book Questioning His Agency Bosses," Teena Thacker, *Indian Express*, September 21, 2007, http:// archive.indianexpress.com/news/cbi-raids-exraw-officer-who-wrote-book-questioning-his-agency-bosses-/219738/.

9. "Reforming Intelligence Agencies in Pakistan's Transitional Democracy," Frédéric Grare, Carnegie Endowment for International Peace, 2009, http://pircenter.org/kosdata/page_doc/p1870_2.pdf – see attempts to charter I.S.I., etc., in 2008 by Bhutto and Sharif with their "Charter of Democracy," pp. 42–43.

10. "Pakistan Army Orders Asad Durrani's Name Be Put on ECL, Launches Probe into His Book," Web Desk, *The News*, May 28, 2018, https://www. thenews.com.pk/latest/322557-pakistan-army-orders-asad-durranis-name-be-put-on-ecl-orders-probe-into-his-book.

11. The accounts of how the I.S.I. processed the proposal came from senior officers at the briefing, and also from officers within the I.S.I. who were briefed after the meetings and spoke with us in five interviews between October 2017 and November 2019.

12. Author tape archive: interview, Rawalpindi, March 2019.

13. "India, Pakistan NSAs Meet in Bangkok," Suhasini Haidar, *The Hindu*, December 6, 2015, https://www.thehindu.com/news/national/national-security-advisers-of-india-and-pakistan-meeting-in-bangkok/article7955001.ece; and "External Affairs Ministry Confirms Meeting of India, Pakistan NSAs in Bangkok," Kallol Bhattacherjee, *The Hindu*, January 12, 2018, https://www.thehindu.com/news/national/india-confirms-nsas-met-in-bangkok/article22424061.ece.

14. Told to the authors by I.S.I. interlocutors with the Saudis in March 2019 and February 2020.

15. "An Extraordinary Link for Archenemies in Spying," James Risen, *Los Angeles Times*, December 31, 1997, https://www.latimes.com/archives/la-xpm-1997-dec-31-mn-3817-story.html.

Part 1: The Back Story

1. Author tape archive: interviews conducted between 2017 and 2020 in the United Arab Emirates and Rawalpindi.

2. "Israeli Spyware Firm Accused of Hacking Apple, Facebook and Google Responds," Zak Doffman, *Forbes*, July 19, 2019, https://www.forbes.com/sites/zakdoffman/2019/07/19/israeli-whatsapp-spyware-now-targets-icloud-google-and-facebook-via-phones-report/?sh=4016be693e9f; and "Israeli Tech Company Says It Can Unlock All iPhones Ever Made," TOI Staff, *Times of Israel*, June 17, 2019, https://www.timesofisrael.com/israeli-tech-company-says-it-can-break-into-all-iphones-ever-made-some-androids/.

3. "Pakistan Journalist Saleem Shahzad Found Dead," May 31, 2011, BBC News, https://www.bbc.co.uk/news/world-south-asia-13599172.

4. Book Excerpts, The Print, August 11, 2019, https://theprint.in/pageturner/excerpt/in-1947-gandhi-told-lt-gen-sen-that-wars-were-inhuman-but-to-fight-for-kashmir-by-all-means/273779/; and *Slender Was the Thread*, L.P. Sen, Orient Blackswan, 1994.

5. Author tape archive: interview in April 2016 with two senior I.B. officers who wrote an unofficial history of I.B.'s evolution, taking in the 1960s wars.

6. Victor Marchetti and John Marks estimated that the C.I.A. portion of the "black budget" was $750 million, as it was 12 per cent of the overall black budget which was then $6.228 billion. See *The C.I.A. and the Cult of Intelligence*, Victor Marchetti and John Marks, Alfred Knopf, 1974, 61, 81.

7. Forty-five per cent of its landmass was ceded to Delhi, with 35 per cent held by Pakistan and the remainder (an area in the north-east of the state called Aksai Chin) under China's control.

8. Deputy Defense Secretary Roswell Gilpatrick to Secretary of State Dean Rusk, August 9, 1961, see the National Security Archive, George Washington University, Washington, D.C., also quoted in *Pakistan's Inter-Services Intelligence Directorate*, Owen L. Sirrs, Routledge, 2017.

9. "Role of R&AW in Liberation of Bangladesh," B. Raman, *Indian Defence Review*, 2013, http://www.indiandefencereview.com/spotlights/role-of-raw-in-liberation-of-bangladesh/; excerpted from *The Kaoboys of R&AW*, B. Raman, Lander Publications, 2012.

10. "RAW Reduced to a Pathetic Parody of a Government Department," Dilip Bobb, *India Today*, July 15, 1981.

11. Ibid.; and also, Delhi High Court, *Satya Vir Singh and Ors. vs Union of India and Ors*, September 25, 1981, ILR 1981 Delhi 713, 1982 Label C 663, https://indiankanoon.org/doc/1937185/?type=print.

12. Ibid.

13. Author tape archive.

14. "Soviet Gave Money to 40 per cent Congress MPs in Indira Gandhi Era: CIA Report," IANS, *Business Standard*, January 30, 2017, https://www.business-standard.com/article/politics/soviet-gave-money-to-40-congress-mps-in-indira-gandhi-era-cia-report-117013000796_1.html.

15. "A.K. Verma's Demise – An Irreparable Loss to Security and Strategic Community," C.D. Sahay, September 5, 2016, https://www.vifindia.org/article/2016/september/05/ak-verma-s-demise-an-irreparable-loss-to-security-and-strategic-community. Also, "Remembering RAW's God of War in the Time of Uri Attack," Sandeep Unnithan, DailyO, September 20, 2016, https://www.dailyo.in/politics/uri-attack-raw-anand-kumar-verma-indian-army-cit-x-rn-kao-boys-rajiv-gandhi-intel/story/1/13004.html.

16. *By Way of Deception: The Making of a Mossad Officer*, Victor Ostrovsky, St Martin's Press, 1990.

17. Author tape archive: interview with B. Raman, Chennai, 2004.

18. Towards the end of the 1990s the G.D.P. for Pakistan was registered at between $50 and $52 billion. See "GDP Growth (Annual %) – Pakistan," World Bank, https://data.worldbank.org/indicator/NY.GDP.MKTP.KD.ZG?locations=PK. Estimates on the heroin business placed the value at towards $65 billion for the same period, see "World Drug Report," United Nations Office of Drug Control, p. 37, https://www.unodc.org/documents/wdr/WDR_2010/1.2_The_global_heroin_market.pdf. According to the U.N., Af-Pak would come to monopolize 97 per cent of the global heroin-morphine market, see https://www.unodc.org/pdf/research/wdr07/WDR_2007_1.2_opium_heroin.pdf. However, critics of R.A.W. analysis in Europe claim this larger number is far too general, and that a regional figure for opium's local value, after the fall of the Taliban, was $4 billion, which was the equivalent of half of Afghanistan's G.D.P. A U.N.O.D.C. report from 2007 agrees with this number, see https://web.archive.org/web/20110618011240/http://www.unodc.org/india/afghanistan_gdp_report.html.

19. The allegation was made against Imtiaz Ahmed, known as Billa, the green-eyed cat, who rose to be a brigadier, but whose close association with Nawaz Sharif saw him fall out of favour with Pervez Musharraf,

leading to Ahmed's jailing. Post-Musharraf, Brig. Ahmed was released and claimed he was the victim of a political witch hunt. See "Former Brig Imtiaz Released from Adiala Jail," *Business Recorder*, September 26, 2010, https://fp.brecorder.com/2010/09/201009261106129/.

20. Author tape archive: eight interviews with Lt. Gen. Hamid Gul between 1999 and 2014, in Rawalpindi and Dubai.

21. Ibid. Gul kept figures too. His calculations were based on direct financing of the military and interest payments on military purchases, which absorbed in 1988 around 4 per cent of G.D.P., officially. The military's own accounting refers to a figure that was commonly 40 per cent higher than the publicly quotes ones. See also the Stockholm International Peace Institute for similar findings. An overview is available here: *Military Budgets in India and Pakistan: Trajectories, Priorities, and Risks*, Shane Mason, Stimson Centre, 2016, https://www.stimson.org/wp-content/files/file-attachments/Military-Budgets-India-Pakistan-Trajectories-Priorities-Risks-Oct2016.pdf.pdf.

22. "Zia of Pakistan Killed as Blast Downs Plane; U.S. Envoy, 28 Others Die," Elaine Sciolino, *New York Times*, August 18, 1988, https://www.nytimes.com/1988/08/18/world/zia-of-pakistan-killed-as-blast-downs-plane-us-envoy-28-others-die.html.

23. References to these robberies and kidnapping are many, see, for example, this one, on a later plan to analyse criminal–terror connections, which reflects on the kidnappings and robberies from an earlier period. "ATS to Monitor Theft, Robberies, Extortion Cases," Nikhil Dixit, *DNA*, March 9, 2009, https://www.dnaindia.com/mumbai/report-ats-to-monitor-theft-robberies-extortion-cases-1237653; and here, "Who Is Aftab Ansari?" *Times of India*, January 25, 2002, https://timesofindia.indiatimes.com/city/kolkata/whos-aftab-ansari/articleshow/1210220186.cms.

24. The quotes are from a secondary Hadith collection, Majmau al-Zawa'id wa Manba al-Fawa'id, written by Ali ibn Abu Bakr al-Haythami. A version was printed by Mu'assash al-Ma'arif in Beirut in 1986.

25. "The Murder of Murtaza Bhutto" was an R.A.W. analytical briefing, prepared by analysts at Lodhi Road, and discussed with us by one of the authors. Author tape archive.

26. Author tape archive: interviews in London and Dubai in 2007, during which Bhutto told us she too believed that the I.S.I. had a hand in her brother's murder.

27. "Court Challenges Put Unusual Spotlight on Pakistani Spy Agency," Declan Walsh, *New York Times*, February 6, 2012, https://www.nytimes.com/2012/02/07/world/asia/isi-in-pakistan-faces-court-cases.html.

28. "Thirty Years Later, We Still Do Not Know Who Betrayed These Spies," David Wise, *Smithsonian Magazine*, November 2015, https://www.smithsonianmag.com/history/still-unexplained-cold-war-fbi-cia-180956969//.

29. "Senior RAW-Man Arrested, Charged with Spying for the US," Inderjit Badhwar, *India Today*, September 30, 1987, https://www.indiatoday.in/magazine/indiascope/story/19870930-senior-raw-man-arrested-charged-with-spying-for-us-799359-1987-09-30.

30. Ibid.

31. We collated twenty-four attempts and warnings by the Defence Ministry, from 2004 to 2018. See also "BrahMos Engineer Arrested for Espionage May Have Been a Target of Honeytrap," Munish Pandey, *India Today*, October 9, 2018, https://www.indiatoday.in/india/story/brahmos-engineer-espionage-honeytrap-1359658-2018-10-09.

32. Author tape archive: interviews with European I.S.I. station chiefs, and counter-intelligence officers in Rawalpindi, August and September 2018.

33. Author tape archive: interview with Indian security services senior officers, from the D.I.A., I.B., and R.A.W., September and October 2017. Also, author interviews with Pervez Musharraf in 2016 and 2017.

34. Author tape archive: interview with Ajit Doval, September 2009.

35. The presence of the car, Cheema, and his suitcase was verified by the airport security log, seen by us in 2004.

36. "Nepal Expels Pak Diplomat," UPI, April 15, 2001, https://www.upi.com/Archives/2001/04/15/Nepal-expels-Pak-diplomat/2509987307200/.

37. Author tape archive: interview with Ajit Doval, September 2009.

Part 2: 9/11 and Its Long Shadow

1. Author tape archive: interviews with Pervez Musharraf 2009, 2011, 2016, 2017, and 2018.

2. Author tape archive: interviews with Porter Goss 2018, Washington, D.C.

3. Author tape archive: interview with George Tenet, 2018, Washington, D.C.

4. Author tape archive: interviews with Mahfouz Ould al-Walid, the Grand Mufti of Al Qaeda, in 2010 and 2012, in Mauritania. He said the phrase was coined by Khalid Sheikh Mohammad, the 9/11 planner.

5. Author archive: a briefing note from Ahmed to Musharraf, dated September 28, 2001, and signed by Musharraf, showing he had read it.

6. Author tape archive: interviews with Musharraf, as above, and also a briefing paper, "Can We Survive a US-led Backlash against Al Qaeda and Taliban?"

7. Ibid.

8. Ibid.

9. Ibid.

10. Two briefs for Musharraf, in response to questions he raised at G.H.Q. – "The Role of the Gun" and "Sectarianism in Pakistan" – both dated October 2001.

11. Author tape archive: interviews with General Ehsan ul-Haq, in 2017, 2018, and 2019 in Islamabad.

12. Author tape archive: interview with Musharraf, 2016.

13. Author tape archive: these accounts were told to the authors by C.I.A. officers serving in Pakistan and India, but also by Musharraf, and the results were seen in media reports shortly after. One example: "Musharraf Dismisses Two Islamist Generals," Luke Harding, *The Guardian*, October 9, 2001, https://www.theguardian.com/world/2001/oct/09/pakistan.afghanistan3.

14. Author tape archive: four interviews with Lt. Gen. Javed Alam Khan in Rawalpindi in 2018 and 2019.

15. This was reproduced in many media outlets, for example, "India Helped FBI Trace ISI Terrorist Links," Manoj Joshi, *Times of India*, October 9, 2001, https://timesofindia.indiatimes.com/india/india-helped-fbi-trace-isi-terrorist-links/articleshow/1454238160.cms.

16. "Our Friends the Pakistanis," James Taranto, *Wall Street Journal*, October 10, 2001, https://911timeline.s3.amazonaws.com/2001/wallstreetjournal101001.html?id=95001298.

17. A Mumbai-based businessman was abducted and shipped to Nepal until a ransom was paid. Others were snatched from Jamshedpur, Rajkot, Patna, Varanasi, Kanpur, and Allahabad, before finally the son of a wealthy shoe magnate was seized in Kolkata.

18. Author tape archive: interviews with Mahfouz Ould al-Walid, former Grand Mufti of Al Qaeda, in 2010 and 2012 in Mauritania.

19. Ibid., and also author correspondence with the legal representatives for Abu Zubaydah, and interviews with al Qaeda clerics in Jordan and Syria, in 2016, 2018, and 2019.

20. Author tape archive: interviews with C.I.A.'s Counterterrorism Center analysts, in 2018 and 2019. Interview with Jose Rodriguez, director of the C.I.A.'s Counterterrorism Centre from May 2002 to November 2004, in Florida, 2019.

21. Author tape archive: interviews with BND (German foreign intelligence service) analysts in 2017 and 2018 in Germany but also Dubai and Pakistan.

22. "Aftab Ansari Has Two Offences in Gujarat: Police," *Outlook Magazine*, April 27, 2005, https://www.outlookindia.com/newswire/story/aftab-ansari-has-two-offences-in-gujarat-police/295035.

23. "Appendix A: The Financing of the 9/11 Plot," in "Terrorist Financing Staff Monograph," National Commission on Terrorist Attacks Upon the United States, https://govinfo.library.unt.edu/911/staff_statements/911_TerrFin_App.pdf.

24. Ibid.

25. "Part of Funding for 9/11 Came from India, Says Top Cop Neeraj Kumar," PTI, *Economic Times*, November 18, 2015, https://economictimes.indiatimes.com/news/politics-and-nation/part-of-funding-for-9/11-came-from-india-says-ex-top-cop-neeraj-kumar/articleshow/49818688.cms?from=mdr.

26. Author tape archive: interviews with Brig. Azmat Hyat in Islamabad, 2019.

27. "Dacoit Leader Malkhan Singh and His Gang Surrender," Sreekant Khanekar, *India Today*, July 15, 1982, https://www.indiatoday.in/magazine/special-report/story/19820715-dacoit-leader-malkhan-singh-and-his-gang-surrender-before-madhya-pradesh-cm-arjun-singh-771949-2013-10-09.

28. "A Nation Challenged: A Suspect; Confession in 1994 Case Evokes Pearl Abduction," Celia Dugger, *New York Times*, February 8, 2002, https://www.nytimes.com/2002/02/08/world/a-nation-challenged-a-suspect-confession-in-1994-case-evokes-pearl-abduction.html?exprod=permalink&partner=permalink.

29. Author tape archive: interviews with Jaish members and officers in Bahawalpur, Pakistan, 1998; and "Masood Azhar Was Mocked," K. Dutta, *India Today*, May 2, 2019, https://www.indiatoday.in/india/story/masood-azhar-global-terrorist-called-motu-at-jihad-camp-1515181-2019-05-02. See also "Exporting Terror," Shekhar Gupta, *India Today*, May 15, 1994, https://www.indiatoday.in/magazine/cover-story/story/19940515-exporting-terror-755620-1994-05-15.

30. Author tape archive: interviews with Syed Asif Ibrahim in Delhi in 2018 and 2019.

31. The fatwa was declared in 1952.

32. Tehrik e-Taliban Pakistan, or T.T.P. – the movement was a coalition formed after the Red Mosque raid in 2007. At least thirteen groups were inside that umbrella with power bases in FATA and elsewhere along the Durand Line, but also, later, in Pakistan's Punjab.

33. "The Terrified Kashmir Families Who Call One of the World's Most Militarized Zones Home," Sophia Saifi, CNN, October 28, 2019, https://edition.cnn.com/2019/10/27/asia/india-pakistan-border-kashmir-intl-hnk/index.html. This piece typifies Western views on Kashmir's militarization. The C.I.A. factbook notes that Kashmir "remains the site of the world's largest and most militarized dispute." See https://www.cia.gov/the-world-factbook/countries/india/. India's security forces maintain that the real number of security services stationed in Jammu and Kashmir is around 400,000, breaking down as 150,000 army, 60,000 R.R. counter-insurgency forces, 130,000 centralized police forces, and 130,000 Jammu and Kashmir police and intelligence officers. See, for example, https://www.rediff.com/news/column/india-has-700000-troops-in-kashmir-false/20180717.htm.

34. In Pakistan-controlled Kashmir.

35. "Kashmir Insurgency," BBC News, http://news.bbc.co.uk/hi/english/static/in_depth/south_asia/2002/india_pakistan/timeline/1989.stm.

36. Author tape archive: we interviewed many of the I.S.I.'s senior executive officers from the U.S. "war on terror" years, within the Analysis, Internal, Counter-terror, and External wings. Interviews were carried out from 2008 until 2020, mostly in Islamabad, Rawalpindi, Lahore, Karachi, Peshawar, and Quetta. But we also conducted interviews in the Gulf states and in Thailand.

37. Author tape archive: five taped interviews with Lt. Gen. Nusrat Naeem in 2018 and 2019 in Rawalpindi.

38. An R.A.W. analysis, dated October 1992, more than 40 pages long, on the funding of the Kashmir project by the I.S.I. made these two allegations, according to the author. This analyst told us it detailed cash flows into the I.S.I. Kashmir project and that it made a recommendation to protest to the U.S. about the "diversion of C.I.A. cash" into an insurgency.

39. The stark assessments on the H.M. and the Hurriyat were dated February 2001.

40. "British Intelligence Tried to Get UVF to 'Shoot Up a School', Documentary Claims," Gerry Moriarty, *Irish Times*, February 20, 2019, https://www.irishtimes.com/news/ireland/irish-news/british-intelligence-tried-to-get-uvf-to-shoot-up-a-school-documentary-claims-1.3800302; and "Security Forces Colluded With Loyalists to Carry Out Killings," Dan Keenan, *Irish Times*, April 18, 2003, https://www.irishtimes.com/news/security-forces-colluded-with-loyalists-to-carry-out-killings-1.356051.

41. Author tape archive: interviews with Yumnam Joykumar Singh in Imphal, Manipur, December 2019.

42. Wikileaks published a classified cable dated April 6, 2005, warning that detention centres in Kashmir tortured captives routinely, and that the Government of India condoned that treatment, as it had snubbed the Red Cross when it made inquiries. https://www.theguardian.com/world/us-embassy-cables-documents/30222. See the cable at https://wikileaks.org/plusd/cables/05NEWDELHI2606_a.html. Also see "Behind the Kashmir Conflict: Abuses by Indian Security Forces and Militant Groups Continue," *Human Rights Watch*, July 1, 1999, https://www.refworld.org/docid/45d0609b2.html.

43. "India's Secret Army in Kashmir: New Patterns of Abuse Emerge in the Conflict," *Human Rights Watch* 8, no. 4 (May 1996), https://www.hrw.org/reports/1996/India2.htm.

44. Author tape archive: three interviews with Kuka Parray, in 1997, 2002, and 2004.

45. Author tape archive: two interviews with Abdul Majeed Dar in Sopore and Pakistan.

46. "The Menace of PSA," A.G. Noorani, *Greater Kashmir*, November 12,

2016, https://www.greaterkashmir.com/news/opinion/gk-exclusive-the-menace-of-psa/.

47. Shortly afterwards, a member of the security forces was murdered, and troops allegedly took revenge, killing fifty to seventy civilians, depending on which sources you read, twenty of them taken from a bus and shot, while 400 to 500 shops and homes were razed. https://www.greaterkashmir.com/news/kashmir/sopore-massacre-when-57-civilians-were-killed-400-shops-and-75-houses-burnt-down/.

48. Son-in-law Hafiz Khalid Waleed was groomed as a potential successor. Brother-in-law Abdul Rehman Makki, who graduated from Medina University, was its strategic force. Son Hafiz Talha Saeed became head of the outfit's university and clerical cell and at one time was launched as a political candidate. Son-in-law Hafiz Khalid Waleed was groomed as a potential successor. Brother-in-law Abdul Rehman Makki, who graduated from Medina University, was its strategist.

49. Author tape archive: four interviews with Rajinder Khanna, in 2018 and 2019 in Mumbai and Delhi.

50. Ibid.

51. We visited in 2007, 2008, and 2010, with members of Lashkar but also with religious students, and interviewed instructors, recruits, undergraduates, and recent graduates. We had briefings with Hafiz Saeed.

52. We visited three times.

53. The I.S.I. estimate of the strength of the LeT was dated to August 2002, and tallied with a second estimate for 2009, showing the outfit flatlining but with far greater numbers than was calculated in the West or India.

54. The I.S.I. report from February 2001 was on Indian intelligence influence on the Lashkar-e-Toiba and Kashmir freedom fighters. Running to 26 pages, it listed incidents and names which led to a conclusion that the outfit was heavily penetrated.

55. Perhaps only the Gaw Kadl mass shooting was worse, when on January 21, 1990 an agitated crowd had massed, after rumours spread of sexual assaults on Kashmiri women, leading to the shooting dead of at least fifty unarmed demonstrators (fatality figures that are disputed). We visited four weeks after the massacre and returned a year later with a team of lawyers.

56. Author tape archive: interviews in Jammu, Kashmir, and Delhi, in 2001, with three I.B. officers who described recruiting post the massacre and how it was used to fracture grassroots networks.

57. "Names of Killer Still Reverberate in My Ears," Aamir Ali Bhat, Firstpost, March 21, 2019, https://www.firstpost.com/india/names-of-killers-still-reverberate-in-my-ears-19-years-after-chittisinghpora-massacre-lone-survivor-recounts-night-that-killed-35-sikhs-6299441.html.

58. The report produced by A-Wing or Analysis, took feeds from C, internal, and the Kashmir desk.

59. Author tape archive: interviews with Rajinder Khanna and four other R.A.W. chiefs, in 2018 and 2019, New Delhi.

60. The report from 2000 concluded that the Ikhwan was more likely to have perpetrated the massacre than Lashkar, and its contents were discussed with us at length. A video emerged which purported to show a retired general saying this too: "Lt Gen Says Indian Army Was Involved in Sikh Massacre of Chittisinghpura," https://freepresskashmir.com/2018/03/20/watch-retired-lt-gen-says-indian-army-was-involved-in-sikh-massacre-of-chittisinghpura/. The Indian defence ministry claims this is a deep fake, but declined to comment on the internal report from 2000, after we submitted our notes, summarizing what it contained.

61. Ibid. A report concluding that government-backed proxies conducted the massacre was submitted to the National Democratic Alliance (N.D.A.) government.

62. "India: Military Court Fails Victims of Kashmir Killings," *Human Rights Watch*, January 24, 2014, https://www.hrw.org/news/2014/01/24/india-military-court-fails-victims-kashmir-killings.

63. Ibid.

64. "Suicide Bomber Targets Badami Bagh Cantonment," Mukhtar Singh, Rediff, December 25, 2000, https://www.rediff.com/news/2000/dec/25jk2.htm.

65. Author archive. A report by I.S.I. C-Wing to D.G.-I.S.I., January 2001, "Badami Bagh, Jaish e-Mohammed, and Political Control."

66. For example, the East African embassy bombings, where explosive-laden vehicles rammed security checkpoints in suicide strikes against U.S. missions that killed 224 and injured more than 4500.

67. He helped found an iteration of Full Moon, a.k.a. the al Badr group.

68. "Militants Attack Kashmir Assembly," October 1, 2001, BBC News, http://news.bbc.co.uk/2/hi/south_asia/1574225.stm.

69. "Case Cracked: Jaish behind Attack," Neeta Sharma and Arun Joshi, *Hindustan Times*, December 16, 2001.

70. Author tape archive: interviews that week with military attachés serving in the European and U.S. embassies.

71. We wrote about this reasoning in our book *The Exile: The Stunning Inside Story of Osama bin Laden and Al Qaeda in Flight*, Bloomsbury, 2017.

72. Author tape archive: four interviews with Lt. Gen. Javed Alam Khan, in 2018 and 2019 in Rawalpindi.

73. "The Rise and Fall of Rajbir Singh," IANS, *Hindustan Times*, March 25, 2008, https://www.hindustantimes.com/delhi/the-rise-and-fall-of-acp-rajbir-singh/story-Sk9JrdkdI61IaCUoutYrnJ.html; but also for context on a trend in Delhi police, see PTI, "SC Upholds Life for 10 Delhi Cops in Fake Encounter Killing," India TV News, May 2, 2011, https://www.indiatvnews.com/news/india/sc-upholds-life-for-10-delhi-cops-in-fake-encounter-killing-7783.html.

74. The reporters were Maneesh Pandey and Shams Tahir Khan for Aaj Tak. See *India Today*, February 10, 2013, https://www.indiatoday.in/afzal-guru-hanging/story/afzal-guru-hanged-helped-the-terrorists-on-promise-of-passage-to-pakistan-india-today-153690-2013-02-10.

75. "And His Life Should Become Extinct," Arundhati Roy, https://www.revolutionarydemocracy.org/afzal/afzal13.htm.

76. "Iftikhar Gilani: No Safeguards in the Official Secrets Act," Mannika, The Hoot, January 3, 2003, http://asu.thehoot.org/media-watch/law-and-policy/iftikhar-gilani-no-safeguards-in-the-official-secrets-act-651.

77. "I Hope My Forced Silence Will be Heard," Afzal Guru, *Outlook*, October 21, 2004, https://www.outlookindia.com/website/story/i-hope-my-forced-silence-will-be-heard/225472.

78. "I Tortured Afzal Guru," Parvaiz Bukhari, Scroll.in, January 13, 2020, https://scroll.in/article/949638/i-tortured-afzal-guru-interview-from-2006-with-arrested-kashmir-police-officer-davinder-singh.

79. The case was heard on October 29, 2003. See "The Case of Afsan Guru," P. Venkatarama, August 4, 2005, *Outlook*, https://www.outlookindia.com/website/story/the-case-of-afsan-guru-navjot-sandhu/228139.

80. This crisis continued until 2015, when the detection rate fell to 25 per cent. See Karn Pratap Singh, "Crimes High Detection Low," *Hindustan Times*, January 5, 2016, https://www.hindustantimes.com/delhi/crime-rate-up-detection-down-delhi-police-solved-only-27-cases-in-2015/story-wDahGWsSQYEkXow0Qdt59O.html.

81. "Crime in Delhi," Satish Golchha, Special Commissioner of Police, http://www.delhipolice.nic.in/CRIMEinDELHI.pdf.

82. State vs Faridullah @ Fareed & Others, June 4, 2010, Delhi District Court, Patiala House, SC No. 45/08 ID No. 02403R0597842005, available at: https://indiankanoon.org/doc/198819232/.

83. "Encounter Specialist Rajbir Singh Killed," PTI, *Hindustan Times*, March 25, 2008, https://www.hindustantimes.com/delhi/encounter-specialist-rajbir-singh-killed/story-GWVpmMv8SFvReVSkelpYYI.html.

84. "Treated Arrested DSP Like Any Other Terrorist," Ashiq Hussain, *Hindustan Times*, January 13, 2020, https://www.hindustantimes.com/india-news/treated-arrested-dsp-like-any-other-militant-police/story-ojA2GgjgndtVw2gTy0fLwL.html.

85. Besides Davinder Singh, others named in the charge sheet are self-styled H.M. commander Syed Naveed Mushtaq alias Naveed Babu, his brother Syed Irfan Ahmad, the group's alleged overground worker Irfan Shafi Mir, alleged accomplice Rafi Ahmad Rather, and businessman Tanveer Ahmad Wani, former president of the Line of Control Traders Association. See "J&K Police DSP Davinder Singh Was Tasked by Pakistan to Establish Contact in MEA: NIA Charge Sheet," PTI, *The Hindu*, August 30, 2020, https://www.thehindu.com/news/national/jk-police-dsp-davinder-singh-was-tasked-by-pakistan-to-establish-contact-in-mea-nia-charge-sheet/article32479851.ece. Davinder Singh denies all allegations.

86. "Terrorist Attack Parliament in India Killing Seven People," Celia W. Dugger, *New York Times*, December 13, 2001, https://www.nytimes.com/2001/12/13/international/terrorists-attack-parliament-in-india-killing-seven-people.html.

87. Author archive. Allegations of torture were made in briefing notes from two Western embassies, seen by us, in February 2013.

88. Author tape archive. An I.B. report we were told about by its author, a senior officer working on the LeT, and a copy was also kept by Thane police, which was discussed with us when we visited there.

89. Ibid.

90. "The Thane Police Claim," *Outlook*, August 11, 2005, https://www.outlookindia.com/website/story/the-thane-police-claim/228231.

91. Thane Police kept a copy of this file, and it was replicated in a brief to

Western intelligence agencies in response to queries over the identification of Hamza. Author tape archive: we interviewed police commissioner, Thane, S.M. Shangari, in September 2002, and in 2003, and he told us he had requested a photo from I.B. post the Parliament attack. He also sent a photo to Delhi and Srinagar of Hamza, after he was captured. Shangari never heard back from the I.B. and there was no follow-up on the man who was sent from Thane to Kashmir.

92. In August 2005, the Supreme Court upheld the Delhi High Court's judgement, acquitting S.A.R. Geelani, while confirming the death sentence awarded to Afzal and modifying the death penalty imposed on Shaukat to 10-year rigorous imprisonment.

93. Author tape archive: Javed Alam Khan, as the former D.G.A., and C.I.A. liaison, was briefed on the terror plot, and told to contain it. Details were shared with Nusrat Naeem.

94. Ḥarkat al-Jihād al-Islāmiyah.

95. "India Accused of Kashmir Massacre," BBC News, February 25, 2000, http://news.bbc.co.uk/1/hi/world/south_asia/656420.stm.

96. "Pak Cross-LoC Raid: Brutality Similar to 2000 Strike by Ilyas Kashmiri," Josy Joseph, *Times of India*, January 10, 2013, https://timesofindia.indiatimes.com/india/Pak-cross-LoC-raid-Brutality-similar-to-2000-strike-by-Ilyas-Kashmiri/articleshow/17961775.cms.

97. Author tape archive: interviews with I.S.I. Counter Terrorism Centre officers, 2018 and 2019, in Rawalpindi and Islamabad, and with Asif Ibrahim in Delhi, 2018 and 2019. See also *The Meadow: Kashmir 1995 – Where the Terror Began*, Adrian Levy and Cathy Scott-Clark, Harper Press, London, 2012.

98. Author archive and tape archive: interviews with S-Wing operatives who confirmed Farooqi's role as a trainer.

99. The Rendition Project, Ibn Sheikh al-Libi, https://www.therenditionproject.org.uk/prisoners/ibn-sheikh-al-libi.html.

100. "C.I.A. Taught, Then Dropped, Mental Torture in Latin America," Tim Weiner, *New York Times*, January 29, 1997, https://www.nytimes.com/1997/01/29/world/cia-taught-then-dropped-mental-torture-in-latin-america.html.

101. See *The Exile*, Cathy Scott-Clark and Adrian Levy.

102. Author interviews with "Aimen Deen" in London 2017. He worked for al

Qaeda and also was an asset for MI6, becoming close to Abu Zubaydah and al-Libi, having frequently travelled to Peshawar and the Khaldan camp. We also interviewed Abu Zubaydah via his legal team, in an exchange of letters to Guantanamo, where he is being held. More of this can be seen on *Forever Prisoner*, a documentary feature produced by us and directed by Alex Gibney on HBO Max in September 2021. Finally, author tape archive: six interviews in 2017 and 2018 with I.S.I. Counter Terrorism Centre and I.S.I. S- and C-Wing officers, who detailed the I.S.I. history in assisting the C.I.A.'s high-value detainee programme for al Qaeda fighters in Pakistan.

103. Work on renditions and the Enhanced Interrogation Program is contained in our forthcoming book, *The Forever Prisoner*, Grove, 2021. See also, "Qaeda–Iraq Link U.S Cited Is Tied to Coercion Claim," Douglas Jehl, *New York Times*, December 9, 2005, https://www.nytimes.com/2005/12/09/politics/qaedairaq-link-us-cited-is-tied-to-coercion-claim.html.

104. Author tape archive: interviews with Lt. Gen. Nusrat Naeem, in Rawalpindi, in 2018 and 2019.

105. "Libya/U.S.: Investigate Death of Former CIA Prisoner," *HRW News*, May 11, 2009, https://www.hrw.org/news/2009/05/11/libya/us-investigate-death-former-cia-prisoner.

106. President Bush revealed the capture at a lunch in Greenwich, Connecticut, on April 9, 2002, describing Abu Zubaydah as a "top operative," https://www.presidency.ucsb.edu/documents/remarks-republican-luncheon-greenwich-connecticut. Vice President Dick Cheney and Condoleezza Rice, then national security adviser, describing the detainee as "chief of operations" for al Qaeda and Osama's "third-in-command," according to Ron Suskind, in his book *The One Percent Doctrine*, published in 2006. The false stories about Abu Zubaydah continued, with President Bush repeating them in 2006. See "President Bush's Speech on Terrorism," *New York Times*, September 6, 2006, https://www.nytimes.com/2006/09/06/washington/06bush_transcript.html?pagewanted=all&_r=0.

107. Author tape archive: interviews with the U.S. and Pakistani teams that captured Abu Zubaydah, including John Kiriakou, formerly a case officer at the Agency.

108. The F.B.I. and Senate Intelligence Committee maintained that

no substantial actionable intelligence was derived from Enhanced Interrogation, only false leads sending officers down time-consuming cul-de-sacs. For a full account, see our forthcoming book *The Forever Prisoner*.

109. Author tape archive: interviews with S-Wing brigadier, 2017 and 2018, in Peshawar.

110. "Germany's Involvement in Extraordinary Renditions and Its Responsibility under International Law," Laura Tate Kagel, *German Politics & Society* 25, no. 4 (85) (Winter 2007): pp. 1–30, Berghahn Books.

111. See "Secret Detention Sites," by the European Court of Human Rights, March 2019, https://www.echr.coe.int/documents/fs_secret_detention_eng.pdf; also see, "The results of inquiries into the C.I.A.'s programme of extraordinary rendition and secret prisons in European states in light of the new legal framework following the Lisbon Treaty," https://www.europarl.europa.eu/RegData/etudes/note/join/2012/462456/IPOL-LIBE_NT%282012%29462456_EN.pdf. Also, "A Staggering Map of the 54 Countries that Reportedly Participated in the C.I.A.'s Rendition Program," Max Fisher, *Washington Post*, February 6, 2013, https://www.washingtonpost.com/news/worldviews/wp/2013/02/05/a-staggering-map-of-the-54-countries-that-reportedly-participated-in-the-cias-rendition-program/.

112. Thailand covertly cooperated with C.I.A. renditions, and received hard cash, support for its own brutal war against Muslims in the south, and a decision not to criticize Thailand for human rights abuses or abrogation of laws. See "An Alliance Gone Bad," Prangtip Daorueng, ICIJ, May 31, 2017, https://www.icij.org/investigations/collateraldamage/alliance-gone-bad/.

113. Author archive: C-Wing bulletin on Saudi princes fighting with al Qaeda, 2002.

114. Taliban asked for political backing from the U.S., Saudi, and Pakistan in exchange for discreetly hunting Saudi royals. A deal agreed, the Saudis went to bat for the Taliban in London and Washington, proposing they be part of a future administration in Afghanistan. The Mullah Omar network searched for the princes. Unsurprisingly, the political proposal went nowhere, with Saudi Arabia and General Ehsan ul-Haq unable to

persuade the Bush White House, even though British Prime Minister Tony Blair was recruited as an advocate for the deal.

115. A reliable account of Daniel Pearl's abduction and murder is available at the Pearl Project, Georgetown University, here: http://pearlproject. georgetown.edu/home.

116. Jamaat ul-Fuqra (J.F., the movement of the impoverished) was dogged by charges of violent acts involving firearms and the stockpiling of insurrectional doomsday manuals. See https://2001-2009.state.gov/r/pa/ prs/ps/2002/7738.htm. See also "A Junior Al Qaeda,"John J. Miller, *National Review*, January 31, 2001, https://web.archive.org/web/20110506010727/ http://old.nationalreview.com/flashback/flashback-miller013102.shtml; and "1999 Patterns of Global Terrorism," U.S. Department of State, 2000. It should be noted, however, that the State Department dropped J.F. from subsequent editions of "Patterns of Global Terrorism." Moreover, the secretary of state has never designated J.F. as a "foreign terrorist organization," which unlike the "terrorist group" appellation carries with it a variety of criminal sanctions. See "Jamaat ul-Fuqra Designated a Foreign Terrorist Organization?" U.S. Department of State, January 31, 2001.

117. See this roundup at "Jama'at al-Fuqara'," Farhana Ali and William Rosenau, *CTC Sentinel* 1, issue 11 (October 2008), https://ctc.usma.edu/ jamaat-al-fuqara-an-overblown-threat/.

118. Robert Muller would be back in the limelight, investigating alleged collusion between the Trump campaign and Russia in the 2016 presidential elections.

119. The indictment over the 1994 kidnapping was publicized on March 14, 2002, when Sheikh was also indicted for the kidnapping and murder of Daniel Pearl. See "Attorney General Transcript, News Conference – Indictment in Daniel Pearl Case," D.O.J. Conference Center, Thursday, March 14, 2002, https://www.justice.gov/archive/ag/ speeches/2002/031402newsconfernceindictmentindanielpearlcase.htm.

120. "The Toughest Boy in School," Alex Hannaford, February 23, 2005, *The Guardian*, February 23, 2005, https://www.theguardian.com/world/2005/ feb/23/alqaida.usa.

121. "The British Jackal," Nick Fielding, *The Sunday Times*, April 21, 2002, https://www.mea.gov.in/articles-in-foreign-media.htm?dtl/18174/ The+British+jackal.

122. "Omar Sheikh, the Path from Public School Boy to Pakistan's Death Row," Simon Jeffrey, *The Guardian*, July 15, 2002.

123. "Omar Sheikh Surrendered to Police, Says Witness," *Dawn*, June 28, 2002, https://www.dawn.com/news/45099/newspaper/column.

124. Author tape archive: interviews with Brigadier Ijaz Shah, Lahore, 2017 and 2019.

125. Brig. Shah welded together new political parties – including an iteration of Sharif's P.M.L., known as P.M.L.-Q. and of Bhutto's P.P.P., known as P.P.P.-Patriots – to shore up the President.

126. Author tape archive: interviews with Musharraf.

127. "Parole Board Declares Never-Charged Abu Zubaydah a Forever Prisoner," Carol Rosenberg, *Miami Herald*, October 27, 2016, https://www.miamiherald.com/news/nation-world/world/americas/guantanamo/article110891862.html.

128. "Al Jazeera Journalist Describes Interview with Sept 11 Suspects," A.P., July 21, 2015, https://www.youtube.com/watch?v=XYK0JKzy5Vg; and also "Covering Al Qaeda," *Arab Media & Society*, October 17, 2015, https://www.arabmediasociety.com/covering-al-qaeda/.

129. The meeting was on April 18, 2002.

130. "Muslim Rebels Kill 30 in Kashmir Army Camp Clash," Rahul Bedi, *Daily Telegraph*, May 15, 2002, https://www.telegraph.co.uk/news/worldnews/asia/india/1394303/Muslim-rebels-kill-30-in-Kashmir-army-camp-clash.html.

131. The man was Mustafa Ahmed Hawsawi, a Saudi citizen, whom the C.I.A. said was an al Qaeda accountant and media manager. See also Mustafa Ahmed al Hawsawi, Guantanamo Docket," https://www.nytimes.com/interactive/projects/guantanamo/detainees/10011-mustafa-ahmed-al-hawsawi.

132. "Raided Family of Microbiologist Denies Official Version of Al Qaida Arrests," Rory McCarthy, *The Guardian*, March 3, 2003, https://www.theguardian.com/world/2003/mar/03/alqaida.terrorism.

133. There was some suggestion that the elderly doctor had served in the 1990s in Sudan when Osama was also there – but this connection was never firmed up by the I.S.I. or the C.I.A.

134. Intercept was on May 30, 2003, according to a transcript we were shown.

135. He was detained in August 2005. A military court in Pano Aqil

Cantonment would sentence Major Adil Quddus to ten years in prison, Colonel Khalid Abbasi to six, and Colonel Abdul Ghaffar to three. Major Attaullah, Major Sarfraz, and Captain Usman were dismissed from service.

136. Author archive.

137. "Nadimarg Massacre: Gunmen Killed 24 Kashmiri Pandits on Mar 23, 2003," Showkat Dar, *Greater Kashmir*, March 23, 2017

138. Author tape archive: interviews with Dr Badroo in 2004.

139. Author archive. The worrying figure was contained in an intelligence estimate dated to the spring of 2003, which the author discussed with us. It took in the sectarians and the Kashmir groups that had ditched the I.S.I. circuit.

140. The comments were made during a visit to the Karachi Council on Foreign Relations on November 13, 2003. See https://2001-2009.state.gov/p/sca/rls/rm/26277.htm.

141. The Jamaat student outfit, Islami Jamiat-e-Talaba, remains one of the biggest in Pakistan.

142. "Nek Mohammed," Rahimullah Yusufzai, *PBS Frontline*, https://www.pbs.org/wgbh/pages/frontline/taliban/militants/mohammed.html.

143. Author tape archive: interview with C-Wing brigadier based in the Punjab, who monitored Jaish.

144. Ibid.

145. April 2003. The three most prominent S.S.G. members in the assassination cell were Mohammad Imran, Mohammad Hanif, and Sheikh Mohammad Ahmed, who formed the group led by Amjad Farooqi and Ilyas Kashmiri, tasked with killing Musharraf.

146. Author tape archive: interviews with C-Wing Punjab officers given the assignment, 2018 and 2019 – Lahore.

147. Author tape archive: interview with Syed Salahuddin, Muzaffarabad.

148. "India and Pakistan Leaders Raise Hope of Détente," Randeep Ramesh, *The Guardian*, January 5, 2004, https://www.theguardian.com/world/2004/jan/05/randeepramesh.

149. Author tape archive: interviews with Pervez Musharraf.

150. Author tape archive: multiple interviews with Brajesh Mishra, 2008 to 2010.

151. Ibid. See also "Brajesh Mishra and Mao's Smile," A.G. Noorani, *Frontline*,

March 16, 2018, https://frontline.thehindu.com/books/brajesh-mishra-amp-maos-smile/article10085029.ece.

152. "Mainstreaming Pakistan's Federally Administered Tribal Areas," Imtiaz Ali, U.S. Institute for Peace, March 2018, Special Report 421, https://www.usip.org/sites/default/files/2018-03/sr-421-mainstreaming-pakistan-federally-administered-tribal-areas.pdf.

153. Author tape archive: interviews with Lt. Gen. Masood Aslam, who served in Waziristan and Swat before becoming the XI Corps Commander. 2017, 2018, and 2019, in Rawalpindi.

154. "India, Israel Advance on Phalcon AWACS Megadeal," Rina Bassist, *Al-Monitor*, September 3, 2020, https://bit.ly/3fqzmyP.

155. Author tape archive: interviews with Lt. Gen. Khalid Rabbani, 2018 and 2019, Rawalpindi.

156. The abbreviation for the Urdu is M.M.A.

157. Author archive, report dated April 2004.

158. "How Jundullah Became Al Qaeda," Ali K. Chisti, *Friday Times*, November 14, 2014, https://www.thefridaytimes.com/how-jundullah-became-al-qaeda/.

159. The medic brothers were sentenced to seven years of rigorous imprisonment on March 14, 2005, only to be acquitted three months later on July 11, 2006.

160. "Report Warned C.I.A. on Tactics in Interrogation," Douglas Jehl, *New York Times*, November 9, 2005, https://www.nytimes.com/2005/11/09/politics/report-warned-cia-on-tactics-in-interrogation.html.

161. "Report Provides New Details on C.I.A. Prisoner Abuse," Mark Mazzetti, *New York Times*, August 22, 2009, https://www.nytimes.com/2009/08/23/us/politics/23cia.html.

162. "A Secret Deal on Drones, Sealed in Blood," Mark Mazzetti, *New York Times*, April 6, 2013, https://www.nytimes.com/2013/04/07/world/asia/origins-of-cias-not-so-secret-drone-war-in-pakistan.html.

163. "Billions in Aid With No Accountability," Sarah Fort, The Center for Public Integrity, May 31, 2007, https://publicintegrity.org/national-security/billions-in-aid-with-no-accountability/.

164. This refers to an August 2004 C.I.S. bulletin on internal security and monitoring, described to us by its author.

165. "Atlas Obscura Society D.C.: The Spies of Georgetown," and here: https://g-turs.com/s-tour/spies-of-georgetown-walking-tour.html.

166. "The Spy Who Was Never," Manoj Joshi, *India Today*, June 6, 2010, https://www.indiatoday.in/india/north/story/the-spy-who-was-never-75972-2010-06-06.

167. "Govt. Orders Probe into Defence Theft," T.N.N. in *Times of India*, October 11, 2003, https://timesofindia.indiatimes.com/india/Govt-orders-probe-into-defence-theft/articleshow/227755.cms. Also see "DRDO Theft: Burglars Had Inside Information," Lalit Kumar, *Times of India*, June 4, 2004, https://timesofindia.indiatimes.com/india/DRDO-theft-Burglars-had-inside-information/articleshow/718272.cms.

168. "The U.S. India Strategic Partnership: An Overview of Defense and Nuclear Courtship," Ashok Sharma, *Georgetown Journal of International Affairs*, July 4, 2013, https://www.georgetownjournalofinternational affairs.org/online-edition/the-u-s-india-strategic-partnership-an-overview-of-defense-and-nuclear-courtship-by-ashok-sharma; and "Unity in Difference: Overcoming the U.S.–India Divide," Ashley J. Tellis, Carnegie Endowment for International Peace, January 21, 2015, https://carnegieendowment.org/2015/01/21/unity-in-difference-overcoming-u.s.-india-divide-pub-57761.

169. "U.S. Unveils Plans to Make India 'Major World Power,'" Agence France Presse, *Economic Times*, March 26, 2005, https://economictimes.indiatimes.com/news/defence/united-states-unveils-plan-to-counter-chinas-rise-from-india-to-taiwan/articleshow/80249913.cms.

170. The agreement dates to June 28, 2005. See also "Wrong Ends, Means and Needs: Behind the U.S. Nuclear Deal with India," Zia Mian and M.V. Ramana, Arms Control Association, https://www.armscontrol.org/act/2006-01/features/wrong-ends-means-needs-behind-us-nuclear-deal-india. Robert Blackwill served in the first George W. Bush Administration as U.S. ambassador to India and then as Deputy National Security Advisor for strategic planning.

171. The pros and cons are well summarized in "The U.S. India Nuclear Deal," Jayshree Bajoria and Esther Pan, Council for Foreign Relations backgrounder, November 5, 2010, https://www.cfr.org/backgrounder/us-india-nuclear-deal.

172. "India Is Building a Top-Secret Nuclear City to Produce Thermonuclear Weapons, Experts Say," Adrian Levy, *Foreign Policy*, December 16, 2015, https://foreignpolicy.com/2015/12/16/india_nuclear_city_top_secret_china_pakistan_barc/.

173. "Security Forces Kill Amjad Farooqi," *Dawn*, September 27, 2004, https://www.dawn.com/news/371810.

174. See "Abu Faraj al-Libi, the Guantanamo Docket," *New York Times*, https://www.nytimes.com/interactive/projects/guantanamo/detainees/10017-abu-faraj-al-libi/documents/11.

175. Comments were made on May 3, 2005, when the CENTCOM commander arrived in Islamabad.

176. "Al Qaeda Number Three 'Captured in Pakistan,'" *Sydney Morning Herald*, May 5, 2005, https://www.smh.com.au/world/al-qaeda-number-three-captured-in-pakistan-20050505-gdl9b8.html.

177. Author tape archive: interview with Lt. Gen. Nusrat Naeem, Rawalpindi, in 2018 and 2019.

178. The Renditions Project, Abu Faraj Al-Libi, https://www.therenditionproject.org.uk/prisoners/abu-faraj-al-libi.html.

179. Author tape archive: interviews with Jose Rodriguez, Florida, U.S.

180. "The Drone, the C.I.A. and a Botched Attempt to Kill bin Laden's Deputy," Jason Burke and Imtiaz Gul, *The Guardian*, January 15, 2006, https://www.theguardian.com/world/2006/jan/15/alqaida.pakistan.

181. "Drone Warfare," *Bureau of Investigative Journalism*, https://www.thebureauinvestigates.com/projects/drone-war.

182. "Pakistan Rally Against U.S. Strike," BBC News, January 15, 2006, http://news.bbc.co.uk/1/hi/world/south_asia/4614486.stm.

183. Author tape archive: author interview with Pervez Musharraf. Eight days later, in Dargai, 130 kilometres north-west of Islamabad, trainees prepared for some square bashing at 5 a.m. Two men wrapped in shawls strolled through the military Punjab Regiment camp heading to the mess canteen kitchen. They switched directions to cross to the square where 130 recruits gathered, chatting and yawning. One of the shawl-wearers detonated a vest, mowing down 38 on the spot, two more dying soon after, flaying scores more, many left physically crippled or disabled by trauma.

184. "Denying the Undeniable: Enforced Disappearances in Pakistan," Amnesty International, 2008, https://www.amnesty.org/download/Documents/ASA330182008ENGLISH.pdf. One group run by families whose members had been abducted represented 563 people.

185. Author archive: I.S.I.-C. report was dated to December 2006 and contained an audit of crackdown numbers, arrests, and detentions.

186. "Love in Lahore," *Dawn*, December 31, 2011, https://www.dawn.com/news/684462. See also *The Taliban Shuffle: Strange Days in Afghanistan and Pakistan*, Kim Barker, Anchor Books, 2012.

187. Author archive: December 2006, bulletin marked from C-Wing and A-Wing brigadiers, to Pervez Musharraf.

188. Author archive: a bulletin from C-Wing general to Musharraf, signed by him, as having been read and received. February 2007.

189. Author tape archive: interview with S.S.G. commanders, in Rawalpindi and Lahore, 2017 and 2018, and with Lt. Gen. Nusrat Naeem, Rawalpindi, 2019.

190. Author tape archive: interview with Musharraf, August 2007.

191. *3 Para*, Patrick Bishop, HarperCollins, 2007, p. 254.

192. Bulletin signed by A- and B-Wing generals, to Musharraf, and also signed by him, as "read and received," December 2006.

193. "Taliban Fighter Tells of Deal Struck with Italian Soldiers in Afghanistan," Tom Coghlan, *The Times*, October 16, 2009, https://www.thetimes.co.uk/article/taleban-fighter-tells-of-deal-struck-with-italian-soldiers-in-afghanistan-snsm7bl7057.

194. Author tape archive: interview with Lt. Gen. Masood Aslam, Rawalpindi, 2019.

195. See the declassified sections of the National Intelligence Estimate, "Trends in Global Terrorism: Implications for the United States," April 2006, made public in November, https://fas.org/irp/dni/trends.pdf. Also see "Spy Agencies Say Iraq War Worsens Terrorism Threat," Mark Mazzetti, *New York Times*, September 24, 2006, https://www.nytimes.com/2006/09/24/world/middleeast/24terror.html. Also, "Iraq Stands on the Brink of Civil War," UN Security Council press release SC/8895, December 11, 2006, https://www.un.org/press/en/2006/sc8895.doc.htm.

196. "India to Invest $500m in Iranian Port of Chabahar," Agencies, *The Guardian*, May 23, 2016, https://www.theguardian.com/world/2016/may/23/india-invest-500m-iran-port-chabahar-modi-transit-accord-afghanistan.

197. Monthly reports and annual compendiums were written by the I.S.I. on Baluchistan and R.A.W. An upscale in reporting came in 2015 and in 2020, detailing claims and incidents. See also "India, Afghanistan Deny Pakistan's allegation of 'Terrorism,'" *DW News*, https://www.dw.com/en/

india-afghanistan-deny-pakistans-allegation-of-terrorism/a-55611636.

198. "Jundullah: Iran's Sunni Rebels," June 2010, Al Jazeera, https://www.aljazeera.com/news/2010/6/20/jundallah-irans-sunni-rebels.

199. "Ideological and Ownership Trends in the Saudi Media," Public Library of U.S. Diplomacy, May 11, 2009, https://search.wikileaks.org/plusd/cables/09RIYADH651_a.html.

200. "Who Supports Jundullah," Muhammad Sahmi, *PBS Frontline*, October 22, 2009, https://www.pbs.org/wgbh/pages/frontline/tehranbureau/2009/10/jundallah.html.

201. "Iran, Still Haunted by Jundullah Attacks, Blames West," Scott-Peterson, *CS Monitor*, December 15, 2010, https://www.csmonitor.com/World/Middle-East/2010/1215/Iran-still-haunted-by-Jundallah-attacks-blames-West.

202. The truce was announced in August 2007. See "Sadr Calls for Mahdi Army Ceasefire," Bill Roggio, *Long War Journal*, August 29, 2007, https://www.longwarjournal.org/archives/2007/08/sadr_calls_for_mahdi.php.

203. "Iran Rebel, on Death Row, Says U.S. Supported Group," Reuters, August 25, 2009, https://www.reuters.com/article/idUSLP446118.

204. Author archive: I.S.I. bulletin from C-Wing on Jundullah and Pakistan actions, triggered by U.S. request.

205. Muhammad Abdullah Gazi was the father, and a biography was released online by Riaz Munsoor, https://archive.org/details/SHAEEDISLAM/page/n5/mode/2up.

206. "Hard-line Pakistani Students Release Chinese Women," Augustine Anthony, Reuters, June 23, 2007, https://www.reuters.com/article/us-pakistan-mosque/hard-line-pakistani-students-release-chinese-women-idUSSP14126820070623.

207. An I.S.I.-C post-mortem about Lal Masjid contained the information, dated September 2007.

208. See "Pakistan Floods Situation Reports," *ReliefWeb*, July 2007, https://reliefweb.int/report/pakistan/pakistan-floods-situation-report-1-02-jul-2007.

209. Author tape archive: interviews with Lt. Gen. Nusrat Naeem, Rawalpindi, 2018.

210. See "Timeline: Twists and Turns in the India – U.S. Nuclear Deal," Reuters, October 2, 2008, https://www.reuters.com/article/us-india-usa-

nuclear-timeline/timeline-twists-and-turns-in-the-india-u-s-nuclear-deal-idUSTRE4912HG20081002?edition-redirect=uk.

211. A brief backgrounder on this and other moves that led to Musharraf's ouster and then his court cases is here: "Why Pakistan's Former Ruler Musharraf Was Sentenced to Death, and What It Means," Madiha Afzal, *Brookings*, December 19, 2019, https://www.brookings.edu/blog/order-from-chaos/2019/12/19/why-pakistans-former-ruler-musharraf-was-sentenced-to-death-and-what-it-means/.

212. The blast was on June 2, 2008, and its mechanics linked it to others for which the Jaish, al Qaeda, Kashmiri, and the S.S.G. were in the frame.

213. Author tape archive: interviews with Lt. Gen. Nusrat Naeem, Rawalpindi 2018, 2019.

214. The Joint Investigation Taskforce into the October 2007 attack in Karachi suggested the batteries could have run down. The best account of the twin attacks is by Owen Bennett Jones. Listen to his BBC podcast, "The Assassination," which began on December 17, 2017, https://www.bbc.co.uk/programmes/p05r6cgx/episodes/downloads. Also read "Questions Concerning the Murder of Benazir Bhutto," *London Review of Books* 34, no. 23, (December 6, 2012), https://www.lrb.co.uk/the-paper/v34/n23/owen-bennett-jones/questions-concerning-the-murder-of-benazir-bhutto.

215. These figures come from the I.S.I. Counter Terrorism Centre, and were shared with the authors, but Action on Armed Violence recorded only 23, in its report "Drone Strikes and Suicide Attacks in Pakistan: An Analysis," by Luqman Saeed, Professor Mike Spagat, and Iain Overton, March 2019, https://aoav.org.uk/wp-content/uploads/2019/03/Drone-strikes-and-Suicide-bombings-in-Pakistan-examined-1.pdf.

216. Author tape archive: interviews with Benazir Bhutto in London and Dubai, in 2005, 2006, and 2007, but also with her backers in the U.S. and U.K., in the U.S. State Department and U.K. F.C.O.

217. Author tape archive: interviews with Benazir Bhutto October and November 2007.

218. "Pakistan: Questions Concerning the Murder of Benazir Bhutto," *London Review of Books* 34, no. 23 (December 6, 2012): 6–10, https://www.lrb.co.uk/the-paper/v34/n23/owen-bennett-jones/questions-concerning-the-murder-of-benazir-bhutto.

219. Author archive: I.S.I.-C Wing bulletin on security, dated October 2007.

220. A U.N. inquiry was commissioned on July 1, 2009 and reported back April 15, 2010. It was led by Hugo Munoz, Marzuki Darusman, and Peter Fitzgerald. Read here: https://www.refworld.org/docid/4bcd50802.html.

221. "Bhutto Said in Will Husband Should Lead Party," Kamran Haider, Reuters, February 5, 2008, https://www.reuters.com/article/idINIndia-31778020080205?edition-redirect=uk.

222. Author tape archive: interview Ajit Doval, 2007, Delhi.

223. The Delhi-based Institute of Conflict Studies which tracks militant violence across South Asia recorded similar numbers. See http://blogs.reuters.com/pakistan/2009/02/04/kashmir-violence-drops-further-but-wheres-the-peace/.

224. "Indians Worry Lashkar Terrorists Are Thriving in Pakistan Kashmir," Cable from U.S. Embassy, Delhi, to Washington, D.C., https://wikileaks.org/plusd/cables/05NEWDELHI8791_a.html.

225. In July 2012, the emir of the Lashkar-e-Toiba, Hafiz Saeed, shared a stage in Karachi with a man called Maulana Abdus Quddus Burmi, where a resolution was passed to "recruit and seek revenge for the atrocities against the Rohingyas." See also Vicky Nanjappa, "Lashkar's Secret Module at Mae Sot," OneIndia, September 16, 2017, https://www.oneindia.com/india/lashkars-secret-module-at-mae-sot-from-where-it-will-launch-rohingya-muslims-2544422.html.

226. Author tape archive: interviews with Rajinder Khanna, Delhi, 2018 and 2019. Also see "I.S.I. Held Training Camps for KLF Men in Thailand," Jatinder Kohli, Hindustan Times, November 9, 2014, https://www.hindustantimes.com/punjab/isi-held-training-camp-for-klf-men-in-thailand/story-wDrAbwtRUkhZaNf1FNcFWI.html. In 2015, the head of the Pakistan Sikh Gurdwara Parbandhak Committee was photographed with Hafiz Saeed, raising questions about their mutual aims.

227. Author tape archive: interviews with SO15 counterterror command officers at Scotland Yard, and with Sir Richard Walton, its former commander. Interviews with "Aimen Deen," who worked for al Qaeda and the Secret Intelligence Service, West London, 2017.

228. "An Intelligence Failure," Richard Norton-Taylor, The Guardian, June 20, 2006, https://www.theguardian.com/media/2006/jun/20/pressandpublishing.terrorism. See also "City Man Jailed for Helping

Terror Group," Coventry Live, March 17, 2006, https://www.coventrytelegraph.net/news/coventry-news/city-man-jailed-helping-terror-3127962.

229. "Ex Teacher Sentenced to 15 years for Aiding Pakistani Terror Group," August 25, 2006, *USA Today*, https://usatoday30.usatoday.com/news/nation/2006-08-25-teacher-jailed_x.htm.

230. Author archive. The report was from June 2009. For statistics on Kashmir, see also https://www.satp.org/terrorism-assessment/pakistan-khyberpakhtunkhwa-2014.

231. "NSA's Changing Counterterrorism Relationship with India," Snowden Archive, June 15, 2009, https://search.edwardsnowden.com/docs/NSA%E2%80%99sChangingCounterterrorismRelationshipWithIndia2018-03-01_nsadocs_snowden_doc; and also, "The Powerful Global Spy Alliance You Never Knew Existed," Ryan Gallagher, *The Intercept*, March 1, 2018, https://theintercept.com/2018/03/01/nsa-global-surveillance-sigint-seniors.

232. Ibid.

233. "How London's 7/7 Bombings Led to Unprecedented Surveillance Tactics," Ryan Gallagher, *The Intercept*, March 1, 2018, https://theintercept.com/2018/03/01/london-7-7-bombings-gchq-nsa-surveillance/.

234. Ibid.

235. Author tape archive: interviews with Lashkar organizers and clerics in Muridke and Lahore.

236. Author tape archive: according to multiple author interviews with S- and C-Wing officers in the Punjab, where Headley had a home.

237. Author tape archive: interviews on both sides of the LoC in December 2008 and January 2009.

238. "Ajmal Kasab Was an Indian – UP Records Show," *Global Village Space*, November 22, 2018, https://www.globalvillagespace.com/ajmal-kasab-was-an-indian-up-records-show/.

239. "NSA's Changing Counterterrorism Relationship with India," *The Intercept*, June 15, 2009, https://theintercept.com/document/2018/03/01/sidtoday-2009-06-15-nsas-changing-counterterrorism-relationship-with-india/.

240. Ibid.

241. Author tape archive: interviews with Lt. Gen. Asif Akhtar, former S-Wing director general, Islamabad, 2018 and 2019.

242. Author tape archive: interview with Lt. Gen. Nusrat Naeem. Also see "Double Game," Patrick Cockburn, *New York Times*, April 25, 2014, https://www.nytimes.com/2014/04/27/books/review/the-wrong-enemy-by-carlotta-gall.html.

243. Author tape archive: interview with Lt. Gen. Nusrat Naeem.

244. It is not clear if Headley succeeded but multiple sources in R.A.W.–I.B. told us that they learned that the U.S. guaranteed Headley that he would not be extradited to India.

245. Author tape archive: interviews with General Khalid Rabbani, 2017 and 2018, Rawalpindi. Author interviews with General Masood Aslam. We also spoke to General Asif Yasin Malik, an XI Corps commander, as well as serving as D.G. Joint Intelligence, D.G. I.S.I., and defence minister.

246. Author archive: sworn statements and affidavits in the Farooq inquiry, taken by Scotland Yard officers and published under disclosure.

247. Author archive: interrogation of Aqeel Ahmad, 2009.

248. "Saffron Terrorism – a New Phenomenon, Says Home Minister Chidambaram," NDTV, August 25, 2010, https://www.ndtv.com/india-news/saffron-terrorism-a-new-phenomenon-says-home-minister-chidambaram-428832.

249. The home minister denied that the secular Congress party was head-butting with the Hindu nationalists of the B.J.P., but instead was dealing with a law-and-order crisis.

250. "Pat Finucane Murder: A Pitiless Act and a Political Storm," Rory Caroll, *The Guardian*, November 30, 2020, https://www.theguardian.com/uk-news/2020/nov/30/pat-finucane-murder-a-pitiless-act-and-a-political-storm.

251. Author tape archive: interviews with the I.B. officers who fed into that inquiry and briefed the home minister, Delhi, 2010 and 2011. Author briefing with home ministry in 2010.

252. "NIA Did Not Allow Me to Drop Muslims from 2006 Malegaon Case," Sunil Baghel and Sharmeen Hakim, *Mumbai Mirror*, September 6, 2019, https://mumbaimirror.indiatimes.com/mumbai/cover-story/nia-did-not-allow-me-to-drop-muslims-from-2006-malegaon-case/articleshow/47822082.cms.

253. Author tape archive: interviews with I.B. officers, and senior I.P.S. officers, including Hemant Karkare, in September 2007 and August 2008.

254. "The Body Politic in Uniform," V.R. Raghavan, *Outlook*, November 24, 2008, https://magazine.outlookindia.com/story/the-body-politic-in-uniform/239011.

255. Author tape archive: interviews with Karkare, see above.

256. Ibid.

257. "Ten Facts About the Malegaon Blasts," The Wire, June 25, 2015, https://thewire.in/law/10-facts-about-the-malegaon-blasts.

258. "Malegaon Blasts 9 Accused Set to Walk Free," Harinder Baweja and Farhan Shaikh, *Hindustan Times*, May 8, 2016, https://m.rediff.com/news/report/-malegaon-blasts-9-accused-set-to-walk-free/20130829.htm.

259. "How Malegaon's Innocent 'Terrorists' Lost Ten Years of Their Life," Harinder Baweja and Farhan Shaikh, *Hindustan Times*, May 8, 2016, https://www.hindustantimes.com/india/how-malegaon-s-innocent-terrorists-lost-10-years-of-their-lives/story-YGqgBk3ejtu1egeIU4etvJ.html.

260. "Abhinav Bharat Was Hijacked by Hardliners: Probe," Chandan Haygunde, *Indian Express*, November 2, 2008, http://archive.indianexpress.com/news/abhinav-bharat-was--hijacked--by-hardliners-probe/380249/.

261. "A Hindutva Plot," Anupama Katakam, *Frontline*, February 13, 2009, https://frontline.thehindu.com/the-nation/article30183701.ece.

262. The Rashtriya Swayamsevak Sangh (R.S.S.) or National Volunteer Organisation, a paramilitary and chauvinist, right-wing Hindu group with at least six million members and formed in 1925. An affiliated group is the ruling B.J.P., or Bharatiya Janata Party. See also "How Hindu Supremacists Are Tearing India Apart," Samanth Subramanian, *The Guardian*, February 20, 2020, https://www.theguardian.com/world/2020/feb/20/hindu-supremacists-nationalism-tearing-india-apart-modi-bjp-rss-jnu-attacks.

263. "Hindu Holy Man Aseemanand in Custody over India Blasts," BBC News, January 13, 2011, https://www.bbc.co.uk/news/world-south-asia-12180193; and also "Swami Aseemanand: Anti Conversion Godman Who Sang, Danced and Prayed with Tribals," Vasudha Venugopal, *Economic Times*, April 17, 2018, https://economictimes.indiatimes.com/news/politics-and-nation/swami-aseemanand-anti-conversion-godman-who-sang-danced-and-prayed-with-tribals/articleshow/63792643.cms?from=mdr.

264. Blasts were in Nanded in Maharashtra, and in Kanpur in Uttar Pradesh, among other places. See "Abhinav Bharat, the Malegaon Blast and Hindu Nationalism: Resisting and Emulating Islamist Terrorism," Christophe Jaffrelot, *Economic and Political Weekly* 45, no. 36 (2010): 51–58. JSTOR, www.jstor.org/stable/25742046. See also "Bajrang Dal Workers Trained in Bomb Making: Cops," News18, October 24, 2008, https://www.news18.com/videos/india/saffron-terrorbajrang-bombs-300178.html.

265. Findings of the N.I.A. inquiry, which were also read into court proceedings.

266. Hemant Karkare memo shared with the N.I.A. and I.B., dated March 2008.

267. "NIA Books Eight Men for Goa Blasts," *Economic Times*, May 18, 2010, https://economictimes.indiatimes.com/news/politics-and-nation/nia-books-eight-sanatan-sanstha-men-for-goa-blast/articleshow/5942645.cms?from=mdr.

268. See "Samjhauta Blasts: LeT Hand Being Probed," *Economic Times*, February 20, 2007, https://economictimes.indiatimes.com/news/politics-and-nation/samjhauta-blasts-let-hand-being-probed/articleshow/1640581.cms?from=mdr. Also see "Samjhauta Express Bomber Admits to Planting Explosive that Killed 68 Passengers," Vikas Kahol, *Daily Mail*, February 15, 2012, https://www.dailymail.co.uk/indiahome/indianews/article-2101162/Samjhauta-Express-bomber-admits-planting-explosive-killed-68-passengers-train.html.

269. "Saffron Terror Role Being Probed," Anirban Bhaumik, *Deccan Herald*, September 20, 2011, https://www.deccanherald.com/content/192456/saffron-terror-role-being-probed.html. See also "Shin Bet and the Challenge of Right-Wing Political Extremism in Israel," Eyal Pascovich, *International Journal of Intelligence and CounterIntelligence* 30, no. 2 (2017), https://www.tandfonline.com/doi/full/10.1080/08850607.2016.1230702?scroll=top&needAccess=true.

270. "NIA Did Not Allow Me to Drop Muslims from 2006 Malegaon Case," Sunil Baghel and Sharmeen Hakim, *Mumbai Mirror*, September 6, 2019, https://mumbaimirror.indiatimes.com/mumbai/cover-story/nia-did-not-allow-me-to-drop-muslims-from-2006-malegaon-case/articleshow/47822082.cms.

271. "No Provision for Victims to Appeal Under NIA Act, " *The Hindu*, March 26, 2019, https://www.thehindu.com/news/cities/Hyderabad/no-provision-for-victims-to-appeal-under-nia-act/article26646680.ece.

272. Author tape archive: interviews with N.I.A. investigators in 2016, 2017, and 2018 in Hyderabad, Bengaluru, Mumbai, and Delhi.

273. Accused were Swami Aseemanand, Kamal Chauhan, Rajinder Chaudhary and Lokesh Sharma.

274. "LeT Behind Samjhauta Blasts: NIA to Quote US Agencies in Court," Neeraj Chauhan, *Economic Times*, May 25, 2016, https://economictimes. indiatimes.com/news/politics-and-nation/let-behind-samjhauta-blasts-nia-to-quote-us-agencies-in-court/articleshow/52430085. cms?from=mdr.

275. "The Samjhauta Acquittals: Hindu Terror Goes Unpunished in India," Apoorvanand, Al Jazeera, March 28, 2019, https://www.aljazeera.com/ opinions/2019/3/28/the-samjhauta-acquittals-hindu-terror-goes-unpunished-in-india.

276. "Militants Attack Pakistani Naval Base in Karachi," Salman Masood and David Sanger, *New York Times*, May 22, 2011, https://www.nytimes. com/2011/05/23/world/asia/23pakistan.html.

277. Author archive: C-Wing, Sindh bulletin, June 24, 2011.

278. "Implications of the Karachi Attack," Shashank Joshi, RUSI commentary, May 23, 2011, https://rusi.org/commentary/implications-karachi-attack.

279. "The Story That Killed Saleem Shahzad," Suhasini Haidar, *The Hindu*, June 2, 2011, https://www.thehindu.com/opinion/op-ed/the-story-that-killed-saleem-shahzad/article2071460.ece.

280. "Al Qaeda Had Warned of Pakistan Strike," Saleem Shahzad, *Asia Times*, May 27, 2011, https://web.archive.org/web/20110916093043/http:// atimes.com/atimes/South_Asia/ME27Df06.html.

281. Committee to Protect Journalists, https://cpj.org/data/?status=Killed& start_year=1992&end_year=2021&group_by=year&motiveConfirmed% 5B%5D=Confirmed& type%5B%5D=Journalist.

282. "The Journalist and the Spies," Dexter Filkins, *New Yorker*, September 12, 2011, https://www.newyorker.com/magazine/2011/09/19/the-journalistand-the-spies?irclickid.

283. "Pakistan's Spies Tied to Slaying of a Journalist," Jane Perlez and Eric Schmitt, *New York Times*, July 4, 2011, https://www.nytimes. com/2011/07/05/world/asia/05pakistan.html.

284. "Pakistan Hits Back at US Commander Over Journalist's Murder Claim," Julian Borger, *The Guardian*, July 8, 2011, https://www.theguardian.com/ world/2011/jul/08/pakistan-denounces-us-journalist-murder.

285. "Strike Two: Ilyas Kashmiri Dead – Again," Qaiser Butt, *Tribune*, June 6, 2011, https://tribune.com.pk/story/182727/strike-two-ilyas-kashmiri-dead-%E2%80%93-again#:~:text=Kashmiri%2C%20who%20had%20a%20maximum,officials%20and%20local%20sources%20said.

Part 3: Back to the Future

1. Author tape archive: interviews in Rawalpindi, 2018 and 2019.
2. "A Jundullah Threat Assessment," author archive. Author tape archive: interviews with Lt. Gen. Nusrat Naeem, Rawalpindi, October 2018.
3. Cathy Scott-Clark and Adrian Levy, *The Exile*.
4. Author archive. The report was generated by I.S.I. Peshawar and dated to the month after the kidnapping was announced.
5. "Progress and Peril in North Waziristan," Michael Kugelman, War on the Rocks, December 11, 2017, https://warontherocks.com/2017/12/progress-peril-north-waziristan/; and "Pakistan Army Is Getting Serious About Defeating Domestic Terrorism," *The Economist*, March 3, 2018, https://www.economist.com/asia/2018/03/01/pakistans-army-is-getting-serious-about-defeating-domestic-terrorism.
6. Author tape archive: interviews with D.I.A., in Delhi, and M.I. and B.S.F. in Srinagar. Author interview with Lt. Gen. Vinod G. Khandare, former D.G. of the D.I.A., and military adviser to the N.S.A.B., Delhi, 2019. By 2012, the number of deaths in Jammu and Kashmir were down to 112, but the trend downwards was noticeable in 2007; see also "Datasheet Jammu and Kashmir," South Asia Terrorism Portal, https://www.satp.org/datasheet-terrorist-attack/fatalities/india-jammukashmir.
7. "Pakistan Seeks UN Probe into Disclosure of Saeed's Info to Indian News Agency," PTI, *Economic Times*, March 17, 2019, https://economictimes.indiatimes.com/news/international/world-news/pakistan-seeks-un-probe-into-disclosure-of-saeeds-info-to-indian-news-agency/articleshow/68450410.cms?from=mdr. See also "Hafiz Muhammad Saeed," U.N.S.C., https://www.un.org/securitycouncil/sanctions/1267/aq_sanctions_list/summaries/individual/hafiz-muhammad-saeed.
8. Author tape archives: interviews in Kupwara, 2010 and 2011. See also "Amid Impunity, Enforced Disappearance Followed by Extrajudicial Executions Continues in Jammu & Kashmir," Jammu and Kashmir

Coalition for Civil Society (J.K.C.C.S.),https://jkccs.net/amid-impunity-enforced-disappearance-followed-by-extrajudicial-executions-continues-in-jammu-kashmir/. See the note below for a version of this reporting.

9.   "The Mass Graves of Kashmir," Cathy Scott-Clark, *The Guardian*, July 9, 2010, https://www.theguardian.com/world/2012/jul/09/mass-graves-of-kashmir.

10. Founded in 2000, some of the J.K.C.C.S. work is here: https://jkccs.net/who-we-are/. Also, author tape archives: interviews with Bashir Lone and others.

11. "Major Booked, Jawan Arrested,"Tejinder Singh Sodhi, *Tribune*, May 29, 2010, https://www.tribuneindia.com/2010/20100530/main4.htm.

12. "The Road to Peace in Kashmir: Public Perception of the Contentious AFSPA and PSA," Ajaz Wani and Dhaval Desai, Observer Research Foundation, August 16, 2018, https://www.orfonline.org/research/43363-the-road-to-peace-in-kashmir-public-perception-of-the-contentious-afspa-and-psa/. And see also, "Getting Away with Murder, 50 Years of the Armed Forces Special Powers Act," *Human Rights Watch*, August 2008, https://www.refworld.org/docid/48a93a402.html.

13. "India: Investigate Unmarked Graves in Kashmir," *Human Rights Watch*, August 24, 2011, https://www.hrw.org/news/2011/08/24/india-investigate-unmarked-graves-jammu-and-kashmir#:~:text=An%20inquiry%20by%20the%20police,of%20violence%2C%20their%20whereabouts%20unknown. See also "Human Rights Panel Tells J&K Government to Complete Investigating 2,080 Unmarked Graves in Six Months," Scroll, November 2, 2017, https://scroll.in/latest/856441/human-rights-panel-tells-j-k-government-to-complete-investigating-2080-unmarked-graves-in-6-months.

14. "SHRC Orders Government to Investigate 2080 Unmarked Graves," J.K.C.C.S., November 2, 2017, https://jkccs.net/shrc-orders-government-to-investigate-2080-unmarked-graves-and-mass-graves-of-poonch-and-rajouri-districts/.

15. J.K.C.C.S., Press Statement, June 29, 2018, https://jkccs.net/in-kashmir-there-is-almost-total-impunity-for-enforced-disappearances-stated-zeid-raad-al-hussein-un-high-commissioner-for-human-rights/. Also, "International Federation for Human Rights, Key Human Rights Issues of Concern in Indian-Administered Jammu and Kashmir," March 2019,

https://www.fidh.org/IMG/pdf/20190315_kashmir_briefing_note_-_
final.pdf.

16. "Report on the Situation of Human Rights in Kashmir: Developments in
     the Indian State of Jammu and Kashmir from June 2016 to April 2018,
     and General Human Rights Concerns in Azad Jammu and Kashmir and
     Gilgit-Baltistan," Office of the U.N. High Commissioner for Human
     Rights, June 2018, https://www.ohchr.org/Documents/Countries/IN/
     DevelopmentsInKashmirJune2016ToApril2018.pdf. Also "Tyranny of
     a 'Lawless Law': Detention Without Charge or Trial Under the J & K
     Public Safety Act', Amnesty International, June 2019, https://www.ecoi.
     net/en/file/local/2016402/PSA-Report_15-FINAL-LOW-Version-2.
     pdf.

17. Author tape archive: interviews with friends and family of Burhan Wani,
     Kashmir, 2012 and 2014.

18. "Narendra Modi, India's PM-Elect, Receives Hero's Welcome in Delhi,"
     Martin Williams and Jason Burke, *The Guardian*, May 17, 2014, https://
     www.theguardian.com/world/2014/may/17/india-narendra-modi-delhi-
     bharatiya-janata-election.

19. "Surat Riots, Investigation and Analysis," Irfan Engineer, Centre for
     Study of Society and Secularism, http://www.unipune.ac.in/snc/cssh/
     HumanRights/04%20COMMUNAL%20RIOTS/A%20-%20%20
     ANTI-MUSLIM%20RIOTS/04%20-GUJARAT/c.pdf. Also, "Timeline
     of the Riots in Modi's Gujarat," *New York Times*, August 19, 2015, https://
     www.nytimes.com/interactive/2014/04/06/world/asia/modi-gujarat-
     riots-timeline.html.

20. "Justice Nanavati-Mehta Commission Gives Clean Chit to Narendra
     Modi in 2002 Gujarat Riots," Mahesh Langa, *The Hindu*, December
     11, 2019, https://www.thehindu.com/news/national/2002-gujarat-riots-
     state-govt-to-table-justice-nanavati-mehta-commission-report-in-
     assembly-today/article30274396.ece.

21. "Undercover, Ajit Doval in Theory and Practice," Praveen Donthi,
     Caravan, September 1, 2017, https://caravanmagazine.in/reportage/ajit-
     doval-theory-practice.

22. "Meet Ajit Doval, the Indian James Bond You Probably Have No Idea
     About," Akarsh Mehrotra, Scoopwhoop, September 28, 2015, https://
     www.scoopwhoop.com/inothernews/indian-james-bond-ajit-doval/.

Also, "Ajit Doval: The Spy Who Came in from the Cold," Vijita Singh, *The Hindu*, July 11, 2020, https://www.thehindu.com/news/national/ajit-doval-the-spy-who-came-in-from-the-cold/article32053422.ece.

23. The journalist was Ghulam Hasnain writing for *Time*. See also, "The Dawood Ibrahim Gang," B. Raman, *Outlook*, October 20, 2003, https://www.outlookindia.com/website/story/the-dawood-ibrahim-gang/221776.

24. From that Board we interviewed Rajinder Khanna, Ajit Doval, Lt General Vinod Khandare, Asif Ibrahim, Tilak Devasher.

25. "See Kashmir Conflict Ebbs as New Wave of Militant Emerges," Jason Burke, *The Guardian*, August 11, 2013, https://www.theguardian.com/world/2013/aug/11/kashmir-conflict-new-wave-militants. Also, "WhatsApp Warriors on the New Frontline of Kashmir's Conflict," Michael Safi, *The Guardian*, July 8, 2017, https://www.theguardian.com/world/2017/jul/08/kashmir-whatsapp-warriors-frontline-conflict-india. And also, "Post Burhan Wani, Hizbul Mujahideen Has Subtly Changed Its Messaging in Kashmir," Rayan Naqah, Scroll, July 22, 2018, https://scroll.in/article/886560/post-burhan-wani-hizbul-mujahideen-has-subtly-changed-its-public-messaging-in-kashmir.

26. "Top Lashkar Commander, Abu Qasim Plotted Udhampur Attack Shot," Mir Ehsan, *Indian Express*, December 25, 2015, https://indianexpress.com/article/india/india-news-india/top-let-commander-and-udhampur-attack-mastermind-abu-qasim-killed-in-encounter/.

27. "Gun Battle in Jammu and Kashmir's Tral Kills Three, Including Two Militants," Shaswati Das, *Mint*, March 5, 2017, https://www.livemint.com/Politics/4M0SDwzLarpItfCJa3YGOM/Kashmir-encounter-Police-constable-militant-killed-in-Tral.html.

28. "Kashmir Went Viral," Riaz Wani, *New Statesman*, August 23, 2016, https://www.newstatesman.com/culture/observations/2016/08/how-death-militant-kashmir-went-viral.

29. "Guns 'N Poses: The New Crop of Militants in Kashmir," Basharat Masood, *Indian Express*, July 26, 2015, https://indianexpress.com/article/india/india-others/big-picture-guns-n-poses/.

30. "If My Son Was Killed in an Encounter, Why His Body Didn't Bear a Bullet Wound?" Basharat Masood, *Indian Express*, April 14, 2015, https://indianexpress.com/article/india/india-others/if-my-son-was-killed-in-encounter-why-his-body-didnt-bear-a-bullet-wound/.

31. "Militant, Soldier, Killed in Kulgam Shootout," Observer News Service, *Kashmir Observer*, May 25, 2015, https://kashmirobserver.net/2015/05/25/militant-soldier-killed-in-kulgam-shootout/.

32. "Murder Mystery of HM Militant Solver, Claims Police," Observer News Service, *Kashmir Observer*, January 6, 2016, https://kashmirobserver.net/2016/01/06/murder-mystery-of-hm-militant-solved-claims-police/.

33. "If My Son Was Killed in an Encounter, Why His Body Didn't Bear a Bullet Wound?" Basharat Masood, *Indian Express*, April 14, 2015, https://indianexpress.com/article/india/india-others/if-my-son-was-killed-in-encounter-why-his-body-didnt-bear-a-bullet-wound/. And also, "Who Is Khalid Wani," Syed Ata Hasnain, *The Quint*, December 16, 2016, https://www.thequint.com/voices/blogs/khalid-burhan-wani-burhan-terrorist-militant-kashmir-elder-brother-and-the-issue-of-compensation-by-the-state.

34. Author tape archive: interviews with two of the I.B. officers investigating Burhan Wani, and a detailed discussion about grid inputs reviewed by them, post the death of Wani.

35. Author tape archive: interview with D.I.A. officers post the death of Wani, Delhi and Srinagar, 2015. D.I.A. analysis for the grid was molecular and explained to us in 2016 by some of the authors.

36. "The Journey of Slain Naseer Pandit from Police to Militant Camp," *Kashmir Scenario*, December 11, 2017, https://thekashmirscenario.com/the-journey-of-slain-naseer-pandit-from-police-to-militant-camp/.

37. "The Curious Tale of Ishaq Newton, a Brilliant Student Who Picked Up a Gun Instead of a Stethoscope," Sameer Yasir, *FirstPost*, March 5, 2016, https://www.firstpost.com/india/the-curious-tale-of-ishaq-newton-a-brilliant-student-who-picked-up-a-gun-instead-of-a-stethoscope-2657352.html.

38. We were told Indian and Pakistani intelligence recorded these calls, as the H.M. was no longer trusted by the latter. The transcripts were reportedly identical, apart from some nuances.

39. "Indian Officers Named in Report on Kashmir Abuses," Jason Burke, *The Guardian*, December 6, 2012, https://www.theguardian.com/world/2012/dec/06/indian-soldiers-report-kashmir-abuses; and International People's Tribunal on Human Rights and Justice, at http://kashmirprocess.org/reports/alleged_Perpetrators.pdf.

40. "The Day They Killed Burhan: Two Years On, a Kashmiri Remembers the Death of the Militant Leader," Adil Langoo, *Caravan*, July 8, 2018, https://caravanmagazine.in/conflict/burhan-two-years-on-a-kashmiri-remembers-the-death-of-the-militant-leader.

41. "The Funeral of Burhan Wani," Qadri Inzamam and Haziq Qadri, *Caravan*, July 10, 2016, https://caravanmagazine.in/vantage/funeral-burhan-wani-unrest-followed-kashmir.

42. "Face in the Darkness: The Victims of 'Non Lethal' Weapons in Kashmir," Billy Perrigo, *Time*, September 6, 2018, https://time.com/longform/pellet-gun-victims-kashmir/. See also "Six Things You Should Know About Pellet Shotguns in Kashmir," Amnesty International, February 1, 2018, https://medium.com/@AIIndia/six-things-you-should-know-about-pellet-shotguns-in-kashmir-48f647691f5c. And also, "India Plans Hot Chilli Grenades," BBC News, June 25, 2009, http://news.bbc.co.uk/1/hi/world/south_asia/8119591.stm. They were inducted into operations in Kashmir in 2016.

43. "India Kashmir: The Teenagers Blinded by Pellets," BBC News, October 28, 2016, https://www.bbc.co.uk/news/world-asia-india-37773759.

44. "India's Crackdown in Kashmir: Is This the World's First Mass Blinding?" Mirza Waheed, *The Guardian*, November 8, 2016, https://www.theguardian.com/world/2016/nov/08/india-crackdown-in-kashmir-is-this-worlds-first-mass-blinding.

45. "Over 200 Militants Killed by Forces in Jammu and Kashmir," *Hindustan Times*, November 2, 2020, https://www.hindustantimes.com/india-news/j-k-over-200-terrorists-killed-by-forces-since-january-this-year/story-iOODQZg1jrj2q3vTqR1NfK.html.

46. Author tape archive: interviews with six officers in I.B. in Delhi, in 2019 and February 2020.

47. "Slain Hizb Commander's Wife Shot Dead in J&K," *Hindustan Times*, November 29, 2006, https://www.hindustantimes.com/india/slain-hizb-commander-s-wife-shot-dead-in-j-k/story-B6K6ma43BhTpwJl6CscAhO.html.

48. The background to this is well set out here: "*Kashmir: The Vajpayee Years*," A.S. Dulat and Aditya Sinha, HarperCollins India, 2015.

49. "Machil Fake Encounter: Army Tribunal Suspends Life Sentence of Convicts; Victim Families Say Fight for Justice Continues," Sameer Yasir,

Firstpost, July 26, 2017, https://www.firstpost.com/india/machil-fake-encounter-army-tribunal-suspends-life-sentence-of-convicts-victims-families-say-fight-for-justice-will-continue-3859129.html.

50. "Kashmir Journalist Shujaat Bukhari Shot Dead in Srinagar," BBC News, June 14, 2018, https://www.bbc.co.uk/news/world-asia-india-44488081.

51. "First Ever Human Rights Report on Kashmir Calls for International Inquiry into Multiple Violations," Office of the U.N. High Commissioner for Human Rights, June 14, 2018, https://www.ohchr.org/EN/NewsEvents/Pages/DisplayNews.aspx?NewsID=23198%20.

52. "Delhi Terms UN Report on Kashmir Human Rights as Fallacious and Motivated," Dipanjan Roy Chaudhury, *Economic Times*, June 15, 2018, https://economictimes.indiatimes.com/news/politics-and-nation/delhi-terms-un-report-on-kashmir-human-rights-as-fallacious-motivated/articleshow/64586898.cms?from=mdr.

53. Author tape archive: interviews with B.S.F. and I.B. officers involved in the Pathankot post-mortem, 2019 and 2020.

54. Author tape archive: interviews with Gulbachan Jagat, former D.G. B.S.F., and also, "Probing Pathankot Attack: Fence Floodlights that Didn't Work, Gaps in Border Patrol, Patchy Police Response," Kamaldeep Singh Brar, et al., *Indian Express*, January 8, 2016, https://indianexpress.com/article/india/india-news-india/probing-pathankot-attack-fence-floodlights-that-didnt-work-gaps-in-border-patrol-patchy-police-response/.

55. Author interviews with I.S.I. Punjab officers, and also officers in the B.S.F. and the R.A.W. in the aftermath of Pathankot.

56. "Treasury Sanctions Indian Narcotics Trafficker Jasmeet Hakimzada and His Network," U.S. Department of the Treasury, February 20, 2019, https://home.treasury.gov/news/press-releases/sm614. See also "Face in the Darkness: The Victims of 'Non Lethal' Weapons in Kashmir," Billy Perrigo, *Time*, September 6, 2018, https://time.com/longform/pellet-gun-victims-kashmir/.

57. Author tape archive: interviews with N.I.A. officers and one Special Judge in September 2019. See also, "N.I.A. Gets Eight Days Custody of Accused," *Hindustan Times*, August 10, 2019, https://www.hindustantimes.com/cities/532-kg-heroin-haul-nia-gets-eight-day-custody-of-accused/story-fXcHwd4Q94t1b52GfTHlmL.html.

58. "NIA Files Charge Sheet Against Narco Terrorist in Heroin Seizure

Case," *Outlook*, May 28, 2020, https://www.outlookindia.com/newsscroll/
nia-files-charge-sheet-against-narcoterrorist-in-heroin-seizure-
case/1848616.

59. Author tape archive: interviews with I.S.I. Punjab officers, investigating
the death.

60. "U.S. Uneasy as Beijing Develops a Strategic String of Pearls," Declan
Walsh, *The Guardian*, November 10, 2005, https://www.theguardian.com/
business/2005/nov/10/china.internationalnews.

61. "Seeking Breakthroughs: The Meandering U.S–India Relationship Needs
a Fresh Impetus," Ashley J. Tellis, *Force*, October 2004, and reproduced
at Carnegie Endowment for Peace, https://carnegieendowment.
org/2004/10/01/seeking-breakthroughs-meandering-u.s.-india-
relationship-needs-fresh-impetus-pub-15980.

62. "Friends, Neighbours of Kulbhushan Jadhav Urge Delhi to Seek His
Release," *Hindustan Times*, April 18, 2017, https://www.hindustantimes.
com/india-news/friends-neighbours-of-kulbhushan-jadav-urge-delhi-
to-seek-his-release/story-8C295Pe8itL2RaAjNOHdIM.html. Also see
the two "confessions" here: https://www.thehindu.com/news/national/
full-text-of-kulbhushan-jadhavs-confession/article17907019.ece; and
see https://www.thehindu.com/news/national/full-text-of-kulbhushan-
jadhavs-alleged-second-confession/article19126804.ece.

63. "Dossiers of Indian Hand in Terrorism Handed Over to the UN Chief:
Aziz," Mateen Haider, *Dawn*, October 2, 2015, https://www.dawn.com/
news/1210439.

64. "Spy Saga Decoded: What India, Pak Said on Kulbhushan Jadhav,"
Saubhadra Chatterji, *Hindustan Times*, April 18, 2017, https://www.
hindustantimes.com/india-news/spy-saga-decoded-what-india-pak-
said-on-kulbhushan-jadhav/story-YXufr60TLSffALM43CH0qL.html.

65. "Kulbhushan Jadhav Was Abducted by Jaish il Adil in Chabahar and
Given to I.S.I.," Manisha Shukla, *DNA*, July 17, 2019, https://www.
dnaindia.com/india/report-kulbhushan-jadhav-was-abducted-by-jaish-
ul-adl-from-chabahar-and-given-to-isi-2772759.

66. Author tape archive: interviews with European intelligence analysts, in
2018, Paris and Berlin. Interviews with U.S. C.T.C. analysts.

67. "R.A.W. Operative Given Task to Sabotage CPEC," *The News*, March 25,
2016, https://www.thenews.com.pk/print/107860-R.A.W.-operative-
was-given-task-to-sabotage-CPEC.

68. "China's $62bn Bet on Pakistan, Letter from Gwadar," Arif Rafiq, *Foreign Affairs*, October 24, 2017, https://www.foreignaffairs.com/articles/china/2017-10-24/chinas-62-billion-bet-pakistan.

69. Author archive: dated August 26, 2018; part of it was included in a brief circulated to the E.U. and U.N. in November 2020.

70. Indian security sources contest this point, saying he had taken premature retirement. However, his service records were removed from public inspection, and there is no explanation for how he obtained two legal passports with false names and misstated religion.

71. "India's Secret War," Praveen Swami, *Frontline*, February 16, 2018, https://frontline.thehindu.com/the-nation/indias-secret-war/article10055129.ece.

72. "We Put Petrol in Afzal Guru's A***," *The Week*, January 14, 2020, https://www.theweek.in/news/india/2020/01/14/we-put-petrol-in-afzal-guru-as-i-had-reputation-for-torture-davinder-singh.html. This condenses the work of Parvaiz Bukhari, who did the interview, some of which was included in *The Hanging of Afzal Guru and the Strange Case of the Attack on the Indian Parliament*, edited by Arundhati Roy, Penguin, 2006.

73. "Alleged Indian Spy Kulbhushan Jadhav Sentenced to Death in Pak," *Business Standard*, April 10, 2017, https://www.business-standard.com/article/news-ani/alleged-indian-spy-kulbhushan-jadhav-sentenced-to-death-in-pak-117041000626_1.html.

74. "Executions as a Matter of Opinion," Manu Joseph, *New York Times*, February 13, 2013, https://www.nytimes.com/2013/02/14/world/asia/14iht-letter14.html. Read a digest of the Supreme Court commentary here, "What Supreme Court Said When It Upheld Death for Afzal Guru," *Indian Express*, https://indianexpress.com/article/explained/parliament-attack-2001-what-sc-said-when-it-upheld-death-for-afzal-guru/. See also the entire judgement, *State (N.C.T. of Delhi)* vs *Navjot Sandhu@Afsan Guru* on August 4, 2005, https://indiankanoon.org/doc/1769219/.

75. "Jadhav Case, Memorial of the Republic of India," International Court of Justice, September 13, 2017, https://www.icj-cij.org/public/files/case-related/168/168-20170913-WRI-01-00-EN.pdf.

76. "Gangs of Lyari, Brutal Tales of Violence from Karachi's Wild West," Imtiaz Ahmed, *Hindustan Times*, April 18, 2016, https://www.hindustantimes.com/world/gangs-of-lyari-brutal-tales-of-violence-

from-karachi-s-wild-west/story-FnnMkjtalnJmGdyobyws6K.html. Also, "Chilling Arshad Pappu Video Goes Viral," *Dawn*, March 23, 2013, https://www.dawn.com/news/797225. And "Lyari Gang War: Arshad Pappu's Death Speculations End with Beheading Video," *Express Tribune*, March 22, 2013, https://tribune.com.pk/story/525034/lyari-gang-war-arshad-pappus-death-speculations-end-with-beheading-video.

77. "Mystery Shrouds 'Gangster' Uzair Baloch's Arrest," Imtiaz Ali, *Dawn*, January 31, 2016, https://www.dawn.com/news/1236534], Web Desk, and "Cops Arrive in Dubai for Uzair Baloch Extraction," Samaa, February 5, 2015, https://www.samaa.tv/news/2015/02/cops-arrive-in-dubai.

78. "Uzair Baloch's Military Trial Completed, Sent to Central Jail Karachi," Aizbah Khan, *BOL News*, April 6, 2020, https://www.bolnews.com/pakistan/2020/04/uzair-balochs-military-trial-completed-sent-to-central-jail-karachi/.

79. "Jadhav Case, Memorial of the Republic of India," International Court of Justice, September 13, 2017, https://www.icj-cij.org/public/files/case-related/168/168-20170913-WRI-01-00-EN.pdf.

80. "Human Shield Case: Jammu and Kashmir Rights Body Seeks Fresh Report on Army Officer Major Leetul Gogoi's Actions," Ishfaq Naseem, Firstpost, August 28, 2018, https://www.firstpost.com/india/human-shield-case-jammu-and-kashmir-rights-body-seeks-fresh-report-on-army-officer-major-leetul-gogois-actions-5063731.html.

81. "Army Honours Officer Accused of Using a Stone Pelter as a Human Shield," Scroll, May 22, 2017, https://scroll.in/latest/838398/army-awards-officer-accused-of-using-a-stone-pelter-as-human-shield-in-jammu-kashmir.

82. "Major Leetul Gogoi Court Martialed," *The Hindu*, August 27, 2018, https://www.thehindu.com/news/national/major-gogoi-to-face-court-martial-over-incident-in-srinagar-hotel/article24790568.ece.

83. Election Commission of India has full breakdowns and can be accessed here: https://eci.gov.in/files/category/97-general-election-2014/.

84. Article 370 was negotiated by Kashmir's Prime Minister Sheikh Abdullah and Indian Prime Minister Jawaharlal Nehru. The article was drafted by Sir Narasimha Ayyangar Gopalaswami Ayyangar, member of the Drafting Committee of the Constitution, who became a minister without portfolio looking after Kashmir Affairs.

85. "Why Article 370 Had to Go," Abhinav Kumar, *Indian Express*, August 16, 2019, https://indianexpress.com/article/opinion/columns/article-370-scrapped-jammu-and-kashmir-5908599/.

86. The quote is from Professor Virender Gupta. See "BJP Says Removal of Article 370 in Jammu and Kashmir Will Give Befitting Reply to Separatists and Pakistan," Firstpost, October 30, 2017, https://www.firstpost.com/politics/bjp-says-removal-of-article-370-in-jammu-and-kashmir-will-give-befitting-reply-to-separatists-and-pakistan-4184403.html.

87. "India's Citizenship Bill Discriminates Against Muslims," *Human Rights Watch*, December 11, 2019, https://www.hrw.org/news/2019/12/11/india-citizenship-bill-discriminates-against-muslims.

88. "Amit Shah 'Termite' Remark on Immigration Unwanted, Says Bangladesh," Deepshikha Ghosh, NDTV, September 24, 2018, https://www.ndtv.com/india-news/amit-shah-termite-remark-on-immigrants-unwanted-says-bangladesh-1921088.

89. "Trump Insists He Witnessed Cheering Muslims on 9/11," Kim LaCapria, Snopes, https://www.snopes.com/news/2015/11/22/donald-trump-cheering-911/.

90. We were offered them by a barrister, via his representative, as were colleagues in the U.S. We met with an I.S.I. station chief in a European capital who confirmed there had been outreach, although he claimed not to know who was responsible. The R.A.W. was keen to get the documents, as they could not be locked by Pakistan, and as such were open to distortion and re-circulation. As a result, the I.S.I. withdrew the ploy.

91. These claims were derived from multiple interviews with the I.S.I. in Peshawar, Lahore, and Islamabad, and are explored more fully in our book *The Exile*.

92. "Doctor Who Aided Hunt for Bin Laden Languishes, Forgotten," *AP*, January 22, 2018, https://www.foxnews.com/world/doctor-who-aided-hunt-for-bin-laden-languishes-forgotten.

93. "Trump Travel Ban, Other Pressures Lead Pakistan to Rein in Islamist Militants," Pamela Constable, *Washington Post*, February 4, 2017, https://www.washingtonpost.com/world/asia_pacific/trump-travel-ban-other-pressures-lead-pakistan-to-rein-in-islamist-militants/2017/02/03/

fb6706ea-ea01-11e6-903d-9b11ed7d8d2a_story.html?utm_
term=.78158a4cd8e1.

94. "Trump Withholding $255m in Aid to Pakistan, as He Accuses Country
of Giving 'Safe Haven' to Terrorists," Serafin Gomez and Alex Pappas,
Fox News, January 1, 2018, https://www.foxnews.com/politics/trump-
withholding-255m-in-aid-to-pakistan-as-he-accuses-country-of-
giving-safe-haven-to-terrorists.

95. "CIA Fails to Organize Prison Break for Doctor Who Helped Find
Bin Laden," *Sputnik News*, April 30, 2018, https://sputniknews.com/
asia/201804301064034449-pakistan-doctor-us-bin-laden/.

96. "The Silence of Aafia Siddiqui," Benazir Shah, Al Jazeera, July 16, 2015,
https://www.aljazeera.com/features/2015/7/16/the-silence-of-aafia-
siddiqui.

97. Compelling work on this was done here: "The Mystery of Aafia Siddiqui,"
Declan Walsh, *The Guardian*, November 24, 2009, https://www.
theguardian.com/world/2009/nov/24/aafia-siddiqui-al-qaida.

98. Ibid.

99. "US President Donald Trump Invites Narendra Modi," BBC
News, January 25, 2017, https://www.bbc.co.uk/news/world-us-
canada-38740090. For an understanding of the deepening defence ties,
read: "India–US Relations in the Age of Modi and Trump," Antoine
Levesques and Viraj Solanki, IISS, March 27, 2020, https://www.iiss.org/
blogs/analysis/2020/03/sasia---us-india-relations-trump-and-modi.

100. "US Envoy Lauds Pakistan's Role in Afghan Peace Talks Process," Munir
Ahmed, September 14, 2020, AP News, https://apnews.com/article/
pakistan-qatar-afghanistan-islamabad-middle-east-9bdf741eac2394ea7c
56bf5dd08dbf5a.

101. "Profile of Pulwama Suicide Bomber: Don't Fall in Love," *Economic Times*,
February 16, 2019, https://economictimes.indiatimes.com/news/politics-
and-nation/profile-of-pulwama-suicide-bomber-dont-fall-in-love/
articleshow/68006566.cms?from=mdr.

102. "Pulwama Attack: Security Forces Have Been Given Free Hand, Pakistan
Totally Isolated, says PM Modi," *Scroll*, February 15, 2019, https://scroll.
in/latest/913372/pulwama-attack-security-forces-have-been-given-free-
hand-pakistan-totally-isolated-says-pm-modi.

103. "India Will Expose Pakistan on Terror Financing at FATF Meeting:
Sources," Namrata Biji Ahuja, *The Week*, August 26, 2020, https://www.

theweek.in/news/world/2020/08/26/india-will-expose-pakistan-on-terror-financing-at-fatf-meeting-sources.html.

104. The F.A.T.F. was formed in 1989 by a G7 summit in Paris. To understand the process and stakes, see "Pakistan Stays on Global Terrorism Financing Grey List," Reuters, October 23, 2020, https://www.reuters.com/article/us-fatf-pakistan-idUSKBN27820B, and the evaluation report, "Pakistan's Measures to Combat Money Laundering and Terrorist Financing," by the F.A.T.F., can be accessed here: http://www.fatf-gafi.org/publications/mutualevaluations/documents/mer-pakistan-2019.html.

105. The Jaish was calling itself the Khuddam ul-Islam in Pakistan and the Majlis Wurasa-e-Shuhuda in Kashmir.

106. "Ticket to Pragya a Symbol to Answer Those Who Demean the Great Civilisation: PM Narendra Modi," *Times of India*, April 20, 2019, https://timesofindia.indiatimes.com/india/ticket-to-pragya-a-symbol-to-answer-those-who-demean-the-great-civilisation-pm-narendra-modi/articleshow/68959461.cms.

107. "Congress Infected by Green Virus: Yogi Adityanath Latest Jab," NDTV, April 11, 2019, https://www.ndtv.com/india-news/yogi-adityanath-says-congress-infected-by-green-virus-2021239.

108. "Mughals Disappearing from Textbooks Across the Country as History Seems Subject to Change," Firstpost, August 7, 2017, https://www.firstpost.com/india/mughals-disappearing-from-textbooks-across-the-country-as-history-seems-subject-to-change-3903053.html.

109. "Why I Will Never Go to Pakistan," Laila Tyabji, The Wire, February 7, 2020, https://thewire.in/communalism/go-to-pakistan-indian-muslims.

110. "Uncovering the IRA," Sean Boyne, PBS, August 1, 1996, https://www.pbs.org/wgbh/pages/frontline/shows/ira/inside/org.html.

111. Adil Hussein Dar, arrested in Shopian in 2017, came from Chatarpura. See "Two Terrorists Killed, One Arrested in J&K," IANS, *Business Standard*, September 10, 2017, https://www.business-standard.com/article/news-ians/two-terrorists-killed-one-arrested-in-j-k-117091000244_1.html.

112. "New Guided Bomb Strikes Afghanistan," Paul Eng, January 7, 2006, ABC News, https://abcnews.go.com/Technology/story?id=98246&page=1; and also, "How IAF Fighter Jets Killed 350 Terrorists in Pakistan's 5-Star Balakot Camp," Live Mint, February 26, 2019, https://www.livemint.com/news/india/how-iaf-fighter-jets-killed-350-terrorists-in-pakistan-s-5-star-balakot-camp-1551173156827.html.

113. "8 Pieces of Clinching Evidence that Show How IAF's Abhinandan Shot Down a Pakistani F-16," Sameer Joshi, The Print, August 20, 2019, https://theprint.in/defence/8-pieces-of-clinching-evidence-that-show-how-iafs-abhinandan-shot-down-a-pakistani-f-16/278752/.

114. "India's Strike on Balakot: A Very Precise Miss?" Marcus Hellyer, Nathan Ruser, and Aakriti Bachhawat, ASPI, The Strategist, March 27, 2019, https://www.aspistrategist.org.au/indias-strike-on-balakot-a-very-precise-miss/.

115. "India Missile Fired Before Mi17 V5 Chopper Crash," Manu Pubby, Economic Times, April 1, 2019, https://economictimes.indiatimes.com/news/defence/budgam-indian-missile-fired-before-mi17-v5-chopper-crash/articleshow/68623744.cms?from=mdr.

116. "Three Days Before Balakot, Arnab Told ex-BARC Chief 'Something Big Will Happen,'" The Hindu, January 16, 2021, https://www.thehindu.com/news/national/three-days-before-balakot-arnab-tells-barc-chief-something-big-will-happen/article33588655.ece.

117. Mohammed Masood Azhar Alvi, United Nations Security Council listing, https://www.un.org/securitycouncil/content/mohammed-masood-azhar-alvi.

118. "NIA Traces Pulwama Mastermind Jaish Commander Umar Farooq's al-Qaeda Link," Kamaljit Kaur Sandhu, India Today, August 27, 2020, https://www.indiatoday.in/india/story/pulwama-terror-attack-case-jem-umar-farooq-al-qaeda-1715434-2020-08-26.

119. "Man Accused of Beheading U.S. Journalist Daniel Pearl Ordered Released by Pakistani Court," Washington Post, January 29, 2021, https://www.washingtonpost.com/world/asia_pacific/daniel-pearl-pakistan-accused-released/2021/01/28/85e3ad14-6140-11eb-a177-7765f29a9524_story.html.

120. "US India Relationship to Remain Strategic Imperative Under Biden," Saheli Roy Choudhury, CNBC, November 9, 2020, https://www.cnbc.com/2020/11/10/us-india-relationship-to-remain-strategic-imperative-under-biden.html.

121. "Top Pakistani Court Upholds Reversal of Conviction in Daniel Pearl Killing," Emily Schmall and Ziar ur-Rehman, New York Times, January 28, 2021, https://www.nytimes.com/2021/01/28/world/asia/daniel-pearl-pakistan.html?searchResultPosition=1.

122. Author tape archive: interview with ISI officer who planned the arrest of LeJ's Rehman.

123. "Qaeda Killer's Veins Implicate Him in Journo's Murder," Spencer Ackerman, Wired, January 20, 2011, https://www.wired.com/2011/01/qaeda-killers-veins-implicate-him-in-journos-murder/.

124. "Backchannel Diplomacy Played Its Part in India, Pakistan Decision to Cease Fire along LoC," Suhasini Haidar and Kallol Bhattacharjee, *The Hindu*, February 25, 2001, https://www.thehindu.com/news/national/analysis-indications-that-india-and-pakistan-have-been-in-back-channel-talks/article33935351.ece.

Select Bibliography

Agee, Philip. *Inside the Company*. Stonehill, 1975.

Al-Haythami, Ali ibn Abu Bakr, *Majmau al-Zawa'id wa Manba al-Fawa'id*. Mu'assash al-Ma'arif, 1986.

Al Asmari, Abdulaziz Abdullah, "Islamic Concept of Intelligence in the Case of Fatah Paramilitary." Brunel University, May 2009, https://bura.brunel.ac.uk/bitstream/2438/3590/4/FulltextThesis.pdf.

Al Naboodah, Hasan M., "Sahib Al-Khabar: Secret Agents and Spies During the First Century of Islam," *Journal of Asian History* 39, no. 2 (2005).

Andrew, Christopher. *Defend the Realm*. Knopf Doubleday, 2009.

———. *The Secret World: A History of Intelligence*. Yale University Press, 2018.

Andrew, Christopher, and Vasili Mitrokhin. *The Mitrokhin Archive: The KGB in Europe and the West*. Penguin, 2014.

———. *The Mitrokhin Archive 2: The KGB in the World*. Penguin, 2015.

Arif, Gen. K.M. *Working with Zia*. Oxford University Press, 2005.

Barker, Kim. *Taliban Shuffle: Strange Days in Afghanistan and Pakistan*. Anchor Books, 2012.

Bhattacharjee, Yudhijit. *The Spy Who Couldn't Spell: A Dyslexic Traitor, an Unbreakable Code, and the FBI's Hunt for America's Stolen Secrets*. New American Library, 2016.

Bergman, Ronen. *Rise and Kill First: The Secret History of Israel's Targeted Assassinations*. John Murray, 2018.

Bishop, Patrick. *3 Para*. HarperCollins, 2007.

Brown, Vahid, and Don Rassler. *The Fountainhead of Jihad*. Hurst, Ithaca Press, 2013.

Brynjar, Lia. *The Society of the Muslim Brotherhood in Egypt*. Ithaca Press, 2006.

Clarridge, Duane R. *A Spy for All Seasons*. Scribner, 1997.

Coll, Steve. *Directorate S: The CIA and America's Secret Wars in Afghanistan and Pakistan*. Penguin, 2018.

Constable, Pam. *Playing with Fire: Pakistan at War with Itself*. Random House, 2011.

Crumpton, Henry. *The Art of Intelligence*. Penguin, 2012.

Deen, Aimen, Paul Cruickshank, and Tim Lister. *Nine Lives: My Times as MI6's Top Spy Inside Al Qaeda*. Simon & Schuster, 2018.

Devasher, Tilak. *Pakistan: Courting the Abyss*. HarperCollins, 2017.

———. *Pakistan at the Helm*. HarperCollins, 2018.

Dhar, Malloy Krishna. *Open Secrets: India's Intelligence Unveiled*. Manas, 2005.

Dulat, A.S., and Aditya Sinha. *Kashmir: The Vajpayee Years*. HarperCollins, 2015.

Dulat, A.S., Aditya Sinha, and Asad Durrani. *The Spy Chronicles*. HarperCollins, 2018.

Durrani, Asad. *Honour Among Spies*. HarperCollins, 2020.

Fair, C. Christine. *Fighting to the End: The Pakistan Army's Way of War*. Oxford University Press, 2014.

Fouda, Yosri, and Nick Fielding. *The Masterminds of Terror*. Mainstream Publishing, 2003.

Gall, Carlota. *The Wrong Enemy: America in Afghanistan, 2001–2014*. Houghton Mifflin, 2014.

Gayer, Laurent. *Karachi: Ordered Disorder and the Struggle for the City*. Hurst, 2014.

Gilani, Iftikhar. *My Days in Prison*. Penguin, 2009.

Gokhale, Nitin A. *RN Kao: Gentleman Spymaster*. Bloomsbury, 2019.

———. *Securing India the Modi Way*. Bloomsbury, 2017.

Grenier, Bob. *88 Days to Kandahar*. Simon & Schuster, 2015.

Gul, Imtiaz. *The Al Qaeda Connection*. Penguin, 2009.

Hamid, Shadi. *Islamic Exceptionalism: How the Struggle over Islam Is Reshaping the World*. St Martin's Griffin, 2017.

Hamid, Omar Shahid. *The Party Worker*. Pan Macmillan, 2017.

———. *The Prisoner*. Pan Macmillan, 2013.

Haqqani, Hussain. *Magnificent Delusions*. Public Affairs, 2013.

Hegghammer, Thomas. *The Caravan: Abdallah Azzam and the Rise of Global Jihad*. Cambridge University Press, 2020.

Hussain, Mujahid. *Punjabi Taliban: Driving Extremism in Pakistan*. Pentagon Press, 2012.

Hussain, Zahid. *The Scorpion's Tail: The Relentless Rise of Islamic Militants in Pakistan – And How It Threatens America*. Free Press, 2010.

Ingram, Martin. *Stakeknife: Britain's Secret Agents in Ireland*. O'Brien Press, 2004.

Jenkins, Tricia. *The C.I.A. in Hollywood: How the Agency Shapes Film and Television*. University of Texas Press, 2013.

Johnson, Lock K. *Secret Agencies: U.S. Intelligence in a Hostile World*. Yale, 1998.

Kiessling, Hein G. *Faith, Unity, Discipline*. Hurst, 2016.

Kux, Dennis. *The United States and Pakistan*. Oxford University Press, 2001.

Mahadevan, Prem. *Islamism and Intelligence in South Asia*. IB Taurus, 2018.

Marchetti, Victor, and John Marks. *The C.I.A. and the Cult of Intelligence*. Alfred A. Knopf, 1974.

Mazzetti, Mark. *The Way of the Knife*. Scribe, 2013.

Mendez, Antonio J. *The Master of Disguise*. William, Morrow, 2000.

Musharraf, Pervez. *In the Line of Fire: A Memoir*. Free Press, 2006.

Nasr, Vali. *The Shia Revival*. W.W. Norton, 2016.

Nawaz, Shuja. *Crossed Swords: Pakistan, Its Army and the Wars Within*. Oxford University Press, 2008.

———. *The Battle for Pakistan: The Bitter US Friendship and a Tough Neighbourhood*. Penguin, 2019.

Ostrovsky, Victor, and Claire Hoy. *By Way of Deception*. St Martin's Press, 1990.

Prados, John. *Presidents' Secret Wars: CIA and Pentagon Covert Operations from World War II Through the Persian Gulf War*. Elephant, 1996.

Raman, B. *Intelligence: Past, Present and Future*. Lancer Publications, 2002.

———. *The Kaoboys of R&AW*. Lancer Publications, 2009.

Rashid, Ahmed. *Descent into Chaos*. Viking, 2008.

———. *Pakistan on the Brink*. Allen Lane, 2013.

Rodriguez, Jose. *Hard Measures: How Aggressive CIA Actions After 9/11 Saved American Lives*. Threshold Editions, 2012.

Schofield, Carry. *Inside the Pakistan Army: A Woman's Experience on the Frontline of the War on Terror*. Biteback, 2010.

Scott-Clark, Catherine, and Adrian Levy. *The Exile: The Stunning Inside Story of Osama bin Laden and Al Qaeda in Flight*. Bloomsbury, 2017.

Sen, Lt. Gen. P. *Slender Was the Thread*. Orient Blackswan, 1994.

Shahzad, Syed Saleem. *Inside Al Qaeda and the Taliban, Beyond Bin Laden and 9/11*. Pluto Press, 2011.

Singh, Maj. Gen. V.K. *India's External Intelligence*. Manas, 2017.

Sirrs, Owen L. *Pakistan's Inter-Services Intelligence Directorate*. Routledge, 2017.

Sood, Vikram. *The Unending Game: A Former RAW Chief's Insights into Espionage*. HarperCollins, 2018.

Storm, Mortem, Paul Cruickshank, and Tim Lister. *Agent Storm: My Life Inside Al Qaeda*. Grove Atlantic, 2014.

Suskind, Ron. *The One Per Cent Doctrine: Deep Inside America's Pursuit of Its Enemies Since 9/11*. Scribner, 2006.

Tirmazi, Brigadier Syed A.I. *Profiles of Intelligence*. Fiction House, 1995.

Wallace, Robert, and H. Keith Melton. *Spycraft*. Plume, 2009.

Wright, Lawrence. *The Looming Tower: Al Qaeda and the Road to 9/11*. Alfred A. Knopf, 2006.

Yadav, R.K. *Mission R&AW*. Manas, 2014.

A Note on the Authors

Former award-winning writers and foreign correspondents for *The Sunday Times* and then *The Guardian*, Adrian Levy and Cathy Scott-Clark have also produced documentaries for HBO, PBS, BBC 1, BBC 2, C4, Facebook, and VICE TV. In 2010, their film *City of Fear*, on Pakistan's bloodiest year, was nominated at the Edinburgh International Television Festival. Their C4 documentary *Torture Trail* won the 2013 Amnesty International award, was shortlisted for the Grierson award, and was a finalist in the Rory Pecks. *Chinese Murder Mystery*, an investigation into a Communist Party killer, was longlisted for a BAFTA and nominated for the Monte Carlo Television Awards. They produced episodes for the Emmy-winning Vice on HBO. Currently, they are producing a feature documentary, *Forever Prisoner,*, directed by Academy Award winner Alex Gibney, investigating C.I.A. enhanced interrogation.

Their first book, *The Stone of Heaven* (2001), was a finalist in Borders New Voices competition. Their second, *The Amber Room* (2004), was a *New York Times* Book of the Year. *Deception* (2008) was a finalist in the Royal United Services Institute, Duke of Westminster's medal for Military History. *The Meadow*, published by Penguin (2012), won the Ramnath Goenka Award. *The Siege* (2013), an account of 26/11, won the CWA Gold Dagger for Non-Fiction. Their sixth non-fiction book, *The Exile* (2017), is a kitchen sink drama of the bin Ladens.

http://secrets-and-lies.co.uk
Twitter: @AdrianMLevy

Index